D0325672

❦ ❦ ❦ ❦ ❦ ❦ ❦ ❦ ❦ ❦ ❦ ❦ ❦ ❦ ❦ ❦ ❦

Doing Research That Is Useful for Theory and Practice

❧ ❧ ❧ ❧ ❧ ❧ ❧ ❧ ❧ ❧ ❧ ❧ ❧ ❧ ❧ ❧ ❧

Edward E. Lawler III
Allan M. Mohrman, Jr.
Susan A. Mohrman
Gerald E. Ledford, Jr.
Thomas G. Cummings
and Associates

✥ ✥ ✥ ✥ ✥ ✥ ✥ ✥ ✥ ✥ ✥ ✥ ✥ ✥ ✥ ✥ ✥

Doing Research
That Is Useful for
Theory and Practice

Jossey-Bass Publishers

San Francisco • Oxford • 1990

DOING RESEARCH THAT IS USEFUL FOR THEORY AND PRACTICE
by Edward E. Lawler III, Allan M. Mohrman, Jr., Susan A. Mohrman,
Gerald E. Ledford, Jr., Thomas G. Cummings, and Associates

Copyright © 1985 by: Jossey-Bass Inc., Publishers
433 California Street
San Francisco, California 94104
&
Jossey-Bass Limited
Headington Hill Hall
Oxford OX3 0BW

Library of Congress Cataloging in Publication Data
Main entry under title:

Doing research that is useful for theory and practice.

(Jossey-Bass management series) (Jossey-Bass social
and behavioral science series)
Includes bibliographies and index.
1. Organizational behavior—Research—Addresses,
essays, lectures. 2. Organizational research—
Addresses, essays, lectures. I. Lawler, Edward E.
II. Series. III. Series: Jossey-Bass social and
behavioral science series.
HD58.7.D65   1985   302.3'5   84-43092
ISBN 0-87589-649-9

Manufactured in the United States of America

The paper in this book meets the guidelines for
permanence and durability of the Committee on
Production Guidelines for Book Longevity of the
Council on Library Resources.

JACKET DESIGN BY WILLI BAUM

FIRST EDITION
First printing: May 1985
Second printing: September 1990
Code 8514

A joint publication in
The Jossey-Bass Management Series
and
The Jossey-Bass
Social and Behavioral Science Series

Consulting Editors
Organizations and Management

Warren Bennis
University of Southern California

Richard O. Mason
University of Arizona

Ian I. Mitroff
University of Southern California

✠ ✠ ✠ ✠ ✠ ✠ ✠ ✠ ✠ ✠ ✠ ✠ ✠ ✠ ✠ ✠

Preface

Doing research that is useful for both organizational theory and practice is a stated objective of our research center, the Center for Effective Organizations, at the University of Southern California. Few of our colleagues argue with the importance of this goal, but many question whether achieving it is feasible. This book is about conducting just such research. It addresses the value and design issues inherent in organizational research and goes on to the fundamental value questions of why we do research and whom we do it for. In the end our argument is that doing jointly useful research is not only desirable—it is necessary.

Part One, "Doing Useful Research: An Introduction to the Issues," includes two chapters, one by Edward E. Lawler III and one by Ian I. Mitroff, that provide important thoughts on basic research design. They also address the philosophical issues involved in meeting both collegial standards of theoretical excellence and practitioner standards of functional utility. They ask some provocative questions, challenging widely held beliefs about how good research should be done.

Part Two, "Alternate Approaches to Doing Useful Organizational Research," focuses on how to conduct research that contributes to both theory and practice. To find out how to do it, we asked researchers who are widely acknowledged to have done exemplary research to write a chapter about their own work. In essence, we chose to ask the experts how they had successfully accomplished what we feel needs to be done by more researchers.

A list of questions that was sent to the researchers as a way of stimulating their thinking on this topic appears as the Appendix to this book. The responses we received were diverse and challenging and demonstrate that few of these scholars follow the traditional prescriptions for doing research.

Each of the authors of Chapters Four, Five, Six, and Seven focuses on his own individual career. The authors' distinguished histories lend these chapters particular interest and importance. In different ways, each author has made seminal contributions to our knowledge about how organizations function.

In Chapter Four, Chris Argyris discusses the relationship between thought and action. He addresses the issues involved in translating theory and research into practice. In Chapter Five, J. Richard Hackman discusses the role traditional research methods have played in his career and how he has modified them in developing his approach. Similarly, in Chapter Six, Richard E. Walton, who starts from a less traditional position than Hackman, tells how he gathers data and learns about organizational issues. In Chapter Seven, Andrew M. Pettigrew argues strongly and convincingly for a "contextualist" approach to research in organizations. Taken together, the chapters by Argyris, Hackman, Walton, and Pettigrew provide a particularly instructive overview of strategies for performing useful research. As these chapters clearly demonstrate, there is no one correct methodology or theoretical framework: there may, in fact, be several.

The two other chapters in Part Two focus on institutional approaches. Chapter Three, by Stanley E. Seashore, provides an excellent discussion of how researchers at the Institute for Social Research think about institutional and organizational issues. This institute's unparalleled success in conducting research of significance for both theory and practice makes it an intriguing subject for discussion. Chapter Eight, by Thomas G. Cummings, Susan A. Mohrman, Allan M. Mohrman, Jr., and Gerald E. Ledford, Jr., discusses the approach to research taken by the Center for Effective Organizations. The center's mission is contributing to the interaction between research and practice; its researchers engage in those projects that hold promise for both.

Part Three, "Comparing Research Approaches," contains Chapter Nine, by Paul S. Goodman, an epilogue by Susan

A. Mohrman, Allan M. Mohrman, Jr., Gerald E. Ledford, Jr., Thomas G. Cummings, and Edward E. Lawler III, and an afterword by Warren Bennis. Goodman's chapter is integrative. He reviews some of the commonalities that emerged from the chapters in Part Two and enumerates the advantages, as well as the limitations, of research strategies designed to produce results with dual relevance. The Epilogue, by Mohrman, Mohrman, Ledford, Cummings, and Lawler, explores the orientation of the chapter authors and their reactions to each others' opinions and ideas. The Afterword, by Bennis, offers observations on the difficulties and rewards ensuing from attempts to do research that is useful for both theory and practice.

Genesis of This Book

During the fall of 1983, the Center for Effective Organizations and the School of Business Administration of the University of Southern California sponsored a conference on research that contributes to both theory and practice. The papers presented at that conference, together with the responses and commentaries written by conference participants, form the chapters of this book.

The two-day conference was an extremely stimulating event. More than twenty people participated in it and their discussions generated considerable controversy and excitement. In many cases, the issues debated concerned the validity and the usefulness of some individuals' entire research output. We have made every effort to convey some of the lively spirit of these exchanges, but since each discussion lasted approximately one hour, we limited ourselves to recording only the highlights.

Overall the book raises important questions concerning the usefulness of research and makes points that should help the reader find answers to these questions. The issues raised are ones that confront every organizational researcher. In the end, of course, each reader must provide his or her own answers, but we feel the chapters offer some excellent statements of how others have resolved them. Researchers differ widely in their approaches to gathering and analyzing data, developing a theoretical framework, and applying a research methodology. This is hardly surprising given the nature of the issues and the variety of strategies that have been successful in the past. Considerable effort was made to include a variety of viewpoints, specialties, and theoretical orientations; we did not intend for the individual chapters to represent a consensus of opinion.

Acknowledgments

We are grateful to a number of individuals for their help. David A. Whetten of the University of Illinois was active in planning the conference. A number of people made valuable contributions to this book. Ian I. Mitroff, Craig C. Lundberg, and Steven Kerr provided useful input during the planning stage. Connie Sutherland, Gretchen Kast, Annette Yakushi, and Carmen Prouty greatly assisted with the arrangements surrounding the conference and the production of the manuscript. The chapter authors proved to be an exceptionally pleasurable group to work with. They were all excited about the topic and were eager conference participants. Our thanks to one researcher who was invited but was unable to participate: Eric Trist, who had initially accepted, was forced to withdraw for personal reasons. His presence was felt throughout, however, because of his pioneering work in this area. Our thanks also go to the commentators, who contributed to an exciting conference and book.

Jack Steele, dean of the School of Business Administration at the University of Southern California, deserves special thanks. His efforts led to the funding of the conference, but more than that, his overall leadership provides a climate that encourages this kind of conference. In particular, his emphasis on making business education both theoretically sound and relevant to the real world has contributed tremendously to the creation and direction of the Center for Effective Organizations and, therefore, to this book.

Los Angeles, California   Edward E. Lawler III
March 1985   Allan M. Mohrman, Jr.
                                       Susan A. Mohrman
                                       Gerald E. Ledford, Jr.
                                       Thomas G. Cummings

❖ ❖ ❖ ❖ ❖ ❖ ❖ ❖ ❖ ❖ ❖ ❖ ❖ ❖ ❖ ❖ ❖

Contents

Preface   ix

The Authors   xvii

Part One: Doing Useful Research:
An Introduction to the Issues

1. Challenging Traditional
   Research Assumptions   1
   Edward E. Lawler III

2. Why Our Old Pictures of the World
   Do Not Work Anymore   18
   Ian I. Mitroff

   Response and Commentary   36
   Steven Kerr

   Group Discussion   40

Part Two: Alternative Approaches to Doing
Useful Organizational Research

√ 3. Institutional and Organizational Issues
   in Doing Useful Research   45
   Stanley E. Seashore

Response and Commentary   60
Craig C. Lundberg

Group Discussion   67

4. Making Knowledge
    More Relevant to Practice: Maps for Action   79
    Chris Argyris

    Response and Commentary   107
    Michael J. Driver

    Group Discussion   115

5. Doing Research
    That Makes a Difference   126
    J. Richard Hackman

    Response and Commentary   149
    Ralph H. Kilmann

    Group Discussion   156

6. Strategies with Dual Relevance   176
    Richard E. Walton

    Response and Commentary   204
    David A. Whetten

    Group Discussion   211

7. Contextualist Research:
    A Natural Way to Link
    Theory and Practice   222
    Andrew M. Pettigrew

    Response and Commentary   249
    Larry E. Greiner

    Group Discussion   259

8. Organization Design for the Future:
    A Collaborative Research Approach   275
    Thomas G. Cummings, Susan A. Mohrman,
    Allan M. Mohrman, Jr., Gerald E. Ledford, Jr.

    Response and Commentary   306
    Lyman W. Porter

    Group Discussion   315

Part Three: Comparing Research Approaches

9. Critical Issues in Doing Research
    That Contributes to Theory and Practice   324
    Paul S. Goodman

    Group Discussion   343

    Epilogue: Walking the Tightrope
    Between Theory and Practice   346
    Susan A. Mohrman, Allan M. Mohrman, Jr.,
    Gerald E. Ledford, Jr., Thomas G. Cummings,
    Edward E. Lawler III

    Afterword: Observations on
    What We Have Learned
    About Useful Research   351
    Warren Bennis

    Appendix: Questions for Chapter Authors   359

    Index   363

❀ ❀ ❀ ❀ ❀ ❀ ❀ ❀ ❀ ❀ ❀ ❀ ❀ ❀ ❀ ❀ ❀ ❀

The Authors

Edward E. Lawler III is a professor of research in the Graduate School of Business Administration, University of Southern California. In 1979 he founded and became the director of the Center for Effective Organizations at the University of Southern California. He received his B.A. degree (1960) from Brown University and his Ph.D. degree (1964) from the University of California, Berkeley, both in psychology. He was formerly a member of the faculty at Yale University and at the University of Michigan, and he served as program director of the Survey Research Center at the Institute for Social Research.

Lawler is a member of many professional organizations and serves on the editorial boards of five major journals. He is the author and coauthor of more than one hundred articles and eleven books. His most recent books include *Organizational Assessment* (1980), *Pay and Organizational Development* (1981), and *Managing Creation* (1983).

Allan M. Mohrman, Jr., is a research scientist at the Center for Effective Organizations, Graduate School of Business Administration, University of Southern California. He received his B.S. degree (1967) from Stanford University in physics, his M.A. degree (1971) from the University of Cincinnati in education, and his Ph.D. degree (1978) from Northwestern University in organizational behavior.

His interests are organizational design, design implementation, and social action approaches to organizational behavior. Currently he is focusing on human resource management, high-technology organizations, and implementation of computer-based and information technologies. He has published in the areas of organization development, participation in decision making, performance appraisal, quality of worklife, and the impact of information technology.

Susan A. Mohrman is a research scientist at the Center for Effective Organizations, Graduate School of Business Administration, University of Southern California. She received her A.B. degree (1967) from Stanford University in psychology and her Ph.D. degree (1978) from Northwestern University in organizational behavior.

Her research has focused on organizational design, innovative organizational systems, and quality-of-worklife projects. She is currently conducting comparative studies of cooperation between labor and management. In addition, she is working closely with several high-technology firms to develop a socio-technical design model for that industry.

Thomas G. Cummings is professor of management and organization at the Graduate School of Business Administration, University of Southern California. He received his B.S. degree (1966) from Cornell University in agricultural economics, his M.B.A. degree (1967) from Cornell University in industrial and labor relations, and his Ph.D. degree (1970) from the University of California at Los Angeles in sociotechnical systems.

Cummings's main research interests include designing high-performing organizations, planning organization change and development, and developing transorganizational systems. He has been involved in several large-scale quality-of-worklife projects and has conceptually developed a new field of planned change called transorganizational development that involves groups of organizations. He has published in the areas of job satisfaction and productivity, systems theory for organization development, labor relations, and organization development and change. Cummings is associate editor of the *Journal of Occupa-*

tional Behaviour and president-elect of the Western Academy of
Management. He was chairperson of the Organization Development Division of the Academy of Management in 1982.

Gerald E. Ledford, Jr., is a research scientist at the Center
for Effective Organizations, Graduate School of Business Administration, University of Southern California. He received his
B.A. degree (1973) from George Washington University, his
M.A. degree (1979) from the University of Michigan, and his
Ph.D. degree (1984) from the University of Michigan, all in
psychology. Ledford has researched a variety of strategies for
improving employee well-being and organizational effectiveness,
including union-management cooperation, organization redesign, innovative reward systems, employee participation in
decision making, and job redesign.

Chris Argyris is the James Bryant Conant Professor of
Education and Organizational Behavior at Harvard University.
He was awarded the A.B. degree in psychology from Clark
University (1947), the M.A. degree in economics and psychology from Kansas University (1949), and the Ph.D. degree in
organizational behavior from Cornell University (1951). Argyris
holds honorary degrees from the Stockholm School of Economics, the University of Leuven, and McGill University. From
1951 to 1971 he was a faculty member at Yale University, serving as Beach Professor of Administrative Sciences and as chairperson of the Department of Administrative Sciences.

Warren Bennis is the Joseph DeBell Professor of Management and Organization at the Graduate School of Business Administration, University of Southern California. He received
his B.A. degree (1951) from Antioch College and his Ph.D.
degree (1955) in economics and social science from the Massachusetts Institute of Technology. He holds honorary degrees
from seven universities. Bennis served as president of the University of Cincinnati during most of the 1970s and was provost
and executive vice-president at the State University of New
York, Buffalo, in the late 1960s. His main research activities

over the past several years have focused on high-performing top executives. He has published fifteen books and more than six hundred articles. The recipient of the Distinguished Service Award from the American Board of Professional Psychologists, Bennis was also honored by the American Psychological Association in 1983 for his contributions to consulting psychology.

Michael J. Driver is professor of management and organization in the Graduate School of Business Administration, University of Southern California. He received his A.B. degree (1958) from Fordham University and his M.A. degree (1960) and Ph.D. degree (1962) from Princeton University, all in psychology. Driver's major research interests are styles of decision making, creative problem solving, career development, and information systems design. He is the author of *Human Information Processing* and numerous journal articles.

Paul S. Goodman is professor of industrial administration and psychology at the Graduate School of Industrial Administration, Carnegie-Mellon University. He received his B.A. degree in economics from Trinity College (1959), his M.B.A. degree from Dartmouth College (1961), and his Ph.D. degree in organizational psychology from Cornell University (1966). Goodman's research interests are in work motivation and attitudes, organizational design, productivity, and organizational effectiveness—topics on which he has authored numerous journal articles and books. He serves on the editorial board of *Organizational Behavior and Human Performance*.

Larry E. Greiner is professor of management and organization in the Graduate School of Business Administration, University of Southern California. He was formerly a member of the faculty at the Harvard Business School, where he received his M.B.A. degree (1963) and D.B.A. degree (1965). His most recent book is *Consulting to Management* (1983, with Robert Metzger). He is currently serving on the editorial boards of the *Journal of Management Case Studies*, the *Journal of Venturing*, and *New Management*, and he is a member of the board of directors of Management Analysis Center.

J. Richard Hackman is professor of organizational behavior and of psychology at Yale University. He received his
B.A. degree in mathematics from MacMurray College (1962)
and his Ph.D. in social psychology from the University of Illinois
(1966). He has been at Yale since 1966. Hackman's research
in social and organizational psychology has addressed the design
of work, the task effectiveness of work groups, and the social
influences on individual behavior. He is on the editorial board
of several professional journals and has consulted with a number
of organizations on quality-of-worklife issues. The author or
editor of five books and over fifty chapters and articles, Hackman
was winner of the Sixth Annual AIR Creative Talent Award
in the field of measurement and evaluation of individual and
group behavior and cowinner of the 1972 Cattell Award of the
American Psychological Association. He is a fellow of that
association in the division of Industrial and Organizational Psychology and in the division of Personality and Social Psychology.

Steven Kerr is research professor of management and
organization and associate dean in the Graduate School of
Business Administration, University of Southern California. He
received his Ph.D. degree in management and organizational
psychology from City University of New York in 1983. Kerr
spent eight years in industry and seven years on the faculty
of Ohio State University. He has coauthored two books and
authored more than forty journal articles. He is a fellow of the
Academy of Management and serves on four editorial review
boards.

Ralph H. Kilmann is professor of business administration and director of the Program in Corporate Culture at the
Graduate School of Business, University of Pittsburgh. He
received both his B.S. and M.S. degrees in industrial administration from Carnegie-Mellon University (1970) and his Ph.D.
degree in management from the University of California, Los
Angeles (1972). Since 1975, Kilmann has been president of
Organizational Design Consultants, Inc., a Pittsburgh-based
firm specializing in the five tracks to organizational success.

Craig C. Lundberg is professor of management and organization in the Graduate School of Business Administration, University of Southern California. He received his B.B.A. degree (1954) and his M.B.A. degree (1957) from the University of Washington and his Ph.D. degree (1966) from Cornell University. Lundberg is the editor of *Organizational Behavior Teaching Review*. In his current research he is focusing on the interfaces between corporate strategy, culture, and development.

Ian I. Mitroff is the Harold Quinton Distinguished Professor of Business Policy in the Department of Management and Organization, Graduate School of Business Administration, University of Southern California. He received his B.S. degree in engineering physics (1961), his M.S. degree in structural engineering (1963), and his Ph.D. degree in engineering psychology (1967), all from the University of California, Berkeley. He has published over one hundred articles and books and is interested in the relationships between managerial practice and theory.

Andrew M. Pettigrew is professor of organizational behavior and director of the Management Change and Development research unit at the University of Warwick, England. Pettigrew received his B.A. degree in sociology from Liverpool University (1965) and his Ph.D. degree in organizational behavior from Manchester University (1970). He is author of the recent book *The Awakening Giant: Continuity and Change in Imperial Chemical Industries*, among other publications.

Lyman W. Porter is professor of management in the Graduate School of Management, University of California, Irvine. He received his B.A. degree from Northwestern University (1952) and his Ph.D. degree from Yale University (1956), both in psychology. Porter is a former dean of the University of California, Irvine, and has been a faculty member there since 1967. Prior to that he was on the faculty of the University of California, Berkeley. His research concerns the relationships between employee and organization, management education and development, and the politics of organizations.

Stanley E. Seashore is program director (emeritus) with the Institute for Social Research, University of Michigan, where he is also emeritus professor of psychology. He received his B.A. degree in economics from the University of Iowa (1937), his M.A. degree in anthropology from the University of Minnesota (1939), and his Ph.D. degree in psychology from the University of Michigan (1954). His research over three decades has focused on the social psychology of organizations, with emphasis on issues of organizational effectiveness and organizational change.

Richard E. Walton is the Jesse Isidor Straus Professor of Business Administration at the Harvard Graduate School of Business Administration, where he was the director of the Division of Research from 1969 to 1976 and is currently course head for Human Resource Management. Walton received his B.S. degree in political science (1953) and his M.S. degree in economics (1954), both from Purdue University. He received his D.B.A. degree in labor relations (1959) from Harvard University. Walton's major fields of interest are organizational change and conflict resolution and behavioral science. His current research involves new technology in the workplace.

David A. Whetten is professor of business administration at the University of Illinois, Champaign–Urbana. He received his B.A. degree (1970) and M.A. degree (1971) from Brigham Young University in sociology and his Ph.D. degree (1974) from Cornell in organizational behavior. He is interested in the determinants of organizational effectiveness, especially successful responses to stressful environmental conditions. As well as being coauthor of recent books on interorganizational relations, organizational effectiveness, and developing management skills, Whetten is associate editor of *Administration and Society* and serves on the editorial boards of *Administrative Science Quarterly* and *Academy of Management Review*.

� with fleur-de-lis ornament row✿

*Doing Research
That Is Useful for
Theory and Practice*

1

Edward E. Lawler III

❧ ❧ ❧ ❧ ❧ ❧ ❧ ❧ ❧ ❧ ❧ ❧ ❧ ❧ ❧ ❧ ❧ ❧

Challenging Traditional Research Assumptions

Research on organizations has increased over its fifty-year history. Starting in the 1950s, the volume has grown dramatically to the point where, today, we find ourselves overwhelmed with research on organizations. New journals are appearing regularly, books are being produced at an increasing rate, and Ph.D. programs are turning out researchers at a high rate.

As the research on organizational behavior has developed and increased in volume, a relatively well-codified set of principles about what constitutes "good" research has emerged. Indeed, today most people in the field can agree on what constitutes a well-designed research study and what represents a good application of the scientific method to research on organizational behavior. This agreement is clearly exemplified by the increasing use of quantitative methods in the field and by the greater sophistication of recent studies with respect to principles of experimental design. To many, the path toward further knowledge about organizational behavior is clear. It leads to more rigorous research with better designs, larger samples, and more sophis-

1

ticated statistical analysis. But is this indeed the best route to lead us toward better understanding of organizations?

Before we can answer this question, we need to ask what constituencies are relevant for research on organizations. Unlike some fields of scientific research, research on organizations has a large, well-defined constituency of practitioners. Indeed, it is this feature of the field, along with a consideration of how data can best be gathered in organizations, that raises the question whether the "traditional" way of doing research is the way most likely to produce useful knowledge about organizations and their management.

This book assumes that research on organizations can serve not only the scientific research community but also those in the society who are generally responsible for and interested in the effectiveness of organizations. In short, it assumes that the research agenda is one that should contribute to both theory and practice. This is an important point because it raises the standard, or perhaps a better way to phrase it is to say that it creates two standards, that any research project must meet. The project must help practitioners understand organizations in a way that will improve practice, and it must contribute to a theoretically and scientifically useful body of knowledge about organizations.

Usefulness of Research for Theory and Practice

Traditionally, researchers of organizational behavior have not focused on the issue of usefulness. We have assumed that if a research project is methodologically sound, it will contribute to scientific knowledge and ultimately to practice. Indeed, many researchers seem to have found comfort and justification for their basic position in Kurt Lewin's statement that nothing is so practical as a good theory. This comfort has often led to their doing studies that focus only on contributing to theory and justifying research that is far removed from practice.

Perhaps because it is not focused on the goal of usefulness, a considerable amount of the research done in organizational behavior has in fact not had an impact on practice. The belief that good scientific research will ultimately win out often turns out to be naive and misleading. For example, the best-known research on organization effectiveness is contained in the book *In Search of Excellence* (Peters and Waterman, 1983). From a methodological point of view, that book is a disaster (no control group, measures not specified, and so forth).

The suggestion here is that if research is to jointly contribute to theory and practice, it must be designed to accomplish this objective. It cannot simply be taken as a matter of faith that adhering to certain scientific research principles will lead to jointly useful research. Indeed, it may be that adhering to principles that were designed to produce research that contributes to scientific knowledge will make it certain that this research will not contribute to practice.

At this point, I need to expand on my earlier statement about how data can best be gathered. Organizational behavior research has numerous characteristics that make it different from research in the physical and biological sciences. The study of organizations and people in them is a much more complex interactive process than the study of most physical and biological phenomena. People in organizations do not become subjects in the same sense that animals, neutrons, and chemical substances become subjects. They are an active part of the research process, and as such, they influence it very directly. Given this difference, it seems quite possible that what is a good research approach for contributing to theory and scientific knowledge in traditional fields of science may not be a good research approach in dealing with organizations.

Indeed, in the case of organizational behavior research there seems to be a particular danger that we will do research that is more a product of the methodology than of the phenomenon being studied. Taken to its extreme, this tendency could lead to a series of theories and findings that meet the test of traditional scientific validity but that are not useful to the practitioner and, indeed, may not be useful to the theorist either, because they do not describe actual organizational behavior. They may fail to be useful because they do not inform the practitioner or the theorist about the realities of the organizational environment. Instead, they frame the issues in such a way, and report on data so far removed from the realities of the complex, interactive, ever-changing world of organization, that they are not useful as a guide to either theory or practice.

It thus seems possible that a whole series of "scientifically acceptable" findings or theories could be developed that would have little or nothing to say about the realities of organizational behavior. How can this be avoided? The argument here is that it can best be avoided by doing research designed to influence both theory and practice.

Theory and practice are not competing mistresses. Indeed, research that is useless to either the theoretician or the practitioner is suspect. If it is useful to the practitioner but not the theoretician, then one must wonder whether it is a valid finding and whether it has addressed the correct issue. If it is useful to the theoretician but not to the practitioner, then one must wonder whether the research is capturing a critical issue. Indeed, it can be argued that we should always ask two questions about research: Is it useful for practice, and does it contribute to the body of scientific knowledge that is relevant to theory? If it fails either of these tests, then serious questions should be raised. It is a rare research study that can inform practice but not theory, or vice versa.

Research on organizations presents the researcher with a series of dilemmas. Hard choices need to be made and value judgments reached about the best way to design research. At this point I would like to raise some of the critical issues that need to be considered in designing research. I will consider how each of them is traditionally resolved and how each might be resolved if the desire is to be sure that the research produces scientifically and practically useful results.

Does Practice Lag Behind Theory?

Traditional wisdom in most scientific disciplines says that practice lags behind theory and research, that improvements in practice follow, often by decades, breakthroughs in research *practice follows theory* and theory. In many areas of organizational behavior the same principle holds. In a number of research and theoretical breakthroughs that have led to changes in practice (for example, the studies on job enrichment and on cafeteria fringe benefit plans), often the lag has been as long as fifteen years between research findings and the changes in practice. But it does not necessarily follow that in all or even in most cases theory leads practice.

Virtually everyone is an observer and theorist with respect to organizations. Many people hold organizational positions that call for them to make organizational design decisions, policy decisions, and practice decisions. Quite a few of them are bright, perceptive people, capable of developing insights into practice without the help of theory and empirical research. So in some areas it is quite possible for practice to lead or at least precede theory. Innovative work designs, policies, and procedures can and do exist before there is a theoretical understanding of why they might work and empirical support for their effectiveness. Skill-based pay is an example, as are high-involvement new plants (see, for example, Lawler, 1978, 1981). Instances in which practice is ahead of theory have some important implications for the kind of research that is done. They suggest that unless scholars and researchers are aware of practice, they may miss out on some important breakthroughs that are relevant to theory and research. Indeed, staying in touch with what is happening in the world of practice may be one of the best ways to develop new theory and to discover new research issues.

In short, what is being suggested is that advances in theory and practice are likely to come about not necessarily as a result of theory leading practice or practice leading theory. Either of these can happen, and, therefore, research ought to focus not only on developing new theory and findings that will guide practice but also on studying practice that can guide theory and new research.

Researchers are prone to ask, "Why don't managers use what we know?" This is a good question, but so is its reverse, "Why don't researchers use what managers know?"

Good point!

6 Doing Research That Is Useful for Theory and Practice

Where Is the Expertise? *Join t expertise*

In traditional scientific research the assumption is that expertise about the phenomenon being studied rests with the research scientist, not with the subject of the research. In most cases this is a safe assumption. But is it a safe assumption with respect to organizations and individual behavior in organizations? As already suggested, often managers and organization members are astute observers of the situation they are in, and their innovations in practice often precede theory. The clear implication is that any research targeted at improving both theory and practice needs to be guided by both practitioners and researchers. To ignore theory is to court rejection from the scientific community, and to ignore what managers already know and are doing runs the very definite risk of producing research that lags behind practice and therefore will not be useful to the practitioner.

The view that practitioners have knowledge about organizations has significant implications for research design. It suggests that, in many cases, members of an organization must be treated as co-researchers; that is, they must have a role in defining the types of research issues that are going to be looked at, and they must be informed of the scientific research issues involved. In short, the argument is that research that is to contribute to both theory and practice needs to be scrutinized by experts in both. Clearly the researcher ought to offer expertise about theory, past research, and methodology, but in many cases he or she has to rely on the members of the organization being studied to provide expertise about practice. For this to happen, the practitioner has to be involved in the study at more than a superficial level and, indeed, has to influence both the kind of topic studied and the methods used.

Role of Research Subjects

Traditional research design is very clear about defining the role of research subjects. It recommends what might be called an ''experimental set'' in which the subject, or respondent, is given a minimal amount of information about the study. The subject is told that the data will be used for research purposes only and that there is therefore no need to be concerned about how the data will affect his or her worklife. This research set clearly puts the subject in a dependent passive role with respect to the research study. It has some advantages, but it may not be the one that produces the best data for determining practice or developing research data that lead to valid theory.

The major problem with this approach is that it assumes people will conscientiously provide data simply because they are asked to and that these data will represent the best information that can be gathered about the subject being studied. An alternative view is that with this approach people might not care very much about giving valid data because doing so is not going to affect their lives and that they have other valid and important data that they could contribute to the study if they knew its focus. The latter would be particularly true if, as suggested earlier, people in organizations have expertise on organizations, just as researchers do. This point raises an interesting challenge for the researcher interested in doing theoretically and practically relevant research. It suggests that a researcher may want to rethink the relationship between the subject and the research so that it becomes a more balanced one in which the subject has knowledge of the key research issues. It also suggests, as discussed later, that better data are produced when the subjects know the study will affect practice in their organizations.

Usefulness of Counterintuitive Findings

Social science researchers seem to love nothing better than a counterintuitive finding. Proving that ''common sense'' is wrong seems to produce a great deal of satisfaction and is highly rewarded in the research community. This is hardly surprising. Counterintuitive findings tend to justify the field because they show that social science theory and research can produce things that are otherwise nondiscoverable. There are numerous examples of counterintuitive findings in the organizational behavior literature, and they are often featured in the textbooks of the field. Indeed, they are used to justify study of organizational behavior because they point out clearly that there is something to be learned here that cannot be learned from the everyday experience of practitioners. And to a degree this characteristic has led us to value counterintuitive findings more highly than research findings that support common sense, elaborate on it, or put it in a more comprehensive package.

It is hard to argue against the importance of counterintiutive findings and the theories that support and explain them. They are an important part of scientific research, but it is also possible that our search for respect, esteem, and credibility has led us to overvalue them compared with less spectacular findings and theory. Often the theory or finding that simply confirms common sense, organizes it better, and allows it to be communicated more effectively is the most useful theory. All too often it seems that the counterintuitive theories on which we focus produce long sequences of research projects that explain relatively few of the phenomena that actually occur in the real world. They end up being artifacts of a particular set of conditions that produce the phenomena we studied. In short, they are catchy, but they do not explain many of the situations that occur in the day-to-day operation of organizations. In my own field of research, for example, the work on effects of overpayment and effects of pay on intrinsic motivation produced catchy findings but ones that in fact seem very limited in the situations where they occur (Adams, 1965; Deci, 1975).

What all this suggests is that if we are to do research that is relevant to both theory and practice, we may have to value highly research that does not produce nonobvious findings but that produces confirmation of "common sense." This follows rather directly from the point that managers can be rather astute observers of common sense and, as such, they know something about organizations.

Project Size

A great deal of the research in organizational behavior can be characterized as small-scale research. It is usually done on a small budget, involves a few researchers, and covers a short time period. There are a number of reasons for the frequency of such research, including the kind of funding available for organizational behavior research and the career considerations present in most universities. All too often this combination of factors leads to organizational behavior research dealing with issues that can be easily studied and works against investigation of major issues that can be studied only in large-scale research projects.

Reliance on small-scale studies may not have hindered the field so much from a theoretical perspective as it has from a practical one. Organizational behaviorists have been able to study a number of interesting theoretical issues without engaging in large-scale research undertakings. However, many practical questions concerning what works and does not work in influencing productivity, organizational effectiveness, and so on seem to demand large-scale, multivariable, complex research. For example, in order to know how such things as self-managing work teams, quality circles, Scanlon plans, and other new management practices work, when they work, and where they work, large-scale studies seem a necessity. Thus, the traditional wisdom that says that a small, "doable" project is better than a large one may need to be changed if research that is relevant to both theory and practice is to be done. Researchers may need to think big, not small, in future research activities.

Researchable Questions

Closely related to the issue of thinking big versus thinking small is the issue of the degree to which available methodology should drive the kind of research question that is addressed. I have often heard the distinction made between interesting questions and researchable questions. As the statement goes, in the field of organizational behavior there are interesting questions and there are researchable questions, and often the two are different.

Often a question is interesting because it is of practical importance. Consequently, to the degree that the field limits

its research to researchable questions, it runs the danger of doing research that does not have practical importance. The implication of this point is clear. If we are to do research that is relevant to both theory and practice, we need to have a definition of "acceptable" or "good" methodology that is driven by the type of question being researched as well as by "traditional" scientific standards of what constitutes good research.

This may sound like a radical point of view, but it is not. It merely suggests that different approaches to data gathering, data analysis, and learning need to be used for different kinds of research problems. This follows rather directly from the view that not all problems can be solved with the same research strategy. The research question needs to drive the kind of data collected, and because methods and questions interact in important ways, the kind of data needed to answer certain questions simply cannot be gathered with traditional research methods. Similarly, traditional research methods produce the best kind of data to answer certain kinds of questions.

Do Practitioners Need Facts or Frames?

The field of organizational behavior is perhaps best at producing facts. The justification for this endeavor is that facts are ultimately a useful product because they allow theory testing, theory construction, and, of course, the improvement of practice.

It is quite possible, however, that the best way to improve practice is not by producing facts but by producing frames, or ways of organizing and thinking about the world. A good case can be made that the most important products of the field of organizational behavior are simple, elegant frames, not findings or hugely complex, ugly, inelegant frames.

The problem with saying we need frames is that it is difficult to identify where they come from and to determine the implication of their source for research strategy. However, drawing from some of my earlier points, at least one possibility is that frames come best from interaction between practitioners and researchers in which the researchers learn from the practitioners and vice versa. Frames, however, may come directly from the insights and research data of the researcher. The point here is not that there is one prescribed, clear-cut, best way to develop frames. It is merely that if part of the research agenda is to influence practice, frames may be the most important outcome of research.

Broad-Brush Versus Fine-Grained Research *more useful*

← Too simplistic –

A number of the early important studies in organizational behavior were fine-grained research. They looked in-depth at a particular interaction or small part of a work organization. The Western Electric studies (Roethlisberger and Dickson, 1939) were of this nature, as was much of the earlier work by William F. Whyte (for example, Whyte, 1955). These studies included dialogue and intensive study of the behavior of small groups and individuals. This type of research has accounted for a smaller and smaller percentage of the total work in the field. Instead we have moved to more and more broad-brush studies that analyze organizations from a distance, either through questionnaires or through secondary data. Organizations are studied by researchers who never see them! The result is rather antiseptic descriptions of organizations and the development of theories from these. To a degree, broad-brush research is the enemy of research that influences practice. Broad-brush research often deals with only a few variables across a large number of people and, as a result, lacks, in the eyes of many practitioners, a truly comprehensive understanding of the workplace. It tends to lead to simple theories that ignore many of the factors the practitioner must take into account in managing the work organization.

It may be that the most useful research is that which takes a more fine-grained approach to data gathering, but there are problems with this kind of research as well. The challenge with fine-grained research is, of course, to extract from it some general conclusions, insights, and frames that contribute to theory. There is also the problem of gathering data in such a way that it is replicable and meets most people's standards for scientifically valid research.

Certainty Versus Usefulness

Traditional science places great emphasis on establishing how certain we are of the validity of a particular relationship or finding. Indeed, most of the research in organizational behavior focuses on validating, extending, and establishing the conditions under which a certain finding holds. This focus reflects the high value placed on certainty in scientific research. But to a degree, certainty may be the enemy of usefulness.

The effort to establish certainty almost always leads to large numbers of studies being done on a single small topic and to more and more careful specification of the phenomenon. Once the phenomenon has been subjected to all the tests of certainty, it often ends up so complex that it is no longer useful to the practitioner. Establishing certainty presents a difficult challenge for the researcher who wishes to do research that is useful for both theory and practice. Somehow the researcher has to satisfy the scientific need to establish that the phenomenon is real and, at the same time, not lose sight of the usefulness issue. Often the conflict between these two demands leads the researcher who is concerned with usefulness and theory to stop doing research on a topic before others would say that the necessary level of certainty has been reached. In the researcher's eyes, however, certainty may have been established because of the kind of data that the researcher has gathered. A practice- and theory-oriented researcher, for example, may place more emphasis on observational data, reports by practitioners, and sense-making insights than would a researcher who is concerned with confidence levels, reliability estimates, and research design.

Study of Change

Assessing organizational change is difficult and often creates conditions that violate traditional views of what constitutes good scientific research. It typically requires a long-term involvement with an organization, an adaptive research design in which methods and questions change over time, and a close working relationship with the organization. All these conditions lead many to argue that it is hard to do "good" research on change. However, many of the most interesting practical questions concern change. Managers and practitioners constantly want to know what happens to Y if they do X, and they also want to know the best way to change organizations toward a particular kind of culture or strategy. Hence there is little doubt that if research is going to be practically useful, it needs to deal with the issue of organizational change.

Although there seems to be some reason for believing that doing good research and studying change are mutually exclusive, a good counterargument can be made. If, as stated earlier, good research is often fine-grained and large-scale, the study of change offers an excellent opportunity to do research that meets these conditions. Members of organizations are often very concerned about and interested in research on change, particularly if it can help inform and direct the change in constructive ways. Consequently, in the study of change, there is often a natural alliance between the researcher who wants to do long-term, fine-grained research on an important organizational change issue and practitioners who want to understand the change and make it effective. Thus, the study of change may be a particularly good opportunity to do research that is useful both practically and theoretically.

If researchers are to do research on change, they need a set of skills often lacking in organizational behavior researchers. Not only do they need to be familiar with and capable of using a variety of research methods, they need to relate to organizations in a way that allows the research relationship to survive over a long period and, perhaps, even to support the change activities going on in the organization. In short, they need to have both research skills and certain consulting skills. If a researcher has these skills and is able to engage the organization in a study of the change process, the probabilty of studying significant problems in a comprehensive way is high.

Indeed, the key question may be: Is it possible to do good research *without* studying change? Given that the key issues in understanding organizations are not static and, as some of the chapters that follow point out, are not the kinds that lend themselves to tightly controlled field experiments, studying change may be the only way.

Consulting and Research

Many researchers take care to separate consulting and research. The two are seen as competing activities because they demand a different relationship with the organization and its members. This is clearly true in the traditional scientific model of what constitutes good research, but it is not so clear if the research agenda is targeted toward influencing both theory and practice.

It can be argued that testing many important theoretical concepts and developing improved practice depends on having some researchers who can engage in consulting relationships with organizations. It is only through this type of consulting relationship that organizations can actually try new ideas and break-throughs in practice.

Some new practices and some new theories can be adequately tested only by putting them in place in an organization. This implies an intervention into an organization's actual operating procedures. Alternatively, one can simply wait for an organization to try something and then capitalize on it as a naturally occurring field experiment or a post hoc study of change. This is often done in the field of organizational behavior, but reliance on this technique places a severe limitation on the development of the field. It requires that new practices be tried by somebody else before the field can progress. A much more attractive alternative is for researchers to help in instituting innovations so that they can study issues that are likely to push the state of theory and practice forward.

Summary

Taken in combination, the points made so far suggest that research that is likely to contribute to both theory and practice can be done but that it may look different from much of the research traditionally done in organizational behavior. To mention just a few points, it is more likely, for example, to involve change, to be large-scale, and to be fine-grained in the depth with which it looks at organizations. This is not to argue that traditional research is to be discontinued or that there is only one right way to do research; rather, there are multiple valid ways to do research on organizations, and the field needs to be eclectic in the approaches it includes. In short, the argument is that there is more than one way of establishing theory and fact. There are multiple ways, and these all need to be used if research that contributes to both theory and practice is to be conducted.

The chapters that follow will touch on the issues raised here from a number of perspectives. By no means do they present a consensus on how research that influences both theory and practice should be done. If anything, the chapters are consistent in pointing out that there are multiple ways of learning about organizations and of doing research. The best approach for a particular situation clearly reflects not only the topic to be studied but the skills of the researcher and the strengths and weaknesses of different methods of data gathering.

Figure 1 elaborates on this point by showing a possible relationship between data and the confidence one has in a finding about how organizations operate. The data gathered may vary from traditional scientific data to no data at all, and confidence can vary from high to low. Where few facts exist but confidence is high, we have entered the arena of value-driven decision making. At the other extreme, when scientific data exist, confidence will be high from a data-based perspective. Yet even where there is a great deal of data, the figure suggests that value contributes to reaching the highest level of confidence. Finally, it suggests that we should have the most "scientific" confidence when we have good traditional data.

Based on the arguments presented in this chapter, it is reasonable to question the nature of the confidence line separating value-driven and data-driven decision making in Figure 1. Figure 1 assumes that the best data are traditionally gathered scientific data. If we assume they are not, then we might draw the line as shown in Figure 2. Ultimately, it is up to each researcher to develop his own relationship between data and confidence in the decisions about what findings to believe and how strongly to believe them.

Figure 1. Possible Relationship Between Data and Confidence.

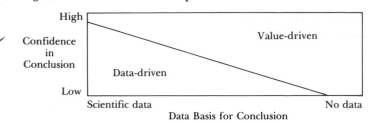

Figure 2. Alternative Relationship Between Data and Confidence.

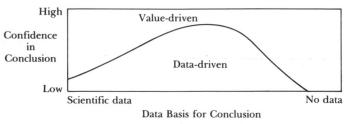

The next chapter by Ian Mitroff directly focuses on the issue of how we know when we know something and makes it clear that there is no right way to establish that we know something. The following chapters look more specifically at how particular leading researchers have, in their own careers, used methods that contribute to research that is relevant to both theory and practice. Their approaches represent a wide diversity of practices, but they are notable in the degree to which they do not follow traditional research approaches. These researchers have found different ways of knowing and learning about organizational phenomena. Indeed, if there is one theme that runs throughout the entire book, it is that there are multiple ways of learning and, therefore, multiple ways of knowing about organizations.

A Nobel Prize–winning economist has observed that the best current research and theory rarely inform contemporary practice in the field of economics (Stigler, 1976). He argues that the kind of data that economists need and the kind of theories they state are so obscure that they bear almost no relation to practice. At first glance, this might seem to be in contrast to Lewin's statement about the usefulness of theory, but I wonder whether Lewin would consider the theoretical work done in economics today good. In fact, I doubt that he would.

There is an interesting possible variant of Lewin's statement about the usefulness of theory: "Nothing is so useful as research that informs both theory and practice." If, indeed, research informs practice, then it is likely to have something to say about the reality of the workplace and to deal with issues that are relevant to practitioners. If it also informs theory, then it must describe more than just an isolated phenomenon or a nonreplicable phenomenon. It must state something that is generalizable across situations and issues. Unfortunately, much of the research on organizational behavior may be better at informing theory than practice. As a result, we end up with many theories that are not useful to the practitioner. We have many theories, but perhaps we have few good theories.

REFERENCES

Adams, J. S. "Injustice in Social Exchange." In L. Berkowitz (Ed.), *Advances in Experimental Social Psychology*. Vol. 2. New York: Academic Press, 1965.

Deci, E. L. *Intrinsic Motivation*. New York: Plenum, 1975.

Lawler, E. E., III. "The New Plant Revolution." *Organizational Dynamics*, 1978, *6* (3), 2–12.

Lawler, E. E., III. *Pay and Organization Development*. Reading, Mass.: Addison-Wesley, 1981.

Peters, T., and Waterman, R. *In Search of Excellence*. New York: Harper & Row, 1983.

Roethlisberger, F. J., and Dickson, W. J. *Management and the Worker*. Cambridge, Mass.: Harvard University Press, 1939.

Stigler, G. J. "Do Economists Matter?" *Southern Economic Journal*, 1976, *42* (3), 347–354.

Whyte, W. F. *Money and Motivation: An Analysis of Incentives in Industry*. New York: Harper & Row, 1955.

2

Ian I. Mitroff

✤ ✤ ✤ ✤ ✤ ✤ ✤ ✤ ✤ ✤ ✤ ✤ ✤ ✤ ✤ ✤ ✤

Why Our Old Pictures
of the World
Do Not Work Anymore

In the beginning
even before the word
was the picture.
Everything came after it,
the road map
of reality.
And the picture
is more enduring.
For the word
itself is
only a picture.

Pictures do not change easily.
They are the bedrock,
the ground of reality.
They *are* reality.

18

And yet
like everything else
pictures do change.
They must
if only
with great difficulty.

What picture
is appropriate
for studying
pictures
changing?

Someone who works as a full-time organizational change agent or organizational development expert once shared with me the following metaphor for understanding why most organizations resist change. I find it an apt metaphor for understanding the nature of change. Picture an organization as a trapeze artist. Suppose that so far in his life the trapeze artist has known only the left-hand swing of the trapeze. He has never taken the bold leap through the air to land on the right-hand swing. He has never directly experienced the right-hand swing, the newer reality to which others are urging him to jump in the promise of a better life, fame, fortune, and so on.

This metaphor, or picture, helps to make understandable the extreme anxiety and severe resistance to change that many organizations experience in confronting change. The metaphor helps us to experience in our gut the anxiety associated with change as a real thing, not as an abstract concept. Asking an organization to change is like asking one to leap through the air, *without a safety net,* to a swing that one has never tested. No wonder organizations often prefer an inferior rung that they know to a superior promised reality that they do not know!

To capture even more aspects of the resistance to change, I have embellished the metaphor over time. For example, I believe that it is fair to describe the new swing that one is expected to jump to as hidden behind a curtain. One cannot even see clearly the new reality that one is being urged toward. Further, imagine that the new swing behind the curtain is swinging back and forth unpredictably. As a consequence, one does not know with much assurance when one should jump or how best to accomplish one's jump.

To extend the metaphor to its fullest, what, then, could possibly cause an organization to jump? Well, a strong push from the environment such as a rotting, deteriorating, or burning platform (that is, a turbulent environment) would surely motivate one to think about leaping (that is, changing). For another, a chief executive officer who was daring or liked to ride the crest of new and even dangerous waves would certainly be a factor. Leaping would be seized as an opportunity, not avoided as a threat.

Whether one accepts or rejects the particular metaphor of organizations as trapeze artists is not the basic point here. The basic point is that whatever one thinks or writes about is based on the presumption of a metaphor of some kind. Countless philosophers of science have pointed out that one is never—repeat, *never*—in direct contact with "reality itself." "Reality" is a theoretical construct whose decription is affected by (filtered through) the particular language (frame of reference) we adopt for describing "it" (see, for example, Churchman, 1971). (Different languages describe different "its.") But since language is at its fundamental basis metaphorical (for instance, we "ground" ideas, we try to "contain" them, we use them as "springboards" to thought and to action, we "chip away" at ideas, we "refine" and we "temper" them, and we even try to "shoot" them "down"), reality is apprehended only in terms of metaphors or, more generally, what I would call an underlying base image or root picture of reality (Lakoff and Johnson, 1980).

In this chapter I wish to discuss three very different basic pictures of the social world, how they have changed in relation to one another, and the kind of research that each seems to warrant. I thus take the notion of a picture very seriously. I believe that the notion of a picture has to do with one of the most fundamental, and for that very reason one of the least studied, mechanisms whereby human beings try to make sense of their world. Pictures have to do with one of the least appreciated aspects of human beings, not to mention scientific theories. This aspect is esthetics.

There is a long, serious, and distinguished history of the study of the truth status of scientific theories—that is, the epistemology, or philosophy, of science. There is also a history, although it is less long and less serious, of the ethics of science and of scientific theories. There is almost no history, let alone serious study, of the esthetics of science. There is little beyond the oft-repeated cliché that the best scientists prefer theories that are beautiful, simple, and elegant.

By the term *esthetics* I mean something far more than beauty. Beauty as such is not my basic concern. By *esthetics* I mean the more general notion that *everyone* has a style, a taste of some kind. For instance, people express their preferences for style in countless ways: in the clothes they wear, the furniture they select, the pictures they hang on their walls; the cars, colors, animals they surround themselves with; the general quality of life they pursue; the foods they eat, how they serve them—in short, elegance or the lack thereof in their lives. By the esthetic dimension of science, especially managerial science, I mean that researchers in different traditions seem to adopt very different underlying pictures of the world and that these pictures grab them at such a basic emotional level that it is almost impossible to have anything even approaching an "objective" discussion across traditions.

If the esthetic dimension is as important as I believe it is, then it may be impossible for the proponents of one picture to convince the proponents of another that the pictures in their gallery are *rationally* superior to those in the galleries of others. Conversion is not, then, solely a matter of logical or rational persuasion but, rather, a matter of Gestalt or picture switch—that is, an esthetic conversion.

The case may be more like two old dowagers walking through an art museum, the one trying to convince the other that the French are better painters than the Dutch, while the other is convinced of just the opposite. If they are to have a critical discussion at all instead of merely shouting at each other, then both have to realize that their dispute is not a matter of truth alone but of different standards of art appreciation. In short, both parties need recourse to a theory of art appreciation, not of truth itself, if they are to have a fruitful discussion. The pictures each prefers are *different,* not necessarily *better.* Each tradition allows one to make certain observations about the condition of the artist and his or her relation to the society, culture, and nature of the artist's time.

In this sense, we have almost no theory of the esthetic dimensions of science, although we do have the dawning recognition that the pictures that managers (practitioners) have of organizations and those that academic researchers have are vastly different. Rather than one being better, it is doubtful that either picture is functional beyond the limited environment in which it operates. Very few academics would know how to recognize and handle a "real world" problem if it bit them. Conversely, very few practitioners would know how to conduct systematic research or to engage in reflective thought about their world.

By this emphasis on esthetics I do not mean to imply that the epistemological or ethical aspects of science are unimportant. On the contrary, they are vitally important. I do mean to imply, however, that they may be secondary in importance. I belive that scientists are no less and no more human than other people (Mitroff, 1974). As such, I believe they get emotionally attached—hooked, as it were—to a basic intuitive conception of the world. Within a particular picture they can ask and pursue questions of truth, ethics, and so on. But first comes the hook, the decision, for all kinds of reasons, to pursue a particular style of life. This is the part that is esthetic, not rational.

For many readers, what I have just said will sound like what Kuhn (1962) has talked about under the heading of "paradigm switch." I believe that the notion of a picture is much deeper. What I am talking about is what *all* scientists, regardless of their particular paradigm allegiance, appear to share—that is, a deep-seated preference for viewing the world in abstract, nearly exclusively cognitive, or "left brain," terms (Mitroff, 1974). For the most part, scientists are "left brain," cognitively oriented creatures, not "right brain," affect-oriented ones. Thus, although Kuhn's notion of a paradigm still applies, there are some general paradigmatic features that all scientists seem to share, notably the preference for certain kinds of general pictures. Put another way, although different scientists like pictures of somewhat different kinds, they all seem to have the same general theory of painting. For all their differences, the pictures they paint tend to look the same. They tend to tell the same kinds of stories in the sense that they hold a common theory of plots.

A valid scientific story is supposedly one that is told in impersonal terms. It removes as much as possible the motives and the true personality of the storyteller. Only the personalities of the characters the scientist studies are supposed to be relevant, not his or her own personality.

Let me turn to three pictures of the world and describe the different kinds of galleries in which each hangs its pictures and thus the different kinds of art collectors to which each kind of picture appeals.

The World as Simple Machine

The oldest picture of the world that still pervades and dominates much of economic and managerial science is that of the world as a simple machine. The classic expression is probably found in the thinking of Milton Friedman, although this picture is found in many places. According to this view, the world of the modern corporation can be decomposed, or partitioned, into three primary entities: the corporation itself, stockholders, and customers (see Figure 1). The reason is the oft-asserted statement that the primary purpose of management (presumably the upper echelons of the corporation) is to serve *the primary stakeholders* in management's environment—that is, the stockholders. From this perspective, all other stakeholders either do not exist or are not recognized as significant. At a minimum, this view assumes that the rest of the environment can be clearly partitioned off from the three stakeholders in Figure 1.

As many writers have noted, among them most promi-

Figure 1. The World as Simple Machine.

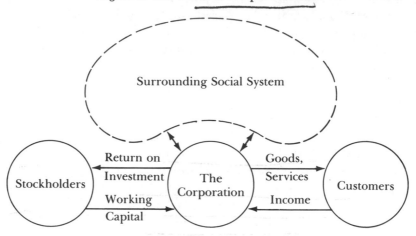

nently Ackoff (1982) and Toffler (1980), this view of the world is founded on a primary, taken-for-granted metaphor of the world as a simple machine. Thus it derives from the industrial revolution, when the entire world, including humans, plants, animals, and the environment, was conceived of in mechanical terms. The metaphor was so strong that to the inhabitants of the time the world was not just metaphorically a machine, it was literally a machine.

Since by definition a machine is something that can be decomposed into its separate components, analysis, or reductionism, was and still is the favored mode of attack in this view. A natural outcome was the partitioning of the universe into distinct and sharply distinguishable causes and effects. From the standpoint of scientific methodology, the classic expression of this philosophy reached its zenith in the work of John Stuart Mill (1872). Everything today that we preach under the label of experimental design is really a direct outgrowth of Mill's canons of induction. If you do not believe the world is literally a machine, as I do not, then this restricts the value you will place on the *wholesale and unlimited* use of experimentation as an appropriate method of knowing for the applied social sciences.

Since a machine is also by definition something that can be objectified—that is, it has no emotions—its working can be described in purely impersonal terms. Hence, economics, for example, offers a natural language in which to describe (better yet, "represent") the workings of society and organizations. Or, one should say, the *kind* of economics we have developed was suited to this representation—that is, the brand of economics that recognizes only the ego component of the psyche as valid and therefore views the human as a rational calculating device, making all decisions on the strict basis of benefits-versus-cost calculations alone. If one grants this supposition as true of everyone, then the behavior of and between individuals could also be described as a series of impersonal economic transactions. Furthermore, since egos are supposedly separable from one another, the properties of each individual were in principle also separable from the rest of the system. To be sure, how individuals behaved was a function of the rest of the system, but supposedly their internal properties were not. Thus, the individual could in principle be removed from and studied in isolation from the rest of the surrounding system. Because of its overwhelming emphasis on the ego, this brand of economics would be better termed "egonomics."

The World as Complex System

Around the 1950s, the picture of the world as a simple machine, which for so long had dominated imagination as a result of the extreme influence of the industrial revolution, began seriously to crumble (Ackoff, 1982). Cybernetics and other methods for describing complex systems with intricate interdependencies and feedback loops were developed. These developments continue to this day.

With these developments came the recognition that the world is a complex system of interconnected elements, not a simple machine of largely independent entities.

It was only a matter of time before this representation spread to organizations and institutions (see Figure 2). Recognition dawned that the modern corporation is increasingly buffeted by a growing number and constantly shifting set of players in a complex system. This broader set of players can be called

Figure 2. The World as Complex System.

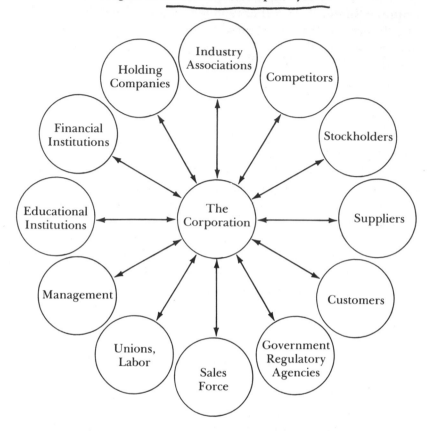

*stake*holders (Ackoff, 1982; Mason and Mitroff, 1981). In contrast to the single class of stockholders—still important, to be sure—stakeholders are all those vested interest groups, parties, associations, institutions, and individuals who exert a hold and a claim on modern organizations. Stakeholders are all those who either affect or are affected by an organization and its behavior (that is, its policies).

It is important to appreciate that this view of the world differs from the preceding one not only in that it contains more parties but also in that the interrelations among them are very different. As to the first difference, the modern corporation has no choice but to recognize that it must contend with a larger set of forces external to it than ever before, whether it likes or agrees with those forces or not. As to the second, in the ''world as complex system'' picture, in principle none of the stakeholders can be described independently of the entire system of which it is a part (Ackoff, 1982). The properties of each stakeholder are not self-contained. Not only do different stakeholders influence one another's surface behavior more and more, but increasingly they also intrude more deeply into the internal properties of all stakeholders. That is, the properties of all those stakeholders external to the organization affect more and more the properties of those stakeholders internal to the organization.

An even more apt metaphor for this picture is that of ''the world as an organism'' (Ackoff, 1982). To take a simple example, the heart and the eye neither function nor exist separately from the brain or the rest of the body—that is, the whole system of which they are parts. A human being is not an organization—that is, a system whose ''parts'' supposedly have an independent and thereby separate existence and will of their own. Rather, a human being is, with respect to his or her physical constitution, a whole system. This even applies to the person's behavioral and mental constitution. A human being is not a self-contained system but, rather, is dependent on the larger social system for his or her existence, beliefs, values, and so forth.

It should be noted that the ''world as complex system'' picture shares some features with the first picture, ''the world as simple machine.'' Both view the interactions between stakeholder entitites as largely rational. That is, in both pictures we are still at the egoic, or surface, level of social analysis (Mitroff, 1983). To be sure, the second picture recognizes the existence or, even more basic, the legitimate right to existence of more parties that have a hold on the modern corporation, but it is still limited in the number of parties deep within the psyche of individuals and of institutions that it recognizes. For this reason, the second picture can still be called ''the world as complex but rational (that is, economic) system.'' A good label for this view is ''systenomics.''

I can only mention in passing the methods of research that this view promotes. Since synthesis of parts into all-encompassing wholes is the main preoccupation of this view, we should not be surprised to find that methods founded on the ever-finer analytic reduction of the world into smaller and smaller atoms are viewed with extreme suspicion, if not disfavor. Instead, methods are promoted that attempt to aid the imagination in envisioning the whole system of which any component must of necessity be a part (Ackoff, 1982; Mason and Mitroff, 1981). That is, as much emphasis is put on the connections between parts as on the parts themselves.

   This does not mean that experimentation is shunned in its entirety; rather, it is insisted that the experimenter is as much a part of his experiments as are his so-called subjects. Even more basic, it is insisted that, as a method of inquiry, experimentation does not stand on its own. Every method is part of the larger system of background ideas that must be presupposed in order to conduct any investigation. None of these ideas can be rigorously controlled, fully known, tested, or removed before the experiment. Thus, experimentation must always be part of some other, larger system of inquiry in order for it to function. These "other systems of inquiry" attempt to supply, by conceptual (that is, nonexperimental) means, the ideas and the tests of those ideas that every experiment requires. There is no such thing— period—as the self-standing, self-contained experiment. Some sort of conceptual analysis must precede and follow every experimental investigation. The nature of these other inquiry systems for supplying and testing needed conceptual ideas has been described elsewhere in extensive detail (Churchman, 1971; Mitroff, 1974).

   To summarize, in dealing with complex systems it may be more important to identify as many potential stakeholders as possible and the broad outlines of the potential interactions (assumptions) among them than to know the behavior of any particular stakeholder in excruciating detail. Since perfect certainty is not accorded the same exalted status in this picture as in the first, getting different pictures of the social system out on the table for explicit debate is regarded as more important than having perfect certainty within any single picture of a complex social system (Mason and Mitroff, 1981). That is, more accurately, Figure 2 is not a single picture but stands for the case of multiple pictures by multiple stakeholders of the social system. In principle there may be as many different pictures of Figure 2 as there may be different stakeholders within any given picture. Little wonder that experimentation *within* any particular picture is not given as much weight as examining the assumptions *between* pictures that warrant belief in any particular picture (Mason and Mitroff, 1981).

The World as Complex Hologram

The last picture I want to present is the one I have come most recently to adopt (Mitroff, 1983). It is important to note that this picture evolved out of pictures one and two. In this sense, although I no longer believe in the adequacy of the former two pictures to capture the complexities of modern social reality, they are necessary in the sense that the latest picture could not have been achieved without them. Though necessary, however, they are no longer sufficient. In this sense, at least, I am no longer personally able to appreciate their way (that is, their esthetic) of viewing the world.

Figure 3 presupposes Figure 2. It starts from it. Indeed, it was out of Figure 2 that Figure 3 was developed (Mitroff, 1983).

Figure 3 adds a number of things that Figure 2 does not contain. First, it adds some additional stakeholder characters that Figure 2, on the whole, is oblivious to. For the most part, these additional characters derive from psychoanalysis in general and from the study of psychopathic and sociopathic behavior in particular (Mitroff, 1983).

Recent acts against corporations, such as the placing of poison in Tylenol, demonstrate that the term *stakeholder,* if it is confined to such parties as suppliers, salespeople, and customers, is far too benign to capture the full nature of the environment in which business now operates. The traditional concept of stakeholders is too limited to capture the range of evil and bizarre characters that now potentially affect the modern corporation. Thus, the first set of additional characters surrounding the

Figure 3. The World as Complex Hologram.

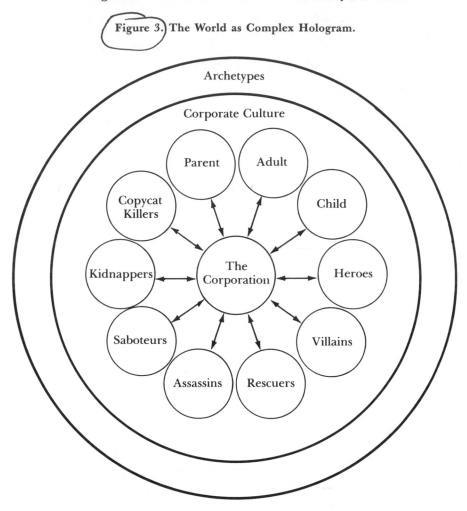

inner circle standing for the corporation is meant to represent the impact of these other very different kinds of stakeholders on the corporation.

For the most part, the stakeholders shown in Figure 2 represent the impact of stakeholders at the sociological, or institutional, level of analysis on the corporation. This level is not wrong; it is merely incomplete. Figure 3 adds another set of stakeholders, which emanates from the deepest impulses rooted in the psychic structure of the human beings.

In addition, Figure 3 is meant to indicate (picture) that

all the stakeholders in Figures 2 and 3 are potentially in contact with one another. When people, either individually or in institutions, interact, they do more than merely engage in impersonal economic transactions. We are more—much, much more—than mere economic calculating machines. We possess more than an ego. We also possess an id and a superego, if one is a Freud, and a complex archetypal structure, if one is a Jung. The point is that whenever two persons or two institutions interact, they do more than merely exchange goods, services, utilities, and so on. To be sure, they do this. However, they also exchange something far deeper. They form images of each other. They project their hopes, fears, dreams, wishes, doubts, worries, joys, and anxieties onto each other. For instance, the recent case of Hitachi's attempt to steal secrets from IBM is a gold mine from a psychoanalytic standpoint. It shows that whenever two competitors interact, they inevitably form distorted pictures of each other. They inevitably see the other as more evil than the other "really" is—or stronger, wiser, braver, and so on.

It would take us too far afield to describe the psychoanalytic mechanisms whereby stakeholders influence one another at this level of social analysis. I have already mentioned one such mechanism—namely, projection. There also exist other well-studied mechanisms, such as compensation, identification, and introjection. Needless to say, we have only begun to study the extreme complexity of the interactions that are possible across both stakeholders and the vastly different kinds of transactions in which they are capable of engaging (Mitroff, 1983).

Human beings are complex not only because they engage in seemingly impersonal economic transactions but also because they engage in psychodynamic transactions *simultaneously*. Thus, once again, it is not so much that Figure 2 is wrong as that it is seriously incomplete. At a minimum there is potentially a *double line* of influence (economic and psychodynamic) connecting each pair of stakeholders in Figures 2 and 3. We are complex because, both consciously and unconciously, we engage in transactions across very different levels of social reality all at the same time and, more often than not, without conscious awareness that we are doing so.

One of the strong implications of this way of thinking is

that at present we have no truly adequate theory of economics. As remarked earlier, current economic theory is largely a theory of transactions that hold only at the level of the ego—that is, conscious reality. We have no theory of economics that describes the ways in which the other aspects of our complex psyche conduct transactions.

Figure 3 differs significantly from Figure 2 in another way. Some of the most recent and radical philosophical speculations concern the proposition that the world may be akin to a hologram (Wilber, 1982). A hologram is a very interesting three-dimensional projected figure. It has the interesting property that if any part of it is enlarged, one does not get merely an enlarged picture of the part being blown up but a fuzzier picture of the whole holographic figure! That is, a hologram has the strange property that the whole is contained in every part but not to the same degree of clarity and sharpness. If a hologram is a good metaphor for a complex social system, then is each stakeholder an imperfect re-creation and projection of all other stakeholders?

Implications for a Theory of Practice

The preceding discussion should help us understand (that is, picture) why we have no real formal theory of practice or any really adequate methods of applied social science. How does one do an experiment on a system of the complexity of Figures 2 and 3? How does one study a complex social system whose constitution is holographic?

If one simplifies the system down to the level of Figure 1, then one can certainly perform an experiment, but what good are the results in helping us understand the behavior of the parts in the context of the whole system? Conversely, how does one put on the psychoanalyst's couch individually, let alone two, three, or more at a time, the various stakeholders of Figures 2 and 3?

One way out of this impasse may consist in combining the insights and instincts of the experimentalist and the psychoanalyst. I think the psychoanalyst is needed both in framing a limited experiment and in interpreting the results carried back into the context of the larger system. I have no qualms about experimentation as such as long as we attempt to get to some of the real psychodynamic factors acting in both the experimenters and the subjects in an experiment. Why do experimenters project what they do on a social situation so that they can later experiment with it—that is, break it apart? Conversely, what must be projected on the results so that we can put the parts back into the nature of the whole?

I think the time is way overdue to take the notion of an esthetic of science very seriously. How do people form pictures of the systems of which they are a part? What kinds of pictures do they form of systems, stakeholders, and assumptions concerning them? Why do we not hire as our associates such characters as graphic artists, set designers, architects, and dramatists to help us draw our pictures of complex systems?

Notice carefully that I am not advocating that we throw out any of the traditional methods in which we have been schooled. These tools are what make us scientists. I am merely saying that they are no longer enough. We need more than ever before to develop our artistic side. Why? Because I think that fundamentally what the applied social sciences are up to is how people make sense of a very fuzzy, large, complex, and loosely coupled whole system. Precision is not how people make sense of their world, no matter how much they would like precision to result.

Paradoxically enough, there is an emerging tool on the horizon that may help to merge as never before the untapped esthetic dimension of science with the more traditional analytic modes of analysis. This is the rapidly expanding graphics capabilities of personal computers (see Mitroff, 1983). Computer packages are available that allow one to create, manipulate, and store exceedingly sophisticated and potent images of stakeholders.

Concluding Remarks

I have always felt that the applied social sciences seriously missed their mark by trying to ape the methods of the so-called more exact sciences (Mitroff, 1974). I have always felt that they needed something different to capture their phenomena, but just what that something was never became clear until the years passed so that this chapter could be written. It now seems clear to me that the inroad into the methods for the applied social sciences lies through a serious appreciation, consideration, and enactment of the esthetic.

Capturing a complex system may be like seating a victim before a police artist. As the artist flips over pages of different kinds of noses, she asks the victim, "Is this nose right?"; then "Is this mouth right?"; and so on. Our task is infinitely more difficult, for we are trying to paint a simultaneous and composite portrait of many more actors who are intertwined in a complex world.

If every individual is as much an innate though naive artist as he or she is an innate though naive scientist, then we owe all persons the dignity of allowing them to express their artistic as well as their scientific side. If they are naive poets as well, then we must also allow them the dignity of speaking in a richer language than scientific prose alone. We need more artists and playwrights in our midst to capture the drama of everyday life. Our traditional media are not up to the complexity of the phenomena we have been trying to capture for too long with only mixed success at best.

Finally, I would like to share some thoughts that came to mind as I read the excellent list of questions compiled by my colleague Ed Lawler to stimulate the thinking of the contributors to this volume. The first thought is that almost all the distinctions that misguide contemporary science (for example, subjective/objective, descriptive/prescriptive, fact/opinion) are appropriate *only* for the first picture of the world (Figure 1). They are either not appropriate for or irrelevant to pictures two and three. For instance, in worlds two and three, there is no such thing as "description" independently of some "prescription," and vice versa (Churchman, 1971). In short, the dominant philosophy of science, which is still largely a holdover from the industrial revolution, is out of date for the pictures of the world that I believe are now more appropriate.

If you think I am overly critical in this regard, listen to the words of the noted philosopher of science Paul Feyerabend: "All the distinctions of the [philosophy of science] discipline (context of discovery/context of justification; logical/psychological; internal/external; and so on) have but one aim: to turn incompetence (ignorance of relevant material and lack of imagination) into expertise (happy assurance that the things not known and unimaginable are not relevant and that it would be professionally incompetent to use them)" (1978, pp. 201–202).

Table 1. Correlation Between Two Kinds of Knowledge.

| | | Academic Knowledge | |
		High	Low
Street Knowledge	High	I	II
	Low	IV	III

The second thought concerns Table 1. I believe that, as a gross oversimplification, there are two very different kinds of knowledge: (1) formal, or academic, knowledge and (2) practitioner, "moxie," or street knowledge. Most of us, perhaps most of the time, are in cell III of Table 1. That is, we have neither in-depth, inside "street" knowledge of the organizations we study (we lack the intuitive knowledge of the real and, for that reason, largely unwritten "rules of the game" that it takes to "make it" in the organization) nor very good formal theories of organizations that explain much beyond the obvious. (I am afraid that much that passes for theorizing in managerial science all too rarely rises above the level of showing that $X = X$.)

Now, traditional academia stresses cell IV. It values formal theory over practitioner knowledge if it even recognizes that practitioners are capable of having anything called "knowledge" at all. Practitioners are, of course, supposed to value or stress cell II over the others.

There is one cell remaining, cell I. Here is where I think our emphasis must be. It is here we must work. I do not believe we can develop anything approaching an applied social science if it is not grounded in and respectful of both kinds of knowledge. To do so, however, requires that we develop very different conceptions of the terms *knowledge* and *theory*.

Lastly, there is the thought that occurred when pondering the implications of Erik Erikson's work. Most of you are familiar with his notion of the life cycle and with the different challenges to one's identity that must be met as one ages. The thought that occurred to me is that as the kinds of questions one asks vary over one's life cycle, so perhaps should the methodology one adopts to pursue the questions. As the questions that once concerned me no longer possess the same force, so also the methods I was once so interested in no longer seem to exert the same compelling force. In brief, most of the methods that dominate conventional social science are appropriate for the earlier stages of the life cycle, what I would call the "engineering" phase of one's career. We have almost no methods or journals for the later stages of life, the reflective, the philosophical. This is intolerable. No wonder the older I get, the angrier I find myself toward what we have done to that once beautiful promise called "social science."

RESPONSE AND COMMENTARY

Steven Kerr

It is generally tolerated as a human frailty that given a nominal data set—wherein categories are mutually exclusive and cannot be described as "greater than" or "less than"—most behavioral scientists experience little difficulty in ranking the data. As an example, Mitroff's chapter offers the example of two dowagers who are foolishly trying to persuade one another of the inherent superiority of either French or Dutch painters. Mitroff points out that the discussion is ultimately pointless, because:

> The pictures each prefers are *different,* not
> necessarily *better.* Each tradition allows one to make
> certain observations about the condition of the artist
> and his or her relation to the society, culture, and
> nature of the artist's time. . . . Rather than one
> being better, it is doubtful that either picture is func-
> tional beyond the limited environment in which it
> operates.

For me, however, the ultimate point of Mitroff's paper
is to argue for the supremacy of his third model, the world as
complex hologram. From his title, "Why Our Old Pictures of
the World Do Not Work Anymore," to his later assertion that
alternative models are "seriously incomplete," it is clear that,
unlike the French and Dutch paintings, Mitroff's figures are
not meant to hang side by side. Rather, his clear intention is
to paint Figure 3 on the canvas where Figures 1 and 2 were
previously visible.

Certainly Figure 3 may be said to be complete. In fact,
I might properly label it "seriously complete." (When I first
saw this depiction of assassins, saboteurs, and copycat killers,
I was afraid that the poor man had been reduced to studying
university committees!) But Figure 3 leads me to ask: What is
the value of a fishing net so broadly woven that fish of any size
may freely leave and enter? Given that Figure 2 is so fully drawn,
of what use is Figure 3 to theory, research, or practice? And
are the new circles in Figure 3 really representative of additional
stakeholders, or has Mitroff merely made some value judgments
about the folks we met in Figure 2? Cannot unions be heroes,
for example, or villains? Cannot customers? Cannot regulators?
And who decides, and using what standards, whether a stakeholder is a hero or a villain? Mitroff begs the question to some
extent by making so many stakeholders in Figure 3 illegal (assassins, saboteurs, kidnappers, copycat killers) and by providing
socially desirable labels for most of the others. In real life, however, researchers might find it most useful to classify stakeholders
according to Figure 2. It is only after a while, and usually when

viewed through value-laden lenses, that the people in Figure 3 come into focus.

It seems a truism to say that every time we simplify we oversimplify; there is nothing particularly wrong with this. Others have pointed out that if a road map were as accurate and as complete as reality itself, it would take as long to negotiate as reality and would probably not be useful. I believe that the most important advantage Mitroff claims for his hologram model is that it provides the most accurate and complete view of organizations in their environment, but the question must be asked: Is realism the ultimate esthetic?

Actually my argument is not with the hologram model per se; that model is, after all, the most faithful of the three to Mitroff's definition of stakeholders. It is the definition itself that troubles me. Let me illustrate its weakness by referring to the Tylenol case, which Mitroff (1983) has so brilliantly analyzed. As I write this, the killer and his or her motive are unknown. If it turns out that the killer is a disgruntled employee, then perhaps we have found a new anchor for our scales of job dissatisfaction. If he or she is an ex-employee, then the case may extend our models of alienation and withdrawal. If he or she turns out to be a dissatisfied customer, there is a different message and a different learning point. But supposing the killer is a certified madman, who randomly selected Tylenol as his agent of destruction. Does such a person fit Mitroff's definition of a stakeholder? Unfortunately yes, since stakeholders are "all those vested interest groups, parties, associations, institutions, and individuals who . . . either affect or who are affected by an organization and its policies." But if the definition includes the Tylenol killer regardless of his motive, then it must also include, for example, the locusts who eat the inventory of an agricombine and destroy its land. And if the definition lets in all these, then who is left out? And if no one is left out, how useful is the definition?

Several of us at the University of Southern California have become interested in a process variable called "fitness for future action." It is a hard construct to measure, hard even to define very well, but it refers to an individual's or a group's capacity to perform in the future, following some performance in the present. As one illustration of the sorts of things we are looking at, Sherif found that sometimes following a loss, teams resort to scapegoating, blame, and occasionally dissolution. Other times, however, the act of losing somehow constitutes a "baptism of fire" that steels a team to the point where it is almost invincible in the future.

Does maximal realism increase or impair fitness for future action? Old wives' tales conflict, and data are sparse. Military training is usually made as authentic as possible, on the assumption that realistic preparation is the best guarantor of combat efficiency. Many management simulations are based on the same assumption.

For an opposite view, consider batting practice prior to a baseball game. Batting practice is of two types. Both types seek to *distort* reality, but in opposite ways. In batting practice most athletes do not care whether they are successful; nobody is there to say whether the output would have been hits or outs. What is important is to improve each player's fitness for future action. What teams *do not* do, though they could, is to locate a pitcher or a machine whose throws maximally simulate competition. Instead they find someone to throw at perhaps two thirds the speed the players will soon encounter, with no curves or other discouragements. Presumably this allows the players to improve their timing, but most importantly, I think, they improve their confidence. On the other hand, immediately prior to batting, players are again offered a distorted reality, but this time in the form of a heavily weighted bat that is *more* difficult to work with than reality. These two preparations—slow batting practice followed by weighted bats—work in opposite directions but have the same rationale, namely, that the best way to prepare for future action is by distorting, not capturing, reality.

Which preparation is superior—making reality simpler or more complex? Are maximally realistic simulations better than either form of distortion? I do not know the answers to such questions, but I would be willing to bet that there is not just one answer. I would wager that no system of preparation is inherently superior, but rather, as Mitroff observed about the paintings, no preparation, and none of Mitroff's models, "is functional beyond the limited environment in which each operates."

I cannot decide whether Mitroff's Figure 3 represents a weighted bat or reality itself, but it certainly does not look much like batting practice, and it is not likely to do much for the confidence of the theorist who must define its constructs, or for the researcher who must operationalize and validate them. Mitroff has himself noted some of the difficulties in working with such a complex version of reality; for example, by asking: "How does one study a complex social system whose constitution is holographic?"

For me Mitroff's chapter, and in particular its advocacy of the world as a complex hologram, has raised interesting and important questions. What remains to be seen is whether such a portrayal of the world impairs or increases our field's fitness for future action.

GROUP DISCUSSION

Mitroff: This raises good points. Let me respond to the central issue, that of complexity. No matter how you start in dealing with complexity, you end up in paradox. The more we sweep into our picture of organizations, the more closely we capture reality, but the picture becomes more complex. If we try to simplify reality, we're in worse shape.

I often say to practitioners, "I'm sorry the world is complex. I didn't create it. The question is whether you want to face up to it and deal with it or not." For example, the psychopath is a stakeholder of all organizations whether they like it or not. The psychopath is probably the best example of what I would call, borrowing from the psychodynamic literature, the shadow of an organization. The current reality is that organizations have no choice but to consider more forces coming from the shadow. Johnson & Johnson lost $100 million on Tylenol. This has to play a role in strategic planning when one thinks about the totality of the forces in an organization.

Once you have a more complex picture, you can raise certain questions that you couldn't raise before. Every organization does not have to consider every one of these stakeholders. But organizations have no choice but to take a much broader view of inside and outside stakeholders than ever before. How do they do it? We have tried to develop methods to guide them and help them set priorities. There will always be oversimplification, but oversimplification of what? So we are back into the paradox concerning the simplification of reality.

Steve raises a very good point when he indicates the fundamental tension, if not contradiction, in my chapter concerning esthetics. In some sense I'm talking out of both sides of my mouth, and I realize this. You can lay out various pictures and have a discussion about the different world views they embody. The choice between them is a matter of esthetics. However, you can discuss esthetic tastes. In order to do that, you have to go to another theoretical base than most of us have grown up with, such as the literature on esthetics and dramatic criticism.

Hackman: How do I know when I'm solving the wrong problem or the right problem? Is the right problem one that is esthetically pleasing to me as a researcher?

Mitroff: I can't give you an absolute answer. The answer has to be relative and, as such, is arguable.

Kilmann: On the issue of complexity versus simplicity, I like to make this an issue of the hologram versus the machine. One contribution social scientists make is in using the complex model, to get practitioners to spend a bit more time thinking and to include more variables and possibilities than they ordinarily do. I have never been in an organization where I had to tell the practitioner, "You're being too broad, you're spending too much time thinking before acting." If you're talking to a manager who is rooted in the Figure 1 machine model, you may get the manager to broaden his stand by moving him toward Figure 2, which is a reasonably open, yet somewhat boundable, notion of the world. But instead, if you try to broaden his view by bringing in the psychopaths of Figure 3, you may just seem incredible.

Porter: Ian, you talk about the ways in which the pictures of the world as a simple machine and then as a complex system can lead us astray. What critique would you make of the hologram as a way of looking at the world? You don't seem to give equal critique to the hologram and the other two pictures.

Mitroff: You're absolutely right—I haven't written a critique of the hologram. I've criticized the machine model because I think it has been so dominant, not because it is all wrong or all bad. The hologram picture doesn't necessarily tell you any better how to grapple with reality, so there are problems with it too.

Seashore: It would appear to me that a general manager of a corporation would be under great pressure to see the world in the way you describe in your third model. That is, he has lived with all kinds of strange events that we do not include in our discipline or in ourselves. He lives with them all the time, and these events are familiar. Perhaps we are carefully trained not to think in that way. The conclusion might be that we ought to get out of his office because we do more harm than good.

Mitroff: It's sad, but I agree with you.

Seashore: If you or I were in the manager's office, who would be consulting whom?

Mitroff: In the last picture, the distinctions vanish. We're co-teachers, colearners.

Pettigrew: I would agree with you about the importance of studying complexity. What is your theory of complexity? When you walk into an organization with the idea that you want to study something that is complex, what do you do? And what is it that makes you believe that you are going to come out with some useful knowledge at the end?

Mitroff: The best answer I can give is that Richard Mason and I are going to try to write that story in two books. In a book on challenging strategic assumptions, we say that there is not only one view of the organization and its problems. Tell me who the stakeholders are and what assumptions you are making about them, how certain you are about them, and how important the various assumptions are. In practice, I don't find much difficulty in doing that. What I do is operationalize in a business context what Graham Allison did in *Essence of Decision,* where he developed three different models of the Cuban missile crisis. We try to institutionalize a debate. We say, before you put all your eggs in one basket, you at least better have a debate.

The research questions are: How do you do that? How do the stakeholders that influence the organization change over time? How do the assumptions change, and what policies result? These questions are highly theoretical to me, and for me the theory is highly relevant to practice.

Wickes: Most of the general managers that I have worked with would understand and be intrigued by the third model. They would call it the craziness or irrationality in the system. The model would help them focus on it. They would pick up on the psychopath all right, but not on some of the others. The model is useful because it begins to help us think about some of the schizophrenia in the system. This particular model encourages general managers to think about the irrational. Once given the idea, they might be able to sort it out and therefore cope with it a little more successfully. [Tom Wickes is vice-president of human resources, TRW Electronics and Defense Sector.]

REFERENCES

Ackoff, R. L. *Creating the Corporate Future.* New York: Wiley, 1982.

Churchman, C. W. *The Design of Inquiring Systems.* New York: Basic Books, 1971.

Feyerabend, P. *Science in a Free Society.* London: NLB, 1978

Kuhn, T. S. *The Structure of Scientific Revolutions.* Chicago: University of Chicago Press, 1962.

Lakoff, G., and Johnson, M. *Metaphors We Live By.* Chicago: University of Chicago Press, 1980.

Mason, R. O., and Mitroff, I. I. *Challenging Strategic Planning Assumptions.* New York: Wiley, 1981.

Mill, J. S. *A System of Logic.* New York: Longmans, 1872.

Mitroff, I. I. *The Subjective Side of Science.* Amsterdam: Elsevier, 1974.

Mitroff, I. I. *Stakeholders of the Organizational Mind: Toward a New View of Organizational Policy Making.* San Francisco: Jossey-Bass, 1983.

Toffler, A. *The Third Wave.* New York: William Morrow, 1980.

Wilber, K. (Ed.). *The Holographic Paradigm.* London: Shambhala, 1982.

3

Stanley E. Seashore

❖ ❖ ❖ ❖ ❖ ❖ ❖ ❖ ❖ ❖ ❖ ❖ ❖ ❖ ❖ ❖

Institutional
and Organizational Issues
in Doing Useful Research

The topic of this chapter posits a deficiency in the relevance of our research to theory building, to practical applications, or to both. This assumption could be challenged by anyone who troubles to review the accomplishments of those present. We have shared a preoccupation with the generation of useful knowledge and, though in varying ways, we have each done something admirable and impressive in the way of demonstrating its utility.

Although we have no ground for apology, as I see it, our aspirations far exceed our performances as specialists in organizational behavior. In many respects, our practice has outrun our theoretical grasp; much of our practice is done in such a way that it cannot feed the theory. Two questions arise: Can we give more attention to theories of kinds that lend themselves to practice? Can we better exploit our practice to serve theoretical developments?

It is timely to examine the ways in which our research might better serve both theory building and effectiveness in practice, for we have unprecedented opportunities and obligations. To support this assertion, I mention only a few factors:

- In recent years we have seen the emergence of theoretical innovations of kinds more friendly to practice than those that prevailed a decade or two ago. The contributions of Argyris and Schön (1978) and Trist (1981) are examples; others could be mentioned.
- In the space of a couple of decades we have substantially increased the cadre of sophisticated researchers and practitioners, and the joining of the two activities has acquired academic standing and some societal respect.
- Management positions in organizations are increasingly filled with people who have had some of the theory and folklore of our specialty, and some of the arts and technology, incorporated into their preparatory education.
- Our opportunities for significant research, practice, or both continue to grow and now exceed our capacities to exploit them. I suppose that all of you present have had to decline attractive opportunities—that is, those of scope, duration, access, and fiscal resources that fit our current needs for optimization of research efforts and for exploration of improved applications of our knowledge.

I expect we will concentrate—and properly so—on a domain of theorizing, practice, and research that is distinctively bounded. We will give a lot of attention to (1) methods that involve action, observation, consultation, and immediately observed sequential events and (2) studies that are site-specific—that is, cases; (3) the reference will be to organizational systems, not much to persons, jobs, technological systems, or population classes; (4) on-site organization members will be considered, tentatively at least, to be active participants in the action and inquiry, not passive informants or subjects; (5) the action initiation will come from thoughtful practitioners or from practical theorists, not from people driven solely by problems demanding solution or by theoretical voids and opportunities.

Such a concentration, if it occurs, is congenial to me. I

think this is the domain where the action is currently hot, where our current theoretical and practical priorities lie, where our past practices have been most deficient. It is what I would like to do better if only I knew how.

Still, I think our joint enterprise needs to be informed by reminder of alternatives, of the limits of a domain of discourse so defined, and of the risks we accept if alternative approaches to theory building and to applications are not advanced in concert.

In this chapter I will attempt a broad view of what is needed to get on with the work of generating knowledge, formalizing theory and transmitting it to those who need it, and inducing its application to problems of the so-called real world of organizational life. We had better do it well. The quality of our lives and our societies may well depend on it.

My argument will be simple and to a large extent will display the obvious. It rests on three propositions:

1. The varieties of knowledge we work with and need exceed the capacities of research methods that are constrained by the unique case, by direct involvement in the phenomena under study, and by "experience" accessible to participants in such approaches to knowledge generation. Some kinds of knowledge and theory can be generated only by comparative study of populations of persons, groups, and organizations rather than a single case; some require distancing from and abstractions from the phenomena under study. We need a broad array of ways to learn, to spin theories, and to act proficiently in organizationally beneficial ways.

2. The practice of our specialty in organizational behavior and the application of what we learn by others cannot be limited to our own hands-on, direct action with individual—and therefore very few—organizations. There are other forms and channels for application. There are more people to be engaged than conceivably can be approached directly by a rather few specialists like us and our colleagues.

3. To get on with our work on organizational theory and practice, we need to attend to our own organization and to its deficiencies and potentials. Physician, heal thyself! We

should do some diagnosing, counseling, and participant action with ourselves.

I think these propositions are self-evident. If they are not, then we have a debate on our hands.

What We Need to Know

The varieties of knowledge we need to have in usable form and transmittable quality can be condensed to a very short list. Here is my version of such a list:

1. The skills, arts, strategies, and ethical guidelines for engaging directly with other persons and in other persons' organizations.
2. Intelligible descriptions of events, states, processes, and illustrative cases that bear on the substance of our professional specialties.
3. Empirical generalizations about the events, processes, states, variable relationships, and the like that recur widely with some prevalence or probability in organizations.
4. Theoretical formulations of knowledge. From the simple to the sublime, these range from mere identification of relevant concepts and variables to framing of theoretical models and formal theoretical systems and to invention of models about theories (paradigm formulation). In short, we need concept names so we can talk to each other and condensed codes (theories) for saying a lot with few words.
5. Knowledge about information—that is, knowledge about epistemological issues, analytical methods, and interpretive methods. There is no such thing as "hard" information of self-evident meaning; it is all as soft as our capacities to use it in some context and to understand its multiple valid implications.
6. A noncryptic measurement technology for getting and displaying quantitative information about persons, groups, organizations, and organizational environments.
7. Knowledge of and sensitivity to our own limitations and potentials as practitioner/theorists.

There are no surprises in that list except, perhaps, for the inclusion of action skills and arts as forms of knowledge that need to be advanced to more describable and transmittable forms. Different methods of inquiry have their respective advantages in generating the different classes of knowledge. Practitioners (we and others) find that a particular instance of application calls on some of these categories of knowledge, perhaps not on others. The issue is one of fit among (1) type of knowledge to be obtained, (2) method of inquiry employed, and (3) context for practical application.

Varieties of Application

As mentioned earlier, I expect and hope that we will focus on theoretical inventions and derived generalizations that are obtained in the context of direct action in and with particular organizational systems. "Direct action" may include such activities as diagnosing, counseling, observing and participating in events, creating opportunities for people to learn and change, and planning actions. Although the parties may aim to learn something about organizations in general, the focus is usually on this organization with all its uniqueness. The joint processes of theoretical inquiry and practical application are not clearly differentiated; each feeds the other and, in principle, all the actors may contribute to both purposes.

One readily grants that this way of going about our work is singularly effective in certain ways. The proof lies in the impressive insights, generated by people here, of kinds not likely to have occurred using other methods. The proof also lies in the occasional instances of impressive consequences for the people and organizations in which this work has been done— that is, the merger of basic research and practice.

Having said that, let's consider other forms of application and other means of knowledge acquisition. I offer a brief defense for some more traditional forms of research, theory building, and practical application. I am referring, of course, to the study of organizational phenomena in ways that (1) emphasize replicable quantification, (2) refer to populations of persons, events, and organizations rather than to single cases or limited sequences of cases, and (3) give priority to teasing out and testing generalizations that are of potentially wide relevance. Theories may result, and usually do, although they tend to be abstracted to the point of diminishing relevance to the real situations we wish to understand as researchers and influence as practitioners.

These more traditional methods have some regrettable features that are not easily amended or moderated. The research results present serious problems of epistemology, of measurement distortion or validity, and of reliance on paradigms that offend one's sense of the intactness of behaving organisms and social systems. Worse, the data and conclusions are not intimately linked to the complex situations and actors for which practical applications are potentially feasible. I could go on, but there is no need for me to do so, as some of you here have rather forcefully explained the frailties of these methods. However, the alternative methods have frailties of their own—most notably a loss of the analytical power arising from the method of comparison.

Some important kinds of information are inaccessible by or inefficiently obtained through direct engagement with single organizations. In addition, some arenas of practical application are virtually inaccessible by direct, hands-on intervention by the theorist or researcher. I think we would be intellectually dishonest and socially irresponsible to ignore them. A couple of examples will make my point clear.

Job Design and Redesign. A great deal has been learned about the generally optimal characteristics of jobs and work environments. It has been learned, for the most part, through studies of diverse populations of jobs and persons or through controlled experiments in search of general principles. The work of Hackman and Oldham (1980) is an example. Furthermore, much of this work is illuminated by reference to a set of criteria, including some, such as turnover rates and delayed health effects, that are discernible only to the researcher with longitudinal population data and not discernible directly to the actors, researchers, or practitioners on the scene.

A plausible case could be made that the application of this knowledge in some particular instance could best be accomplished through a process for on-site exploration of outcome priorities and local determination of how best to accomplish the optimizing. However, it is a fact—and will remain a fact for a long time—that most jobs are designed by people other than those who will perform them or supervise and manage them and by people other than us and our colleagues. The work setting and organization may not yet exist. For the most part, the practitioner will be a consultant or a work system designer who can do his or her own job better by employing the principles. Methods of action research, local experimentation, and negotiation would severely limit the application and might often be intolerably costly. The practitioners in such a case are distant from the research that feeds their professional practice.

A similar case could be made with respect to compensation, benefit, and noneconomic reward systems, which are normally determined by fiat or labor management negotiation in the absence of guiding information derived from research elsewhere and some theories generated in other organizations or in laboratories.

— *Models of Desirable Organizational Characteristics.* Some of the knowledge and theory produced by us and our colleagues refers to organizational states, changes, and outcomes that occur on a scale that appears to preclude the close joining of research and practice. The "practitioners" in such an instance may well be persons unconnected with the organization and local phenomena that are the subject of research or persons who are general managers rather than specialists in organizational behavior.

To illustrate, I refer to a recent doctoral dissertation (Denison, 1982) that asked whether, over a long span of time, business organizations acquiring the properties advocated by currently popular prescriptive models of organizational functioning do or do not show advantage by hard criteria of long-term economic performance. The researcher worked with organizations large enough to have had at least a ten-year span of public reports in the Standard & Poor annual volumes. He obtained a number of measures of organizational properties specified by a defined model, using questionnaire methods, and traced their associations with the fiscal performance indicators for five years prior to the measurement year and for five subsequent years. The model gets general support, but some organizational properties appear to offer a fairly immediate fiscal return, others a delayed return following an early negative effect.

This research was, in some ways, primitive. However, it made a contribution to theory on the sequencing and/or phasing of organizational changes; it also affirmed that one of many alternative models seems to connect as expected with time-extended events in the real world. The associations are strong. It is a marvel that they could be discerned at all with measures of known deficiencies, amid all the surrounding "noise" of economic cycles, market changes, product shifts, and the like. The comparative method displays its power.

I should think that managers considering what sorts of organizations they aspire to have would be interested in this information, not to mention investors considering where to place their next bets. It is not easy to imagine how these results could have been obtained through case studies or interventionist research methods. Nevertheless, the observed practices feed the theory, and the theory plainly can feed improvements in practice.

The common features of these two examples are that the optimum approach to inquiry, at least in early stages of theory building and application, hardly allows effective use of case study and inquiry embedded within concurrent organizational activities. Furthermore, the aspiration to discover general principles—perhaps even universals—is complementary to and not epistemologically at odds with approaches that are limited to a particular organizational setting.

I think we are forced to invent ways to join theory, research, and practice that allow us to translate the general principles into practice (usually by someone other than the antecedent researcher) and to ensure that the practice can feed back to the general principles to enlarge, modify, or void them. Under our present practices, the conjuncture of research and practice is frail, and the practitioners seem uninterested in contributing to theories of the kinds used for illustration. We are not organized very well to get our work done in optimum ways.

Knowledge from Practice and Practice for Knowledge

The task of joining theoretical research and practice is impeded by inherent problems, some of which I have mentioned, and also by current orientations and practices, which can be altered. A view of the situation, in highly simplified form, might look like this:

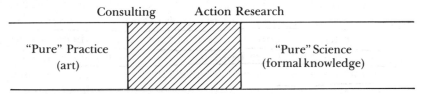

	Consulting	Action Research	
"Pure" Practice (art)			"Pure" Science (formal knowledge)

At the left is represented the practice of the arts and skills of organizational intervention, change, and therapy. In the extreme instance, which we have all occasionally observed, the practitioner professional or manager is quite unable or unwilling to describe what he or she did, or how, or why, but merely observed that "it" worked or did not; a contribution to knowledge is unlikely to occur. Nothing is transmitted except the knowledge that "something" "worked." At the right is represented "pure" science, undertaken to generate empirical generalizations or theories and to test their validity under controlled conditions. The methods are fully described, the design and interpretive rationales are public, and the conclusions are open to disproof. There is maximum effort to avoid the complexity of "natural" events and organizational processes. Any contribution to practice is, at best, qualified and distant in time and, at worst, nil.

The diagram indicates an intermediate range, suggested by the shading and labels, in which, as a practitioner, one hopes to add to knowledge and potentially can do so and, as a researcher, one hopes to accept and capitalize on the complexity of the phenomena one helps to create or encounters serendipitously. The consultant/practitioner aims to describe and evaluate his or her "case" in language relevant to the formalization of knowledge and with some discernible implicit or explicit theory to guide the choice of concepts and their names. The action researcher tries to carry along some of the baggage of the formal methods of science and may even use some elements of experimental design; he or she will surely attempt to draw credible evidence from the work and to formulate some interpretation in language applicable to practice in other organizational situations. Some division of work must occur, but merger of functions in the same person (or team) is to be desired.

The joining of research and practice can occur in the shaded middle range. It appears to be our task to find ways to get more knowledge from the consultants and more usable theories and empirical generalizations from the action researcher—that is, to expand the shaded area. At present, in my view, we are wasting a prime natural resource by our failure to develop ways to capture the observations and experiences of consultants and of thoughtful managers for use in building a transmittable base of knowledge. There are some exceptions, of course—take Barnard (1938), for example. We also induce waste by training most of our younger colleagues in overly narrow methods of research and narrow ideas about the nature of useful knowledge.

The Parties at Interest

Most of us, most of the time, work within an overly rigid and simple conception of the parties at interest and of potential sources of help in conducting research that is useful for both theory and practice. The people we encounter in our work tend to get put into classifications that constrain our images of how we can use and serve them better.

Suppose that we came to regard organizational practitioners (that is, managers) as potential researchers, consultants as potential subjects or informants, informants as clients, subjects as colleagues, action researchers as teachers, disciplinary colleagues as consultants to us, and so on. Suppose also that we came to regard the advancement of theory, knowledge, and practice not as a task for organizational behavior specialists with academic roots or connections but rather as a task that, by its intrinsic nature, requires a joint effort by the full community of interested parties. Would (could) we then organize ourselves for the task in new ways—ways that exploit these parties more effectively, that salvage more of the information that gets generated and lost, that connect research and practice more closely or more often, that make our product more widely public for evaluation and potential application, that make our choice of issues for research and intended impact more attuned to ''reality'' as defined by the community of parties at interest?

I am well aware that many of us strain in that direction. Like you, I have done some consulting in ways that openly included a basic research component. I have been a party to some action research projects in which, in the end, it was difficult to distinguish the nature of the contributions of the people coming from different roles, and I felt myself becoming, in part, a well-served client. I have engaged in ''post mortems'' and ''debriefing'' exercises with trusted colleagues to share information, quandaries, insights, and comparison of cases. I have engaged in field studies in which professional consultants (among others) were subjects of study. I have even published case studies in sufficient detail to invite revisionist interpretations by managers as well as by disciplinary colleagues. None of this is exceptional, and it is certainly not unique. Nevertheless, we tend to favor certain parties and ignore others—for example, academic colleagues over client/subjects, or vice versa. We do not very seriously try to induce organizations to become autonomous experimenting organizations, except in isolated cases. The prevailing norms and habits of our trade tend to be exclusionary and to keep clients and subjects, particularly, in their proper (subordinate) place. We get an indecent and dysfunctional pleasure out of arcane knowledge and work methods. We do not work very much with accountants, engineers, economists, strategic planners, or physicians.

And let us not forget that many—perhaps most—of our prospective user/practitioners cannot be directly parties to the action. They are in Congress, or in India, or in a software sweatshop on Route 128, or in the M.B.A. program at Harvard.

I should not press this theme too hard. Let me just say that if we can successfully urge the organizations we work in to improve their coordination systems and processes and more

Collaborator

fully to exploit their resources in problem solving, then we might be able, with some success, to apply similar principles to our own case.

What to Do About It?

It is easy to offer prescriptions for the remedy of our deficiencies and lost opportunities as described in the preceding pages. I suppose it all has to be worked through in some organic fashion in a participatory mode, using our best contemporary paradigms and a bit of political clout. Some suggestions can be made to stimulate thought and discussion.

1. Much of the needed research and theory building must be done in ways insulated from site-specific complexities. Can we promote the idea that such inquiries are merely preparatory and must be accompanied by case studies of application? In some topical areas can we assign *negative* value to empirical and theoretical reports that do not seriously address issues of practice and fit to context?

2. Can we force dynamism into our theories by insisting on more intensive use of historical data and longitudinal research designs?

3. Can we make some consulting (not all) a less solitary activity and more of a joint, or information-sharing, activity? One model is the clinical case-review conference procedures found in health service delivery institutions. Another is found in the spontaneous and continuing work groups, of small and invitational membership, in which consultants (or researchers or both) review their practices, invite advice from peers, plan joint inquiries across a set of organizations, and identify issues for mutual persistent attention. I understand there may be a dozen such groups at this time, some of long duration, such as the "No Name Group," the "Friday Group," and the "Mayflower Group." In such stable peer groups, confidentiality is not an issue and one's professional reputation is not at stake when goofs, quandaries, and disasters are discussed along with tentative theorizing.

4. Can we legitimize a "clinical" component in our prac-

tice and in our training of younger colleagues? The meaning of *clinical* here is not easily explicated with brevity, but note that it is a posture of diagnosis and of trial therapeutic practices oriented toward theoretical insights and the production of illuminating case summaries.

5. Can we codify (just a little) our norms for case reporting so that the conclusions or issues identified are more than just incestuous products of selective information and prejudged conclusions?

6. Can we reform our institutions where new colleagues are trained so that some encouragement is provided for those who aspire to work in hybrid theoretician/researcher/practitioner roles? To do this would require several changes—for example, changes in the provisions for supervised internship-like experience, moderation of the demand for early publication by new Ph.D.s, and provision of publication outlets hospitable to non-quantitative inquiries.

7. Can we fill the void (destroy the barrier) between researchers and practitioners by instituting publication outlets for researchers who have something to say of a practical nature? It is hard to break into the *Harvard Business Review,* and there are few alternatives. Books on organizational theory currently sell well, but they require extraordinary writing skills and single-minded themes to reach the manager/practitioners.

8. Can we promote more productive research and practice by increasing the amount of work done by interdisciplinary teams over extended time periods? Existing institutions (with some exceptions) do not facilitate such work through funding, extended on-site engagements, and maintaining team integrity over long periods.

Some Personal History

Contributors to this conference were asked to comment on past conditions and events that may help to account for our current views about theory and practice in organizational behavior. My own case illustrates the thesis that we, collectively, are likely to engage in the kinds of research and practice that are compatible with the institutional and organizational contexts in which we work.

I have never had trouble with a sense of incompatibility between "basic" and "applied" research or with the notion that one can be a practitioner or a theoretician but not both. The dichotomies never made sense to me except as poles on descriptive continua having no intrinsic imbalance of merit. My theoretical contributions, such as they are, have nearly all arisen from research projects having an unmistakable intention to support practice, and in some instances they arose as a by-product of excursions into hands-on change activities. This ease with the labels may be associated with my early exposure to research in and on organizations.

My first significant employment was with an industrial firm, one of the U.S. Steel rolling mills. I was hired as a clerk in the personnel office, 62.5 cents per hour, with some collateral duties to help a senior consulting industrial psychologist with his on-site work. Though devoid of proper training, I very soon was fully engaged in some traditional kinds of psychological research—validating selection tests; testing the associations between visual capacities, job performance, and accidents; developing and testing in use an improved merit rating scheme; and the like. In that context, there was no doubt whatever that research should be practical in purpose. Within a year or so I became the head of personnel research on the firm's corporate staff, with opportunities to expand the range and improve the quality of my research, all of which arose from issues raised by line managers or other staff units. There followed a five-year stint with a consulting firm, A. T. Kearney & Company, with clients raising problems of personnel selection, training, compensation plan management, and organizational design. In all, there were ten years of professional development as a researcher/practitioner, after which I entered a doctoral program at Michigan to become, properly credentialed, an organizational psychologist officially authorized to engage in theorizing.

At the Institute for Social Research, 1950–1983, I was again in an institutional setting where a problem orientation is valued along with aspirations to add to the common fund of useful information and theory. Most of my work during those years was supported by business and industrial organizations, public service agencies, and other organizations having priorities of a practical sort along with some appreciation of the link between good theory and good practice.

What next? One might think that being asked to write an autobiographical note signals the end of one's career, and that may be the case more than I am willing to concede. However, there is one matter that I find especially threatening, challenging, and significant for our field of inquiry, and I hope yet to help do something about it.

Although there are several areas of productive dispute among us, one relating to the study of organizational systems stands out in my mind. The matter rests on basic differences in the models or paradigms with which we work—our image of what it is we try to understand, explain, and influence. From this basis, the matter unfolds into specific, contemporary differences in teaching, in research strategies and priorities, and in the professional services that we provide. Readers of this chapter will need only a few code words and phrases to understand the thought.

We have a history of significant accomplishments in describing the structures of organizations and some of the microprocesses that are associated with desired and undesirable states and outcomes. We have only a short history, but some significant accomplishments, in attempting to treat groups and organizations in accordance with their emergent, evolutionary, and hence complexly differentiated characteristics. We risk the emergence and institutionalization of opposed camps, with powerful ideas about organizational uniqueness and dynamics arrayed against equally powerful ideas of others concerned with organizational structures, states, and universalities. Some might think the differences are merely a matter of esthetic preference or transient tactics, but it has become apparent that as an organization changes, it not only becomes different from its former state but becomes in some degree incomparable. To risk an analogy, it is as though the sciences of biological maturation and disease etiology were to attempt separation from anatomy and biochemistry, when their complementary natures need to be exploited.

My own intellectual origins and predilections are somewhat one-sided in this matter, though not by deliberate choice. Much of my work has been in the mode of "scientific rigor" so deplored by Argyris and others. However, in the mid-1950s I served apprenticeship with the National Training Laboratory network, with the aid of Bradford, Bennis, Shepard, and Blake. I spent a year, 1965–66, with Trist and Emery at the Tavistock Institute to try to gain some understanding of their methods of diagnosis and intervention strategy. In the late 1960s I worked on systemic intervention projects with Floyd Mann, who is a master of that art. These efforts persuaded me that direct interventions in the form of action research had better be left to others.

Nevertheless, I think the merger of approaches, both in practice and in theoretical formulations, will be needed and will be accomplished—in part by those who can alternate their style of work and in part by others, myself included, who can work in teams of mixed approach.

RESPONSE AND COMMENTARY

Craig C. Lundberg

Professor Seashore's chapter is replete with modest optimism, gentle chidings, considerable wisdom, and several suggestions for enhancing research that is useful for both practice and theory. Seashore writes from the perspective of many years as an applied researcher and, more significantly, from a perspective that does not insist that all knowledge should be directly relevant to practitioners or have immediate practical relevance. He rightly, I think, reminds us of the considerable progress already obtained and notes the many difficulties and crucial choices facing further progress.

This chapter contains a lot to which we can nod affirmatively. Yes, some emerging theories are more friendly to practitioners. Yes, there is a great potential in researcher/practitioner collaboration. Yes, we do need to be more cognizant of the limits of what can be done to produce knowledge that is jointly useful to theory and practice. Yes, we do require a broad array of ways to learn, act proficiently, and spin theories. Yes, we should have more longitudinal research projects. Yes, we need to more fully and faithfully capture the insights, observations, and experience of thoughtful managers and consultants and, where possible, encourage organizations to become experimenting ones. And, yes, we probably should attend to our own organizations, research the research process more, and be less wasteful in the training of our younger colleagues and managerial students. These points are well taken, useful to hear, but not altogether surprising.

Consistent with his personal style, Professor Seashore has both subtly and modestly proffered several of his own beliefs about research strategy, design, and methods. In the spirit of his chapter, I would like to respond to some of the challenges and preferences he presents, perhaps thereby contributing to the increased differentiation and precision he calls for as well as expanding our available options.

Let me begin by reminding Professor Seashore (and the other contributors to this volume) of two discriminations that need to be kept in mind. Both concern the loose use of the term *theory*. Technically, *theory* refers to conceptual edifices that have substantial internal consistency and have withstood considerable testing and verification and, hence, are said to be reasonably well validated. Models are also conceptual but are distinguished from theory by their tentativeness or incompleteness. Given these meanings, most use of *theory* in this volume is simply wrong— we may desire and actively seek theory that informs both research and practice, but at present, realistically, we are only formulating and applying somewhat crude models.

Further, there are models and theory at several "levels"; that is, they vary in scope. Conventionally we specify three levels: general or grand, midrange, and micro. These three levels of models or theories inform one another—for example, as when higher levels subsume lower ones—and all function to select and

Figure 1. The Relations Among Models
and Theories, Facts, and Paradigms.

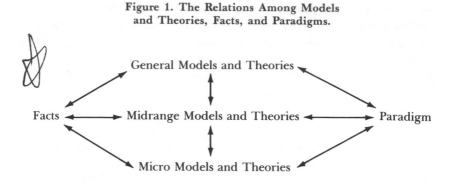

interpret appropriate facts (facts, in turn, shape and verify these models and theories). Facts, of course, are not equivalent to phenomena. Models and theories reflect a paradigm. Figure 1 shows the relations just recounted. Will each level of model or theory be equally functional in guiding research for both practice and theory? Probably not.

Another of the issues Professor Seashore and colleagues ignore is the appropriateness of the dominant social science paradigm and the models and theories derived from it for conducting research with a joint utility for validating theory and enhancing managerial practice. If, as has been stated, the present dominant paradigm is a unidirectional, causal one (Benson, 1977; Mitroff and Pondy, 1978; Lundberg, 1981), then our discomfort with the spate of overly reductionistic, overly analytical, overly rational, too often microlevel contemporary "theories" that abound is hardly surprising.

Professor Seashore may—again, along with the other contributors herein—have unrealistic expectations for theories and models. It appears that he assumes theory can serve all sorts of purposes—a theory can be scientifically valid, relevant to particular practitioners, and general, all at the same time. I doubt this is possible. Let me adapt Weick's (1979) characterization of Thorngate's (1976) postulate of commensurate complexity. As shown in Figure 2, any given model or theory exists at some one point on the clock—but not at more than one point simultaneously. This volume essentially seeks theories and research

Figure 2. Alternative Zones and Tradeoffs for
Theoretical Relevance, Validity, and Generality.

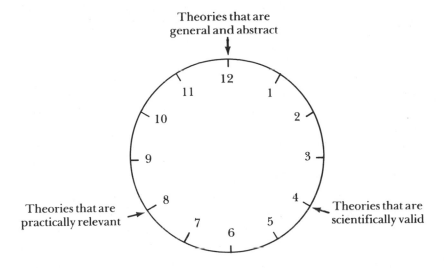

that lie in the area between four and twelve o'clock. Figure 2 illustrates two often underappreciated points. One is that there are many combinations of purposes that theory can provide beyond those "pure" ones represented by the twelve, four, and eight o'clock positions—and we might actively seek such diversity as long as we understand that all are legitimate. A second point relates to our focus on research that is useful for both theory and practice. Figure 2 indicates that the zones four to eight o'clock and eight to twelve o'clock are appropriate—but not the same, a point blurred by Professor Seashore. In his chapter, he asks for replication, better measurement, quantification, and the like, on the one hand, and teasing out and testing generalizations, using populations of units over even limited sequences of cases, and translating general principles into practice, on the other. In addition, he hopes for practice to "feed back to the general principles to enlarge, modify, or void them." I submit that these are rather different research ideals or purposes—and cannot be expected from a single research strategy, design, or set of methods.

The task of joining "theoretical research and practice," according to Seashore, falls to activities and roles that occupy the midzone between "pure" practice and "pure" science. Although he admits that this is a simplified view, it may also be misleading. Let us accept the continuum laid down. At one pole is managerial art, or pure practice, and at the other pole theoretical science, or pure science. I suggest that parallel consultancy *and* research roles and activities reach from pole to pole. Consultancy roles of expert, designer, facilitator, and so on and researcher roles of conceptualizer, field experimenter, action researcher, and so on occur all along the continuum—the sophistication of their enactment in a particular project determining where on the continuum they appear. Managers and scientists are here viewed as being engaged in an inquiry process—that is, asking and answering questions so as to learn. We tend to see scientific research and practitioner problem solving as substantially distinct, probably because practitioners emphasize goal relevance and timeliness more than scientists do (Thomas and Tymon, 1982), but this is more myth than reality. The myth is perpetuated by conceptions of science and scientists as objective, a perspective persuasively eroded ever since Berger and Luckmann's (1967) treatise on the social construction of reality. Mitroff's (1975) evidence that scientific ideas are tested not only against theories but also against networks of social and personal relations nails the point.

"Useful" knowledge, for either practitioners or researchers, simply means knowledge that is capable of being used advantageously or beneficially (Louis, 1983). Professor Seashore notes that the ladder of abstraction is relevant to usefulness; but he does not say explicitly that practitioners prefer the more concrete because of its descriptive relevance and its evaluative potential for specific circumstances, while theoreticians often settle for the more abstract because theory verification, not outcome effectiveness, is of primary interest. I suggest that usefulness is also a function of a judgment of the potentiality or capability of knowledge before the fact. Advocacy, therefore, is a second major dimension of usefulness. Figure 3 displays the two dimensions just noted and characterizes the researcher role of each quadrant. The researcher in each role, to produce useful knowledge, will go about it in a different way. Managerial researchers will, given their predilection for advocacy and the concrete, develop what

Figure 3. Researcher Roles in Relation to the Abstract/Concrete
and Advocate/Nonadvocate Dimensions.

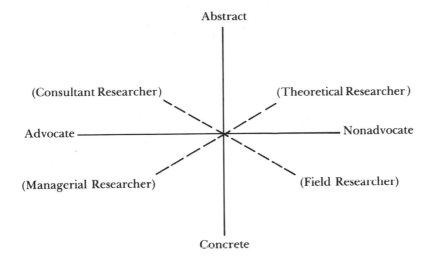

Vaill (1975) has termed "practitioner theories"—that is, theories
from the actor's point of view. Consultant researchers will, in
part influenced by the variety of experiences they observe, develop
local contingency models that frame the significance of certain
circumstances. Field researchers will go beyond rich description
to develop cause maps and complex reflexive models—for example, Weick (1979). Theoretical researchers, at least those who
wish to contribute useful knowledge, will move toward what
Mohr (1982) terms "process theory," which moves both time
and discrete events to the fore to establish necessary precursors
for outcomes.

On close reading of Professor Seashore's chapter, I find
him ambivalent about site-specific studies—that is, cases. On
the one hand, he expects his colleagues in this volume to concentrate on such studies and urges codification of the norms for
reporting on them. On the other hand, he urges populations of
units over single cases, proposes that research and theory be insulated from site-specific complexities, and states that the optimum approach "hardly allows effective use of case study and
inquiry embedded within concurrent organizational activities."

No doubt this ambivalence reflects his institutional affiliation and intellectual experiences. I would argue, however, that he dismisses the utility of case studies somewhat too easily. That we have often got, in Seashore's words, "just incestuous products of selective information and prejudged conclusions" is a fairly common observaton. Before throwing the baby out with the bath water, let me note a few research-functional aspects of cases. Case studies that are comparative can provide both modal analysis and descriptions of dynamics far beyond conventional survey work. In fact, Professor Seashore is a coauthor of an excellent recent example (Cammann, Lawler, Ledford, and Seashore, 1984). Examination of extreme cases may also provide more understanding of a phenomenon than empirically common ones (Pondy and Olson, 1977). The need for longitudinal research that Seashore advocates is most often satisfied by cases, and it is through such cases that processes generally, and change processes specifically, have been most illuminated. If it is empirical generalization that is sought, there are now available experimental single-case designs (for example, Hersen and Barlow, 1976). Single-case experimental designs and other idiographic research endeavors (that is, case studies), in fact, have been legitimized recently both by persuasive arguments of method such as action research (for example, Susman and Evered, 1978) and by exemplar ethnomethodological studies (for example, Gebhart, 1978).

I wish to conclude this commentary by echoing the note on which Professor Seashore concludes his chapter. He states his belief that progress in conducting research useful for both theory and practice will be accomplished in part by teams and in part by those of us who can alternate our style of research. I wholeheartedly agree. The three figures presented in this commentary are intended to provide some suggestive guidance toward style alternatives and team compostion. Seashore's chapter is a model of gentle, overly modest, and careful optimism. I suspect it is this matter of emotional tone that ultimately separates us. I would have him dream more boldly, advocate more ardently, and let his passions as well as his intellect lay down challenges for us.

GROUP DISCUSSION

Lundberg: Are there some exemplars around, maybe in your own works, maybe in the work of others, that you think contribute to both theory and practice?

Seashore: I must say I got a singular pleasure out of a period of work with Alfred Marrow, who owned a firm we studied, and the colleagues I worked with in the inquiry. Several people generated things that are of value and made a connection with things that firms might do. The chairman of the board and the president of the company were as much a part of the research design as anybody else and, in fact, set the climate when it came to making some decisions. We worked quite intimately with the firm's financial officer, the accountants, and the engineers and others of that sort on the scene. The study extended over the scheduled period of some three or four years. We went back after five more years to make a total of eight, I think—in short, a time span almost long enough for studying organizational change and the stability of changes and some of the conditions and intrusive events and forces that might disrupt the organization. In that case it went the way the book said it should. I started three or four other, similar events that didn't work the way the book said they should have. I'm not in the mood to start a ten-year project right now, but somebody has to.

Lundberg asked Seashore about his preferred research style, to which he replied: My own preferred style of research involves a study of cases—in particular, studies of sets of cases in ways that allow comparison. And I think there is great power in that, but it can't do everything. I also think that a lot of kinds of inquiry cannot be conducted effectively except at some distance from the organization that is being studied. There are some generalizations that can only be discovered and certainly can only be tested working with large populations with data that extend over considerable spans of time and data that members of the organization can't give you. Why? Because they don't know when they are going to die. They can't tell you what their death rate is.

They're still alive. Things like that. So I think we need those generalizations, knowing their frailties.

Lundberg: One thing that strikes me is, there is a quality of self-reflection among the colleagues at this table. I'd like to hear you say a little about whether you think you are a self-reflective practitioner/researcher.

Seashore: Oh, yes. I would describe myself in the words you use, but the balance of the weight among them, I think, differs a bit among all of us in the room. Reflective, a little bit; researcher, in capital letters; practitioner, in lower-case letters; and changing from time to time. If I were to redesign my own career or design somebody else's, I would recommend changing the style of work from time to time. I haven't changed enough or often enough. I suppose I regret being, in some ways, constrained by an institutional setting where I had to carry on an institutionalized pattern of study and, in fact, thought well of doing so.

Hackman: Because of the nature of the Institute for Social Research (ISR) and the kind of contract research that is done there, a lot of the research in your career has been team research. I'd be interested in your reflections on the advantages and disadvantages of doing studies as teams, as opposed to solo research.

Seashore: I suppose it's partly an esthetic choice, but it seems to me that most of us, most of the time, can double our generation of ideas and understanding of information if we work with others. Debate can ensue and decisions can be challenged. I value that. It does take time. I have been connected with a number of studies that have had a component of the activities that involved investment of large amounts of skillful time in organizations. I have had people around me who could spare the time and who had the skills more than I did. It was a division of effort. I felt that was highly useful. I think team research is adequate for some of the problems that now baffle us. Individuals can no longer deal with the kinds of issues we are raising—at least, not entirely.

Goodman: Let's think about ISR and the large number of research activities that have been occurring there. Were there some mechanisms that you think were more significant than others that translated that work into practice?

Seashore: A lot of the work we did never did, or did not in the short run, get translated into any effective action. Even though the intent and the focus were to do and learn something useful, our energies and attention and perhaps our inclinations were more to the research than to the practice. I think over the long haul ISR has had a very big impact indeed—not by people on our staff directly, but because some of our research has entered the common culture. People who read the newspaper have come to think that way a little bit.

I have been around the ISR long enough to have observed three rather intensive and heavily invested efforts to include what we called an action component to our research. These efforts survived for three or four years. It was then found that the people we brought in to carry out the intense and continuing fieldwork needed for that kind of research were simply not honored in the ISR building. Why? First of all, they weren't there. People didn't see them very much. Second, they were characteristically people who liked the action but didn't care much to put words on paper. So they didn't earn the kinds of credits that sustain a person in the kind of environment we have. Very able people; I could name some of them, you would know them. And they did some extraordinarily fine work, but it did not survive in our environment. Our latest try had a longer, richer, and much more successful life, and I think the next try will be a winner. But the institute had its origins in mass data survey-type research, and that's what was rewarded and honored.

There was a short discussion about the reputations of such ISR personalities as Rensis Likert, Kurt Lewin, and Floyd Mann, who were well known in the field for their action orientation but were regarded as idealists rather than academics by some at ISR. This discussion led Chris Argyris to comment:

Argyris: For researchers with the mechanistic view, there is a psychological need for distancing. I am attributing that people who eventually got tired of psychological distancing in one form or another had to leave.

Kilmann: I wonder, rather than putting a lot of reponsibility on the institution, whether we're really talking about the choices that individuals make about how they spend their time and how they feel they're contributing. I know people who get blocked with writing, and for them writing a paper is an absoutely agonizing experience. I also know, on the other side, how absolutely exhausting it is to do intervention work—long-term projects of three to five to ten years, many times losing sleep because you worry about an intervention. It's a kind of responsibility that is perhaps more difficult than research. It wouldn't surprise me if some people played out more the research side because for some of them it might be easier. There is a very different energy, involvement, and commitment. I know research can be very involving; it's clear, but there's something different going on. You can get tired; you can get exhausted by a client.

Lawler: Chris, I agree with you. Most of the people I saw in the institute wanted to work on pretty much their own problems that were theoretically important. They wanted to work on the field situations, but they didn't want to get very close to the field. They wanted to pretty much work on applied problems that were theoretically important.

Hackman: There are pretty good counterforces still out there. Everybody you have named (Rensis Likert, Kurt Lewin, and so on) and almost everybody around the table, I have heard at some point or another referred to as a flake because he wanted an organization to succeed. It is somehow morally wrong to want to do work that helps some people have a more effective organization. So when an esteemed colleague says to me (this happened just a few weeks ago), "Gee, Hackman, you *used* to be a pretty good scientist," that strikes a very powerful deal in me because I really see myself as a good scientist and I want to be esteemed by my colleagues as a good scientist. But I am trying to help my organization succeed right now, and that kind of rules me out.

Mitroff: What kind of mentality wants to say that Lewin or Likert maybe *once* was a good scientist? When one becomes an advocate, is one less a scientist?

Ledford: Why do we care so much whether they think that what we do is legitimate? The important thing is to find a critical number of people who share similar ideas, and it doesn't have to be everybody at whatever institution you're a part of. There has to be some way for them to work together in some kind of sustaining life, and I think probably everybody at this table has found things like that. Why do we keep trying to change the minds of people who are analytical scientists?

Lawler: Well, that's a good question. They threaten us, they challenge us, they compete with us for students, resources, ideas, attention. Richard, would you say you were a researcher/scientist when you got into that action role? If the answer to that is yes, would you say anyone in an action role is therefore a researcher/scientist? If you would say no to that, what distinguishes you from everybody else out there in an action role?

Hackman: Yes. No. Maybe. Yes, and no, not everybody is. I really do see my primary commitment as to learning. The test of my ideas and of what I do is whether I'm generating some things that please me. I also find that I can be successful in helping other people understand how to create various kinds of patterns of behavior in social systems.

Lawler: So the way we're going to tell you apart from the run-of-the-mill action person who is out there is that you're going to produce a different product.

A. Mohrman: The question that I locked onto is, if one becomes an advocate, is one less a scientist? The only way I can deal with that question is to remove the problem by saying social science is by definition advocacy. It's a study of advocacy, and because we are social animals, we are involved in the very thing we are studying. Somehow that's the only way I personally can reconcile this kind of thing.

Argyris: There is one problem of advocacy that I own up to. When I read back some of the stuff I've written, I see gaps that I can explain only on the basis of my emotionality to the advocacy. But the truth of the matter is that I never faced up to those until later. So I think there are difficulties with being an advocate, and I don't want to hide behind them. Now, the one thing that makes me feel less guilty is that I also see gaps in the other people who say they are not advocating.

Bennis: I'd like to discuss a couple of questions. First of all, I think there's probably more of a tendency to be reflective of personal issues in a conference like this than maybe ten years ago. I think this questioning is not being met with disdain as, in light of ten years ago, "What is all the personal and subjective crap about?" We can approach the reflective/subjective and certainly the personal-knowledge kind of question. But there are a couple of questions that it raises in my mind that are really fascinating. Why are guilt-inducing questions even asked? What about our own superegos here about what is proper, correct, right? Are we very vulnerable to this very model that we are trying to operate somewhat against, or is the action model in an adversarial situation with our model of science? Were we brought up with the tight-lipped logical positivism of the fifties or sixties, so that we really have in our hearts and in our soul somewhere this sort of what's right and what's wrong? I think I can say without fear of contradiciton that it has never been said of me that I used to be a good scientist. So I can raise this question without fear. So the question is, why this guilt? I feel that same superego.

The second question is really an important one that I would like us to explore. Chris [Argyris] was saying, look, this mechanistic style of research leads to a distancing from people. That may have real implications for ways we approach data and ways we look for the problems. It would seem to me that if an action orientation doesn't preclude the closeness to people, then I would also maybe have blind spots for those of us who get more involved in the action advocacy. It would be interesting to look at the affective styles along with our cognitive styles and what they mean in terms of the research products themselves. Do the products reflect these kinds of subjective biases?

I'm puzzled about this next issue. We here represent many of the cultural gatekeepers, for heaven's sake. The chances are that if I attribute a remark to someone in this room, there is at least a .5 probabilty of my being right. So we are the people who shape the future. And yet, what is the thing that creates the ambivalence, the guilt? How does whatever it is in our culture that creates blind spots work, which serves in such a guilty way to show that we're not living up to whatever we think we're supposed to?

Argyris: I have another feeling: "By God, they don't respect me." Not guilt. I rarely felt guilty about not doing rigorous research. So if somebody said that to me, that wouldn't make me feel guilty, but I would feel disrespect. And I would feel that the discussion was closed, that the other person who was doing the disrespecting was closed to exploring.

Walton: Warren [Bennis], you introduced another dimension, which is that affective styles influence the choices we make about what we want to do and how we go about doing it. I think that may be much more important than the attention we've given it so far. I wonder if you would elaborate on that.

Bennis: I've thought about it here and there, but I hadn't thought about it specifically with organizational behavior knowledge. For example, it was very clear to me when I was at MIT that Edgar Schein and I had very different styles of how we developed things. We used to kid a little bit about the hedgehogs and the foxes. Ed was the hedgehog who would go after one problem without diverting. You know one thing about a hedgehog: At their best they're adorable, and at their worst they're dull. And I was a fox because I would predict so far in the future that no one could truly disprove it. So our styles really have a great deal to do with the kinds of problems. I'll tell you, I felt a little the way Chris does. I felt sort of rejected by those others more than I felt I rejected them. One thing about foxes is that they embrace, almost by definition, perhaps too much. I always felt Chris didn't as much as I, which is what I respected him for. Foxes aren't particularly treasured. There's not even a hedgehog in me trying to come out. In me I have a feeling of envy toward people who've continued the long stay of research. Let's say it's true that people with an ambivalence or who are opposed to an action orientation have distanced themselves from direct relationships with others. They've got a repressed emotionality vis-à-vis the people they work with. What does that mean in terms of research? And what about those who do get involved? You can look at this as a continuum between "attack and research." Like what was said about the reporter: Will the reporter who is standing at the elbow of history take down the middle initials? Well, there are some of our colleagues who spend their entire lives taking down middle initials. And then the people who get overly involved with their subjects—and I was wondering what the areas of strengths would be and the blind spots.

Driver: One of the things that strike me about our field is how little we have turned it on ourselves. One of the learnings we've had in organizations is that when we go in, we work with the various cognitive styles. We get them to a position where they can talk about things without the kind of animosity that otherwise exists. It creates a little bit of distancing, but not too much. You can talk about your style, the fox, with a little more humor and a little more fun. It allows you to put teams together; it allows you to see strengths and weaknesses; it allows you an awful lot of things in organizations that we've been doing over the last ten years. I don't see it used at all in the academic world. I don't see us at all trying to entertain each other's styles or trying to put any of these tactics to use. So I would strongly support your commitments to trying to turn that process technology inward on ourselves. I think it will get us out of the person-to-person attacks and into some discussions of complementarities and other phenomena.

Walton: If we take seriously what we've just said, the institute, the Center for Effective Organizations, and the Harvard Business School would do well not to have so much convergence in

what we're trying to do and how to do it. It's one thing to have
a distinctive competence, so that people know they are at one
place versus another. But there is a need to have different people
interacting with each other with different affective styles and
different cognitive styles. You need a degree of diversity within
an institution.

Kilmann: I'd like to make a comment on the issue of security,
insecurity, and egos. I can reflect on a number of faculty meetings with just four and five persons, and the last thing that's
going to be discussed is how each one feels insecure, threatened,
or unsure of his or her own identity. Yet we spend so much
time trying to present such a strong, positive image. I also think
that if one suffers from worrying about identity, it's easy to come
on with that hard-line research attitude, because there's a lot
of safety in that. That's the way we've been trained, and we
can fall back on that. I think it's much harder to come on strong
and say: "I reject it for these reasons, and I'm going to go in
this direction because the newer directions are totally uncertain."
I can also recall only one or two conversatons with maybe four
or five faculty members when it got down to the level of these
kinds of insecurities and egos. After that kind of meeting there
wasn't the possibility of threatening one another as much anymore. It's as if since we could acknowledge this to one another,
it took away a lot of the power about worrying what our identi-
ties are.

Mitroff: I think the premise, unstated but really stated, is that
playing a different game, in which the standards of excellence
are no less but I would say even higher and harder, is that of
a social artist. I'm not just trying to play with words, but I think
it is a social scientist/artist. To me what infuses your work is
not only the futurism, but it's the playfulness of ideas. I do think
there is a change. I think about the recent books, these best-
sellers in the *New York Times* on business. Although they aren't
done primarily by academics, the field is moving toward that
in some funny way. I feel it is. It's moving toward it, and we
may make jokes and take potshots and all the rest, but I have
a feeling that down deep in all of our hearts is the unstated

ambivalence, "Golly, we wish that we had had all the potshots for writing one of those best-sellers." Maybe not all of them. I think it is the social art that has not been given its due expression. It deserves its day in court. We need more people who will say, "I'm going to create a better story or a different story, if not better. A different way to tell the story." I think Warren's analogy is very relevant. It's a continual battle between the hedgehog and the fox. What I think we haven't done is, perhaps, advance the fox methodology as much as we'd like to think. Don't turn away from the hedgehog. But what is it like to really be foxy?

REFERENCES

Argyris, C. and Schön, D. A. *Organizational Learning.* Reading, Mass.: Addison-Wesley, 1978.

Barnard, C. *The Functions of the Executive.* Cambridge, Mass.: Harvard University Press, 1938.

Benson, J. K. "Innovation and Crises in Organizational Analysis." In J. K. Benson (Ed.), *Organizational Analysis: Critique and Innovation.* Beverly Hills, Calif.: Sage, 1977.

Berger, P., and Luckmann, T. *The Social Construction of Reality.* Garden City, N.Y.: Anchor Books, 1967.

Cammann, E., Lawler, E. E., III, Ledford, G. E., Jr., and Seashore, S. E. "Management-Labor Cooperation in Quality of Worklife Experiments: Comparative Analysis of Eight Cases." Technical Report No. 21-26-80-18. Washington, D.C.: U.S. Department of Labor, 1984.

Denison, D. "The Climate, Culture, and Effectiveness of Work Organizations: A Study of Organizational Behavior and Financial Performance." Unpublished doctoral dissertation, University of Michigan, 1982.

Gebhart, R. "Status Degradation and Organizational Succession: An Ethnomethodological Approach." *Administrative Science Quarterly,* 1978, *23* (4), 553–581.

Hackman, R. and Oldham, G. *Work Redesign.* Reading, Mass.: Addison-Wesley, 1980.

Hersen, M., and Barlow, D. *Single Case Experimental Design.* New York: Pergamon Press, 1976.

Louis, M. R. "Useful Knowledge and Knowledge Use: Toward Explicit Meanings." In R. Kilmann and others (Eds.), *Producing Useful Knowledge for Organizations.* New York: Praeger, 1983.

Lundberg, C. "On the Paradigm Orthodoxy of the Organizational Sciences: Consequences for Theory and Research— Toward an Alternative Strategy and Inquiry." *Proceedings of the Eastern Academy of Management,* 1981, pp. 8-13.

Lundberg, C. "Toward Theoretical Development: Paradigmatic Influence, Theoretic Structure, and Inquiry Strategy." Paper presented at a meeting of the Western Academy of Management, Vancouver, Canada, April 1984.

Mitroff, I. I. "On Mutual Understanding and the Implementation Problem: A Philosophical Case Study of the Psychology of the Apollo Moon Scientists." In R. L. Schultz and D. P. Slevin (Eds.), *Implementing Operations Research/Management Science.* New York: Elsevier, 1975.

Mitroff, I. I., and Pondy, L. R. "Afterthoughts on the Leadership Conference." In M. W. McCall, Jr., and M. M. Lombardo (Eds.), *Leadership: Where Else Can We Go?* Durham, N.C.: Duke University Press, 1978.

Mohr, L. B. *Explaining Organizational Behavior: The Limits and Possibilities of Theory and Research.* San Fancisco: Jossey-Bass, 1982.

Pondy, L. R., and Olson, M. L. "Theories of Extreme Cases." Paper presented at meeting of the American Psychological Association, San Francisco, August 1977.

Susman, G., and Evered, R. "An Assessment of the Scientific Merits of Action Research." *Administrative Science Quarterly,* 1978, *23* (4), 582-603.

Thomas, K., and Tymon, W. G., Jr. "Necessary Properties of Relevant Research: Lessons from Recent Criticisms of the Organizational Sciences." *Academy of Management Review,* 1982, *7* (3), 345-352.

Thorngate, W. "'In General' vs. 'It Depends': Some Comments on the Gergen-Schenker Debate." *Personality and Social Psychology Bulletin,* 1976, *2,* 404-410.

Trist, E. *The Evolution of Socio-Technical Systems*. Toronto: Ontario Quality of Working Life Centre, 1981.

Vaill, P. "Practice Theories in Organization Development." In J. D. Adams (Ed.), *New Technologies in Organization Development*. Vol. 2. La Jolla, Calif.: University Associates, 1975.

Weick, K. *The Social Psychology of Organizing*. (2d ed.) Englewood Cliffs, N.J.: Prentice-Hall, 1979.

4

Chris Argyris

❖ ❖ ❖ ❖ ❖ ❖ ❖ ❖ ❖ ❖ ❖ ❖ ❖ ❖ ❖ ❖ ❖

Making Knowledge
More Relevant to Practice:
Maps for Action

Elsewhere, I have tried to describe the conditions that tend to inhibit the production of valid and usable knowledge, especially when diagnosing and changing the status quo (Argyris, 1980, 1982a, 1983). In this chapter I should like to describe some concepts and research methods that can be used to develop usable knowledge that also adds to basic theory. In describing the methods in some detail, I also hope to show how they illustrate a more general perspective for making knowledge more relevant to practice.

The Meaning of Practice

Practice may be defined as the implementation of a set of ideas in order to achieve intended consequences in the world

I wish to thank Dianne Argyris, Robert Putnam, and Diana Smith for their many helpful comments.

of practical affairs. The act of implementation may be at the level of formulating a policy or executing it. The focus of this chapter is on producing social science knowledge that practitioners can use in taking action, such as executing policies. The domain of focus is on human beings as they are interacting in order to achieve their intended goals. I take it as a given that it is individuals who will do the actual implementing, the acting, even though they may be serving as agents for an organization or group.

Maps for Action

If we are to be of help to practitioners as they act, we need to consider what kind of knowledge individuals require and use while acting. Fortunately, recent research provides many insights into how people make sense of their worlds in order to act. For example, they organize data into patterns, store these patterns in their heads, and then retrieve them whenever they need them.

Humans probably use several mechanisms to store these patterns. The one we will focus on here is called "maps for action." These maps represent the behaviors that people use to design and implement their actions. These maps are the key to helping us to understand and explain why human beings behave as they do, because they represent the problems or causal scripts that individuals use to inform their actions.

I want to emphasize that these maps are constructions formulated by researchers, and, as such, they are hypotheses to be tested. Further, action maps are never completed, because all the features of situations cannot be fully known. Ironically, then, maps are most useful if they contain designed ignorance. Or, to put it another way, a map for action may be viewed as the researcher's constructions of the actor's views of the strategic variables that determine the essential formulation of a solution (Ansoff, 1979, pp. 220–222).

One of the central arguments of this chapter is: If human beings use maps for action to inform their actions, then one way for social scientists to help ensure that the knowledge they pro-

duce will be usable is to organize, or package, it in the form
of maps for action. I will present several examples of action maps
that we have developed, discuss their underlying properties, and
make explicit how they can be tested and how they add to knowledge while also making it more likely that the knowledge will
be usable in action.

Example I: Conflict Avoidance and Directive Control

The first map was developed by Diana Smith and me.
We were trying to make sense of the data obtained during a
weekend workshop attended by six senior members of a professional firm and their spouses. The objective of the workshop
was to help the participants understand and cope more effectively with the pressures they were experiencing.

The map (Exhibit 1) begins by identifying the factors that
all participants agreed created the pressures and problems that
they experienced. As indicated in column 1, these factors are
related to work requirements (frequent travel, long and unpredictable hours at work, and so on) and home requirements (being with spouse and children, chores related to home, and so
on). Next, the couples identified what may be called structural
solutions to deal with the pressures (column 2). These consisted
of a range of rules that were not to be violated, such as "Divide
tasks" and "Define personal turf." At times these rules were
effective, but at other times they were not, as any number of
unexpected factors led to violations that, in turn, led to the difficulties that the couples were trying to solve. The frequency
of rule ineffectiveness was high enough for the couples to agree
that this was a major source of conflict. The couples identified
two major patterns they used to deal with such conflict (column
3). Some spouses acted to avoid conflict (CA); others became
aggressive and controlling (AC). Men were as likely to be in
either category as women. Sometimes conflict avoiders acted
aggressively but only when they felt there was absolutely no other
recourse left to them.

In column 4 we note the most frequent reactions used by
the individuals to deal with the conflicts and pressures. The CAs

Exhibit 1. Action Map for Example I.

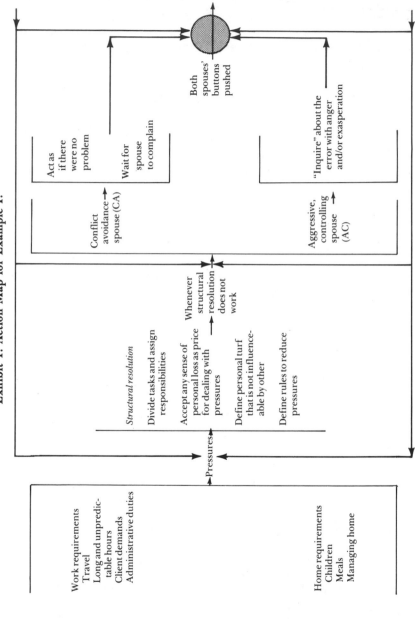

Work requirements
Travel
Long and unpredic-
table hours
Client demands
Administrative duties

Home requirements
Children
Meals
Managing home

Pressures

Structural resolution

Divide tasks and assign
responsibilities

Accept any sense of
personal loss as price
for dealing with
pressures

Define personal turf
that is not influence-
able by other

Define rules to reduce
pressures

Whenever
structural
resolution
does not
work

Conflict
avoidance
spouse (CA)

Act as
if there
were no
problem

Wait for
spouse
to complain

Aggressive,
controlling
spouse
(AC)

"Inquire" about the
error with anger
and/or exasperation

Both
spouses'
buttons
pushed

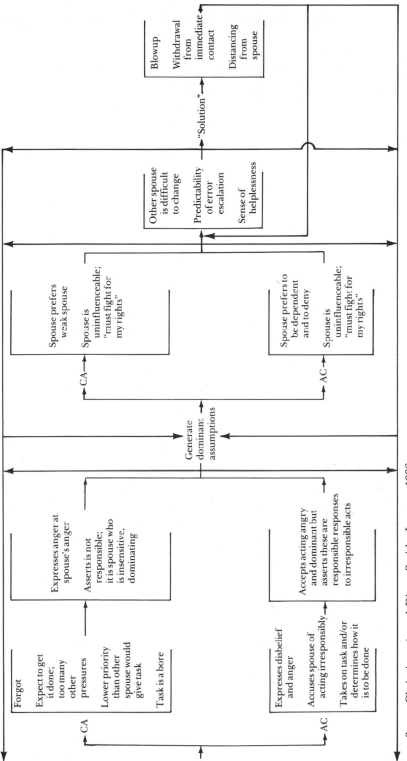

Forgot

Expect to get it done; too many other pressures

Lower priority than other spouse would give task

Task is a bore

Expresses anger at spouse's anger

Asserts is not responsible; it is spouse who is insensitive, dominating

CA →

Spouse prefers weak spouse

Spouse is uninfluenceable; "must fight for my rights"

Generate dominant assumptions

Expresses disbelief and anger

Accuses spouse of acting irresponsibly

Takes on task and/or determines how it is to be done

Accepts acting angry and dominant but asserts these are responsible responses to irresponsible acts

AC →

Spouse prefers to be dependent and to deny

Spouse is uninfluenceable; "must fight for my rights"

Other spouse is difficult to change

Predictability of error escalation

Sense of helplessness

"Solution"

Blowup

Withdrawal from immediate contact

Distancing from spouse

CA

AC

Source: Chris Argyris and Diana Smith, January 1982.

acted as if there were no problem and waited for the spouse to act. The ACs acted relatively quickly but usually tried to do so by hiding their exasperation and anger with disingenuous inquiry. The passivity of the CAs and the aggressiveness of the ACs tended to trigger automatic emotional responses. It was as if they had a psychological button that was pushed. In column 5 we note these typical reactions. As a rule the CAs would try to downplay their errors either directly or indirectly by saying that they had other chores or much higher priorities. The ACs would then express disbelief and outrage at such responses and question the CAs' sense of responsibility. This, in turn, would make it possible for the CAs to become angry and accuse the ACs of being hostile. The ACs would accept that they were acting in a hostile manner and then hold the CAs responsible (column 6).

In Exhibit 1 we show that all these reactions feed back to reinforce the previous actions. The feedback processes in this system are not error-correcting but error-enhancing. Living under these self-sealing, escalating processes is difficult for all concerned. One way to live with these conditions is to formulate an explanation for the dysfunctional behavior of the other. The explanation becomes a dominant belief or assumption about the other. Hence, the CAs come to believe that the ACs prefer weak spouses and are uninfluenceable, and that they (CAs) must fight for their rights. The ACs, in contrast, come to believe that the CAs prefer to depend on them and to deny that this is the case. The ACs also come to see their spouses as uninfluenceable, so that they too must fight for their rights (column 7). These conditions lead all parties to conclude that the other spouse is difficult to change, that escalating error and a sense of helplessness are a way of life (column 8). The outcome of this state of affairs is either to experience blowups or to withdraw and distance from each other or both (column 9).

Example II: Moving Toward Genuine Matrix Management

In the second example (Exhibit 2), we present a map of the operation of a top management group in a larger organization (developed primarily by Diana Smith). The group contained the fifteen top executives of the firm, representing all the major functions. Its purpose was to act as the highest governing body for the important strategic issues of the firm. The members had committed themselves to creating group dynamics and a group culture that would make it possible for them to discuss issues that are typically undiscussable, to constructively confront one another's ideas, and to encourage risk taking and new trust.

The members believed that if they were to succeed, two types of conditions would have to be developed. First, there were structural conditions. For example, policies would be developed to guarantee members organizational power to act forthrightly and candidly; rewards, including financial ones, would be available to those making important contributions to the development of the group; organizational policies would be implemented guaranteeing the job safety of individuals who, in acting forthrightly, might offend or upset members with more seniority; and finally, rules would be developed by which counterproductive actions by any members would be discussed. Second, group members would develop the skills required to produce actions consistent with the structural arrangements so that the structures would come to life and be put into practice as intended. Otherwise, if individuals were structurally protected to confront constructively but when they did so, the actions themselves were destructive, then the structural arrangements would soon lose their credibility.

The top group met about once a month, usually for twelve to fifteen hours, to deal with strategic issues. Tape recordings of sessions were sent to researchers whenever they were not present. After a year of operating, a good deal of concern was expressed that although important structural safeguards were in place, the actions of some members were counterproductive to the ideal of an effectively functioning strategic group that they were trying to approximate. The most pressing problem was that many of the younger officers felt that the four senior executives were not acting consistently with the collegial model. The president was seen as overcontrolling. He agreed that at times he acted this way because the others were creating a vacuum

Exhibit 2. Action Map for Example II.

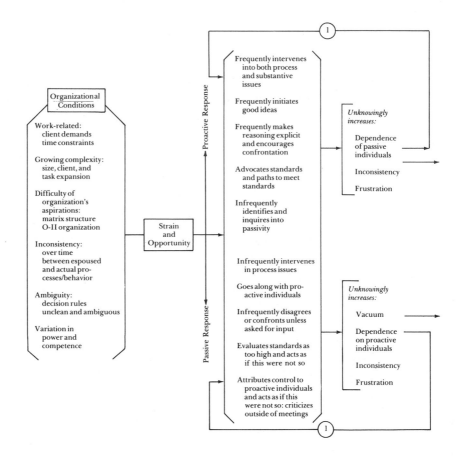

Source: Diana Smith and Chris Argyris, February 1983.

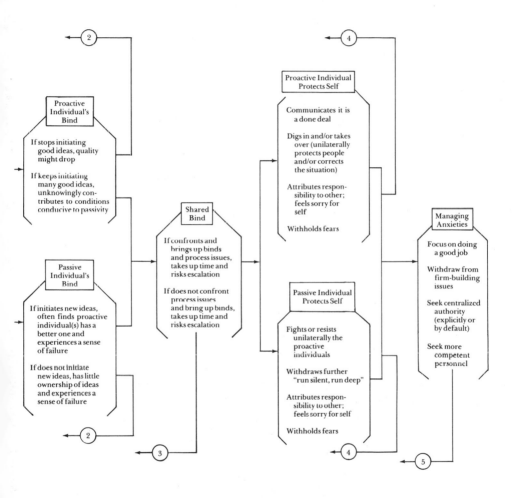

2

Proactive Individual's Bind

If stops initiating good ideas, quality might drop

If keeps initiating many good ideas, unknowingly contributes to conditions conducive to passivity

Passive Individual's Bind

If initiates new ideas, often finds proactive individual(s) has a better one and experiences a sense of failure

If does not initiate new ideas, has little ownership of ideas and experiences a sense of failure

2

Shared Bind

If confronts and brings up binds and process issues, takes up time and risks escalation

If does not confront process issues and bring up binds, takes up time and risks escalation

3

4

Proactive Individual Protects Self

Communicates it is a done deal

Digs in and/or takes over (unilaterally protects people and/or corrects the situation)

Attributes responsibility to other; feels sorry for self

Withholds fears

Passive Individual Protects Self

Fights or resists unilaterally the proactive individuals

Withdraws further "run silent, run deep"

Attributes responsibility to other; feels sorry for self

Withholds fears

4

Managing Anxieties

Focus on doing a good job

Withdraw from firm-building issues

Seek centralized authority (explicitly or by default)

Seek more competent personnel

5

that he had to fill for the sake of the organization. The three other senior executives were seen as a good deal more passive, not confronting the president. As a result, the younger officers felt that they had to "play it safe." The metaphor in good currency was "Run silent, run deep."

Turning to Exhibit 2, the map begins with the conditions that all participants agreed were governing constraints.

Organization-Governing Conditions (Column 1). The first column represents the conditions that all participants agree are constraints that cannot be ignored. All actions by the members must take these constraints into account. Six such governing conditions were identified.

1. High demands are placed on the professionals to meet clients' requirements. For example, the professionals typically work a ten- to twelve-hour day and frequently work on Saturdays and part of Sundays.
2. The firm is growing so fast that the board of directors has asked the chief executive officer to reduce the pace of growth. The fast rate at which new clients are added places heavy demands on the professionals.
3. A third governing condition is the inconsistency between the participants' espousal of the ideal and their inability to produce such actions as often as they wish.
4. As a consequence of conditions 1, 2, and 3, the participants are faced with another governing condition—namely, they are having difficulties in creating a learning environment and group dynamics during the group meetings that are consistent with their ideal, which could be described as Model II. (If unfamiliar with the details of Model II, please see Argyris, 1982a.)
5. There is a high degree of ambiguity around the decision rules related to the substantive features of the business as well as around the rules for moving toward the model of group functioning to which the members aspire.
6. Finally, the members agree, and the researchers confirm, that the individuals have different degrees of competence in skills as well as different degrees of power. An example

of the latter is that the matrix includes the chief executive officer, three senior partners, and vice-presidents.

Passive Proactive Response (Column 2). These conditions create all sorts of strains and opportunities for learning. Individuals report that they respond (and they are observed to respond) to these governing conditions with varying degrees of proactivity. Hence, we show a continuum of passive to proactive responses.

Examples of the proactive responses include (1) intervening in both process and substantive issues that are critical to effective transition, (2) initiating and advocating ideas that are judged by the group members to be useful and good, (3) frequently making the reasoning behind actions explicit and encouraging confrontation of them, (4) advocating high standards both technically and in the management of the human processes within the group and organization, and (5) frequently identifying and inquiring into passivity.

The individuals who act more passively tend (1) to infrequently intervene in process issues, (2) to go along with proactive individuals' contributions, (3) to infrequently disagree or confront unless asked, (4) to evaluate standards as too high and act as if this were not so, and (5) to attribute control to proactive individuals and act as if this were not so—that is, to criticize proactive individuals privately.

Consequences of Proactive and Passive Responses (Column 3). Proactive individuals, who often make valid interventions, tend to facilitate dependence of passive individuals. These actions reinforce the inconsistency between the espoused aspirations and the actual individual actions and group dynamics. Finally, the proactive members feel frustrated with the lack of involvement by those who act more passively and who simultaneously condemn them for being more proactive.

The passivity tends to create a behavioral vacuum that the proactive members believe they must fill. The passive actions also reinforce the dependence on the proactive individuals, the inconsistency, and the frustration.

These two sets of consequences feed back to reinforce respectively the original responses. Hence, individuals who act more proactively defend themselves by maintaining or reinforcing their proactivity, while individuals who act more passively defend themselves by reinforcing their passivity.

The Paradoxes of Proactive and Passive Actions (Column 4). In addition to respectively reinforcing the preferred response patterns of individuals, the actions and consequences described so far lead to a third order of consequences that are paradoxes. A paradox occurs when individuals are in a situation in which whatever response they make in order to be constructive is also counterproductive.

The paradox experienced by the proactive individuals is: If they stop being proactive with admittedly good ideas, the quality of the group's performance will drop. If they keep initiating good ideas, they will reinforce a passivity that will also lead the group's performance to drop, as well as inhibiting the move toward Model II and an O-II world (see Argyris, 1982a).

The paradox experienced by the passive individuals is: If they initiate new ideas, they will often find that the proactive individuals have better ones, and hence they will feel disappointment of failure. Yet, if they do not initiate new ideas, they will experience little ownership of ideas and still experience failure in not producing their own ideas and not moving toward II and O-II.

This set of paradoxes reinforces the particular responses because the actors tend to continue their preferred ways of responding when dealing with the paradox.

The Shared Paradox (Column 5). These paradoxes, in turn, lead to another paradox that all participants have. When individuals confront the process issues, they are likely to take up precious time in an already full agenda and risk error escalation, particularly since they are apt to raise the dilemmas consistently with their predispositions. But if they do not confront the issues and bring up the paradoxes, the resulting dynamics will also take up time and lead to error escalation.

This shared paradox both reinforces the previous factors and leads to self-protective responses aimed at managing the paradoxes. Thus, the highly proactive individuals tend to become impatient with passivity, to take action and to take over, and to communicate that "it's done." If confronted, they tend to dig in and to place the blame for their unilateral actions on the passive actors. Finally, they tend to withhold their fears about the effectiveness of the matrix as well as the probable long-run failure of the experiment.

To protect themselves, the passive individuals tend to resist the proactive individuals—either covertly or overtly. Most often, however, they tend to withdraw even further, withholding their fears and holding the proactive individuals responsible for both their withdrawal and their fears (column 6).

These fifth-order consequences then feed back to reinforce the previous consequences and simultaneously lead to a set of final consequences related to how individuals manage the stress. They include (1) focus on performing one's own job very well, (2) withdrawal from firm-building and matrix-building issues, (3) seeking more centralized authority, and (4) seeking more competent personnel (column 7).

These consequences will help to produce high-quality individual performance but can also lead to an organization increasingly full of stress, which, in turn, may hinder the building of an organization that can ensure high performance over time.

Features of the Maps

The maps purport to identify and to describe the interdependence of the variables that the actors define as relevant. By *interdependence* I mean how a given variable influences and is influenced by the other variables. For example, the passive actors and conflict avoiders have an impact on the proactive or aggressive actors, and this impact, in turn, has specified consequences on the variables that follow plus feedback consequences on the variables that precede it.

Embedded in the map is a microtheory of how the variables developed and how they are presently forming a self-maintaining and reinforcing system. Both these features contain what I should like to call "sloppy causality." The causal assertions are sloppy in that they are not formulated in rigorous and unambiguous terms. But it may be that sloppy causality is the most rate causality that the participants will ever be able to use.

is is true, then the feature that social scientists will have to address is how human beings achieve "satisficing" accuracy by using causal theories that are sloppy.

The maps depict a story or drama that unfolds with predictable repetitiveness (Mangham, 1978) at different levels of analysis. The maps begin by specifying conditions that are external to couples' actions yet help to drive the actions. For example, the couples choose to have their professional careers, to raise children, to be active neighbors. The executives choose to design a top-level matrix group to administer their firm, they choose to make their firm a fast-growing one, they choose to create a world with many ambiguities, and they choose to be in a world where there is variation in power and competence. Yet, once created, these conditions come back to roost, requiring these individuals to take them into account.

The maps indicate the pressures and strains that these governing conditions create, followed by the ways the participants predictably and repetitively choose to act to deal with the pressures and stresses. Next are the second-order consequences of these choices as well as the way they feed back to reinforce the previous factors. The maps continue with third-order, fourth-order, and so on consequences plus their feedback. Some of these lead to dominant assumptions and beliefs (Example I); others lead into paradoxes and then to dominant assumptions (Example II). The sequence in each map appears to start with governing conditions and then to go to strategies, behavioral consequences, norms, assumptions and beliefs, and further behavioral consequences. The exact nature of these conditions and sequences and of the feedback mechanisms depends on the context being studied.

Since participants, past or present, are able to identify the story embedded in each map, and since the story appears to exist over time and through the turnover of actors, the maps are also maps of social systems. The patterns they depict form a social system in the sense that the patterns exist even though the participants who wish to alter them appear unable to do so; and even as participants come and go, the essential components of the system depicted in the map remain.

These maps contain a frequently identified feature of "supraindividual" systems: They are created by individuals, yet once created, they become self-maintaining and it is difficult for the individuals to change them. They also contain another feature of supraindividual systems that is rarely emphasized: These maps cannot be changed directly by supraindividual factors. As we shall see, in order to help individuals we must first begin by altering their individual theories of action that lead them to produce the automatic responses (such as conflict avoidance or acting proactively) that, in turn, lead to the second-, third-, or fourth-order consequences that become supraindividual conditions.

Both maps suggest that there is a low probability that the system will become self-corrective or that the drama will change significantly. So far, almost all the maps developed, at the beginning of the relationship, have the features of feedback processes that inhibit the detection and correction of error, that escalate mistrust and defensiveness, that enhance self-fulfilling and self-sealing processes.

These general features of maps are caused by the theories of action that human beings use to deal with such problems. These theories-in-use appear to be the same for most participants; hence the similarities among systems, and hence the supraindividual features described earlier. But if most individuals have the same theory-in-use, then the individuals are the carriers of the supraindividual systemic features. In other words, (1) it is individuals who "cause" the supraindividual systems; (2) it is the supraindividual systemic features that "cause" the individuals to act and reason as they do; hence, (3) the system cannot be changed without altering the individuals' reasoning processes, which (4) are so protected by socially learned defenses that change must *begin* at the individual level; but (5) these changes are related to the theories-in-use, which are learned through socialization and hence are supraindividual variables.

It is this intimate connection between individual and supraindividual factors that makes these maps generalizable beyond the context in which they were developed. For example, "button pushing" has been identified among senior-level executives (Argyris, 1976). Moreover, it appears that, in classes held in a university setting to help students learn Model II, the students act in ways that are consistent with the features of the map in Example II. Students are under time pressures during the classes or are constrained in how often they can meet in small sections outside class. They experience a growing complexity and ambiguity because they often act inconsistently between their espoused theory and their theory-in-use and feel stuck in their inability to change their theory-in-use. There are also varying degrees of power, the instructor and the teaching assistants having more than the students.

At the outset, the instructor is more proactive than the students. She or he frequently has important things to say and advocates high standards. In the classes, the number of participants is large (over fifty), and hence the instructor does not often deal with passivity, because she or he is kept busy dealing with the issues by the more proactive students. The passive students tend to criticize the proactive students and, at the outset, the instructors outside class. They experience the sense of inconsistency and frustration that the passive members of the matrix team described in Example II. The paradoxes identified in the matrix example also exist in the classroom.

Finally, the maps do not identify how many individuals are members of the system, their age, sex, educational status, or social status, or many other demographic factors often studied by social scientists. The hypothesis is that the intimate connections among (1) the individuals' theories-in-use, (2) the systems depicted by the map, and (3) the operation of cultural factors through which the individuals learned their theories-in-use are so powerful that many members in this system will act consistently with the system. If any are found not to do so, then we would predict that they would describe themselves as individuals who are bucking the system. The hypothesis of the powerful relationship is therefore disconfirmable, a topic discussed below.

Creating the Action Maps

The first step in creating an action map is to describe the governing conditions that the players agree on. In Example I, all the couples agreed that the beginning of their problems was due to the pressures they were experiencing from work and home requirements. They then listed the features of these requirements that, up to that point, they had considered as givens—that is, as unlikely to be changed. In Example II, all the participants were able to agree on the governing conditions described in the first column that existed as they were trying to create an effective matrix organization.

The next step is to identify the strategies with which participants deal with the givens. For example, in Example I, we identified two strategies that the participants used to deal with the pressures. One was structural and the other behavioral. In the structural strategy, the couples tried to define rules and responsibilities that, if each spouse carried out, they hoped would reduce the pressures. The couples reported that the structural strategies worked for a while but did not solve the basic problems. After lengthy discussions, the basic problems, as they experienced them, turned out to be the behavioral strategies that individuals used to resolve conflicts. Example II illustrated the problem of an increasing discrepancy between the espoused theory of management (a matrix Model II) and the actualities plus the theory-in-use that produced the discrepancy. The logic was similar. We began with the governing conditions, then the behavioral strategies such as (1) the strain and opportunity, (2) the proactive and passive responses, (3) the consequences of each of these responses, (4) the separate binds that resulted for proactive and for passive players, as well as (5) the binds that resulted for both, (6) the ways individuals protected themselves, and (7) how they managed their anxieties.

Embedded in the maps is a theory of defense. For example, we hypothesized that the proactive and passive actions lead to dependence and frustration among the participants. Then we hypothesized that these effects lead to different sets of binds and a joint set. The binds could not be derived without a theory of human defensiveness. We then hypothesized how these binds lead to organizational consequences, such as the proactive individuals making decisions unilaterally, while the passive individuals go to meetings and withhold important views while acting as if they were not doing so.

Once the map was formulated, we then asked ourselves

whether there were any episodes that contradicted it. If there were, then the map would have to be revised unless it could be shown that they were irrelevant to the map. The final map had to be acceptable to those involved as explaining all the relevant issues and problems that they were trying to solve. In fact, the first step in ascertaining the validity of the maps was to examine, discuss, and revise them with the players until they considered the maps authoritative descriptions of their context. These discussions were often time-consuming: Most actors checked the causal relationships depicted in the maps; oftentimes, they disagreed about the consequences; and individuals spent much time tracking themselves through the map. For example, some conflict avoiders went through all the consequences carefully. The proactive players sought data from the group to test the extent to which they produced dependence in others. Players also spent time discussing the content of the double binds.

In authenticating the map, the participants also set the stage for changing it should they wish to do so. Change cannot occur without having a map of the present state of affairs, including why the players remain boxed in even though they prefer a different state of affairs. If they did decide to begin to change the system, then an additional set of data became available to test features of the map. In Example I, for instance, a strategy for change that focused on changing the spouses' dominant assumptions without changing their own and/or others' automatic reactions and skills for dealing with conflict, we would predict, should fail. Or, in Example II, even if the group were to double the amount of time available in group meetings, the shared bind should not go away. Or requiring, cajoling, persuading the proactive to remain silent and the passive to become more proactive should not resolve the binds that each group experienced.

Methods for Obtaining the Data Used in the Maps

In obtaining the data on which the maps were based, the key requirement was to get as directly observable data as possible. (For detailed descriptions of how to execute methods for obtaining such data, see Argyris, 1982a.) Such data could be obtained through observations, backed up, if possible, with tape recordings. The exact number of observations depended on the nature of the conditions. For example, if the content and dynamics of the meetings were repetitive and routine, then the sample could be small. There might be as few as two observations of group meetings and probably not more than ten.

The second requirement was that the conditions for study be such that the actors would produce their everyday actions even though they might feel embarrassed or threatened. The third requirement was that they have the opportunity, with the help of the researchers, to reflect on their actions. Fourth, the actors should provide additional data that could not be collected by observations or tape recordings—for example, the reasoning processes that led them to act as they did and any thoughts and feelings that they suppressed.

The fifth requirement was that the data collection be repeated several times in order to check and recheck the actors' learning and their conclusions. The sixth requirement was to create an opportunity to explore what changes would have to be made in individual, group, intergroup, and organizational behaviors to reduce the counterproductive features. Such discussions could especially serve to test the participants' commitment to the validity of the maps.

The Testability of the Maps

The maps represent the numerous variables, plus their interrelationships, that the actors use to make the problem manageable and to have a basis for a solution. The first test, therefore, is to obtain information on the variables included in the map. One way to achieve this is to show the map to the participants and obtain their reactions. As mentioned earlier, this step often requires at least several hours of discussion to examine differences and objectives and to redesign the map.

A second way to test features of the map is to make predictions about the future state of affairs. For example, we would predict that if the members of the couples group are left to their own devices, no actions will be observed over time that will alter the defensiveness and self-fulfilling, self-sealing, error-escalating processes even though the players have now confirmed the map as a valid description of their universe. The patterns in the map should be self-maintaining over the years. A third test is to predict conditions under which the players will leave the system or will consider it a failure.

A fourth type of test is to use the map as a basis for designing concrete and implementable learning environments to change the counterproductive features of the map. The theory of instruction to be used in these seminars can also be inferred from the map. The learning activity and change program, therefore, will be "derived" from the action map and hence can be used as a test of various features of it. For example, what individuals' attitudes, skills, and values will have to be unfrozen to help passive and conflict-avoiding individuals become more proactive and confront constructively? What skills and competencies do all the participants require in order to deal directly with paradoxes and double binds? Turning to the levels of group and intergroup dynamics, how can win/lose, competitive dynamics be reduced? How is it possible to create a culture in which the undiscussable becomes discussable and alterable?

None of these questions can be answered without specifying the processes by which individuals can unfreeze the old and produce the new. Once these processes are specified, they should be consistent with the relationships defined by the map. For example, the button pushing in the couples group cannot be altered simply by altering the avoiding of conflict or acting less aggressively. The basic assumptions that each spouse develops about the changeability of the other must also be dealt with. In Example II, it is not enough to alter the passivity; one must alter the way the members deal with the double binds. Indeed, one cannot be altered without altering the other.

If educational experiences can be developed or structural arrangements implemented that alter the counterproductive features (for example, self-sealing processes, escalating error) without altering the variables identified in the maps, then the hypothesis that the variables and their interrelationships are both fundamental and strategic will be disconfirmed.

The Nested Features of Maps for Action

I have been describing maps for action as constructions of what researchers hypothesize to be in the players' heads, both explicitly and tacitly, in order to explain their actions. The constructions are therefore hypotheses and are subject to testing. I have identified several tests that we have used, ranging from reworking the map with the players until all authenticate it to making predictions under the same conditions to making predictions under different conditions.

One way to create different conditions is to help the players change the social system in which they are embedded, including changing the actions that contribute to maintaining it. When individuals cooperate to produce change, gaps become evident in the maps that hitherto were often not realized. When the participants authenticate such actions as "inquires," "expresses disbelief," "acts as if there were no problem," "is proactive," they do so because they have experienced many situations in which those actions occurred. They can illustrate the meanings for these terms with actual behaviors from their direct experiences or from the stories they have shared with one another.

But when participants wish to change the actions so that they can reduce the counterproductive features described in the maps, they do not have experience to use as a basis to create the new actions. Players who act primarily as passive may "know" what new actions mean, they may "know" what active behavior looks like from observing the more proactive, but they do not "know" how to produce it. Indeed, if they did know, they would have done so long before we arrived.

In order to begin to change actions, it is necessary to gain the cooperation of the other participants so that they are willing (1) to begin to change the system and (2) to help one another strive to change their individual actions. These conditions are usually met in our intervention programs, or else we could never go ahead with these programs. Nevertheless, these conditions are not adequate to produce change in individual actions; that is, even with system support and good intentions, these efforts fail. The insufficiency of the efforts shows that individuals must hold another program in their heads that leads them to produce the actions they wish they could eliminate or reduce. If they are unaware of that program, then a program must also exist that keeps them unaware. Hence, an additional map or set of maps is required if the systemic conditions described in the two examples are to be altered.

An example is the action of being "passive." One of the most frequently observed actions that passive individuals use when they try to act more proactively is "easing in." Easing-in is used when individuals slowly unveil the information they wish to communicate in order to minimize making the other defensive. Often they ask questions in a nondirective mode such that, if the other answers correctly, he or she will realize what the hidden meanings are (Argyris, 1982a).

One way to help individuals change their easing-in actions is to help them generate a map for action that they probably use to produce such behavior. The following list states the master program that individuals probably have in their heads to produce easing-in. It begins with the rules (1 and 2) that the actors know how they wish the others would behave and that they do not intend to tell them. Next (3) is the rule that the actors should formulate any questions such that, if the others are able to answer them, they will figure out what the actors are hiding. Next (4-7) are the actors' expectations about the others' willingness to collude with them. Finally (8a-8e) are statements about how the actors will act if the others do not act as expected.

1.   I know how I want you to behave, and I am not going to tell you directly.
2.   I will not tell you that this is the case.
3.   I will ask you questions such that, if you answer them correctly, you will understand my position.
4.   I will expect that you will see all this without my saying it overtly.

5. I will expect that you will not discuss it.
6. I will expect that you will go along.
7. If you have questions or doubts about my intentions, I will expect that you will not raise them and will act as if you did not have doubts.
8. If you do not behave as I expect, I will—
    a. give you more time to think "constructively" by continuing my questions.
    b. eventually become more forthright about my views.
    c. try to argue you out of your views.
    d. conclude that your defenses are too high to permit you to learn or too difficult for me to handle.
    e. compromise and/or withdraw and act as if I were doing neither.

Examining this map, we can identify some important assumptions embedded in it. First, the map focuses on how the actor should behave. It informs the actor to expect the others to behave as the actor expects them to. It does not tell the actor to test his or her impact on the others, especially for unintended consequences. Nor, therefore, does it encourage inquiry into the actor's actions. If the actor follows this program rigorously, and if the others do not behave as expected, then it follows that they are to blame. Hence, embedded in the program for being passive are rules that produce a high degree of unilateral control over the others and a high degree of blindness about the unintended consequences of one's controlling actions.

Using this map, the passive actors (easing-in, conflict avoiders) can begin to gain insight into the reasoning processes that help them to create some of the systemic consequences of defensiveness, escalating error, helplessness, and distancing described in the models.

The actors can then help to alter the program by trying to master another program that, like the first one, has built into it the intent (1) to communicate difficult or threatening information and (2) to minimize the actor's responsibility for making the others defensive but adds some additional factors, such as (3) facilitating testing of, inquiry into, and constructive confrontation of the actor's actions. This new program is as follows:

1. I know how I believe that you (or I) should behave given the difficulties identified, and I will communicate* that to you.
2. I will act in ways to encourage you to inquire* into and to confront* my position.
3. I will expect* that you will inquire into and confront my position whenever you believe it is necessary and I will tell* you my position if you ask.
4. I will check* periodically to see whether you are inquiring and confronting. I will hold you responsible for continual designed congruence between your actions and your thoughts.
5. If I infer incongruence between thoughts and actions, I will test* it with you openly.
6. a. If I learn* that the incongruence is unintentional, then I will act to help you by going back to numbei 1.
    b. If I learn* that the incongruence is intentional and you are knowingly hiding this fact, then I will feel that I cannot trust you and will go back to number 1.

Notice that several key words in the map are starred. These words are so general that they could be executed in a Model I or Model II manner. All should be executed in a Model II manner in this program. These words are key to producing the new program. Although the individuals may understand their meaning, we find that they are rarely able to produce the corresponding actions under on-line conditions. What they require, in addition to unfreezing the old program, is to learn a theory-in-use with which to communicate, inquire, confront, tell, and so on, so that they will not produce the unintended consequences in the two examples described at the outset. Once this new theory-in-use is mastered, it can be used to produce any actions that do not create the unintended consequences, as long as others aspire to the same conditions and the system permits alteration of the two conditions that I have suggested tend to exist with clients who are genuinely interested in correcting the dysfunctionalities of the existing system. This, in turn, requires both (1) examining and interrupting the old program and (2) something similar to learning the new program or skill. You need a map of the actions to take the opportuniy to practice the actions depicted in the map repeatedly and to get frequent and accurate feedback on how well you are doing (Argyris, 1982).

Concluding Comments

I have tried to show that the practical problem of communicating scientific knowledge to practitioners in a form they can use is less a cosmetic issue and much more an issue of how we conceive of research designed to produce usable knowledge.

The approach embedded in this chapter and that embedded in normal science are similar in that both emphasize the importance of (1) describing and understanding reality as is, (2) specifying causal relationships that lead to explanations, and (3) producing generalizations that are subject to (4) public testing and refutation. The differences begin when we examine the source of the criteria for accomplishing these features. For example, in normal science objectivity, precision, and completeness are key features. Objectivity is often accomplished by distancing the researcher from those being studied. Precision is achieved through the use of quantitative language. Completeness is obtained through development of long-range research programs.

The approach embedded in this chapter does not ignore objectivity, precision, and completeness. It takes the position that the criteria for these should take into account the features of the way the human mind works when human beings try to use the knowledge that social scientists produce. For example, quantitative precision can lead to information-rich generalizations that either are not usable under on-line conditions or, if used correctly, could create conditions that would negate the predictions embedded in them. Distancing and objectivity may reduce some kinds of distortions and increase others. Moreover, if those being studied model their behavior after the researchers, they may distance themselves from the researchers when informants are distorting information. Finally, the aspiration for completeness may inhibit effective action in a given situation, because it is unlikely that one can know everything ahead of time; and if one aspires to being complete, one can create conditions of unilateral control over others that, in turn, may alter the validity of the data obtained.

Both approaches seek involvement by those being studied. But the nature of the involvement can be quite different. Social scientists using the normal science approach hope and expect that individuals will participate for the sake of producing valid knowledge. Those who are more applied have an additional hope that sound research will provide a basis for subject involvement.

The approach embedded in this chapter takes a view that builds on the one just described. It suggests that one is more likely to reduce distortion and enhance the production of valid information if the individuals see that participating in research will lead to important learning for them. By *important learning* I mean learning that goes beyond understanding and explanation to producing desired changes and, therefore, learning new values and skills as well as creating new kinds of social systems.

Take the idea of altering the actions of the participants in the two groups in this chapter. All their actions are highly skilled and often reinforced by the system in which they are embedded. Therefore, their sense of competence is related to their ability to continue to produce their actions. But altering their automatic, highly skilled actions requires time. More important, it requires that they become aware of the defenses of which they have been unaware; of unfreezing any defenses that exist that lead them to continue their actions even though those actions are counterproductive. Finally, it requires opportunities for the practice and iterative learning of new skills. All these conditions are rarely achievable under the condition of the participants' being subjects. The more appropriate metaphor may be the one of clients. Participants engage in research because in doing so they can be helped to act more effectively and to design and implement organizations that encourage new actions.

Finally, there is the issue of "ultimate" values, often recognized but rarely discussed. One such value is that we hold sacred the right—indeed, the obligation—of researchers to study whatever intrigues them. The constraints for researchers as described in books on research methods have been less in what to study and more in how to study. But if practice of rigorous research is based on a theory-in-use that is consonant with those used to manage hierarchical organizations, then adherence to these concepts may very well influence the choices social scientists make about what to study. For example, less attention may be paid to developing normative views, views that not only question the status quo but produce knowledge about how to alter it. Further, less attention may be paid to the possibility that research to produce understanding on an issue may be designed quite differently than research on the same issue intended to produce understanding for the purpose of action.

A second ultimate value is related to the kind of world that we prefer to support. It is not true, I believe, that social scientists are neutral about the kind of society in which they live. Even the most "anti" applied researchers value a society in which they are free to conduct research. Such societies would have to value experimentation and learning, which, if truly unfettered, would also require the valuing of risk taking and trust. Such a society, in turn, is unlikely to come to exist without human beings who are willing to accept personal responsibility for their actions (Argyris, 1982a). If the maps we have developed as a result of our research are any indication, then understanding and effectiveness (individual or organizational) will not occur unless the players take seriously their personal causal responsibility for creating, maintaining, and changing those systems.

But this may be so because we choose to conceptualize the order of the universe in the way we do. Others may believe that individuals are not personally causally responsible for the universe in which they are embedded. For example, there are organizational ecologists (Hannan and Freeman, 1977; Brittain and Freeman, 1980) who are creating an ordered universe in which the individuals in organizations are seen as not responsible for the growth and death of their organizations. This view of the order contradicts our view, and vice versa.

The differences go beyond the issue of freedom to construe realities in different ways. All scientists believe that the universe that they are studying is ordered and that the key to understanding it is to specify the order. A second assumption is that a universe will not contain contradictory orders. Einstein believed that it was necessary and possible to unify Newtonian and quantum physics because nature would not play tricks on physical scientists by permitting two theories to be valid that contained fundamental views about physical reality that were contradictory.

Unlike the physical science universe, both orders I have described may be valid even though conflicting, because in the domain of human conduct different and contradictory orders may be possible. Physical nature may not play tricks, but human beings can create social universes that do.

But if several orders exist, if they contain contradictory values, then perhaps social scientists should be required to make explicit why they chose to develop the order they developed. The answer must go beyond the obvious, "because it is a valid view." The question to be answered is "Of the several views that are valid, then why did you, as a social scientist, choose the particular focus?" For example, in my case, I am interested not only in understanding (explaining or predicting) a particular order but also in furthering, reinforcing, and supporting the world view that human beings are causally responsible, that they are the creators of the universe in which they are embedded. I am interested in furthering the probability that human beings will be in charge of their destinies. This does not mean that I should not make explicit how social systems may facilitate or inhibit human proactivity. Indeed, it is because they probably do both that they must be studied (that conforms to the requirement to study the universe as is). But, once having generated the map, I then seek to understand what it would take to change the status quo. The additional map of how to change the status

quo not only tells us much about the status quo (a basic requirement of social science) but provides human beings with liber-
ating alternatives.

RESPONSE AND COMMENTARY

Michael J. Driver

Argyris seems to me to have zeroed in on one of the most critical
problems in current social science research: the "user gap."
On reading journals and attending conferences in the academic
world, one encounters sets of variables and models that are often
ingenious, fairly rigorous or mathematical, and sometimes complex. On reading journals and attending conferences in the
human resource (HR) practitioner area, one finds almost no
transfer of these academic models. In fact, overlapping atten-
dance in these two sets seems rather minimal (Driver, 1983).
When one moves further into the world of practicing managers,
the gap seems wider still.

Argyris blames three factors for much of this: (1) complexity of academic models, (2) generalizability problems, and
(3) unfamiliarity of terms.

With respect to complexity, he implies that some models
are far too complex for use by practitioners. I agree, but with
several caveats. My concurrence is based on evidence of cognitive styles of IIR practitioners in several organizations. Using
the model of "decision style" (Driver, 1979, in press), we have
found a striking difference in decision style between members
of HR departments and members of other organizational units.
In general, the HR practitioners show a moderate to low information use, narrow-focus decisive style—particularly at a conscious level. This stylistic pattern precludes an enthusiastic use
of complex or changeable academic social science models.

Our studies suggest, however, that operating managers
may not suffer from the same problem. In many sites, managers

Figure 1. The HR Lens Effect on the "User Gap."

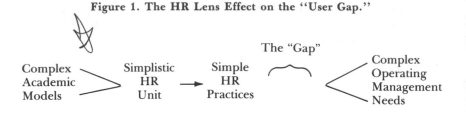

outside HR show fairly complex, multifocus styles of thinking. As seen in Figure 1, the "gap" between academia and managers may be largely attributable to an "HR lens" that blocks transmission or implementation of complex ideas.

This analysis suggests two solutions for academics: (1) increase cognitive complexity in the HR field and (2) deal directly with managers, engineers, and so on. Argyris seems to embrace the second solution directly and the first only indirectly.

A second problem Argyris identifies is generalizability. He points covertly to the caution that must be used in taking social science results across varied environments. He suggests that one must re-create the study environment to use a study's results. Given the absence of a good set of environmental descriptor dimensions, one must agree with him. Practically, this observation suggests that organizations must conduct their own research. However, another approach might be to try to build a set of transsituational dimensions. Such dimensions might tell what changes to expect in relationships between variables when changing from one environment to another.

For instance, time pressure could be considered a transsituational dimension. From a systems perspective (Driver, 1983), time pressure has a curvilinear relationship to information used in systems. Argyris, using case examples, notes that managers and students alike, under time pressure, drop the more complex information approach that he calls Model II learning for the simpler Model I approach. Using a transsituational approach, one could thus forecast what learning model would "work" given information on time pressure in a situation.

Clearly, using only one transsituational dimension is grossly inadequate. What is needed is a minimum set of critical environmental dimensions that can aid in determining the applicability of research findings across environments.

Finally, Argyris attacks the "formidable jargon" of social science, which he feels appalls practitioners. His suggested solution—action maps—directly attacks this third deficiency in social science applications. With the idea of maps developed jointly by academics and managers, Argyris strikes at the heart of jargon. It seems clear that if models are built by managers or others in organizations, the terms will not be unfamiliar to them.

Some other advantages of this approach are the following:

1. Individuals in the organization construct the model. They will tend to "own" the model—it is not some alien construct from academia. Use should increase with ownership. Changing the model should be easier because participants can conduct daily "reality tests" of ideas they fully understand. By involving the participants, we increase their sense of competence to analyze and solve problems on their own.
2. By constructing maps, we raise the awareness of all concerned. Argyris rightly notes that behavioral systems are not self-correcting. Higher awareness all around makes a participative self-correction (without intervention) increasingly likely.
3. The "mapping" approach requires awareness of the need for a complex set of changes if problems are to be corrected. Argyris cites a need for changes in each perceiver's self-awareness and in his or her perceptions of others, the behavior of others, and in-system properties. This system view would be a strong antidote to simplistic efforts to solve organizational problems by focusing on only one factor.
4. Argyris makes some good suggestions on checking the validity of maps. Subjecting them to verification through prediction of intervention applications is appealing, if a bit risky.

In general, the mapping approach has the benefit of being highly involving and usable for organizational problem solving. Although Argyris worries about oversimplification, this innately system-oriented approach is unlikely to be too simple—with one exception, to be noted later. On balance, this approach seems to be a strong alternative to the standard method, which treats participants as passive recipients of academic "wisdom."

The mapping approach seems to have some potential problems, which, if solved, could further strengthen it. One concern is for the accuracy of the concepts (especially intrapsychic concepts) that surface during map making. Describing behavior at the start seems straightforward, but when causal explanations surface (for example, active versus passive orientations), one wonders about their accuracy.

Figure 2. Factors Involved in Surfacing Concepts for Map Making.

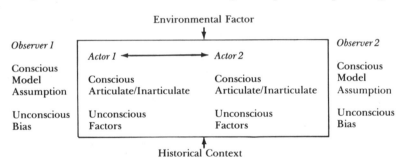

Figure 2 represents some of the subtleties involved in surfacing concepts. Consider only two actors in a situation. Each constructs a map mainly from conscious, articulate constructs. Each may have some ill-defined, inarticulate ideas that could be "teased out" by a perceptive other. Each also may have a number of powerful unconscious factors shaping his or her interaction. Left to their own devices, these two persons are likely to build a map using constructs from the conscious, articulate layer only. If they disagree, the stronger person's constructs are likely to prevail. Occasionally, an inarticulate, conscious idea might emerge through interactive dialogue.

What happens to this process when trained academic observers are present? It is a bit like the proverbial blind men with the elephant. Each observer will see factors through the screen of his or her training and unconscious biases. For instance, if observer 1 in Figure 2 is steeped in cognitive theory, he or she is likely to focus on conscious constructs that the actors use and to clarify some inarticulate terms. Observer 2, however, might be a Freudian analyst who will disregard conscious statements to infer unconscious factors. What a Jungian analyst might do almost boggles the imagination. The critical issues are: (1) How do we know what is real? and (2) How do we know we have included all critical factors?

There are several kinds of reality distortions possible: inadequate self-awareness by actors, conformity pressure by strong actors, conformity pressure by the academic observer (often unwitting), biases in observers, and abnormal situational or cultural history factors.

Leaving the last aside for later, how might mapping avoid distortions and deletions? Argyris suggests that discussion might resolve these problems. Possibly, but the problems of subtle conformity pressures and "folies à deux" are not eliminated. Prediction and intervention are powerful tests but could be risky if the problem is critical or explosive.

One suggestion is to use psychological assessment in conjunction with the mapping process. For example, if an active/passive dimension surfaces, one might use some standard measure of activity/energy to get an independent, standardized measure of the distribution of this quality among actors. If the assessment confirms the proposed factor, it adds an objective check to the process; if it disconfirms the factor, perhaps a reanalysis of the map would be in order.

Another possibility is to do a thorough psychological assessment of actors ahead of any map making. Once maps are constructed by Argyris's procedure, two checks can be made using the assessment data. Presumed factors that emerge during the mapping process can be checked (as above), and other, possibly inarticulate or unconscious factors of even greater weight might be seen and subsequently woven into the map. For instance, although an active-passive factor might be confirmed, test data on participants might show that an even more crucial latent factor is a positive-negative self-concept.

One final idea might be to use several observers of varied training and use consensus among diverse observers and participants to establish accuracy and completeness of the factors that surface during mapping.

A second major concern with the mapping approach is generalizability. It seems that, as presently developed, the mapping process is intensely situational and the concepts developed may be highly ideographic, permitting little generalization to other situations. Argyris seems to offer a possible solution. He notes the existence of "higher-order programs" that control particular behavior in a situation. In my view, he is getting close to describing general cognitive styles that are used by actors transsituationally. By using these broader styles, one can begin to transfer understanding gained in one situation to another and inductively build a scientific theory. One could use Argyris's method to surface the traces of the style in concrete behaviors and then test participants (before or after) to get a closer fix on the actual styles present.

The cognitive-style approach does not obviate the need for mapping. It merely embeds maps in a deeper layer of cognitive structure, permitting the evolution of testable scientific theory. Moreover, the style approach offers a partial solution to the situational/generalization problem. For instance, decision-style theory (Driver and Streufert, 1969) suggests that cognitive styles change systematically as key environmental dimensions change. These dimensions are environmental complexity, negative input, positive input, and uncertainty. Taken together, they constitute "environmental load." As seen in Figure 3, information use varies curvilinearly with load. Other information behaviors are also seen to vary predictably with load.

Consequently, if, in a mapping situation, one finds persons with a high-information style acting in a given way, one can look at load factors in the situation to determine generalizability. In another setting with similar loads, one could expect similar behavior; however, even with people of similar styles, if the load level is different in a new situation, one would expect different behavior. For instance, if in a particular conflict situation one finds high-information types using a Model

Figure 3. Information Use Styles in Relation to Environmental Load.

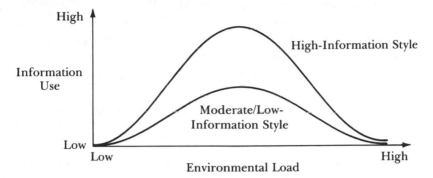

II learning behavior given moderate load, one might expect the same in any other situation in which styles *and* load were the same; conversely, if load varied, one could predict a shift even by high-information users to a simpler style—for example, Model I learning.

A third concern with mapping as presented here concerns the predominance of cognition over motivational factors. Argyris, at times, seems to be saying that if a person is made aware of his or her own program and is shown an alternative, better program, he or she will change behavior appropriately. This type of cognitive shift may indeed occur for some people, but I doubt that it would occur universally. For some people, a behavior program may be rooted in a powerful, unconscious motive, such as fear of failure. To really change the behaviors, one would need to surface this deeper motive and reduce the fear. This is not a purely cognitive event and would require changes in affective motivation (see, for example, Jung, 1957).

An answer to this concern might be to measure actors' motivational (for example, emotional) as well as cognitive areas. In some cases, projective measures such as the Thematic Apperception Test might be used to penetrate deeper layers. Remedial actions might go well beyond purely organizational skills and require trained therapists. If the mapping technology is not to falter whenever deep motivational processes are involved, something like the approach suggested here is needed. (Another idea would be to use diversely trained clinicians as observers.)

A final concern with mapping is that it may be too complex. Looking at Figure 2, we see that if awareness of all the relevant factors in a situation is raised, it may put all actors and observers into cognitive overload, a state that would motivate retreat to some simpler, more "workable" approach. A reactive solution to this problem might be to premeasure cognitive style or liking for complexity (see, for example, Bryson and Driver, 1972). Clearly, if the participants' styles and preferences lean toward the simplest mapping, information overload would rapidly produce burnout. In my view, only people with a more complex style could do a complex map (or even do Model II learning). Hence, observers could be guided by such premeasures in how complex a model could likely be built.

Equally critical might be a measure of observers' styles. It would seem unlikely that a noncomplex observer would build more than a relatively simple—possibly oversimple—map. Perhaps practitioners could learn to match problem/case complexity to observers' styles. On a more proactive note, one might want to develop methods for increasing the complexity of participants or observers before tackling a complex map (Athey, 1976).

In sum, the mapping approach does not seem to be beset by insoluble difficulties. If diverse observers and means of psychological assessment are used, I believe, this tool will be a powerful approach to bridging the "user gap."

One final comment on the general strategy recommended by Argyris: Instead of trying to match maps to participants' naive concepts, why not first educate the participants in more sophisticated concepts—that is, make the inarticulate articulate—and then do mapping? Our work with managers suggests that they can learn complex social science concepts. Pretraining could greatly enhance mapping. A caveat idea is that our experience is with managers in technical engineering firms. In nontechnical firms, managers may be less complex—here, the purer Argyris method may be better.

In similar fashion, preassessment results can be shared with participants to arouse consciousness of unconscious factors (for example, unconscious decision styles). Here again, our experience is that, when handled correctly, such feedback is immensely valuable. In conjunction with map making, this kind of prior self-awareness raising could be very potent in aiding the surfacing of unconscious factors.

In any event, the movement of social science toward a more self-awareness-building, participative strategy in theory construction could go a long way toward spanning the user gap.

GROUP DISCUSSION

Driver: I guess what I'm saying is that each of us brings to interactions we engage in or relationships we observe a set of assumptions about what are the critical factors, both conscious and unconscious, that operate—which, I think, reflects a little bit on our own past disciplines and our own peculiar assumptions. What I'm raising here is, how do we ever get a sense of really clearly describing the situation? How do we know when we have a clear description? Should we start adding more observers? That is one way of looking at it. Should we consider the possibility of backing up the inferences made by some measurement like psychological testing, so that we can then get a second reading on whether our particular attributions are correct?

Walton: I think the answer to your question is quite plain. Sure, we can add observers, we can bring in instruments, we can even use tape recorders, all kinds of things. The prior question is whether when you add an observer to the map, you have not merely elaborated the map, but it is now a map of a different territory.

Driver: What's the real territory? How do you know?

Walton: I assume that observers bring in a set of assumptions that reflects their background, their training, and what they've been taught. Now, they come into any interaction, and their perception of that interaction is flavored by that particular set of assumptions. For example, as Chris [Argyris] saw passive/active, maybe I was looking at it and saw a different thing. You look at it and see something still different, and the participants probably might tend to agree with any one of us. To use them as your criterion for what's real or not real then assumes that they can fully understand what's going on at these deeper levels of themselves. My own concern is that I think people can be got to the easier, more conscious aspects of themselves, but if you know anything about therapy, it is very hard to get people to get in touch with deeper issues.

Kilmann: I guess the issue of multiple observers to me largely comes down to questions of interjudge reliability.

Driver: The reliability of what?

Kilmann: Well, I think there is a well-established methodology for training observers and then getting—

Driver: You're not catching my point. Reliability on what?

Kilmann: Oh, that's my separate issue. I'm saying one side of it is the interjudge reliability. The other side is, what variables and what domains do we allow people to look at? The kind of issue that comes to mind is, I have found in general that scientists as well as managers tend to focus on the observable tangibles, not just for methodological reasons but for personal reasons. If you can touch it and see it, it's more likely to be controlled. As we've talked about in the last two days, context is clearly something that is difficult to conceptualize, pin down, and measure. I think we all know that the same is the case for the unconscious. I would be concerned about rationalizing a theory of action simply because we can account for it, measure it, and therefore say it's important, while we tend to discount this whole other range of variables, which I think at some level we all acknowledge can very much come back to haunt you. Are we spending so much time on pinpointing and making more exact and precise the observables that we're missing those very intangible pleasant things?

Walton: Another issue that I really like and I heard Chris getting at is, if we could surface these unconscious contextual variables in the minds of these actors, their power over the situation increases. Does this make sense, Chris?

Argyris: First of all, the positivistic side would say that I have to make sure that what you just said was not a curve; that is, if I use *passive/active* to describe a situation, an independent observer would use *passive/active*. We could give the observer a tape, or we could have him or her sit there and observe. Most important, the clients would make up their minds about whether that passive/active set of categories makes sense. I'm interested in pushing understanding for two reasons: disconfirmability and action. I'm interested in getting enough of a picture that would make me feel like I've understood it enough so that I can say, "Well, it's open to being disconfirmed." The other reason is, it's not simply what did I learn, but how can that learning lead to action, because moving toward action would give me even further ways of testing.

Driver: I have a concern about asking the actors to be your test of validity. How do you know it isn't your plausibility rule that is getting the acceptance?

Argyris: That's why I feel it is absolutely necessary to include intervention and change. Because if there are reasons that either my view or their view distorts, and if I develop a theory of instruction for their change program that's based on unwittingly distorted data, it will come out.

Driver: So that's also been your answer to the question of observers.

Argyris: That's right. I find people are not about to go through these learning experiences for fun. They're very tough on "Is this trip necessary?" I find that's why the change program becomes a test of the probable degree of validity. We can still be all wrong. They could have changed well and so on, and we would have never known we got the distortion; I own up to that possibility. I would say that's true for any research of whatever variety.

Driver: I was wondering about how you would feel about going over testing measures after your assessment as another way of looking and sharing that with them.

Argyris: I would not. I was thinking, as you were talking, of the gentleman who said, "The best theory is the theory with the least number of concepts and the greatest comprehensibility." Occam. I have a kind of Occam rule, which is "Use the least number of instruments needed to produce understanding, disconfirmability, and competence." If I keep doing this and it doesn't work and somebody says, "Hey, Chris, use this testing," I use it. But if you ask me a priori, would I use it, I would stay as close as I could to a complementary, equal relationship. I wouldn't rule those out, however.

Driver: You heard my proviso on using testing as shared back with the person involved?

Argyris: But the testing instrument is unilateral.

Driver: As opposed to your interpretation and explanation to these people of what their maps are all about?

Argyris: Well, not only mine, but they're doing it also. They're doing it of each other, they're doing it of me. In that sense, it is more complementary.

Driver: One of the second issues I wanted to raise is, I noticed to my great surprise, running through this chapter, some of the thinking I attribute to Herbert Simon rather than Chris Argyris: If you can give them a better program, they'll adopt it. That bothered me.

Argyris: When you said if Herb believes that if you give them a program, they'll adopt it, then that part of Herb I would not accept. What I believe is that if human beings become aware of the program that is presently in their heads, they can then make a choice about whether they want to alter it. They then begin to try to alter it, but then they see they've also got to change their governing values, because they can alter it in the Model II direction and hang on to Model I governing variables. One man once said, "I've got to learn this stuff to zap the other guy." That's Model II behavior in the interest of Model I governing values. My view would be that the way to change governing values is to help people become skillful in a new program. They can produce it under zero to moderate stress. If I've communicated that somehow if they got this map, then they've got what they need—no, it's going to take a lot of work and practice before they are able to alter it.

Mitroff: I want to raise something slightly different. I found the chapter interesting, but I would have found it more interesting to see the maps of the theory-in-use versus the espoused theory of researchers and the different maps that they have of science. Because methods and maps of the world have been a major theme of this conference, I think it's important to get at the maps of the observers.

Argyris: Two doctoral students and I are now writing a book that I think is getting at the question you're asking. In effect, what we are saying—to refer for a moment to the chapter by Cummings and his colleagues—the relational aspects are important, and we have a normative theory that says Model II is a better theory-in-use to have as a researcher if you want to get double-loop inquiry. Second, our theory addresses how you teach Model II. You have to get into certain kinds of relationships in order to teach it. But in order to teach Model II, you also have to focus on the researchers' view of research, what they come with. They begin to develop, if you will, their maps of their action maps of research as well as their values about why they're even in the field of research in the first place.

Greiner: Might that map turn out to be even more adequate than the map they started with?

Argyris: I can only speak for myself. I keep finding new data as I listen to my behavior and tapes, so that I have to take a look at my own maps. That's true for all these maps. They're continually subject to redesigning. But the keys are: Can the map predict under any condition that exists for those human beings, and can it lead to learning on an action basis, not just insight? For me insight without action is irresponsible, because what it does is permit people to distance themselves from their own personal cause of responsibility. The person can say, "But, gee, I learned." That is not taking a look at your personal responsibility for acting.

Driver: Chris, the last point I wanted to raise is, do you see this leading cumulatively to an increasingly large set of underlying dimensions like the two you use in your chapter? Do you see, eventually down the road, a series of generalized characteristics that you can help train people to look for when they go into situations like this? Where do you see this leading in the long run, or do you see it as a series of clinical encounters—I guess that's another model—that you never generalize, that each time is a fresh encounter?

Argyris: No, I'm interested in generalizability beyond the individualized situation, but the kind of generalizability that doesn't kill the uniqueness of a situation. My metaphor is a good camera that aerial photographers use. The operational definition of a good camera is that the higher it can go up, the more it can comprehend without being able to lose its ability to look at a footprint. That's the kind of theory that I'm interested in. I think, for example, the button-pushing maps and the maps of passivity are generalizable. The maps of passivity are generalizable for people who are trying to move from Model I to Model II, be they in a business firm, in a school, or anywhere. My fear is that I don't want people to go into a situation with a passive/active map as one of the tools they have in their heads to use. But I don't for a moment think that asking them to do this means that's what they're going to do. They may, in fact, use those maps to move too fast in imposing on the situation.

Kilmann: I'd like to ask a question on context. I see the model more as an interpersonal one. And let me think for a moment about group dynamics. A very simple rule has been that groups are more than the sum of the individuals. Now, I envision an executive session where if you deal with the rules that they use with one another, you might miss some of the group norms that are above and beyond what the individuals created. Because as new executives come into the group, they get trained and socialized to these new rules. And in a different setting, in a different membership, the executives might use different kinds of behaviors.

Argyris: But quite the opposite happens. I think that the map is both an individual and a group one—it can be used for both levels of analysis. It's not something more than its parts. For example, one person will say, "Well, I place myself in the passive on these and these dimensions and the active on these and these dimensions, but I believe the norms of this group are as follows." Or somebody would say, "You can't do that," and the reply would be "What do you mean, I can't do that?" So they soon get to group norms. I think maps can be used at any level. It's not an interpersonal thing, but as I tried to mention in my chapter where I think you're right, I do have the bias; I don't know of any research that has ever produced double-loop change by structural change. The only way that I know you can produce that is to change the way human beings reason, and then they can alter the structure.

Kilmann: Okay. But then, you're willing to reason with them in the group context.

Argyris: Oh, yes, and in the organization.

Lawler: When we broke for lunch, we had some head of steam up on some issues that Porter raised about the chapter by Cummings and his colleagues. I found myself at lunch trying to think—okay, where would Chris be in answer to some of the very questions that Porter raised? Like one that runs through a lot of the chapters: the conflict between being a consultant or a service giver and being a data gatherer.

Argyris: In terms of bridging it by doing research about mapping, which is what the clients want and what I need? I'm trying to connect. What's the answer you see in my chapter?

Lawler: I think your chapter is saying that you get access to data because of the role relationship you develop with the people. You get a unique kind of access and a unique kind of understanding because you're offering the service.

Argyris: Yes, but I want to own up to, and I think Cummings and his colleagues would, that that doesn't mean that we're not subject to another set of distortions. The difference, however, is that they become part of what's discussable. The first time I ever did research, I'll never forget it. It was White Bache. I went through eleven organizations; they all turned me down. So Bache called some guy who is a Yale alumnus and said will you be kind to Chris Argyris and let him come into your bank and interview some people. So he said sure. So I went in and interviewed fifty people, did my study, sent it to the American Sociological Review, and it was accepted. And I went and gave the people some feedback, and they said to me, "We like this. Would you come in now and do a total bank study?" Which I did. Needless to say, I was very pleased, but I got almost diametrically opposed data. And I had interviewed twenty-five of the same people that I interviewed before. So I got angry. How could they do this to me, you know? And so I went to the president and I said this is what's happening. And he said it's not my problem, it's yours. Why don't you go talk with them? So I said I would like to, and I had nineteen of them come into a room, and I said, "You can tell me what's going on." They said, "Professor, it ain't so difficult. Four weeks ago, whatever it was, it was be-kind-to-Chris week. So some of us answered the questions in a way, who cares, and some said what the hell, it's not going to be threatening, tell the truth. Now you come back as a consultant/researcher. Those of us who are now frightened distort the data, and those who think they might get some help give you the truth." At least it's now discussable. I think an awful lot of that goes on in more traditional research, which I think is what some of us are trying to overcome. We're not saying we have the truth and we don't get distortions; we at least say the client is so concerned about getting knowledge that she or he is going to confront you on every little step.

Lawler: You made an interesting assumption in your presentation that I think Cummings and his colleagues also made. That is, if it's going to make a difference in their lives, they're going to tell you the truth.

Argyris: Or they will lie. It's both possibilities. Neither approach saves itself a priori. What you at least have a decent chance to do is to keep asking questions of this group, because you're not only asking them with distance mechanisms like questionnaires, you're asking them in an on-line, interactive manner where their lives may be influenced by what kind of training or whatever they are going to go through.

Lawler: You make it more difficult for them to live the lie; there is no question about that. They can't just put a check mark on a questionnaire.

Kilmann: Or for you to live a lie.

Lawler: Yes, or for you to live a lie.

Mitroff: I wonder if I could raise a different kind of question altogether. Let's say I'm a manager sitting here or a chief executive officer of a very large organization who is in need of excellence. And I've read *In Search of Excellence.* I've read maybe even Robert Reich, and I need to get my company going, or I am head of industrial policy of the United States. And I turn to Chris and say, "Now, Chris, what has this got to do, what insights, if any, has this got to do with telling me how to seek excellence in my individual corporation or for industrial policy of this nation?"

Argyris: Well, I will beg off on the nation but at least stay with the company, okay? I'd start with several answers. One is that the CEO tends to put her or his arms around complexity by a process she or he calls strategic planning. There is a problem of strategic planning once you've even formulated the plan or got some idea of where you might go with it. It has to do with the implementation of it, which then gets into issues of learning—how do you detect and correct errors in your plan? Our approach, Mr. CEO, will help you take a look at to what extent your organization—and we'll start at the top for a moment —is able to detect and correct errors in its plan and know when it cannot detect and correct errors. And by the way, Mr. CEO, if this works well, that's detecting/correcting anywhere, anything that this group does. That's the direction I would go in. That's exactly the kind of question that's often asked by CEOs who say, "Why the hell should we have you in?"

REFERENCES

Ansoff, H. I. *Strategic Management.* London: Macmillan, 1979.

Argyris, C. *Increasing Leadership Effectiveness.* New York: Wiley-Interscience, 1976.

Argyris, C. *Inner Contradictions of Rigorous Research.* New York: Academic Press, 1980.

Argyris, C. *Reasoning, Learning, and Action: Individual and Organizational.* San Francisco: Jossey-Bass, 1982a.

Argyris, C. "Research as Action: Usable Knowledge for Understanding and Changing the Status Quo." In N. Nicholson and T. D. Wall (Eds.), *The Theory and Practice of Organization Psychology.* London: Academic Press, 1982b.

Argyris, C. "Usable Knowledge for Double-Loop Problems." In R. Kilmann and others, *Producing Useful Knowledge for Organizations.* New York: Praeger, 1983.

Argyris, C., and Schön, D. A. *Theory in Practice: Increasing Professional Effectiveness.* San Francisco: Jossey-Bass, 1974.

Argyris, C., and Schön, D. A. *Organizational Learning.* Reading, Mass.: Addison-Wesley, 1978.

Athey, T. "The Development and Testing of a Seminar for Increasing the Cognitive Complexity of Individuals." Unpublished doctoral dissertation, Graduate School of Business Administration, University of Southern California, 1976.

Brittain, J. W., and Freeman, J. H. "Organizational Proliferations and Density Dependent Selection." In J. R. Kimberly, R. H. Miles, and Associates, *The Organizational Life Cycle: Issues in the Creation, Transformation, and Decline of Organizations.* San Francisco: Jossey-Bass, 1980.

Bryson, J., and Driver, M. "Cognitive Complexity, Introversion, and Preference for Complexity." *Journal of Personality and Social Psychology,* 1972, *23,* 320–327.

Driver, M. "Individual Decision Making and Creativity." In S. Kerr (Ed.), *Organizational Behavior.* Columbus, Ohio: Grid Press, 1979.

Driver, M. "A Human Resource Data Based Approach to Organizational Design." *Human Resource Planning,* 1983, *6,* 169–182.

Driver, M. "Cognitive Psychology—an Interactionist View." In J. Lorsch (Ed.), *Handbook of Organizational Behavior,* Englewood Cliffs, N.J.: Prentice-Hall, in press.

Driver, M., and Streufert, S. "Integrative Complexity." *Administrative Science Quarterly,* 1969, *14,* 272–285.

Hannan, M. T., and Freeman, J. H. "The Population Ecology of Organizations." *American Journal of Sociology,* 1977, *82* (5), 929–964.

Jung, C. G. *Aion.* Princeton, N.J.: Princeton University Press, 1957.

Mangham, I. *Interactions and Interventions in Organizations.* Chichester: Wiley, 1978.

5

J. Richard Hackman

❧ ❧ ❧ ❧ ❧ ❧ ❧ ❧ ❧ ❧ ❧ ❧ ❧ ❧ ❧ ❧ ❧ ❧

Doing Research
That Makes a Difference

In concluding a retrospective review of his research on purposive behavior, E. C. Tolman wrote:

> I started out . . . with considerable uneasiness. I felt that my so-called system was outdated, and that it was a waste of time to try to rehash it and that it would be pretentious now to seek to make it fit any accepted set of prescriptions laid down by the philosophy of science. I have to confess, however, that as I have gone along I have become again more and more involved in it, though I still realize its many weak points. The system may well not stand up to any final canons of scientific procedure. But I do not much care. I have liked to think about psychology in ways that have proved congenial to me. Since all the sciences, and especially psychol-

Preparation of this chapter was supported in part by a contract from the Office of Naval Research (Organizational Effectiveness Research Program, Contract No. 00014-80-C-0555 to Yale University). Some of the material included is adapted from the author's chapter "Psychological Contributions to Organizational Productivity" in A. P. Brief (Ed.), *Research on Productivity* (New York: Praeger, in press).

126

ogy, are still immersed in such tremendous realms
of the uncertain and the unknown, the best that any
individual scientist, especially any psychologist, can
do seems to be to follow his own gleam and his own
bent, however inadequate they may be. In fact, I
suppose that actually this is what we all do. In the
end, the only sure criterion is to have fun. And I
have had fun [Tolman, 1959, p. 152].

This quotation, printed and framed, was given to me by Neil
Vidmar when I received my doctorate in social psychology in
1966. Neil and I had been in school together throughout our
undergraduate and graduate years, and we agreed that Tolman's
criterion was a good one for a psychologist to keep in mind while
pursuing a career of research and scholarship.

Neil's gift is still on my wall (he had to order twenty-five
copies to get the printer to produce one, so I always have a fresh
copy), and I still believe what it says. Moreover, it is my strong
(albeit undocumented) impression that most of us do our best
work when it feels more like play than like toil.

So when a graduate student asks me what would be ''a
good thing to study,'' my answer invariably is something enor-
mously unhelpful like ''whatever it pleases you to study.'' This
is not always believed, because I teach in an organizational behavior program located in a management school, and the presumption that research should inform managerial action permeates the place. But I am deadly serious: I strongly prefer to
see a student do first-rate scholarship that has uncertain relevance
for action than second-rate work that is immediately applicable
to some organizational problem.

For this reason, I approach our conference with a measure
of ambivalence. On the one hand, what pleases *me*, what I find
the most fun to do, is to wrestle with problems of improving
the effectiveness of social systems. So I am personally engaged
by the topic of our conference and pleased to have been invited.
On the other hand, I would be dismayed if we were to find
ourselves talking, even implicitly, as if the only worthwhile research in organizational behavior were that which contributes
simultaneously to theory and practice.

I say all of the foregoing because this chapter calls into question many well-accepted dicta about theory and method in organizational behavior. It *describes* what I think I have learned over the years in attempting to simultaneously build theory and improve practice, but it *feels* as if I am turning my back on big hunks of my training as a social scientist. And although I am convinced that the lessons I have learned make sense for me, for the kind of research I choose to do, these lessons may have little relevance for basic research in social science that makes no presumption of applicability.

Background

To provide a context for interpreting my comments, let me say a few things about the phenomena I study and the kinds of theories I like to build. I have, for more than fifteen years, been trying to understand the factors that influence how people do work and to frame that understanding in a way that invites constructive change in how work is structured and managed. My dissertation was on small-group performance, and that topic has provided fun and frustration in approximately equal measures ever since. I also have spent some time studying individual motivation and performance, with special emphasis on the design of the tasks people do at work. And recently I have been trying to learn how organizations can become more effective by fostering and supporting greater self-management among organization members.

The notion of "performance effectiveness" is common to the several themes in my research. As I intend to spend the rest of this chapter discussing strategies for generating usable research and theory about performance effectiveness, let me take a few paragraphs to explain exactly what I mean by the concept.

I define an individual, group, or organization as carrying out work effectively if the following three criteria are met:

1. *The productive output of the performing unit exceeds the minimum standards of quantity and quality of the people who receive, review, and/or use that output.* There is no unidimensional, objective criterion of performance effectiveness in most organizational

settings—and even when there is, what *happens* to a performing unit usually depends far more on others' assessments of the output than on any objective performance measure. So it is necessary to pay attention to the evaluations made by those who have a stake in the group's output—even though this may require us to deal with multiple and conflicting assessments of how well a unit is performing.

2. *The process of carrying out the work enhances the capability of the performing unit (be it an individual, a group, or an organization) to do competent work in the future.* Organizations are not single-shot systems, and the way any single task is carried out can strongly affect the capability of a performing unit to accomplish subsequent tasks. A unit that "burns itself up" in the process of doing a task is not viewed as effective even if its product in that particular instance is fully acceptable.

3. *The work experience contributes to the growth and personal satisfaction of the persons who do the work.* Sometimes the process of carrying out a piece of work serves mainly to block the personal development of individual performers or to frustrate satisfaction of their personal needs. In such cases, the costs borne by individuals in generating the work product are so high that the performing unit is not viewed as effective even if its product is fully acceptable.

This way of thinking about performance effectiveness, then, involves far more than simply counting outputs that meet a predetermined quality standard. The use of client evaluations of work products, for example, shifts primary control over the choice of assessment standards from researchers to those who use and are affected by what is produced. And the social and personal components of the criterion are explicitly normative in asserting that some group and individual outcomes are generally to be preferred over others. These are relatively nontraditional ways of thinking about performance effectiveness, and they impose on the researcher both a greater measurement challenge and a higher data-collection work load than are usually encountered in assessing work outcomes.

Yet the criteria themselves are modest. All that is required to exceed minimum standards for effectiveness is output judged by those who receive it to be more than acceptable, a performing unit that winds up its work more competent than when it started, and performers who are more satisfied than frustrated by what has happened. The challenge in my work has been to develop ways of understanding, designing, and managing performing units that increase the chances that these modest criteria can be met. And what I have to say about research strategy in this chapter is based on my history of trying to make some progress on this general issue.

I will frame my thoughts as a series of assertions, each of which summarizes something I think I have learned about what is required to develop usable research and theory about performance effectiveness as I have defined the concept. Each assertion begins with a negative learning, something I have found *not* to work as well as I once hoped and expected. Then I will raise some alternative ways of proceeding with research that may circumvent the difficulty—including some strategies I am using in my current research on team effectiveness and others that remain to be explored in the future.

Assertion One: Laboratory research methods are not much help in developing practical theory about performance effectiveness—but for reasons different from those we usually cite when complaining about laboratory studies.

It is sometimes argued that laboratory research, because of the inherent artificiality of the situation, is not useful for understanding organizational phenomena. I disagree. If the phenomena addressed by some organizational theories are actually created in the laboratory, and if appropriate choices are made about relevant variables (that is, what variables to manipulate, to control, to measure, and to ignore), then laboratory research can provide powerful tests of conceptual propositions, including propositions about behavior in organizations (Runkel and McGrath, 1972; Weick, 1965). Moreover, certain research objectives (for example, discovering what *can* occur rather than documenting what *usually* occurs) can sometimes be better pursued in the laboratory than in more "realistic" field settings (Mook, 1983).

There is, however, a real risk in studying performance

effectiveness in the laboratory—a generally unrecognized risk that has less to do with the absence of mundane realism in the laboratory than with the kinds of variables about which one can reasonably expect to learn using laboratory methods. Consider, as an example, research on small-group behavior and performance. Laboratory studies of small groups tend to focus on individual, interpersonal, and group-level variables, holding constant (or ignoring) the relationship between groups and the contexts in which they operate. Indeed, laboratory researchers learn quickly that one had *better* control variables such as task characteristics, experimenter/subject relationships, reward-system properties, and the demand characteristics of the research setting.[1] Not to do so is to invite these variables to overwhelm the more subtle intra- or interpersonal phenomena one is trying to study.

But what if contextual and environmental variables should happen to be among the most powerful influences on group performance? This is not an unreasonable possibility (for example, Hackman, in press; Pfeffer and Salancik, 1978). It just may be that, in the interest of good experimental practice, some of the variables that most strongly affect group behavior and productivity are usually fixed at constant levels in laboratory research, *thereby ruling out any possibility of learning about their effects.* By contrast, these same features of the group and its external relations receive special attention in many state-of-the-art action projects in which self-managing work teams are created in organizations (for example, Poza and Marcus, 1980).

Although this example is taken from small-group research, contextual and environmental variables typically are ignored or fixed at constant levels in laboratory experiments on other

---

[1]This does not mean that contextual forces are absent. They are present in the person of the *experimenter:* it is he or she who picks the place where the study will be conducted, recruits the subjects and forms them into groups, selects and assigns the group task, decides what rewards will be available and administers them, provides groups with the information and resources they need to do their work, and establishes the basic norms of conduct that guide behavior in the setting. In essence, the experimenter creates an organization that serves as the context of the group, serves as the top management of that organization, and (if expert in his or her role) makes sure that the contextual factors are as nearly the same for all groups as possible.

performance-relevant phenomena as well. This is readily understandable, because it is extraordinarily difficult to manipulate such factors well in the laboratory, as researchers who have tried to create temporary but real organizations for research purposes will attest. But the example does raise questions about the usefulness of laboratory methods in research on performance effectiveness.

The liabilities of the experimental laboratory for developing practical theory, then, have little to do with the artificiality of the setting as such or with the limited ecological validity of the setting (Berkowitz and Donnerstein, 1982). The problem, instead, is that those variables that lend themselves to study in the laboratory may be less important in influencing performance effectiveness than those that are difficult or impossible to deal with in that research setting.

What research strategies might be preferable to the laboratory for studying the relationship between a performing unit and its organizational/environmental context? Neither organizational sociologists, who *are* interested in the links between organizations as total systems and their environments, nor we organizational psychologists, who tend to discard the complexity—and the guts—of contextual phenomena to make them researchable using standard methods, have made a great deal of headway on this question. (Both sociologists and psychologists have, however, shown an interest in organizational design, an important question but a different one.)

Clearly, understanding contextual and environmental relations requires that substantial variation exist in the features of the performance situation. This suggests that a field setting may be called for—but merely conducting the research in a "real" organization does not automatically take care of this requirement. One can no more learn about contextual influences in a single, homogeneous unit of an organization during a period of relative stability than one can in a laboratory, since all members of that unit work within essentially the same context.[2]

[2]This lesson was learned, or should have been, by those job-design researchers who attempted to assess the relationship between job characteristics and work outcomes by studying their correlations in a single organizational unit where all employees performed the same basic job.

Particularly inviting are settings where organizational changes are taking place. The changes may involve planned alterations of the work context, or they may be responses to a changing external environment. In either case, there is variation in the phenomena of interest, and therefore study of those phenomena is possible. Another alternative is to gather data from a number of performance situations and conduct comparative analyses. I have used these strategies in my current research on work group effectiveness and with each of them have found it necessary both to use multiple data-collection methods (observational, interview, survey, and archival techniques) and to collect data from multiple perspectives. Just as no one method can adequately capture the complexity of contextual influences on group behavior, neither is there any single accurate description of the context or how it operates. Because there are many separate (and not necessarily correlated) truths about the context of a group, any reasonably complete understanding of contextual influences requires that they be examined from multiple perspectives, using a variety of measurement devices.

A seemingly very attractive research strategy would be to conduct a field *experiment* (or quasi experiment) on the impact of the work context. If appropriately designed, a field experiment could provide access to the contextual variables of interest, the opportunity to manipulate those variables to create the needed variation, and researcher control over factors (such as assignment of participants to conditions) that otherwise might confound the results. Unfortunately, as will be seen later, field experiments, for all their advantages, also have some serious problems as devices for developing usable knowledge about performance effectiveness.

Assertion Two: The field experiment may be a fundamentally inappropriate device for developing practical theory about performance effectiveness.

Several years ago Clayton Alderfer and I wrote a proposal for a field experiment to compare team building and job design as points of intervention for initiating performance-relevant organizational changes. The proposal was well received, and we were encouraged by all who read it to proceed to find a site and conduct the experiment. Over the next two years, Clay and I spent a great deal of time together—attending meetings, hearing about impending reorganizations, watching managers with whom we were about to contract for the research be transferred, and reassuring each other that the project was worth the investment we were making in trying to get it under way. Eventually we decided it was not, and we abandoned our plans.

Recently some colleagues and I did succeed in negotiating something almost as good—a decent quasi-experimental design in which a performance-relevant independent variable would be manipulated at different levels for different groups and follow-up data would be collected longitudinally. This time the reorganization and managerial realignments occurred *after* the study had begun, and these events were supplemented by the dissolution of about half the groups we were studying.

Organizations do not hold still while we negotiate entry, make our intervention, and wait for an appropriate time to collect follow-up data. Although it took me too many years to learn this, it is not a surprising learning, and it simply attests to the difficulty of negotiating and executing field experimental research. It is not the point I want to make here.

The point is this: If we had been able to successfully negotiate a field experiment, execute it, and gather follow-up data on schedule, we would then have needed to worry about the external validity of the findings—their generalizability to other organizations. Why? Because any organization that could and would hold still long enough for such research to be done and would relinquish to researchers the level of control needed to run an experiment (for example, determining how people are assigned to conditions, designing the intervention and the measures, deciding when they will be administered) would be a pretty strange place, unlike the great majority of work organizations to which we would wish to generalize our findings.

So there are three ways to lose in field experiments on performance effectiveness: (1) we can fail to gain entry, (2) we can fail during execution, or (3) we can succeed in getting the study done just the way we wanted it done. Field experimental designs are not, I fear, a very good way to generate usable findings about performance in organizations—not because organizations are uncooperative or because researchers are incompetent but because the field experimental *model* is inappropriate for such research.[3]

What, then, are some alternatives to field experimental designs? The usual response when this question comes up is to suggest that a quasi experiment be conducted. Yet quasi-experimental designs which require researchers to have control over significant organizational interventions or which need organizational realignments to be put on hold until time-series data have been collected are subject to many of the same problems as true experimental designs.

Rather than continue trying to force the world to fit the designs we know and know how to use, I suspect we need some innovative thinking about methods for studying productivity in organizations. Can we, for example, find ways to create mutually beneficial *partnerships* with organizations, in which researchers and organization members collaborate to learn about factors that influence individual and group performance?[4]

The researchers in such a partnership would bring some special expertise to it—for example, regarding the construction of reliable measures whose validity can be assessed or the invention of methodological strategies that allow for relatively unambiguous attributions of causality. Organizational representatives would also have much to contribute—for example, regarding special constraints on what can be done in the organization, special opportunities for learning that may be coming up, issues of special importance to organization members, and concepts that have special meaning or history in the organizational cul-

---

[3]A well-documented case analysis that illustrates many of the built-in limitations of the field experimental model is provided by Blumberg and Pringle (1983). Their report describes what happened when a "good" experimental design was used to study the outcomes of a quality-of-worklife program in a coal mine. In essence, the research design prompted a number of unanticipated and unfortunate consequences (such as widespread conflict and dissension throughout the organization), which, in turn, contributed to the premature demise of the very program whose effects were being researched.

[4]For ideas about how to do this, see Alderfer, Brown, Kaplan, and Smith (in press) or Hakel, Sorcher, Beer, and Moses (1982).

ture. By working together, researchers and organization members should be able to tailor the research to the particular constraints and opportunities that exist in the social system. Moreover, since the aim of the research would be to generate learnings about real organizational concerns, *both* partners should be motivated to ensure that the data be trustworthy and meaningful and that inferences be logically sound and backed by data.

A research partnership requires a commitment by both partners to develop ways of learning that subordinate neither party's legitimate needs to those of the other and to seek out and exploit opportunities for learning as they develop in the social system. Fulfilling this commitment demands great sensitivity to questions of timing, creativity in finding ways to learn from events that have not been designed for learning purposes, and willingness of the researcher to share control over the research process with people who are much more concerned with organizational needs than with the dicta of research methodology.

Collaborative, opportunistic research is demanding, often frustrating, and altogether a chancier enterprise than I personally find comfortable. It offers a means of generating learnings that may not be obtainable in other ways, however, and it frees researchers from the burden (and ultimate futility) of trying to find organizations that will let them have the level of control they need to satisfy the stringent requirements of field experimentation.

Assertion Three: Searching for unitary causes of performance effectiveness can make it harder, not easier, to learn about the organizational conditions that foster good performance.

When something happens in an organization that improves productivity, managers are happy and psychologists are frustrated. "What actually *caused* the improvement?" we ask. And we begin to take apart the inevitably fuzzy and multifaceted change, first conceptually, then often empirically—perhaps in a laboratory experiment that isolates the suspected cause or using structural modeling techniques with survey data. We want to rule out as many possible explanations for the observed phenomenon as we can. We want to pin down the *true* causal agent.

Consider, for example, the review by Locke and his colleagues (Locke, Feren, McCaleb, Shaw, and Denny, 1980) comparing the efficacy of goal setting, compensation, participation, and job enrichment. This review provides an excellent comparative evaluation of the programs reviewed, and it is a valuable contribution to scholarly thought about behavior in organizations. But empirical studies and review articles that seek to isolate unitary causes may not be of much help in generating theoretical propositions and research findings that can be *used* to improve performance. Influences on performance do not come in separate, easily distinguishable packages. They come, instead, in complex tangles that often are as hard to straighten out as a backlash on a fishing reel. Indeed, to try to partial out and assess the causal effects of each piece of a multifaceted organizational change may lead to the conclusion that *nothing* is responsible for an observed improvement in performance—each ingredient of the spicy stew loses its zest when studied separately from the others.

Teasing out the separate effects of various interventions does, of course, help us obtain a sense of how potent they are when isolated from other factors that may also enhance or depress performance. The problem arises from the fact that there are many ways to be productive at work and even more ways to be nonproductive. If our attempts to understand what causes productive work behavior focus on single causes, we are unlikely to generate a coherent understanding of the phenomenon. There are simply too many ways to get there from here, and the different routes do not necessarily have the same causes.

Systems theorists call this aspect of organized endeavor "equifinality" (Katz and Kahn, 1978, p. 30). According to this principle, a social system can reach the same outcome from various initial conditions and by a variety of means. Equifinality encourages us to view the management of work performance as essentially involving the *creation of multiple conditions*—conditions that support high productivity but also leave individuals and groups ample room to develop and implement their own ways of accomplishing the work within them.

The best way to improve performance, then, might be to alter *several* factors all at once, to create a "critical mass" of favorable conditions, and to deliberately foster redundancy among positive features of the performance setting. Unfortunately, when one looks through the literature to see how scholars in organizational behavior think about and study performance phenomena, one sees theories and research paradigms that are conceptually clean and often elegant—but provide little help in learning about messy, overdetermined organizational phenomena.

If performance outcomes are in fact overdetermined—that is, if they are products of multiple, nonindependent factors whose influence depends in part on the fact that they *are* redundant— then we will have to find some new ways of construing and researching performance phenomena. The comfortable "X is a cause of Y, but their relationship is moderated by Z" kind of theorizing will have to go, for example. Moreover, several key assumptions of our powerful multivariate models, models designed specifically for analyzing causally complex phenomena, would be violated so badly that we could not use them for studies of influences on work performance (see James, Mulaik, and Brett, 1982). Are there alternative approaches that might be adopted for studies of work performance, approaches that would fit better with the phenomena?

One possibility, which has received surprisingly little attention, would be to bring the case study out of the classroom and put it to work in scholarly pursuits. It is true that case studies, as traditionally prepared, may give too much credence to the interpretations favored by their authors. Selective emphasis of material and choices about what data to include and exclude are real problems (although these problems are shared by writers of quantitative empirical studies to a far greater extent than we usually admit). Can we think of ways to present case studies that invite disconfirmation and tests of alternative interpretations? Would it be possible, for example, to carry out competing analyses for each interpretation of a case that we generate—one that seeks to make the best case possible for the interpretation and one intended to cast the greatest possible doubt on it? Would such an approach to case analysis and presentation foster learning by other scholars and contribute to the accumulation of knowledge across case studies? We are trying this kind of approach now in attempting to learn as much as we can from our detailed, descriptive analyses of task-performing teams. And although it is too early to assess the ultimate efficacy of the approach, we certainly are learning a great deal in trying to use it.

Another possibility, heretofore used more by coroners, detectives, and aircraft accident investigators than by scholars of organizations, is the "modus operandi" method (Scriven, 1974). If one can generate a list of the *possible* causes of some outcome or event and has some knowledge about the special "signature" of each one, then it is often possible to use logical, historical, and microexperimental techniques to disentangle the probable causes of that outcome—even when it is complexly determined or overdetermined. The modus operandi approach, which, so far as I know, has not been used in the study of work performance, provides an intriguing alternative to standard quasi-experimental and correlational studies of organizational phenomena.

Whatever the new devices we come up with for trying to develop usable knowledge about overdetermined organizational phenomena, I suspect that they will involve thick, systematic description of those phenomena and that they will require interpretations that cross traditional levels of analysis (that is, link individual, group, organizational, and/or environmental variables). We may even see greater recognition of the value of multiple perspectives on the same data, from people in different groups with different "stakes" in how those data are interpreted. What we will see less and less, I hope, is analyses of the causes of performance outcomes that isolate causal agents from the social systems in which they operate.

Assertion Four: Contingency models of behavior in organizations are of little practical use in managing work performance.

Contingency theories of behavior in organizations typically hold that the relationship between some predictor variable (for example, how a job is designed) and some outcome variable (for example, quality of performance) depends on some third variable (for example, some characteristic of the performer or attribute of the work situation). Contingency theories contrast with universalistic models of behavior at work—that is, those that posit that a given variable will operate in more or less the same way for all people and situations normally encountered in work organizations. Such theories have been much in vogue in industrial/organizational psychology during the last decade and have been prominent in my own work.

Where do contingency models come from? Sometimes they are generated out of a researcher's desperation. Findings that were supposed to match other findings do not, and the researcher goes on a search for the reasons the expected replication did not occur. Such searches are almost always successful: A plausible explanation having to do with individual differences or situational attributes can be found for virtually any unexpected finding. Unfortunately, as Hunter, Schmidt, and Jackson (1982) note, variation in findings across studies or samples is often the natural statistical result of small sample sizes, restricted range of variables, and/or unreliability of measures. Contingency theories based on such variation will not hold up when properly tested. However, contingency models based on an in-depth understanding of the phenomena and thoughtful conceptual analysis can be quite helpful in sorting out complex phenomena. The normative model of leadership decision making proposed by Vroom and Yetton (1973) is a good example of a conceptually sound contingency theory.

To assess the usefulness of a contingency model as a guide for organizational practice, we must ask two questions. First, does the model predict the outcomes of interest more powerfully than simpler "main effect" models that address the same phenomena? And, second, is the model framed in a way that makes it *usable* by practitioners in their work?

Unfortunately, the answer to both questions for contingency models having to do with work performance appears to be a qualified no. Although there are some exceptions, the general direction in research guided by contingency thinking has been to make more and more distinctions and to add ever more conditions and qualifications to general propositions. The point of diminishing returns is reached soon: Increments in explanatory power come more slowly than increases in model complexity.

Moreover, research in cognitive psychology casts doubt on our ability to process multiple contingencies in making decisions about our behavior (see, for example, Slovic, 1981). Indeed, one distinguished contingency theorist has even had a black box constructed to guide managerial decision making. The manager sets various switches in accord with the characteristics of the decision situation, pushes a button, and has electronically revealed the course of action that, according to the theory, should be followed. So far the theorist has chosen not to market the device (its construction was something of a lighthearted enterprise), but it nicely symbolizes the difficulty of using complex contingency theories as behavioral guides.

Are there alternatives to contingency models that would provide more powerful and practical conceptual tools for managing work performance? One intriguing lead is offered by the theory of multiple possibilities set forth by Tyler (1983). Whereas contingency theory assumes that if we knew the right moderating variables, we would be able to predict and control behavior in virtually any situation, multiple possibility theory holds that such an aspiration is ill conceived. Instead, the theory maintains, there are *many* possible outcomes that can emerge in any situation, and the particular outcome that is actualized is not completely determined by the causal factors that precede it. Thus, multiple possibility theory envisions a world with some "play" in the system, and it encourages attention to human choice as a factor that transforms multiple possibilities into single courses of action.

Multiple possibility theory nicely complements the system theorists' notion of equifinality, discussed in the preceding section. Where equifinality alerts us to the fact that the same outcome can occur in response to many causes, multiple possibility theory posits that the same cause can generate a variety of outcomes. Taken together, the two notions call into question standard stimulus-response models in which situational causes are tightly linked to behavioral effects—whether directly ("Introduce this management practice and performance will improve") or contingently (" . . . performance will improve, but only for certain kinds of people under certain circumstances").

If we were to take seriously the notions of equifinality and multiple possibilities, would that signal an abandonment of "scientific" approaches to understanding behavior in organizations? Not at all. But it would require that we generate qualitatively different kinds of scientific models of organizational behavior and that we invent some new methods for assessing the validity and usefulness of those models.

What kinds of theories, for example, would exploit rather than suppress the systemic context in which work is done? Can we envision performance models that deal explicitly with the ways that symbols, language, and physical place affect both how people comprehend their workplaces and how they assign meaning to what happens within them? What would be the attributes of a performance model that would allow us to learn about self-reinforcing spirals of performance, illuminating how the choices people make at a given moment affect their capabilities for future performance—often resulting in well-performing units finding it easier to perform even better, while poor performers become ever poorer? What would be required of scientific models that are oriented more toward understanding the conditions and contexts that shape the choices people make about their behavior than toward pinning down the immediate, proximal causes of particular performance outcomes?

What kinds of methods would be needed to generate moving pictures of performance as it changes over time, rather than still pictures of what is happening at a given moment? How could we go about studying multiple, redundant influences on performance in ways that yield more than mere descriptions of what happens in work organizations—that, instead, offer insight into the kinds of organizational conditions that foster and support excellence? What methods might be used to learn about factors that have powerful *cumulative* influences on work behavior but whose effects are almost impossible to discern at any given moment?

In my view, these are substantial conceptual and methodological challenges and certainly not ones for which I have ready answers. But if we could begin to confront them, then we might find ourselves on the way toward the development of scientific models of work performance that are considerably more congruent with the realities of the social systems where work is done than the deterministic contingency models we presently favor. And, in the process, we just might generate some guidelines for managerial action that would be both powerful in affecting work performance and *usable* by people who design and manage work organizations.

Is disaffection with current conceptual and research paradigms great enough that organizational psychologists are likely to explore a radically different approach to their subject matter? I think not—even though there is real movement in related disciplines toward the development of alternative kinds of knowledge and ways of knowing (for example, McGuire's, 1983, contextualist theory of knowledge in social psychology). Indeed, I see signs in organizational behavior that at least some of us feel that the best remedy for the disease we are now experiencing would be a return to more orthodox scientific models and methods. I remain hopeful, nonetheless, that at least a few of us will venture into the relatively uncharted territory I have tried to sketch here and report back on what is found.

Assertion Five: Evaluation research that assesses currently popular productivity improvement programs allows both managers and scholars to avoid addressing fundamental questions about how organizations are designed and managed.

How can one argue about the value of evaluation research in our field? The history of management is filled with fads and fashions that, when subjected to empirical assessment, have proved to be of little value. And, occasionally, research has shown that some management devices, appropriately used, *can* improve work performance in organizations.

We have done MBO, job enrichment, T-groups, goal setting, zero defects, brainstorming, and a multitude of others.

Now we are examining newer programs, such as quality circles, quality-of-worklife programs, and gain-sharing plans. Soon still others will emerge, and we will take a look at them. Part of the burden of being a social scientist interested in organizational performance, it seems, is that one must be ready to gather up one's methodological tools and pack off to evaluate the latest productivity improvement scheme. Although we sometimes risk losing a few consultant friends along the way, the work is important and ultimately constructive.

It also is insufficient and is a diversion from what we really ought to be doing, if we aspire to research that has significant implications for organizational effectiveness. What bothers me is not what typical productivity improvement programs do but what they do *not* do. Understandably, managers would like to obtain improvements in productivity with as little effort, anxiety, and disruption of standard organizational practices as possible. As a consequence, productivity improvement plans that gain easy acceptance by the management community tend to be those that do not call into question (1) the authority structure of the organization, (2) the core technology used by the organization in making its product or providing its service, or (3) fundamental managerial values and assumptions about how human resources are used in the organization and about the personal and financial rights of employees.

By studying only programs that are readily acceptable to management, we close off the opportunity to learn what might happen if some of management's unquestioned ''givens'' were altered. Worse, we may unintentionally and implicitly support the notion that relatively modest, nonthreatening programs are the best that behavioral scientists have to offer. The result can be a continued collusion between ourselves and managers, an unstated agreement that the search for ways to improve work performance will not seriously address the possibility that the way work is designed, organized, and managed in this society underutilizes and misuses human resources.

We obviously cannot study what does not exist, so what are we to do if we harbor a suspicion (as I do) that many opportunities for improving performance effectiveness lie hidden in management's unexplored forbidden land? Three possibilities come to mind.

First, we can watch for occasions when unexpected or unintended changes in authority structures, technologies, and human resource strategies *do* occur and be prepared to exploit the learning opportunities these occasions provide. When a crisis occurs, for example, an organization may temporarily operate in ways that management would find wholly unacceptable during normal operations. If we are present, prepared, and not already fully occupied with evaluating the latest productivity program, we may be able to capitalize on such occurrences—and just might generate findings showing that ''unacceptable'' ways of operating actually result in improved performance effectiveness.

Second, we can seek out organizations that go about their business in ways that differ markedly from standard corporate practice. We have much to learn from public and nonprofit organizations, for example. And of special interest are work organizations that have chosen a deliberately democratic model of governance, such as worker cooperatives. Some of these organizations manage the productive work of the firm using interesting, nontraditional structures and systems. They can serve as a kind of laboratory for examining the impact on performance effectiveness of ways of operating that are quite unlikely to appear spontaneously in more traditional businesses.

Finally, we can prepare ourselves to help *create* nontraditional organizational forms when opportunities present themselves and carefully document what happens and what is learned in the process. Creation of new plants, for example, has provided some valuable opportunities to learn about alternative ways of improving productivity, even in corporations whose headquarters operate quite traditionally (Lawler, 1978). This option may be the most engaging and promising alternative to evaluation research on productivity improvement programs. It is also the most challenging, in that it requires not only a model of the conditions that foster work effectiveness but also a theory of action to guide implementation and management of the innovative system (Argyris, 1980). It is hard to deal with "What is to be done" and "How and when should we do it" questions at the same time. It surely is worth the trouble to try.

Yet we may have to go even further. If we seek to do research that can have a significant impact on organizational performance, we may have to start dealing explicitly with the assumptions and values held by managers in the organizations where the research is conducted. And to ask managers to examine their unstated assumptions and values requires that we be aware of our own—and be willing to make them explicit. If our research is intended to generate knowledge useful in improving productivity, for example, then we must be prepared to assert that we believe improved productivity to be a positive outcome, something worth espousing and supporting.

One can, of course, take the contrary position, that research and practice aimed at productivity improvement are *not* desirable for this society at this time in history. But if we choose the view that higher productivity is beneficial and involve ourselves in research or action intended to promote it, then it seems to me we are obligated to do that work as well and with as much impact as possible. And this will, on occasion, require us to confront managers directly about what is and what is not open to change in an organization.

Conclusion

We just may be leaving the period of history when people write of the great promise of "applied behavioral science." Implicit in the whole of this chapter is the view that it is probably futile to try to take the results of basic research in the social sciences and apply them intact to solving organizational problems. In fact, the reverse may be true: Application-focused research may be more useful in generating advances in basic knowledge than basic research is in generating applications. The history of experimental psychology, for example, shows that many of the most significant and fundamental conceptual problems in that field had their origins in work that initially was focused specifically on solving real problems of human perception and cognition (Garner, 1972). It may be that the best way to generate advances in basic theory is to do research that seeks solutions to real problems and to keep one's eyes open for fundamental conceptual issues as one proceeds.

In organizational behavior, this approach will require that our research be tailored to the special circumstances of the social systems in which we conduct our studies and to which our findings ultimately are intended to apply. The theory and method of the social science disciplines were not, by and large, designed for that task—and I believe them to be insufficient for it. Moreover, they have led us to study factors that have ripple rather than tidal effects on organizational phenomena. We need now to open ourselves to the larger organizational forces and to develop conceptual models and research methods that address them directly —rather than persist with our well-worn traditional models, hoping that one day we will find places to apply them or, worse, that one day organizations will change to fit with them. This position can create some dilemmas for those of us who work in organizations where management is willing to accept from behavioral scientists only those contributions that do not call into question unstated assumptions about such matters as the choice of technology, the distribution of authority, the allocation of gains realized from productive work, and the strategy of the firm in obtaining, developing, and using human resources.

If our professional judgment is that such issues may be key to performance effectiveness in an organization, should we insist that they be addressed and decline invitations to work on problems that divert attention from them? Or should we pitch in, try to find constructive things to do within existing constraints, and hope that opportunities for real contributions to productivity improvement will develop at some later time? Such choices are, obviously, much easier for an academic than for someone whose livelihood depends on keeping a job in the organization where the work is being done. But even academics, including me, too often find reasons to defer discussions about organizational values and assumptions and about what may be required if there is to be any real chance of achieving nontrivial gains in organizational effectiveness.

Lest there be any misunderstanding, let me state that I am not advocating that we go on strike for greater impact. All I am suggesting is that we make explicit the values on which our work is based, that we assess the usefulness and the impact of what we do with respect to those values, and that we try to avoid getting ourselves into a position in which our work unintentionally impedes progress toward the very ends we seek. Those of us who study performance in organizations or who attempt to promote it should never have to respond, when asked why we are doing what we are doing, "I had no choice." As professionals, we always have a choice.

Such a reorientation will require, for most of us, both a good measure of inventiveness and some fundamental changes in how we think about and go about our work. But it will not require us to abandon the core values that underlie scholarly work. Traditional conceptual values, such as parsimony and sound logic, are just as essential for research on real problems as for paradigm-driven studies of interest only to other academics. And traditional methodological values—such as the disconfirmability of findings, measures whose reliability and validity are publicly demonstrable, and means of inference that allow for relatively unambiguous and logically defensible attributions of causality—are, if anything, more critical for research whose findings can substantially affect people's lives than for paradigmatic research. The values are much to be cherished, and in my view they should be rigorously taught to each cohort of fledgling organizational scholars. They are the bedrock on which scholarly work in organizational behavior is done, and they provide a firm enough foundation to allow structures to be built that are, if unconventional, more suitable for our phenomena than those previously built by other scholars for other purposes.

The reorientation about which I have been speculating in this chapter is not a simple undertaking, and (if my own experience in trying to behave in accordance with my words has any generality) it invokes no small measure of ambivalence, for at least two reasons. First, despite my intellectual confidence that new conceptual and methodological approaches are required in organizational behavior, experimenting with those approaches occasionally makes me feel as if my deviations from traditional ways of pursuing scientific values were somehow heretic and sinful. Second, when one is trying to do something which one does not know how to do and for which there are no ready models, failure is always a real possibility and is probably more likely than success. Such ambivalence tends to be accompanied by anxiety, which, in turn, can block intellectual work and make it hard to get *anything* done, let alone something new and possibly interesting. But ambivalence and anxiety are also reputed to be the precursors of creativity, so there is always hope that something worthwhile will emerge if one sticks with it long enough.

These, then, are the kinds of questions and issues, both emotional and intellectual, that I am wrestling with these days as I continue to try to develop practical theories of individual and group performance effectiveness. I am finding the challenges—to my imagination and to my courage—substantial. I am awfully glad I have Tolman's quotation mounted on my wall, because sometimes I need a little reminder about how much fun I must be having.

RESPONSE AND COMMENTARY

Ralph H. Kilmann

I have never done anything "useful." No discovery of mine has made, or is likely to make, directly or indirectly, for good or ill, the least difference to the amenity of the world. I have helped train other mathematicians, but mathematicians of the same kind as myself. . . . Judged by all practical standards, the value of my mathematical life is nil. . . . That I have created something is undeniable: the question is about its value. [The things I have added to knowledge do not differ from] the creations of the great mathematicians, or of any of the other artists, great or small, who have left some kind of memorial behind them [Hardy, 1967, pp. 150–151].

> I think that it is a relatively good approxima-
> tion to truth . . . that mathematical ideas originate
> in empirics, although the genealogy is sometimes
> long and obscure. But, once they are so conceived,
> the subject begins to live a peculiar life of its own
> and is better compared to a creative one, governed
> by almost entirely aesthetical motivations, than to
> anything else and, in particular, to an empirical
> science. . . . As a mathematical discipline travels
> far from its empirical source . . . it is beset with very
> grave dangers. It comes more and more purely
> aestheticizing, more and more purely *l'art pour l'art*
> . . . whenever this stage is reached, the only remedy
> seems to me to be the rejuvenating return to the
> source [von Neumann, 1956, p. 2063].

Closing the gap between theory and practice is generally
viewed as bringing the practice of management up to speed with
the accumulated knowledge in the organizational sciences. My
concern is with a different sort of gap—the one between our
accumulated knowledge and the research methodologies we use
to develop new knowledge. Essentially, as we learn more about
human behavior and the functioning of complex organizations,
we should be able to develop more sophisticated (and realistic)
ways of studying human behavior. The alternative is to ignore
what we know and to continue studying behavior as it was conceived when our research methods were initially developed and
originally accepted in the profession. The consequence of this
knowledge/inquiry gap is that we currently may be studying behavior in a way that systematically prevents us from developing new knowledge. As a result, the theory/practice gap will close
by a decrease in the relevance of the theory, not by an increase
in the quality of the practice (Kilmann and others, 1983).

Richard Hackman's chapter brings the knowledge/inquiry
gap to life. Hackman summarizes his fifteen years of research
on performing units as three general principles: ''All that is required to exceed minimum standards for effectiveness is output judged by those who receive it to be more than acceptable,
a performing unit that winds up its work more competent than

when it started, and performers who are more satisfied than frustrated by what has happened. The challenge in my work has been to develop ways of understanding, designing, and managing performing units that increase the chances that these modest criteria can be met.''

Figure 1 shows these principles organized into a simple two-by-two model by adding on a fourth principle that Hackman implicitly argues against: using a single criterion of performance outcomes—such as any output-to-input ratio. Figure 1 organizes all four principles using the simple distinctions of technical versus human and micro versus macro. Both these distinctions occur repeatedly in most contingency theories of management and organizations (Kilmann, 1983b). Here, the macro/technical aspect (cell 2) emphasizes multiple performance criteria according to different stakeholder assessments; the macro/human aspect (cell 3) highlights the growth and learning of the performing unit as a whole; the micro/human aspect (cell 4) indicates the growth and personal satisfaction of the particular members of the performing unit.

Figure 1. Principles for Performing Units.

Technical

Cell 1 Single-criterion performance measures: output to input ratios	**Cell 2** Multiple criteria via different stake- holder assessments
Cell 4 Growth and personal satisfaction of members; having fun	**Cell 3** Growth and learning of whole system; increasing capacity to perform well

Micro (left) · Macro (right)

Human

Applying this accumulated knowledge of performing units to the research enterprise (as in the knowledge/inquiry gap) leads to some interesting conclusions. To begin with, it seems that most of the research in the field has concentrated on a single-criterion method of inquiry. In essence, the micro/technical principle argues for simple cause-and-effect relations in which the broader context and other phenomena are ignored. The laboratory experiment, designed for studying behavior in this way, has become the hallmark of scientific work in the organizational arena. However, the three principles that Hackman includes in his accumulated knowledge on performing units do not allow for tight experimental designs and controls. On the contrary, the study of multiple criteria of performance via different stakeholders (both inside and outside the organization) precludes the traditional experimental designs in research. In addition, the principles of growth of the whole performing unit (macro/technical) and personal satisfaction of the individual members (micro/human) tend to defy the laws of simple causal relations (Mitroff and Kilmann, 1978).

Only in a simple-machine view of the world (cell 1) could one expect simple cause-and-effect methods to add to our store of knowledge. If we now recognize and accept multiple criteria and complex human interactions as the phenomena of performing units, we must revise our research methodologies so that these sorts of phenomena can be studied. We therefore need research methods that view the world as a complex hologram, allowing for multiple, redundant, overly determined, and equifinal possibilities. If Hackman's knowledge of performance units is taken seriously, it becomes virtually impossible to argue for the experimental method to study human behavior today. It is time to close the knowledge/inquiry gap if we wish to move the field forward—if we wish to keep the theory/practice gap pushing practitioners to apply truly new and useful methods for managing problems in today's organizations.

Applying Figure 1 to the research enterprise as a performing unit also suggests that our research is acceptable to the criteria of only a few stakeholders (cell 2)—ones that are internal to the research system, not outside in the broader community. For example, the stakeholders most satisfied by the current research are (1) other academics, (2) academic journals, (3)

research universities, and (4) various funding agencies. Those
stakeholders who appear to be most dissatisfied by the current
research are (5) practicing managers, (6) management consultants, and (7) the public at large. The latter stakeholders are
presumably the clients of the organizational sciences.

Continuing, it is not clear that the scientific enterprise
is more competent now than it was a few decades ago (cell 3).
In fact, if the scientific enterprise is performing research in
simple-machine terms, then the research-performing unit may
have reached its highest level of incompetence. In order to advance, the knowledge of managing complex organizations today
requires methods that are in tune with complexity, uncertainty, imperfection, and not being in control. Applying the research
methods that worked yesterday to today's problems has reached
the limit of research performance.

Furthermore, it seems that the members of the performing unit—academics—are generally satisfied with their jobs and
their profession (cell 4). This is a dangerous situation, especially
if researchers, such as Hackman, suggest that their own personal satisfaction is reason enough to engage in the scientific
process. It is as if production workers in a nonacademic performance unit—in industry—were to suggest that happiness on the
job is the bottom line, not performance. If we do not accept
satisfaction as the only reason to be employed, then we should
not accept this for academics either. Besides, we learned many
decades ago that a satisfied worker is not necessarily a productive worker. Receipt of rewards that lead to satisfaction must
be made contingent on performance; otherwise, members may
do the minimum to get by and to remain in the organization.
I wonder whether the latter is indeed the case for most academics!

Measures of performance must reflect the entire range
of multiple stakeholder criteria if behavior to gain rewards is
to result in effective performance. Yet it seems that performance
in a research unit is geared largely to numbers of publications
in academic journals, judged by the traditional academic criteria
of certainty, simplicity, control, and the like. Thus, the worst
scenario in academia today is that researchers are performing

for single criteria of performance for yesterday's world. They are also satisfied in doing this, so that there is little impetus to search for alternative modes of inquiry. Having multiple criteria for multiple (external) stakeholders and developing the capacity for improving the research unit's ability to address today's problems with updated research methods are not being applied to challenge the performance of the research enterprise.

A Solution?

"Doing research that makes a difference" must, therefore, alter the design of research units, the performance criteria that guide their behavior, and the capacity of the system to adapt to the knowledge it creates—to practice what it preaches. It is time to recognize that the predominance of research striving to obtain precise cause-and-effect relations is ill suited to today's holographic world. We have to stop this myth of complete simplicity and total control. Researchers, as Hackman suggests, should return to the case analysis as a way of capturing the dynamic complexity of organizational behavior. Using multiple observers who have different perspectives and paradigms would help to achieve some form of validity. Debating these different views of the same situation would bring out the different values and assumptions of the analysts. Such a "dialectical science" seems much closer to what we know of organizations than the traditional experimental models of science, which clearly no longer fit with our inventory of knowledge (Kilmann, 1983a).

Hackman's chapter also suggests another way of highlighting the need to move to other kinds of scientific inquiry given what we now know of organizational functioning. It seems important to distinguish researching the separate parts of an organization from researching the context within which these parts exist and function. Experimental methods have worked best at isolating and studying the parts while ignoring the context or assuming that it was irrelevant. What if the context is the primary determinant of organizational behavior, such as history, culture, political and economic setting, and actions of external stakeholders? If this is the case, then studying the isolated parts within the organization is misplaced effort. Topics such as goal setting, motivation to perform, communication processes, and influence processes, while subject to study in a laboratory situation, are easily overwhelmed by the contextual factors operating in any living organization.

It seems that the field of organizational studies has developed in a backward manner—worrying about individual pieces of a very restricted puzzle before knowing (or caring) whether the context (the major determining factor) can be understood and managed. The dilemma that most concerns me is the choice between getting a precise understanding of an insignificant process of cause-and-effect pieces and getting a rough approximation of some contextual change that does make a substantial difference on multiple outcomes that matter to practitioners (and other external stakeholders). Stated differently, if everything taken together makes a difference while nothing by itself does, then *isolating the parts to discern their separate effects in the experimental tradition is to learn more about the nothings.* Research methods must be devised and encouraged to address the important contextual factors in a total package in all their glory.

Hackman's most important suggestion for me is his emphasis on forming an active partnership between academics and practitioners in learning about organizational functioning. This model of inquiry seems most similar to action research and interventions for the purpose of improving effectiveness of the organization as well as enhancing its capacity to improve in the future (much like the accumulation of scientific knowledge). If such an arrangement accomplishes these purposes and provides joy to all the participants as well, then Hackman will continue to have fun and the organizational sciences will have learned from the past. If this path is taken, the value of our science, to the broader community or to ourselves, will not be nil. At the same time, we will be getting back to the basics—the empirics—just in time to be relevant to today's organizational world. We will have returned to the source and will have rejuvenated the organizational sciences.

GROUP DISCUSSION

During his presentation, Kilmann drew concentric circles. The outer circle represented the context of history, culture, stakeholders, and so on. The inner represented the isolated organizational topics, such as goal setting and motivations. Kilmann estimated that the context might well explain 80 percent of organizational behavior and the microdynamics 20 percent.

Mitroff [addressing Hackman]: In your verbal presentation, you implied that somehow if we can depart from the criteria that govern normal science—the innermost circle there—it would mean somehow that we're being unfaithful to the original oath that we all took when we became ordained scientists. You expressed the guilt in most of us. The sad thing, really, is that contemporary modern philosophy of science has moved increasingly over the last twenty years away from that inner circle so radically and so drastically that, just as Dick [Walton] could talk about the tremendous lag between what we know in academia and what managers/practitioners consider, there is also an incredible lag between what we were taught is scientific method and the new philosophy of science. The new philosophy of science, as much as I am aware, is oriented to the 80 percent and was such a severe counterreaction to the 20 percent that it's almost—if you think I was radical or being argumentative, there are people like Paul Feyerabend at Berkeley who have almost just completely dumped on the 20 percent to the point where they wanted to get rid of those who espoused the notions of the 20 percent inner circle. Now that's not true for the field generally. But I think there is a lag for us, so I think one of the things this kind of a meeting can do is try to help purge or share some of that guilt and say, you know, philosophy of science has moved way beyond. In effect, we are annunciating that the very criteria you're talking about have become elevated to the status of formal criteria for judging theory. It sounds very, very strange, but it's a radical departure from positivism. So you do not have to feel guilty anymore.

Hackman: Let me make a process comment. I use terms like *vomit* and *oh, gee whiz* when I'm embarrassed and unsure. I have had to take on some of my colleagues in psychology who think this is unmitigated heresy, and I have no problems with that. We just sort of slug it out. There's no problem at all there. I know the regular methods, and I know them real well, so I am comfortable saying, "And here's how it's different and here's how it ought to be," and carrying on that argument and standing up straight and looking somebody in the eye. But I don't know what the criteria for testing the theory are—so when I talked about it earlier, I was looking down, I used terms like *vomit*, okay, because I don't know philosophy of science. I feel terribly guilty that I don't know philosophy of science. I know what I've got to do is experiment with some other ways of doing it, but I read that stuff and I get bored and I can't understand it. So I say, well, I'm a bad little boy but. . . . So to talk to a group like this of people who know that stuff makes me real embarrassed and defensive and ineffective.

Mitroff: Richard, [during the discussion of Pettigrew's chapter] we were engaging in what I think Abe Maslow called "science as a safety defensive mechanism," not as a growth experience. I think a lot of the questions addressed to Andy were all appropriate but had what I would say is a defensive character—asking Andy to prove and show his points exactly. Questions of clarification are legitimate to understand how one goes about doing a contextual study. I could understand, but I think it would probably be more helpful if you had discussed your anxiety because I see a lot of that discussion as working out our defensiveness and—

Porter: What would be nondefensive questions?

Mitroff: That's a legitimate question. The questions yesterday weren't inherently defensive in themselves, but I picked up— you asked me quite frankly—a hostile, aggressive, anxiety edge. You hear it reflected in my voice now, too. I'm no different. I share the same feeling. It's not so much the nature of the questions but the spirit and the tenor, is what I felt. I don't know whether the rest of you did, but I'll put myself on the line, and Richard [Hackman] told us about his. I was terribly put off, distressed by what happened around Andy's chapter. Not because the questions were invalid, not because they were inappropriate, not because many of us are struggling to understand what he was saying. It was like saying ''I can defend myself à la macho science,'' rather than saying, ''Let us walk with you, Andy, let us make the assumption that you're bright, what can we learn?'' That's what I'm saying is missing. And that turned me off. It angered me. I feel that if we're not above that, we should be able to talk about it, as Chris said we could perhaps talk about our ambivalence.

Greiner: But you're into dialectics, aren't you?

Mitroff: Larry, I'm into dialectics, but I also hope we could talk about the personal source of it and get over some of the anxiety. It wasn't dialectic. I think that was something more of a personal nature or process. We weren't managing our own process. I don't pretend to be an expert in that area. But I'm giving you what I felt. Intellectually I can take the dialectic.

Argyris: This could get us off. My own feeling is that I don't share that view. I share the view that it ought to be discussed. I don't share his [Mitroff's] view of what happened. And what impressed me, he's looked at the causal responsibility of the group and not of Andy, as if Andy didn't do anything to attract it. I don't know if that's what we ought to do. Shall we get into this or go back?

Lawler: We could try to sense the group and see where the group stands on whether we want to spend five minutes or ten minutes or the day.

Kilmann: Since I'm supposed to at least be the discussant, let me summarize it this way. I think we just talked briefly yesterday, that there are going to be some undercurrents of some of the insecurities, holding on to some of the old paradigms. I think when any group like this gets together, some of that may be going underneath. But I don't know if we want to spend—I don't think in this setting that kind of thing is going to get worked out. I think it's useful to acknowledge it and see it, and then maybe in more of the questioning we can perhaps be more sensitive just to explore and to be here to learn. But beyond that, I don't know if we want to take the time, to go into it now when there are some more content issues.

Lawler: Let me try one last observation that might facilitate the flow of events from here on. It seems to me that there is an undercurrent that we described accurately, I think. My estimate is that it's a much lower level than Ian's estimate. I think it's maybe 15 to 20 percent. And when I was listening to Ian, I thought it sounded more like 70 to 80 percent. I think what Ian just said and what Ralph just said to a degree tended to almost treat people who would hold a more traditional view of science as retards who somehow haven't reached the age of enlightenment, and therefore those of us who are more enlightened have to be tolerant of their interpersonal hang-ups and insecurities while they're going through this inevitable transition. I think that polarizes the group more than it really needs to.

Kerr [to Mitroff]: Getting back to your chapter, do these pictures get to hang side by side, or are we insisting that the old one gets pulled down and given to Goodwill and the new one goes up on the wall? . . . Well, we're having part of the process conversation.

Argyris: Well, it seems to me, I guess I would think you were part right, and yet, you know, in a way you either have a group and they deal on company manners or they don't. And company manners are great. Everybody has a surface politeness. They save the stabbings for the dinner and the after-dinner conversation. That's how we live our lives. In a way you have people amazingly willing to share their anxieties and their fears and say when they feel embarrassed and why they feel embarrassed. You get that far away from company manners and you don't permit any kind of sloppy process. You say we're in a collective group process and we've spent a day denying it. We're not experts in anything. We're a bunch of confused, tormented souls. And so, what happened yesterday won't even make my top fifty list of nasty, ugly, ganging-up, scapegoating, ego/vanity flashes. I doubt that it would impress other people—I doubt that it would make your list of top fifty. So I'm saying if we agree to stay at this level of interpersonal disclosure and wrestling with things that are really deeply troubling to us, and that's as bad as it gets, don't feel angry, feel grateful because it could be a lot worse. And the only way I know to prevent it is back to company manners. Nothing ventured, nothing lost.

Going back to substance, I don't want to buy Lawler's notion that he was angry at the traditionalists, because I'm not a traditionalist and I don't share his view. And I think the traditionalists—and I'll put Lyman and Paul on that list for the moment—weren't defending normal science yesterday; they were asking questions of validity. How do you know what was occurring? So I think what they were doing is forward-looking. To say that that's more traditional is not, to my point of view, a valid framing of it.

Seashore: I have to add one more thing here. I think we all sensed the hostility and anxiety, and I think you've missed the direction of it. I think a number of us have the uncomfortable sense of having revealed a domain of ignorance and incompetence and the effort was to try to understand that.

Lundberg: I thought it was a highly symbolic event in the light of the conference. It just so happened to be Andy. It could have been others, I think. He made us face our communal ignorance and uncomfortableness in a way that was mighty uncomfortable. Yes, we sparked a little bit. What was fascinating was how it ended. [Richard Hackman's] summary in trying to understand, Andy's incredible joy at seeing him understand, and having heard for the umpteenth time, we understood a little better. What I find fascinating is that much of what looked like dumping, we did with Andy, we could do with you. Your chapter is full of the same stuff. And what's interesting is that we are not going to do that. We're going to move on somehow, I think.

Walton: I don't feel any guilt, and I don't want to put the people who do simpler research out of business. I think what we're doing, what most people are reaching for here—either they start out reaching for it or are moving toward that—is middle-range theory as opposed to very simple theory. They're not satisfied with theories of why, not satisfied with contingency theory. They want more. One way, at least I have found, to build middle-range theory is to really go out and do what Andrew said, hopefully do it well, to come back and really inductively develop out of that some concepts and kind of try and push them into a theoretical framework. At the same time, if I'm about my business, and I did this more in my earlier stages than I did later, I went to the sociopsychological experimental literature, and I found that by the time that I had developed a way of thinking about it, you could arrive at the same theory two ways: You could get a lot of theory by putting together the "X varies with Y under conditions B but not C." And so I find that I use that experimental literature. I use the "X varies with the curvilinear relationship between stress and communication effectiveness." I use it. It becomes embedded as one proposition that is interrelated with other propositions. I think I've been working off of the intellectual capital that has been built up by the simpler theories. Now, I would like the bulk of the efforts to be moving toward larger interests of middle-range theory, but I must say I still find merit in the knowledge and the methods that produced a lot of the psychological and sociological literature.

Goodman: Let me ask the question of both of you. You use what other people have done in that kind of experimental literature to help you think about things, as you've been expanding and looking at possible methods, whether you see a role taking ideas that you've learned in the field or in the different kind of groups you're looking at and then going back and doing some experiments. Are you doing anything like that? Is that still a reasonable thing to do?

Hackman: Sure, sure. It's a reasonable thing to do, but in the context of the research stream. The need to get a little clearer can give rise to doing an experiment on that because you know what variables it's okay to control and it's not okay to control. So, yes, and then, damn yes. I don't know if the first three pages had their intended impact on my chapter or not, but it was a very explicit attempt to say, without a sledgehammer, let's follow our own light. This is my light and it does not mean that your light, your basic researcher who doesn't care so much about applicabilities, is not a good light. I want to keep that picture up on the wall as well.

Having said that, I really do believe that. But I'm back to *vomit* again when I look at the job-design literature. Okay? Ed might have kind of started it and Oldham and I kind of picked up on it, and I don't know if anybody notices or not, but I quit some years ago. And I quit kind of out of despair because of what was happening to what I thought was a pretty interesting line of research. With our journal stakeholders and our scientific paradigms, a lot of people said, well, we have to control this, understand all this stuff, and started going in and doing laboratory experiments of the moderating effect of growth needs on reaction to enriched versus unenriched jobs and created conditions where the context is totally controlled, where there is essentially no variance in the job because you cannot manipulate a job enough to get the phenomenon there, where there are essentially no individual differences because the subjects are taken out of the same subject pool, and then they do a study and they don't find much. So somebody else does a follow-up, and the business of science goes about tracking down something, and the phenomenon is gone. The phenomenon isn't there, even the individual differences thing. Ed and I were talking, early on, about whether the differences in growth-need strength moderate how people react to jobs. It's a pretty interesting question. But now the question for me is, seeing as how that didn't pan out so well, if you're going to have a high-commitment work system, and if you take other researchers' findings that one's life experience, including one's job experience, does shape the kinds of needs and values one has, and if you take as a criterion that effective performance involves, as a value or normative statement, individual growth as well, the question isn't can we pin down the moderating phenomena, the question is how can we create systems that further a certain kind of outcome. Whole different question. So the phenomena and the value thing led me to such despair about the job-design literature that I just couldn't even stay in it anymore. I don't even read this stuff anymore. And you say you disagree with that.

Walton: I was thinking of the practice side. On the practice side, I think people could take that [framework about job design] if they took it simply, without understanding the context and so forth, they could misuse that as well. But that tool, that framework, is a very useful tool in the hands of people who understand how organizations change. And, therefore, that's what I'm saying. It's an oversimplified version of reality, but it is more complex than the previous propositions. And it's a very useful tool. What your paper does is, it goes further than I think I would go in the sense that it's asserting that they're not relevant to practice. They're not relevant to practice by themselves, but none of us is going to develop a theory that you can transfer into an organization and have it work by itself. It's always going to be embedded in local knowledge.

Argyris: I'm going to focus on only the value side for a moment. I'm going to do some lawyering and I want to ask you [Walton] two questions and, if you would, give me a yes or no on this. Would you require all social scientists to have the criterion of personal satisfaction in growth and learning?

Walton: No.

Argyris: Second, how would you feel about social scientists who did research on decreasing growth, decreasing personal satisfaction and learning. Would you permit it?

Walton: I would permit it.

Argyris: Okay. I wouldn't, and let me tell you why. There is a whole issue of whether you ever get valid knowledge. You might be like a businessman who milked the business or like the people who milked our country and so on. You might for a couple of years get your data, but the population will arise. You're living near a community that might decide this. Just imagine your being at Cambridge in front of that group that's trying to throw out the biological scientist, they don't want to permit these people to do basic research anymore. And [Derek

C.] Bok [president, Harvard University] says, "What do you mean? Scientists have a right to do what they want as long as they are not harming people." These people are saying, "Sorry, no more. None of that." Now I said I was on the side of the scientist. I think we're going to be in real trouble. Just imagine if you're out there answering those questions in front of 700 hostile Cambridgites who now see social scientists, let's say, as Communists or something. And you say yes, I'm willing to permit someone to do research that could lead to—that's designed to better understand—decreasing personal growth and learning. I think we'd be in trouble. Who do you think is going to permit this to continue? In [Richard Hackman's] sense, it's the experimental method. That's where he's raising some of these issues.

Walton: I'm not going to do the experimental method, but I would permit somebody to create conditions in which people are disaffected from the social system and in which—

Argyris: Okay. That's the value system we all should talk about because I wouldn't.

Lawler: There's another theme in this that somebody mentioned earlier, that of consulting to organized crime or the Ku Klux Klan, which is an old example. It has been argued that if we are going to be allowed to pursue our trade in this society, we have to be willing to consult with the Ku Klux Klan and organized crime.

Walton: I would never consult with an organization that has as its objectives the antithesis of personal growth and destroying people's humanity. I never consult with them.

Seashore: I think there's a little miscommunication here, because it's possible to permit research on ill health without implying that you're promoting ill health.

Argyris: No, I'm talking about if you imagine yourself in front of people asking you questions and say yes, I will defend the right of someone to design research whose intention is to produce propositions that will help people to reduce their growth, reduce their satisfaction—that's basic research. But would you?

Lawler: I see a difference. I can remember you standing up in front of people and advocating OD people consulting with the Ku Klux Klan.

Argyris: Sure. But do you remember the rest of the sentence? It had to do with conditions that had to do with valid information, free and informed choice for the people in the organization, including the customers. Well, you know, when will the Ku Klux Klan permit its customers and itself to have the notion of valid information, free and informed choice?

Lawler: I think to a degree that's a qualification that would get you personally out of consulting. I don't think it would answer that screaming mob in Cambridge wanting to know why you would advocate allowing social scientists to consult with the Ku Klux Klan.

Argyris: It follows. You see, I think [Richard Hackman's] values are not any longer personal. He said, "These are for me, this is what makes life fun," and if somebody else might have something else to say, then I think we are in an era when we no longer have that choice. That is, our society is not going to let us do the kinds of things of which we would have normally thought, "Of course, social scientists have the right to choose whatever they're going to say." It's happened, needless to say, in government, but it's going to happen with the citizens.

At this point the discussants switched topics.

Lawler: Richard [Hackman], let me try a point. I was thinking back to your chapter and Dick's [Walton's] and Andrew's [Pettigrew's] trying to see what were the similarities and differences. I think that in some ways they are very close. It seemed to me you and Dick talked more about a personal odyssey of how you learn and how you go through it, whereas Andrew tried to a degree to put a name on it and describe a way of going about it, not Richard's way or Dick's, but a contextual model. He began to formalize it more and to some degree moved toward creating a group of followers, a name that people could rally around, saying I'm this kind of researcher. Am I right that I didn't see that in what you two were doing?

Hackman: Absolutely.

Lawler: Is that unintentional? Intentional? What?

Hackman: Intentional.

Walton: Mine is the shortest answer. I just haven't thought much about it. I'm indebted to somebody who articulates the method. I thought a lot about intervention, I haven't thought about how I research it. Chris bangs away at me for that.

Hackman: I thought about it a little bit, and it was intentional. I have a lot of sympathy for what Andrew is writing about in terms of the kind of research he is addressing. I would rather that he not label it contextual research so that he does not make it easy for us to identify ourselves as in this camp or that camp. I think that can be a little risky, particularly when you don't yet know for sure what you're doing. I think Andrew doesn't. I think he is still in the middle of the struggle as well. I worry about that premature label.

Lawler: Good point. Let me try another theme, which I hear sometimes from graduate students. "Gee, it's wonderful that you, Richard Hackman, do all these great things and it's wonderful that you, Dick Walton, do all these great things, but what hope is there for me? Obviously, I can't emulate you or copy you, you've got all these different kinds of experience and so forth and so on. Unless you give me something as a guide and some way of getting into that kind of activity, the world seems hopeless to me."

Pettigrew: I think that is precisely the sort of motive force for my proceeding to try to formalize it, precisely because that question has been put to me time and time again, particularly by doctoral students, who, as I tried to say, have a conception that other kinds of research methods have been codified, have been formalized, have been written down, and it says they are accessible in some way or another and to some degree or another. But when we talk about that kind of research we were talking about [when discussing my chapter], we are talking about something that has been codified less, that appears to be less accessible. Therefore the question is: Whatever it is, how do I go about trying to learn it? I think there has got to be some evidence of trying to formalize it and describe it for people to appreciate. Then others can say, "Well, all right, I want to do it that sort of way. Now I understand more clearly what it is." But at the same time, we must be cautious, of course, that it doesn't start to appear as another ladder to get to the biggest and the brightest sun. I think the danger of that would be not that it becomes formalized, because I think that is part of the process of appreciation and part, therefore, of the process of learning. But, in fact, it becomes so formalized it starts to appear as another technology. That's when I would start to say, I want to butt out at that point in time.

Hackman: I want to respond. I think that one of the things we went over was, we were asking Andrew to do even more of that which he should not have been doing in the first place: "Tell us what the steps are that you go through to do this." I think there is a response to the question. But I take sharp difference with Andrew. I think it has to be at the level of questions you ask yourself of your methodology rather than the steps in the methodology that you use. If somebody tries to emulate what I do, he's going to go astray, because what I did was tailored for this particular conceptual issue I'm exploring or this particular site or set of observations that I have.

What I hold dear, what I cherish—I don't know if I said this at the end of the chapter or not—what I cherish is criteria I was taught about what a good method should do for you. When students ask, "How should I do this?" I say, "Come up with some ideas, be inventive, let's be creative, let's speculate about some wild ways that you might go about this." But then we've got some criteria. We're going to ask: Do those methods allow you to keep the phenomenon that you're studying, or do they destroy the phenomenon? Do they allow you to find out that you're wrong? Do the concepts have some conceptual integrity? We know some things about what conceptual integrity means. Is it possible to assign some relatively unambiguous meanings to them? There's a whole thing coming out of psychometrics and other literatures about how you assign meaning to concepts. You can kind of go down that line. Chris has his, you know, The Big Three, that have been with him always, and he has used all kinds of different methods, but he can always justify his methods in terms of his three criteria. I don't have mine in a nice list. I'm still struggling with them. I want the criteria to be there and then say, "Let us, dear graduate students, be inventive about how we go about trying to study this phenomenon, testing our methods against these criteria," rather than laying out experimental design 11-A.

Lawler: Let me just make a strange intervention here. First of all, I would say those are relatively positivist views of the world.

Hackman: I don't care how you label this. I really don't care.

At this point Lawler made an attempt to invite some of the gallery of new and aspiring Ph.D.s to respond to Pettigrew's position versus Hackman's. Responses were tentatively offered, and discussion quickly shifted back to the main table.

Argyris: To me, now, I think I begin to understand the trouble I had. I think Andy [Pettigrew], when he talks about craft, is talking about precisely what you [Richard Hackman] told him not to. Let me illustrate it by using you and me. I have these criteria. But often you said to me early, "Now look, Chris, what led you to ask that question? What led you to do this? What led you to do that?" I didn't know. [*Referring to the dialogues Schön wrote about in* The Reflective Practitioner—*see Chapter Seven*] I've been trying to figure what are the questions you ask people who are, so to speak, stars. Schön didn't ask the architect for general criteria. He said, "Now the student came over here. She put this design right in front of you. You then said this." And so on. That's the dialogue that went on. For me, Andrew was focusing on those rules that are skillful and effective but passive. It seems to me I wouldn't want to rule those out. So you need both. You need the criteria, but I would want to watch you in action and start asking you some questions.

Greiner: The really impressive thing that I got out of listening to both of you [Richard Hackman and Andrew M. Pettigrew] is, you intensively try to get familiar with the phenomenon and you just work and work at it. My hunch is that you just don't come at it through research. That circle up there [*referring to Kilmann's diagram*] is too closed for me because there are a lot of ways to get knowledge. You somehow try to immerse yourself in that phenomenon however you come at it. It's not the method that is driving you anymore. Is it?

Hackman: No. Maybe you're right. Of course it's not. That raises a whole other set of questions on which it would be nice to have a conference some time, which is: Where do our problems come from? I think there is probably some interesting psychology in me that I have not explored about how come I'm so interested in groups and in work and in change. These are the things that have been kind of themes in my work. That probably has more to do with how I got myself brought up and is probably neurotic, and I know there is a lot of energy there. My stance is, if you are a little freaked out about something, it's important. For depth-type reasons, you might want to go with it.

Lundberg: The first part of your [Hackman's] chapter, your assertions part, I really liked that. It is very articulate, it flows marvelously and hits a lot of my biases in a comforting way. I reread it last night and I came away from it feeling that it's a little bit like throwing the baby out with the bath. Is my hunch right that it's probably a little overstated, that you're trying to make your point and, in that pointmaking, throwing the baby out with the bath? Are you really going to abandon field experiment?

Hackman: I'm not going to abandon lab experiments, because there are occasions when, with the right set of variables and the right question, they can be terribly informative to do. I really have very fundamental doubts about the viability of field experimental and field quasi-experimental designs as a way of doing the kind of research we are talking about at this point.

Lundberg: Maybe it's what you understand to be a field experiment versus what I do. I think we may get in trouble there. I use it pretty loosely. I'm willing to do it post hoc.

Hackman: Then we might not differ so much. It has to do with issues of control in the role of research and in the role of the organization and with the degree to which social systems hold still while data are collected. That strikes me as impossible.

Driver: We've heard an awful lot about context, environment, and some people call it the E-type of variable. I got a sense of despair from you that the P-type of variables, the person variables, are just not going to give us any leverage in building even medium-size theories, not to mention larger-scale ones. I would like to rise to their defense as I heard you do with the laboratory method—which I agree with, by the way. I think there is a vast body of literature that I think for some reason has been very poorly utilized in organizational behavior: the entire psychological testing literature, the entire body of psychometric literature. Why that has happened, I'm not sure. I think it's as rich a field and as useful as the historical contextual world Andrew [Pettigrew] was articulating. I would like to suggest that it would be a grave mistake to throw it out, particularly since one of the major stakeholders, the manager, would find it absolutely ludicrous for anybody to walk into his or her office and say individual differences don't matter. I have to think that somewhere in this discussion of research we really need to come to grips with why we perhaps have been avoiding this individual difference variable and the literature that is behind it.

The second comment has to do with the practitioner issue, and again the same sentence practically triggered this, Richard.

Hackman: What's the sentence?

Driver: Here it is. "Is the model framed in a way that makes it *usable* by practitioners in their work?" That triggered something that I've been wrestling with for some time. It has to do with the complexity of the user relative to the complexity of our models. Are we to be limited by the complexity of practitioners and what they can handle and understand in the kind of models and structures we build? In the kind of models and structures you built, I thought I heard you saying, in that sense, yes, we should. That if the users can't handle the additional complexity of adding five or six more variables, we better be damn careful about adding them in and keep our models down to a simple level. Did I hear that right? I would differ with that again. I would think that that would be a very dangerous type of limiting process.

Bennis: Two questions that I would like to elaborate on—something that is interesting to me and is obviously of interest to you. Ralph raised a question about your fun issue, and I guess I share Ralph's feeling that it's an important idea: fun and excitement and all those things that we have that really energize us. Without wanting to put you in the pocket of being a world saver, is it really just that in the end? Or could you elaborate?

    The other question has to do with your saying to Pettigrew not to label someone. I really identify with what you said: "Let's not use that word, because it labels people and puts them into categories." But it seems to me that as a conceptualist, which you are, you also know that we build knowledge and that so-called compilation of learning by labeling things. That's giving people something to shoot at and shoot for. How do you resolve these things to be true? Labeling to divide where you don't advance and labeling things to advance. They are both real questions that I obviously don't have an answer to.

Hackman: Karl Weick and I were sitting around a conference much less engaging than this one, writing each other notes, a few years ago. We were playing the epitaph game. What would we like on our tombstone? The three options were "He had fun," "He understood the world," and "He saved the world." Neither of us was willing to accept "He had fun." Karl and I had a difference on whether the ultimate was "He understood the world" or "He saved the world." I would kind of like to save the world if I had the time to do it. What I was trying to say in the chapter was, I do my best work, and I think most of us do our best work, when we're having fun. What is fun for me is to try and get this marriage working somehow. It's also frustrating and so forth. But when it works, it's really a kind of a joyful deal. That's where the fun and the saving the world come together for me. I don't see it as a moral responsibility, which is why I can be pretty accepting of other people who are doing things that I don't think are having negative consequences on the things I value, if they're having fun. I learn an awful lot from people who just frankly don't give a damn about the things that we're talking about in this conference. Dick was saying a similar kind of thing. I want to value that, I want to support it. And even use it.

I am wrestling with the other question, too. If you want to have influence—and part of the deal is having influence, obviously—I'd like to influence researchers. One of the ways to do that is give them alternative pictures or visions or ideas. I know how you make things comprehensible and use them to buy people. You put some names on them and you wrap them up in a way that they can understand them and use them. I find a great instinct to do that because I don't want just to be sitting here doing my own thing. I want other people to learn from my mistakes, and so I need to do some packaging. This may be a case example of the ambivalence that we were talking about—that I want to do that, but I'm real scared about doing that because I see what happens when you have Campbell and Stanley come out or when you have whatever people latch on. Now we have a methodology.

Argyris: I am going to try another answer to your [Bennis's] question. I think we must categorize. I think the danger that Richard [Hackman] points out is right, but the way to deal with it is to be confrontable on the categorization process. When I turned to Andy and said, "Andy, have I asked you an inappropriate question?" I am sure Andy didn't say, "Yes, Chris, your question was inappropriate." All right, now I would say, the problem is not whether Andy develops the category scheme, it is how we then deal with discussing the category scheme. That's where I would say we have to take a look at it.

Pettigrew: When I said your question was inappropriate, what I was really trying to say was that your question was unanswerable. The question was being posed in terms of what proportion of the problem you were looking at can be called contextual. I don't know. I haven't been in the situation that you were describing.

Argyris: Now you're beginning to have the kind of dialogue that would be helpful, because then the next question arises, what makes that question unanswerable?

REFERENCES

Alderfer, C. P., Brown, L. D., Kaplan, R. E., and Smith, K. K. *Group Relations and Organizational Diagnosis.* New York: Wiley, in press.

Argyris, C. *Inner Contradictions of Rigorous Research.* New York: Academic Press, 1980.

Berkowitz, L., and Donnerstein, E. "External Validity Is More than Skin Deep." *American Psychologist,* 1982, *37,* 245–257.

Blumberg, M., and Pringle, C. D. "How Control Groups Can Cause Loss of Control in Action Research: The Case of Rushton Coal Mine." *Journal of Applied Behavioral Science,* 1983, *19,* 409–425.

Garner, W. R. "The Acquisition and Application of Knowledge: A Symbiotic Relation." *American Psychologist,* 1972, *27,* 941–946.

Hackman, J. R. "The Design of Work Teams." In J. W. Lorsch (Ed.), *Handbook of Organizational Behavior.* Englewood Cliffs, N.J.: Prentice-Hall, in press.

Hakel, M. D., Sorcher, M., Beer, M., and Moses, J. L. *Making It Happen: Designing Research with Implementation in Mind.* Beverly Hills, Calif.: Sage, 1982.

Hardy, G. H. *A Mathematician's Apology.* Cambridge: Cambridge University Press, 1967.

Hunter, J. E., Schmidt, F. L., and Jackson, G. B. *Meta-analysis: Cumulating Research Findings Across Studies.* Beverly Hills, Calif.: Sage, 1982.

James, L. R., Mulaik, S. A., and Brett, J. M. *Causal Analysis: Assumptions, Models, and Data.* Beverly Hills, Calif.: Sage, 1982.

Katz, D., and Kahn, R. L. *The Social Psychology of Organizations.* New York: Wiley, 1978.

Kilmann, R. H. "A Dialectical Approach to Formulating and Testing Social Science Theories: Assumptional Analysis." *Human Relations,* 1983a, *36* (1), 1–22.

Kilmann, R. H. "A Typology of Organization Typologies: Toward Parsimony and Integration in the Organizational Sciences." *Human Relations,* 1983b, *36* (6), 523–548.

Kilmann, R. H., and others (Eds.). *Producing Useful Knowledge for Organizations.* New York: Praeger, 1983.

Lawler, E. E., III. "The New Plant Revolution." *Organizational Dynamics,* Winter 1978, pp. 2–12.

Locke, E. A., Feren, D. B., McCaleb, V. M., Shaw, K. N., and Denny, A. T. "The Relative Effectiveness of Four Methods of Motivating Employee Performance." In K. D. Duncan, M. M. Gruneberg, and D. Wallis (Eds.), *Changes in Working Life.* Chichester: Wiley, 1980.

McGuire, W. J. "A Contextualist Theory of Knowledge: Its Implications for Innovation and Reform in Psychological Research." In L. Berkowitz (Ed.), *Advances in Experimental Social Psychology.* Vol. 16. New York: Academic Press, 1983.

Mitroff, I. I., and Kilmann, R. H. *Methodological Approaches to Social Science: Integrating Divergent Concepts and Theories.* San Francisco: Jossey-Bass, 1978.

Mook, D. G. "In Defense of External Invalidity." *American Psychologist,* 1983, *38*, 379–387.

Pfeffer, J., and Salancik, G. R. *The External Control of Organizations.* New York: Harper & Row, 1978.

Poza, E. J., and Marcus, M. L. "Success Story: The Team Approach to Work Restructuring." *Organizational Dynamics,* Winter 1980, pp. 3–25.

Runkel, P. J., and McGrath, J. E. *Research on Human Behavior.* New York: Holt, Rinehart and Winston, 1972.

Scriven, M. "Maximizing the Power of Causal Investigations: The Modus Operandi Method." In W. J. Popham (Ed.), *Evaluation in Education: Current Applications.* Washington, D.C.: American Educational Research Association, 1974.

Slovic, P. "Toward Understanding and Improving Decisions." In E. A. Fleishman (Ed.), *Human Performance and Productivity*. Hillsdale, N.J.: Erlbaum, 1981.

Tolman, E. C. "Principles of Purposive Behavior." In S. Koch (Ed.), *Psychology: A Study of a Science*. Vol. 2. New York: McGraw-Hill, 1959.

Tyler, L. E. *Thinking Creatively: A New Approach to Psychology and Individual Lives*. San Francisco: Jossey-Bass, 1983.

von Neumann, J. "The Mathematician." In J. R. Newman (Ed.), *The World of Mathematics*. New York: Simon & Schuster, 1956.

Vroom, V. H., and Yetton, P. *Leadership and Decision-Making*. Pittsburgh: University of Pittsburgh Press, 1973.

Weick, K. E. "Laboratory Experimentation with Organizations." In J. G. March (Ed.), *Handbook of Organizations*. Chicago: Rand McNally, 1965.

6

Richard E. Walton

❖ ❖ ❖ ❖ ❖ ❖ ❖ ❖ ❖ ❖ ❖ ❖ ❖ ❖ ❖ ❖ ❖

Strategies
with Dual Relevance

What distinguishes research that is potentially useful for both theory and practice? What strategies of the researcher are necessary for such research? How does an author's personal experience illustrate the issues, dilemmas, and synergy involved in pursuing research relevant to both theory and practice? These, paraphrased, are questions that the seminar organizers have asked each author to address.

I will begin by reviewing the nature of my personal research efforts. I start here because I prefer to rely considerably on processes of inductive logic, especially early in my mapping of an intellectual puzzle. Then I will turn to the other two questions, formulating several generalizations consistent with my experience.

A Case History of One Researcher

My research career can be described in terms of three broad content areas. During the 1960s I was concerned about conflict and conflict management. Beginning about 1970 my

176

primary focus was on work innovations that promoted both human and economic values. Recently, my interest has shifted to change and development in interinstitutional systems—in particular, those systems that may play a strategic role in social and economic development. Within each area there was a nature to the series of particular intellectual puzzles that attracted my interest (see Figure 1).

Conflict Management. My interest in conflict began with an effort to make systematic sense of labor/management negotiations. When Robert McKersie and I completed our *Behavioral Theory of Labor Negotiations* in 1965, we claimed it was a theory of "social negotiations" and illustrated its applicability to international and race relations. Two subprocesses of negotiations—bargaining and problem solving—were found to be also at the heart of intraorganizational conflict and cooperation. John Dutton and I studied and theorized about interdepartmental conflict. I engaged in little, if any, consulting activity that contributed either to the negotiations book or to the articles on interdepartmental conflict.

Another conflict management puzzle was in a multilateral setting in which the parties had an option not only about whether they interacted in a conflicted or cooperative mode but also about whether they interacted at all (*Conflict and Integration in the Federal Bureaucracy,* 1971). The theoretical formulation of the problem was "system building among institutions in loosely interdependent networks." It drew on eight documented attempts in the federal government to integrate the efforts of a number of independent agencies—in foreign affairs (State, Defense, Central Intelligence Agency, Agency for International Development, Peace Corps, and Commerce, in overseas missions and in Washington, D.C.) and in domestic affairs (Housing and Urban Development, Labor, Health, Education and Welfare, and the Office of Economic Opportunity). I served as a consultant to many of these efforts, which, conducted over several years, both applied my theoretical framework and contributed to it.

These works were followed by an effort to theorize about third-party intervention. *Interpersonal Peacemaking* (1969) was based on several case studies of my attempts to help resolve con-

Figure 1. Evolving Topical Focus of Intellectual
Activity and Illustrative Products.

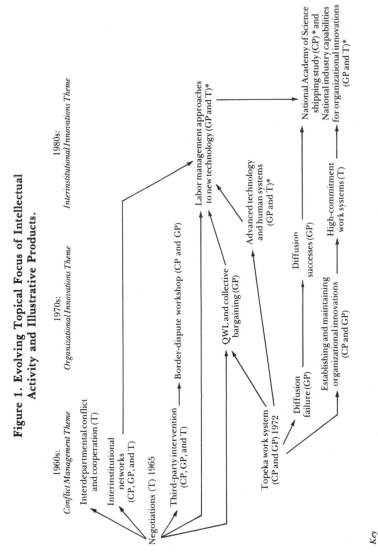

Key
T = Systematic theory
CP = Specific client practice contributions
GP = General practice recommendations and ad hoc hypotheses
 * = Ongoing projects in fall 1983

flicts between managers. It specified the dynamics of conflict episodes, the conflict management functions performed by third parties, the tactical implementation of these functions, and their role attributes that enable a third party to perform these functions. Generalizations were formulated at a middle level of abstraction and were proposed as applicable to third-party interventions in other forms of social conflict, ranging from intergroup to international conflict.

In the fall of 1969 I participated as a member of a third-party team in a two-week workshop to search for solutions to the border disputes in the Horn of Africa. Members of the elite (but not official government representatives) from Somalia, Kenya, and Ethiopia had been enlisted in an innovative experiment in informal diplomacy. Three Yale members of the third-party team were African experts; I was included as one of the conflict resolution experts. This practical experience drew on all the theory and practice previously described, and it resulted in research papers that attempted to derive the practical lessons from this social innovation. The workshop was assessed as a mixture of technical successes and failures, but in the acid test it has failed twice in the fifteen years since to prevent the renewal of border war between Ethiopia and Somalia. The United Nations Institute for Training and Research supported further work on the workshop idea for small-country conflicts, and similar interventions were organized for Northern Ireland and Cyprus.

Work Innovations. My interest in the field of work innovations began in 1968, when I was presented with an opportunity to help design a new plant organization and to influence the development of the young organization. The opportunity grew out of an established consulting relationship. The client and I had become discouraged with the limited effect of process interventions in turning around organizational patterns of alienation when structures could not also be altered to support positive commitment. We seized the opportunity to make structural changes in the design of rewards, jobs, roles, and hierarchical relations. The plant was the General Foods pet-food plant in Topeka, Kansas. The plant's effectiveness in economic and human terms was extremely encouraging. I attempted an early delineation for *Harvard Business Review* readers of the general design principles of the work organization and of contextual conditions that promoted the success of the plant.

At the time, the plant was considered a radical departure from conventional plant organization design. It violated most of the conventional wisdom of management practitioners. Yet it was, in conceptual design, less a discovery of fundamentally new organizational principles than a full-blown, carefully designed, operational application of principles that had long been enunciated by Chris Argyris, Rensis Likert, Doug McGregor, and other behavioral scientists. Their ideas certainly were in the back of my head and influenced me, but the organization design was more a product of inductive reasoning by the managers—a process of examining their own assumptions about people and analyzing the actual work processes required to manage the plant technology.

My attention soon shifted to the diffusion question. What dynamics explain why a complex work innovation can be judged successful yet fails to be diffused throughout the same organization? I studied a dozen work innovations similar in spirit to the Topeka system, and I developed a set of explanatory hypotheses. I did not attempt to combine the hypotheses into a systematic theoretical framework; rather, I tried to ensure that each hypothesis would be taken into account by practitioners.

A similar motivation to influence practice underlay two research projects with Len Schlesinger dealing with (1) the dilemmas experienced at the supervisory level in highly participative organizations and (2) the issues associated with introducing work innovations in the context of a collective bargaining relationship. Each contained some insights that could have been pressed further for their theoretical implications but were not. We were more interested here in the practical implications.

My interest in theorizing about the work-restructuring phenomenon came in the late 1970s. I formulated a theory of "high-commitment work systems," based partly on the longitudinal study of four new plant organizations through the first two and one-half to six years of their existence. I had consulted with and observed those organizations over their lives. One plant was a failure. The others represented varying degrees of success. Trend lines depicted the rises and dips (or declines) in the level of member commitment in each organization. Propositions were developed to explain (1) the increases and decreases in commitment over time within the same organization and (2) the differences among plants in level of commitment achieved. This systematic, retrospective, and comparative analysis clarified for me a number of organizational dynamics that I had not fully appreciated. For example, the skill and problem-solving requirements of the task technology *declined* during and after start-up, whereas the corresponding capabilities of human resources *increased* during these early phases of organizational life. These developmental trends combined to create a ''skill gap'' during early start-up and a ''skill surplus'' during steady-rate operations. Moreover, each trend separately had exactly a contradictory implication for the appropriate developmental trend of the organization structure. The increasing certainty of the task technology indicated a structure that evolved from ''organic'' to ''mechanistic'' in form (after Burns and Stalker), whereas the increased expertise, problem-solving capabilities, and shared understandings suggested that the organization could become increasingly ''organic'' in form. Thus, together the two trends created dilemmas and inherent need for structural compromises. These longitudinal and comparative analyses also yielded insights into the phased development of ''meanings,'' or organizational ideologies, which was as important as the evolution of structure. As Andrew Pettigrew and others have noted, the modus vivendi and the modus operandi each require attention, and their interrelationship has to be orchestrated.

About 1980, I became particularly interested in advanced information technology after I recognized its tremendous potential to transform the nature of clerical, professional, and managerial work as well as craft and semiskilled blue-collar work. A vast literature exists on the social impact of new technologies. I did not aspire to add incrementally to this literature on social and human impact; rather, I wanted to move directly to questions about the processes required to modify the impact. My preliminary research confirmed that this new technology often had profound organizational consequences, that these effects were sometimes positive and sometimes negative, and that they were mostly unexpected. Analysis of this new-generation technology indicated to me that it is less deterministic than earlier work technologies, offering the designer more technical routes to the same economic result, each route having different social implications. With this encouragement about both the importance and the feasibility of socially sensitive design, the research question for theory and practice became: What changes in conventional processes for designing, approving, and assessing technology result in applications that are not only technically sound and economically justified but also organizationally congruent?

Armed with a question that was both theoretically interesting and of strategic practical relevance, my research associates and I were ready to document a number of positive case histories of designs that consciously attempted to incorporate social criteria. Earlier, we had documented some negative cases—in which the social dimension had been ignored in the technology development process—and these cases had yielded some hypotheses about the changes in roles, participants, procedures, rewards, and design concepts that would probably be required in order to produce socially sensitive designs. But these were speculative hypotheses that needed to be improved or replaced.

Unfortunately, we did not locate any positive cases, nor were we offered any opportunities to help create positive cases. What we needed was a Topeka-type opportunity for "action research"—that is, to participate in pioneering new design processes. Some potentially suitable possibilities did appear and were explored, but none materialized.

There were, to be sure, documented instances in which the design of equipment and operational procedures in plants, refineries, word-processing centers, and accounting departments had been influenced by sociotechnical concepts. I had participated in sociotechnical designs of this type and had found they were relevant. However, none of these new technical systems met the criteria for what we believed would transform future work organizations—namely, systems which cut across many normal departmental boundaries, which are on-line, and which comprise a network of terminals accessed by a large number of clerical, professional, and managerial workers in the performance of their normal duties.

Interinstitutional Innovations. While waiting for the right opportunity to pursue the questions about technology design methods framed above, I became interested in how U.S. labor unions were currently approaching the new computer-based technology and how they might approach it in the future. The Communications Workers of America and two other unions representing Bell System workers had negotiated a clause in the 1980 agreements establishing joint Technology Change Committees to review new technologies at least six months in advance of their introduction. In addition, I became aware through a colleague, Leslie Schneider, of technology agreements in Norway and other European countries that had enabled the unions to influence workplace applications of new technology.

A broad possibility suggested itself. Whereas work restructuring and quality of worklife had been pioneered in the early 1970s in nonunion work organizations, new approaches to the design of work technology might this time be pioneered in the collective bargaining framework.

With Leslie Schneider, I am currently investigating union and management approaches to new work technology in several industries. What are the different approaches—for example, unilateralism, traditional adversary bargaining, and joint problem solving and planning? What are the dilemmas and consequences of each approach under varying conditions? What explains why a particular approach is taken? We expect to develop some theories that make sense of these phenomena and to derive their action implications.

Recently I began another activity that could contribute to both practice and theory. In April 1983 the National Academy of Sciences established a committee charged with making recommendations for "effective manning" in the U.S. maritime trades in order to enhance the competitiveness of our shipping industry. The committee comprises a representative of labor, a ship owner, other maritime specialists, and myself as a specialist in change processes. To achieve an understanding about the nature of manning and organizational innovations implemented in many other Western countries but not yet in the United States, we visited Norway, Sweden, Denmark, West Germany, Holland, and the United Kingdom, meeting with labor union officials, ship owners, government officials, and maritime academics in each country. The shipping industries in a few countries have developed organizational innovations during the past fifteen years that have enabled them to reduce manning safely to levels that are sometimes as low as 50 percent of U.S. manning. The objective of this public service assignment is to influence an area of U.S. practice, but the by-product of my early work on the assignment is a new research agenda. The comparative data on six European countries have sharpened my interest in an important intellectual puzzle and yielded pieces that may be part of its solution.

The puzzle: Why is an industry in country X better able than the same industry in countries Y and Z to develop and diffuse organization innovations that improve productivity and international competitiveness? The question can be asked with respect to steel, automobiles, electronic consumer products, or computers. I suspect the answers are partly the same and partly different, depending on the industry.

The opportunity: I have comparative data on the types of organizational innovation and the level of diffusion that have been achieved in each of the six northwest European countries. The six countries can be ranked in terms of the amount of change over the past fifteen years. I have analyzed the factors that help explain the amount of change and the lack of change in each country—hence, the rank ordering.

The shipping industry is especially suitable for analysis because ships can be directly compared. A Norwegian ship and a U.K. ship may have been built to similar specs in the same Korean shipyard and may incur similar capital and fuel costs. They may be competing for the same trade on the same deep-sea routes. In these circumstances, it is easy to appreciate that operating costs, primarily crew costs, become a critical competitive factor. When companies are no longer competitive in a given service with national crews, they either sell the ships and shrink their fleet or reregister a ship under a flag of convenience and hire less expensive foreign crews. Thus, there are some ready indicators of innovation and change and of the loss of competitiveness.

In proposing a theory to explain the capability of a national industry for the organizational innovations required to remain competitive, one needs to consider what roles are played by the following factors: competitive threat and other change motives, the types of visions of organizational alternatives that characterize the industry, and the nature of the change process employed. In particular, one must inquire: How much does organizational innovation and change depend on institutional factors at the industry level as contrasted with motives, visions, and process skills at the enterprise level or, indeed, the ship level? How do factors at these several levels relate to one another?

Some Issues in Contributing to Both Theory and Practice

When I talk about the requirements of research with dual relevance, I will, implicitly, be referring to the type of research activity outlined in the preceding section. Other chapters will outline different types of dual-purpose research.

First, I will propose a mix of research and other learning activities that can be instrumental in making a dual contribution and explain why; I will also explore the implications of alternative sequences of these intellectual activities.

Second, I will explore how the choice of topical questions affects one's ability to make dual contributions. This discussion will illustrate ways in which the dual commitment can influence the evolution of the topical focus over time.

Third, I will propose how a dual commitment to practice and theory influences one's selection of theoretical variables and frameworks, the choice between theory testing and theory generating, and concern about methodological rigor.

Research and Other Learning Strategies with Dual Relevance

The first implication of the preceding review of my efforts to contribute to theory and practice is that some integral activities are clearly not research as we customarily use the term. To make sense out of my experience, I need to introduce an additional concept broader than "research strategy"—hence, "learning strategy."

Figure 2. Orientation of Written Products.

Practice Orientation of Products		No generalization specified	Ad hoc insights, hypotheses, and generalizations offered	Systematic theory discussed
	General implications for practitioners indicated		Problem-focused articles on QWL diffusion, collective bargaining, super-vision, and so on	Third-party theory Negotiation theory
	Implications for particular clients indicated	Unpublished consulting reports		
	No practice implications specified		-	Work systems theory

Theory Orientation of Products

Learning activities include certain types of consulting projects as well as research (field investigations, literature review, writing). The possible orientation of the written products that result from these learning activities can be visualized in a matrix showing different types of relevance (see Figure 2). One can distinguish three degrees of relevance to practice: A product may have no specified implications for practice; it may be related to a particular client's problem; or it may be relevant to practitioners generally. These three possibilities are presented on one side of a matrix along with a similar three-way distinction in terms of the generalizations offered: The product may contain no generalizations; it may contain ad hoc insights, hypotheses, and generalizations; or it may contain a discussion of systematic theory.

I have found that over a period of time the efforts to produce a mixture of written products (as indicated in the three-by-three matrix in Figure 2) were instrumental in producing dual relevance. The matrix clarifies that some written products by themselves do not have dual relevance. However, the cumulative learning associated with unpublished client reports is likely to be incorporated subsequently into theory statements. And theoretical ideas, in turn, are tested and made more operational when one applies them to a concrete situation. Thus, even where dual relevance is not found in a single project, it is found in the portfolio.

At different times and for different topics my learning strategies have comprised different patterns of interaction among research and consulting activities. In some cases the involvement has been broadly *sequential;* that is, one activity on the same topic has been completed before another has been started. The broad sequence can move from theory to practice or vice versa.

My interest in conflict resolution started with a relatively pure theory effort and culminated in a predominantly action-oriented project, the border dispute workshop. In contrast, the organizational innovation interest was launched with the Topeka consulting project and culminated in the theory of high-commitment work systems. Thus, my experience fails to point to an inherent advantage in either sequence. It may, however, be significant that, as a younger scholar, I started with theory and moved toward practice on the same subject, but in midcareer, I started with an action project that eventually yielded a theoretical formulation of the same phenomenon.

In some cases, the involvement in consulting and research activities on the same topic has been highly interactive. For example, I developed the theory of third-party peacemaking during a year in which I was myself very active as a third party. One result of the interactive process is that this particular theory had the most apparent implications for practice, in comparison with my other systematic theories.[1] This fact suggests the following generalization: The more interactive the client practice-oriented activities and the theoretical activities, the greater the practice implications of the theory.

---

[1]The negotiation theory is shown in Figure 2 to have specified general implications for practitioners, but it was less directly relevant than third-party theory. The work systems theory was still less directly relevant, and it is categorized as having specified no practice implications.

The advantages derived from shifting one's attention from theory to practice and vice versa are especially strong for practices that involve diagnosing and solving concrete problems, as is often required in consulting.

This advantage is partly due to *intellectual synergy*. All researchers attempt to develop strategies for generating synergy in their activities. I am suggesting that there is a particular type of synergy deriving from dual-relevance learning strategies. One's theory influences one's practice, which provides the basis for revising one's theory, which can be tested in practice, and so on. The practical dilemmas one encounters provide clues about the existence of theoretical dilemmas. Practical experience is especially helpful in distinguishing causal variables that probably have high leverage from those with minor influence.

Synergy derives in part from one's being literally forced to move up and down the abstraction ladder—to be very operational and literal when grappling with the concrete problem and to become abstract and conceptual about the class of problems during the theory-generating phase. Incidentally, the intellectual skill of applying concepts and of conceptualizing observed phenomena may be one of the most critical skills enabling dual contributions to theory and practice.

Synergy is produced also because the combination of theory and practice facilitates both intuitive and analytical processes. That which is intuitively discovered in my grappling with the practical gets clarified analytically; clarified propositions get internalized by me and eventually become tacit as I go about my practice. They are "forgotten" in the same sense as the rules of a golf swing are, ideally, forgotten in a golf match.

A pattern of intellectual activities with dual purposes has other efficient and practical advantages. Access is a big one. One may have better access to certain types of data as a consultant than as a researcher.[2] Compared with research subjects,

---

[2]Here and elsewhere I make a distinction between consulting and research that many other dual-relevance researchers do not make. Some researchers enter into a relationship with the client or subject as a "consultant/researcher" or "action researcher" or simply "researcher." For me, these potentially synergistic and mutually advantageous activities are nevertheless conceptually separate.

the client often is more highly motivated to ensure that all the relevant data get on the table; the investment the client is willing to make and the quality of his or her attention are often higher. The tendency for clients to be active and challenging and to provide on-line feedback about the relevance of ideas can benefit the person who is interested in formulating theory.

In addition, resources are saved by shortening the feedback cycle by which general ideas are formulated, tested, and revised. Much of the data gathering has dual relevance, and so does some of the analysis and conceptual work.

The shipping study illustrates these practical advantages. Because I was part of a National Academy of Sciences committee with an industry-level action assignment, I shared in access to comparable labor leaders, ship owners, and government officials in six countries—access of a quantity and quality I could never have arranged as an independent scholar. Thus, in some respects, the theory-oriented data benefited from the dual purpose, making the research more effective. Further, it was more efficient. I was entirely freed from concern with the logistics of arranging travel and scheduling three dozen meetings with approximately a hundred officials in six countries.

The shipping study also illustrates some issues and dilemmas of dual-purpose intellectual activity.

If one starts with an action assignment, the assignment not only shapes the nature of the theoretical questions that one will find interesting but also constrains the methodology one can use in contributing to theory. In fact, the theoretical question about the determinants of national industry adaptation developed in my mind only during the field trip. However, even if I had formulated the theory question earlier, the timing of the European field trip, which I could not control, would have limited my ability to peruse existing theory before gathering data. The prescribed itinerary of the traveling committee put additional constraints on the data gathered in the field. During the trip, while one was wearing a client-specific hat, one had to give priority to data and analysis that had leverage on action questions, regardless of whether they were adequate for developing or testing theory.

The general point is that where a single cluster of intellectual activities serves a client's needs, yields general implications for practice, and also forms the basis for theory development, role clarity and flexibility become important assets and the lack thereof an important liability. At any given time one role and role relationship will be primary. It is important to be clear about which is the primary role relationship and to honor all the obligations associated with it: One day the role may be that of consultant, and the search for solutions to the client's problems takes precedence; the next day the role may be that of social theorist, and the search for generalizations takes precedence.

The dual role has some other disadvantages. There is increased potential for subjectivity—for example, for self-serving or defensive explanations of a phenomenon—when one has been both an actor in and an observer of the situation.

That my dual orientation has put me at risk in this respect is illustrated by a recent article (Whitsett and Yorks, 1983, p. 105) reviewing Topeka, in which the authors state, "Walton, whose credentials and important reference groups are rooted in social science, has been walking the tightrope walked by most management theorists." They acknowledged that I had recognized the potential role conflict involved but concluded that I did not keep my balance on the tightrope. Their observations are instructive about the potential risks. They reported that my "purpose in writing was to persuade managers into action, not advance the basis of scientific knowledge" (p. 104). My actual intention was to do both. They interpreted my assertion that the broad principles underlying the Topeka work structure are widely applicable as "a political argument, not a scientific one" (p. 104). In fact, I was making two separate but related assertions: (1) that, on the basis of limited empirical evidence and available theory, I was confident that these principles are widely applicable to American work organizations and (2) that, on the basis of my diagnosis of society and my personal values, I favored the wide application of these principles.

The authors also concluded that I "wrote more confidently than was warranted" (p. 105), explaining this by the fact that, as an active change agent, I wanted the plant to succeed.

This criticism and the need to address the issue in the present chapter on dual-relevance research prompt me to distinguish three possible objectives for a researcher who would write on the projects in which he or she has played an active role. Each objective has a different potential for role conflict.

One objective might be to contribute to our understanding of the effects of particular design and implementation choices and to increase our understanding of the reasons for particular outcomes. This has been a major interest of mine—to understand the failures as well as the achievements of the interventions and to learn from them. But won't my professional pride predispose me to find that actual developments are consistent with original assumptions and intentions? I have not worried about lapses of this type, because my curiosity is a countervailing force to the potential bias; I am equally interested in discovering what we planners overlooked, what we did not forecast, and in explaining why. Although others may not accept such reassurance from the researcher himself, it does not serve science to exclude from consideration accounts by researchers who were also actors. In addition to the unusual access to the research site, the action researcher has the advantage of understanding the original intentions and assumptions. However, such accounts are more useful if the scientific and practitioner communities also have access to the accounts of others who were *not* involved as actors. Fortunately, in the case of Topeka, Edward Lawler and Robert Schrank, in separate investigations, also provided data to the public domain. Schrank offered a causal interpretation for the positive attitudes and work patterns that differed from mine. The combination just described reduces the audience's vulnerability to the action researcher's biases and yet enables the researcher to contribute to the audience's cumulative learning.

A second objective might be to advocate to practitioners a certain approach to a class of design or implementation problems. I believe this can be done by an action researcher if the advocacy is based on the limited direct evidence, coupled with a careful articulation of the reasoning that supports the approach.

A third possible objective is to offer an authoritative,

balanced evaluation of the potential effects of the kinds of interventions documented. Here the action researcher's evaluations are and should be considered most suspect, especially when the researcher clearly is an advocate. This last objective involves the greatest inherent tension with one's role as a change agent.

Others may find these distinctions in purpose too finely drawn. For me, however, they are important ones. Generally, I have intended the first two purposes but not the third.

Topics and Questions with Dual Relevance

An important aspect of producing knowledge with dual relevance is selection of the topical domain and formulation of the questions within that domain.

Formulating Appropriate Questions. An appropriate question is one that is interesting on two counts. First, the question is theoretically interesting; that is, there is a gap in theory or a weak theory and a scholarly audience that will appreciate the contribution to theory. Second, the question is practically interesting; that is, there is an undefined area of practice or an ill-defined set of practices and a practitioner audience.

Finding the questions that are interesting on both counts involves a number of steps and requires a variety of skills, as well as a sense of timing.

A thought process that may help one identify a particular question with dual interest is to start with the practical puzzles, paradoxes, or dilemmas. What is it that perplexes practitioners? Difficulties in practice can often be translated into theoretical puzzles. Having formulated the theoretical puzzle that underlies the practical problem, one must then discover whether the theoretical puzzle has already been satisfactorily solved. If not, one must decide whether one wants to attempt the theoretical solution. If it has been solved, one may decide to provide additional testing of existing theory.

The shipping study illustrates the foregoing sequence of thought processes and some of its implications. I started with the action questions for the U.S. shipping industry, and then I formulated an underlying question in the spirit of descriptive theory:

> Assume that one can observe that in a given international industry (for example, steel, autos, or shipping), different countries will manifest different rates of innovation and diffusion of organizational practices that increase productivity. What factors explain these intercountry differences? What concepts and hypotheses, within what theoretical framework, help make systematic sense out of these explanatory factors?

Then, assuming that this theoretical question was an apt one given the practical issues already before me, the question became whether some existing theory purported to explain this type of phenomenon. If it did, then I would view the shipping investigation as an opportunity either to disconfirm or to provide additional support, illustration, and refinement for existing theory. If no existing theory claimed to solve the puzzle, or if the theory appeared inadequate on its face, then I could proceed with the hope and expectation that the analysis of data in one or more industries might provide the basis for suggesting some new theory. The question of the adequacy of existing theory gives rise to a new question: where to look for the theory. Economic theory of industrial structure and competition? Sociological theory of diffusion? Literature on managerial innovation? Organizational theories regarding work restructuring? Theories about effects of national differences in character? Literature on negotiations, regulations, or trade unions? Do existing theories address only an aspect of the theoretical problem posed, or has someone already attempted a middle-range theory that perhaps synthesizes propositions drawn from these various disciplines?

The illustration contains a number of implications. Working from practice to theory requires that one be reasonably familiar with the existing stock of theory. This can be a major difficulty, because the problems in practice can be informed by so many basic and applied disciples.

Influencing the Evolution in Research Topics. With respect to the organizational innovations, I pursued a logical sequence of research and action questions, each new question being formulated as developments in practice made it salient: What organizational design principles are capable of improving human development and economic performance? What conditions and processes serve to launch and sustain a new and innovative organizational unit? Which dynamics promote and which inhibit the diffusion of innovations within the same organization? What is the potential for integrating work restructuring and collective bargaining? And so on.

If this sequence can be considered moving *forward* with practical developments in work restructuring, then the sequence of research questions I have posed about social criteria and technology can be said to have been moving *backward* and *sideways* as I searched for an understanding of why practice developments were *not* occurring and tried to locate areas where they might be about to occur. In other words:

1.   Because we failed to find research sites with positive cases in which organizational criteria had been used systematically during the development of complex office technology, we had to be satisfied with our documentation of negative cases of omission and with analysis of the questions "Why?" and "So what?"

2.   Then came a move sideways to examine union and management approaches to the introduction of new technology. Perhaps in collective bargaining we would find a sharper concern about work-force implications of technology and therefore more interest in modifying the procedures and roles involved in developing, approving, and introducing new technology.

3.   When we discovered a relatively modest trend in this direction and substantial adherence by the parties to their traditional approaches to technology issues, we amended our research question. For example, we became more interested in clarifying the historical roots of the current strategies used by particular unions (for example, Communication Workers of America and the United Auto Workers) to protect their members from the adverse effects of new technology. Perhaps this understanding would provide the basis for hypothesizing what changes in union objectives, processes, and attitudes—as well as what coordinated changes in mana-

gerial behavior—might lead to a joint approach to managing the work-force effects of new technology.

In each case—work innovations and new technology—the pattern of evolution of research questions is explained in part by the fact that in practice I was promoting a class of social innovations. In the first case, my involvement near the leading edge of practice helped enhance both the content and the timing of my writing on practice issues and related theory. In the second case, my diagnosis of societal needs, the sense of urgency that that engendered in me, and my preoccupation with understanding and promoting *positive* solutions helped cause what could be regarded as false starts. I had to review assumptions once a research thrust was initiated. Had I been less concerned about promoting practice, I might have recognized more quickly the need to explain *current* practices better—especially their root causes. The sequence embedded in this learning process has had some advantages, but it does serve to illustrate two contrasting evolutionary patterns of research interests, both geared to interests in practice.

Theory and Methods with Dual Relevance

Selecting Appropriate Variables. The practice-oriented researcher is interested in a subset of the variables of interest to an organizational sociologist or a social psychologist. What types of variables and what types of theoretical configurations are of interest to the researcher oriented to both theory and practice?

Figure 3 contains an illustrative, general framework for theorizing about organizational phenomena. It indicates that organizational outcomes, such as economic performance and human development, are a function of some contextual conditions and some managerial design and policy choices and that some of these influences on performance are "direct" and some are "indirect," in that they act first to shape attitudes and relationships, which, in turn, influence the outcomes. There are, of course, feedback processes and other dynamics that are neglected in this simplified diagram.

Figure 3. Organizational Variables.

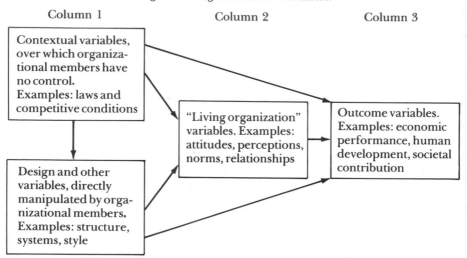

Consider how the "living organization" variables in column 2 might be of interest. A theory that includes these social psychological variables is more likely to have practical implications if it treats them as dependent variables explained by variables drawn from column 1 and/or as independent variables that explain the outcomes in column 3. Theories are least likely to have practical relevance if they describe only associations among variables drawn from column 2. In contrast, as a social psychologist, I might be interested in the interrelationships among these living organization variables without reference to the types of antecedents in column 1 or the types of consequences in column 3. As a social psychologist, for example, I might be interested in the relationship among social cohesion, trust, and interpersonal communication; and as a management theorist, I would be interested in these variables if they were also linked to some managerial lever and some performance criterion or other outcome variable.

Consider the two types of variables represented in column 1. Theories that include manipulable variables are more likely to have practice implications than those that do not. Therefore, some of the independent variables studied ought to be those over which the target practitioners have control. National cultural attributes may be less controllable for the practitioner audiences than structural design choices. Some of the dependent variables studied ought to be those outcomes that the practitioner values inherently. To illustrate, the level of economic performance is more likely to be of inherent interest to managers than the question whether workers extend their work relationships to off-the-job social activities.

Theories that comprehend more causal variables, albeit less rigorous in specifying precise relationships among variables, are more practical than X-varies-with-Y theories.

My interests in conflict illustrate these points. They gravitated quickly from a fascination with the dynamics of conflict in themselves to an interest in understanding how to influence these dynamics. My theoretical interest became one of differentiating conflict that had good outcomes from conflict that had bad outcomes and then discovering the antecedents of the good outcomes. The practical implications flowed naturally from conflict theory with this type of structure. To become more practical, I did not need to become less interested in theory; I needed only to select an appropriate configuration of variables.

Generating Hypotheses Versus Testing Them. Is one type of research more useful than the other for practice? Consider research at one end of a spectrum: Research may be designed to test well-formulated hypotheses where the results may increase one's certainty about the relationship among variables from probabilities of, say, .85 to .95. In effect, the research replaces moderately high certainty with very high certainty. This type of contribution to knowledge is valuable to the basic social sciences.

Toward the other end of the spectrum, research may be intended to formulate concepts and hypotheses where the results may increase certainty about a phenomenon only from a probability of .2 to .6. It may be more apt to say that the result of this research is a *decrease* in uncertainty as a result of the tentative mapping of previously uncharted territory.

During my tenure as director of research in a professional school, I tried to assess what type of research was useful to practicing managers, and I concluded that the latter type of research was of much more use than the former. Managers are accustomed to making decisions under relatively high levels of uncertainty. They have little interest in the kind of knowledge about causes and effects that merely increases the certainty of an already apparent relationship. They are decidedly more interested in either conceptual knowledge that helps them order their thinking about an action area or plausible hypotheses that have not previously occurred to them.

From the foregoing reasoning, I would argue that dual relevance is more likely to result from research that is designed to *generate* concepts, hypotheses, and theory than from research that is designed to *test* hypotheses and theory. My own research experience tends to be consistent with this argument. My comparative field research on interdepartmental relations and my laboratory experiments on bargaining were designed to test hypotheses; they made the least incremental contribution to practice, if indeed they made any.

Let me be clear. I believe research at both ends of the spectrum makes important, essential contributions to theoretical knowledge. As a member of the social science establishment, I would not rank hypothesis-formulating activity over hypothesis testing. As a researcher in a professional school, I value hypothesis generation more highly.

Rigor and Relevance: Does Practice Affect Rigor? There is not always a trade-off between rigorous methodology and relevance. If the practice problem is one that happens to include few variables, all quantifiable, then rigorous methodologies may be powerful in producing practical solutions. However, the more strategic practical problems tend to be relatively complex and to include variables that are not quantifiable. Therefore, an interest in these practical problems leads the researcher/modeler to make trade-offs. To capture more of the complexity, one sacrifices precision in the specification of variables and elegance of form of the overall model of the problem.

General Strategies

Here I will elaborate on a number of general aspects of the learning strategy described and analyzed in the chapter so far.

Research Strategy. I have alluded to but have not described how I go about my research. My research strategy and methods generally follow those proposed by Glaser and Strauss (1967). In addition, I try to observe certain specifications which, as associate editor of *The Journal of Applied Behavioral Sciences,* I proposed (Walton, 1972) and which would make analytical case histories a better basis for the inductive development of intervention theory and method.

Occasionally I will start a study by reviewing or refreshing my familiarity with the relevant literature. However, this preliminary phase often will be relatively cursory. My notion of the data I want (and sometimes of the questions I am chasing) will evolve as I gather the data.

In the field, I try to develop rich descriptions of the situation. I search for comparative data between organizations or between different time periods in the same organization. During the early stages of making sense of the data, I rely mainly on inductive processes. I immerse myself in the data, let them sink in, and then gradually organize them, searching for themes, contrasts, and causal relationships among aspects of the situation studied. Often it is only after I have developed a conceptual map of the phenomenon and have formulated some hypotheses that I review the literature systematically.

For me, as for Glaser and Strauss, the "strategy of comparative analysis for generating theory puts a high emphasis on *theory as process*; that is, theory as an ever-developing entity, not as a perfected product"(1967, p. 32). I also agree with their thinking about the different forms of theoretical exposition: "Grounded theory can be presented as a well-codified set of propositions or in a running theoretical discussion, using conceptual categories and their properties" (p. 31).

Values and Diagnosis of Society. Especially in dual-relevance research, it is important not only to be clear about one's personal values but also to have formulated one's diagnosis of society. The latter sounds presumptuous; nonetheless, it is necessary. Values specify the broader range of problems and outcomes one cares about. The diagnosis determines the narrower set of problems that are urgent and significant.

In my case, three values in particular have helped me define the types of outcomes I study and promote. The first value is the efficient use of natural resources—raw material and human effort—to produce goods and services. Efficiency is an aspect of the more fundamental value of conservation, although it is seldom appreciated in this light. Second, I have a deep commitment to human development. Third, I believe in pluralism—strong institutions in industry, labor, government, the news media, academia, and so on. Highly relevant to my research and practice has been my dual commitment to competent, strong, legitimate management in the private sector and a competent, strong, legitimate free trade union movement. Perhaps it is understandable, therefore, that I regard the management of differences as one of society's most strategic social processes.

My diagnosis of society in the 1960s centered on the need to develop our capacity to manage conflict—to use conflict management to balance the power and to resolve differences between the disenfranchised and the established institutions and among established institutions.

In the early 1970s I concluded that breakthroughs in redesigning work organizations could more readily occur in new plants, which invariably would start out without a union. Despite what was regarded as an even-handed treatment of management and trade unions in my earlier books on professional engineering unions and labor negotiations, many trade unionists saw my new plant work as helping to create models that could be and were being used by some managements to avoid unions.

Later, after a number of new high-commitment work systems demonstrated the types of human and economic gains that were possible, I turned my interest to the potential for integrating collective bargaining and these new work structures. Some trade unionists disapproved of my earlier work, whereas some executives who would like to weaken the union movement disapprove of the thrust of my more recent work.

Intrinsic Motivation or Professional Rewards? Why pursue dual relevance? It helps to care genuinely about both theory and practice. I suspect that is a general proposition. It certainly applies to me. I have not analyzed how the absence or presence of professional rewards or institutional support mechanisms has affected my orientation to theory and practice. I would emphasize the importance of intrinsic interest.

Motivationally, it is hard for me to engage in intellectual activities that do not offer the potential for payoff in both currencies: The activity must lead to some change, solve some real-world problem; it must lead to increased cognitive clarity on my part. Ideally it will lead to written generalizations, but at a minimum it must be clarifying for me personally. I lose interest steadily in any consulting on problems where I find I am not still learning at a significant rate. And I also lose interest in intellectual puzzles for which I do not see action implications.

My own dual interest influenced my educational choices, which, in turn, reinforced my theory and practice commitment. I received an M.S. in economics (Purdue) and a doctorate from a professional school (Harvard Business School); I did postdoctoral work in social psychology at the University of Michigan and spent a sabbatical leave at the psychology department at the University of California, Los Angeles. I have taught courses in several disciplinary departments as well as in professional programs. I identify myself professionally as a behavioral scientist.

Of course, caring about contributing to both practice and theory is not sufficient. The intellectual activities of contributing to each need to be mutually facilitative. If each aspect did not in some way benefit from the other, there would be less research with dual relevance.

Summary and Conclusion

My approach to this chapter illustrates one approach to generating new knowledge. I have examined a number of activities of one scholar, contrasted and compared them, sought to understand their functional interdependence. Then I invented some conceptual distinctions that made the contrasts and comparisons appear more systematic to me, and I formulated some ad hoc hypotheses that had face validity and were consistent with my observations—all very speculatively and tentatively.

The chapter distinguishes three possibilities: a research

career oriented to the development and testing of theory, a research career oriented to the development of guidelines for action, and a consulting practice giving direct assistance in the solution of practical problems. Research careers with dual relevance are those that combine the first two career options. Although the consulting practice is by definition not required, a review of my case history indicates that it was an integral part of my "learning strategy" and therefore played a critical supporting role in my two-pronged research strategy.

Reflecting on my own case, I believe the combination of the three orientations enabled me to be more productive in each area than if I had concentrated on any one area alone.

One advantage of the three-pronged learning strategy is the additional *intellectual synergy* that can be derived from (1) testing one's own theory and theorizing about one's own tests, (2) applying one's abstractions and abstracting from one's own action, and (3) combining one's analytical and intuitive processes. There are also *practical advantages:* better access, efficiencies in data gathering, and additional resources.

The potential *disadvantages* that my experience illustrates arise (1) because opportunities to contribute directly to the solution of practical problems may not accommodate an ideal sequence of activities for developing or testing theory and (2) because there are potential role conflicts when one is actor, advocate, and researcher.

My experience did not point to an advantage of one learning sequence over the other—that is, from theory-oriented to practice-oriented activities or from practice-oriented to theory-oriented activities. However, the potential costs and benefits that I have attributed to a three-pronged learning strategy may be heightened when the strategy involves a highly interactive process of searching for solutions to a concrete problem and conducting research on the same type of problem.

Certain research choices appear to be favored in work that contributes to both theory and practice. One attempts (1) to include in one's theoretical framework a causal network of variables that acts as a bridge from factors manageable by actors to those of ultimate value to actors, (2) to select problems in which the research is expected to reduce confusion and uncertainty rather than to replace moderately high certainty with high certainty, and (3) to be willing to make trade-offs between, on the one hand, traditional concepts of "rigor" and "elegance" and, on the other hand, an interest in capturing more of the complexity of the phenomenon.

The temperamental qualities helpful to the dual researcher or the three-pronged learner would appear to include an appreciation of the intrinsic rewards associated with each of the three types of contributions and a disciplined attention to the different requirements associated with each activity, accompanied by a willingness to "sin bravely," because lapses may well occur.

The ultimate effectiveness of the dual-relevance research strategy (and of the three-pronged learning strategy in which it may be embedded) also depends on the quality of the broad topical focus selected, duration of sustained attention to this broad topic, and the sequence of particular research questions within the broad topic.

In my case, my work was assisted by the fact that in the 1960s social conflict was a highly salient issue in our society— for example, civil rights, anti–Vietnam War activities, and other direct challenges to established authority.

My attention to social conflict moved from one institutional setting to another: labor/management, civil rights, intraorganizational, interpersonal, and international. In each shift the questions were: What can be transferred? What is different in the new social setting? The theoretical focus was also constantly changing: What are conflict dynamics? What are tactical opportunities for participants in conflict systems? What are leverage points for third-party peacemakers?

General academic and practical interest in work reform during the 1970s was as high as interest in the management of social conflict had been in the 1960s. Within one broad focus on work innovations, my attention shifts followed a relatively determined logic as each of a number of questions became salient. In each question there were an interesting theoretical issue and an urgent practical problem. It was, however, the practical problems that triggered my research activity—until the end of the decade, when I turned my attention to systematic theory.

My current interest in innovations in interinstitutional

conflict resolution and joint planning has roots in both earlier fields of interest. Does rapid progress in work reform necessitate the invention of new interinstitutional structures and processes involving management, trade unions, and other stakeholders, such as public agencies? What factors will explain whether the enabling structures and processes will emerge? What factors explain why national industries as a whole do or do not adapt organizationally to remain competitive in international markets? I expect that my activities in this area will be equally influenced by the compelling nature of the theoretical puzzles I find here and by the urgency of the related practical problems.

RESPONSE AND COMMENTARY

David A. Whetten

I appreciate the opportunity to study Richard Walton's thoughtful and highly personal assessment of what is required to make important contributions to both theory and practice. As one who has had numerous conversations with colleagues during the past three or four years about the desirability, advisability, and feasibility of pursuing a dualistic approach to research, I found several points in this chapter very enlightening. Walton is one of a handful of organizational scientists who are widely regarded as having made important contributions to both theory and practice, and it is therefore very instructive to read such a frank and insightful account of his personal odyssey.

My comments on his chapter will first summarize what I consider the key points. Although this underscoring obviously reflects my own biases and concerns, it provides a vehicle for highlighting some of the important contributions contained in the chapter. Then I will shift my focus from the individual experiences of Richard Walton to the prospects for shifting the "center of gravity" in the orientation of the field as a whole. One of the purposes of this conference is to encourage more researchers to pursue a dualistic orientation. Therefore, it is important that we examine the applicability of the author's approach for the bulk of researchers in the field. Although it is clearly instructive and personally gratifying to know that a few key individuals have succeeded in pursuing this dualistic orientation, if on closer scrutiny we conclude that the conditions necessary to accomplish this feat are not generally accessible to the population of organizational researchers, then we risk espousing an elitist model of research. Stated another way, whereas I could have chosen to quibble with the author over some of the cooking instructions in his recipe for success, I am far more concerned about whether the key ingredients are available to most cooks.

Highlighting Important Contributions

Walton's chapter makes several important contributions to our understanding of dual-relevance research. First, in keeping with the title of this conference, the author clearly advocates that research should be viewed as a tool for enhancing *both* practice and theory. Unlike some others who have emphasized only the value of generating more profound insights for practice, using a particular action research model, or have suggested ways to graft a research agenda onto consulting arrangements, this chapter demonstrates a genuine dual commitment to both theory and practice. A critical component of Walton's approach to this dualistic orientation is his emphasis on the frequent movement back and forth between the worlds of theory and practice. Referring to Figure 2, he argues that the potential of any given project to make contributions to both theory and practice is enhanced when the "general learning style" of the investigator is balanced between intervention and reflection. To Walton, making a dual contribution represents something far more significant than token statements, at the end of a study, of the implications the theory has for practice. Indeed, this pattern of iterative, total immersion in the two spheres of activity is so deeply ingrained in Walton's professional career that at times the distinction appears artificial.

Second, he does not, however, ignore the challenging nature of the dual-orientation role. He carefully delineates the potential role and value conflicts he has experienced and offers some suggestions for resolving them. For example, he urges researchers to clarify their personal values and professional goals and to use these as reference points for assessing their motives for engaging in a particular project. He also argues that when an organizational scientist is acting as both researcher and consultant, generally one of these roles has primary emphasis in the view of the client/host organization. Walton reminds us that the scientist as consultant needs to ensure that his or her actions do not violate those expectations.

Third, Walton defines "implications for managerial practice" broadly. So much of the recent discussion of "relevant research" seems to have the limited objective of getting researchers out of their behavioral labs and into organizations. Although this is, in most cases, a necessary condition for making a meaningful contribution to practice, it is far from sufficient. Very little of the current research being conducted inside organizations by academics will influence the broad practice of management. It is either thinly disguised theoretical research or contract research that at best will aid decision makers in a single organization (for example, validating their performance appraisal system, evaluating the effects of a limited change in management policy). In contrast, Walton argues that research that makes significant contributions to practice wrestles with complex and challenging organizational problems whose solutions have far-reaching consequences for the design and administration of organizations in general. Many behavioral scientists lament the fact that our profession is not called on more often to help key government and industrial leaders solve the numerous pressing societal problems for which our expertise is clearly appropriate. Dick Walton is a person whose work clearly has been influential in these high-level policy-making circles, and it is instructive to observe that his influence is partly due to the broad scope of the practical problems he has tackled. Again, research that makes a contribution to practice should not be confused with research conducted on practitioners (instead of college sophomores). Although Walton correctly argues that research designs that enable the investigator to become immersed in the phenomenon being investigated are more likely to produce important new insights, an often overlooked point is that our potential for making significant, lasting contributions lies as much in the scope of our work as in its location.

Fourth, expanding on this point, Walton argues that the choice of variables and methods significantly influences the contribution of a study (see Figure 3 of his chapter). As demonstrated by his career, in which he has investigated topics ranging from interpersonal conflict resolution to the effectiveness of the shipping industry, most topics in our field lend themselves equally well to theoretical and to practical treatment. Therefore, the extent to which a given study is likely to make an important contribution to either theory or practice is influenced by the questions we ask, the data-collection devices we use, the rules of evidence we require, and so forth. In this regard, I found his distinction between research that is intended to reduce the uncertainty of a given outcome and research intended to stimulate discussion of previously unconsidered alternatives informative. Research focusing on explaining the variance in an otherwise obvious set of relationships is inherently less likely to make a contribution to theory and practice than research that illuminates previously obscured organizational issues.

Fifth, Walton's chapter reinforces the importance of doing research that stimulates the researcher's intellectual curiosity. Engaging in professional activities that are personally rewarding and challenging increases the likelihood that they will make contributions to the thinking of others. This observation is consistent with research by Daft, Campbell, and Hulin showing that studies having the greatest impact on the field are intrinsically interesting to the researcher. Although this seems like common sense, it is unfortunate how seldom it is reflected in common practice.

Sixth, Walton reassures us that making dual contributions to theory and practice is a long-term endeavor. Not every single written product or even every research project need reflect a dualistic orientation. For those interested in making contributions to multiple audiences, he argues that we will generally have a greater impact by focusing on one cell in his Figure 2 at a time. His emphasis on building up a publication portfolio that is well distributed across the entire matrix will in the long run, one hopes, stimulate others to venture beyond the security of familiar, well-worn cells.

Implications for the Field

Walton's chapter helps clarify and reinforce a number of key points about the research process, but at the same time his personal odyssey raises some troubling concerns about the field in general. Most fundamentally, why are such a small percentage of active organizational researchers currently conducting research that makes a contribution to both theory and practice, and what would it take to change this condition? Assuming that these twin objectives are not in principle mutually exclusive, what are the necessary and sufficient conditions required for researchers to make important contributions to both? Specifically, taking Walton as a case in point, is his success primarily attributable to the strength of his commitment to the dualist perspective, coupled with his profound insights into what it takes to implement it? Or are there other necessary ''exogenous conditions'' reflected in his case history that bear examination? For example, I am struck by the breadth and balance of his training (Harvard D.B.A. plus postdoctorate work in social psychology); the range of courses he has taught (labor relations, social psychology, management); the diversity of professional roles he has occupied (from director of research to consultant); his affiliation with an institution that is well known for its abundant resources, supportive climate for intensive research projects, and ready access to business organizations; and the impressive number of unusual invitations he has had to study important organizational problems.

For me, one sobering outcome of Walton's very thoughtful and illuminating description of his research career is an increased awareness of the myriad institutional, personal, and professional obstacles in the way of individuals who desire to make contributions to both theory and practice. In particular, I was struck by the diverse and time-consuming set of activities described by Dick in his examples of research projects with dual objectives. In comparing those with the research designs described in most *Academy of Management Journal* and *Administrative Science Quarterly* papers, the distinction between a research generalist and a research specialist comes to mind. Assuming it is appropriate to characterize the modal researcher in our field as a specialist interested mainly in adding to a specific theoretical body of knowledge, it is instructive to consider what (besides desire) is required for him or her to make the shift to a generalist orientation pursuing dual contributions.

Whereas the specialist can do adequate research with only limited in-depth knowledge of one discipline, the generalist must feel equally at home in several bodies of knowledge in order to truly understand complex, multifaceted real-world problems. The generalist must also have competence in several forms of data collection and analysis. But particularly he or she must feel comfortable with a clinical approach to investigation that is unfamiliar to most theory specialists. The goal of the theory specialist is to be able to predict or explain a given organizational phenomenon; the generalist needs to understand how to change it. As a result, the generalist needs a much broader and deeper understanding of fundamental organizational processes. This, in turn, requires much greater access to information in organizations. Whereas the specialist can be satisfied with an agreement for the organization to provide a limited range of "sterilized data," the generalist needs to personally experience the raw data in their natural state. This requires becoming as conversant with the world of practice as with the realm of theory. As Walton points out, consultants are more likely to gain this exposure, and this is a role many "pure researchers" deliberately avoid.

These differences in the nature of the research activities of the specialist and the generalist suggest some important distinctions between the personal characteristics of the two types of researchers, as well as their university setting and professional support structure. Individuals pursuing dual contributions seem to have interests more akin to those of an engineer than a traditional scientist, and an entrepreneur more than an intellectual.

The generalist seems to have a strong need to tinker, while the theory specialist is more inclined toward reflection. Hence, the dualist is more likely to have the cognitive style of an accommodator, who begins an investigation with few preconceived ideas about what information is important to examine, which models are relevant, or whether previous conceptions of the phenomenon are even valid. In contrast, the theory specialist is more likely an assimilator, who relies heavily on explicit or implicit models as frames of reference for organizing and explaining new information and is less receptive to the need to redefine or discard accepted schemes.

The institutional context of researchers also has a significant impact on the nature and scope of their research products. The theorist works best in a university that places a high premium on research productivity and evaluates researchers' impact on the basis of their contribution to basic knowledge. In contrast, dualists operate best in a university setting that has a much higher tolerance for research projects with a long gestation period. Further, to foster a dualistic orientation in university settings, a researcher's impact must be assessed on the basis of a much broader range of professional contributions, including activities outside the academy. And in order to facilitate access of researchers to organizations, it is helpful for the university to have a high profile in the business community, as is most likely in large urban centers.

Finally, there are important differences in the characteristics of the profession that foster a specialist or dualist research orientation. The theoretical specialist can be trained in a traditional graduate program in which specialized knowledge and research skills can be acquired in a reasonably short period. In contrast, the breadth of the training necessary for making dual contributions would require a much more comprehensive and hence longer training program. To encourage more generalist research in the field, our research norms and opportunities would also need to be altered so that, for example, journal articles were required to discuss implications for practice as well as theory, and greater emphasis was placed on writing books. The nature of our professional meetings would also shift from emphasizing rarefied discussions of the implications of emerging theoretical frontiers for future research projects to a greater emphasis on articulating the emerging problems in the practice of management. Furthermore, critiques of papers would consider evidence of utility as much as validity.

This comparison between the specialist and dualist research orientations is obviously oversimplified and extreme. We all know individuals who have made the transition with a minimum of trauma, often without moving to a different institution or changing their professional association membership. However, I feel it is still useful to recognize that, for many in our field who desire to shift the focus of their research, the gap I have portrayed appears truly formidable. They are required to develop new patterns of thinking and skills for collecting and analyzing data and to cultivate new opportunities for doing research and outlets for publication. Giving up the certainty of research decision rules based on statistical significance and percentage of variance explained entails a risk of considerable magnitude. This is accompanied by a shift of status from expert to novice and a change in identity from pure to applied that often leads to one's motives being questioned by colleagues and former mentors. This shift also requires a fundamental redefinition of our relationship with practitioners. They are no longer merely "sources of raw data" for our subsequent analysis. Instead they become full partners in a collaborative search for insight and understanding based on the premise that they have just as much to contribute as the researcher.

In conclusion, for me the major contribution of Walton's chapter is the cogent and timely suggestions for how to pursue a dualist research strategy. What remains is further consideration of how these ideas can be implemented on a broad scale under nonideal circumstances.

GROUP DISCUSSION

Driver: One of the things that I am struck by as I look at this is the question of where do people start in all this process. I think you made some assumptions, Dave [Whetten], that I'm not sure I can completely buy. Can we ever get specialists out of their disciplines, particularly if the publishing industry and the journals increasingly reinforce specialization? And do the people who do break out of it ever go through this conversion? One of the things that strikes me as I'm looking around this room is how many of us went through this kind of doctoral program versus a doctoral program in some less disciplined, less structured area that is so broad that we never got squashed in like this. Essentially, we may have had a broader view to start with. I'm wondering if the model that fits, say, psychology training really does fit those of us who maintain the generalist's posture.

Seashore: There's one element in a scheme like this that is missing, perhaps. I think it has to do with the question of when specialization and generalization might first occur. Now, in medicine we have a model of the internship, which has two features: Internship is one way to specialize further. At the same time, it's a way to practice your arts in a complex environment, generalizing, if you please. Now, I would guess that none of us in this room had a proper internship exposure. I'll bet that if we could design programs for the students we're working with, we would all put in something that is like internship.

Lawler: *Question is addressed to Walton:* I heard you sort of being unashamedly opportunistic in your research interest and activities. I heard you sort of saying, ''I was really interested in this issue, but the cards didn't get broken correctly, so I skipped over it and did this.'' Is that a fair characterization?

Walton: Yes.

Lawler: Certainly that's not what you were taught, were you?

Walton: Well, I didn't go through a classic Ph.D. program, so I don't fit what I think is the more typical pattern. Most of the people who went through the program that I went through never became as interested in theory as I was. So I really got my discipline training at the University of Michigan after I got my doctorate from the Harvard Business School. So I picked that up as a post-doctoral [experience]. In a sense my activities were narrow to begin with. In college, I hadn't written theory, and at that point in time I wouldn't have written it. And in some sense I was narrow in my professional activities and was not involved in practice for a few years.

Argyris: I remember that God-awful fear I had when all of you came to Yale that somehow the department was going to have a particular view. If Chris [Argyris] at that time was interested in T-groups, then everybody had to be interested in T-groups. And the big fear I had was that somehow the department was going to create a norm that something was in and something was out. I think I was blind to the extent to which I felt free to advocate my position and think that it wasn't upsetting other people.

   I wonder what senior people do when they are heading departments or whatever to create some of the climate that we're talking about? Maybe there's something we can do at the undergraduate and the graduate level.

   The thing I felt pretty good about was to try to find places where I could use my status to bring in a younger person. And I did it two ways. I literally, I guess you'd say, bribed the people on top. I'd say, "Well, here's my normal fee, I'm going to cut it 40 to 50 percent. You've got to give the younger person (a) a chance to come in and (b) some money." I thought that some people, therefore, got immediately very close to the top and then they couldn't think like "techies" anymore, so to speak, because those people up there were asking them questions.

Mitroff: I'm not sure the only way to get a disciplined mind, which is the most important thing and not the same as a disciplinary mind, is to go through the current specialties. I know what that produces. I am less convinced from my own personal life that people who are at a younger stage ought to suffer the same path that I have. I don't believe in childbeating. I believe in breaking the pattern. I really mean that. Why can't we break the pattern?

Lawler: I can remember Chris—thinking back to our days at Yale—one of the opportunities we had there was to create a Ph.D. program. Each one of us, I think, wanted to recycle our own graduate training program. It was very interesting. Chris eloquently described the Cornell program as what we should follow at Yale. And I described the Berkeley program, and Richard [Hackman] described the Illinois program, and we ended up not being (at least not in our initial thoughts) very creative about how to break the mold. Ultimately, through banging off of each other, we did some things that were different from any one of us. But there was a real tendency to try to replicate what we had gone through as the initiation rite that everybody else had to go through.

Hackman: I don't think we ought to run people through the horrors of the initiation rites that some of us had to go through, but I do want to put in a good word for discipline. Not disciplines, but discipline. This may be real conservative and old and stuff, but I think it's real important to get competent at something that is your base, that you know you're good at, from which you can then move and explore. I think there has to be a comfortable home where you're really confident. One of the things that childbeating does—no, forget the childbeating. One of the things that going through some kind of a discipline-focused program does is give you a good base from which to move. And as I look at the people around the table who have innovated, most of them had something from which they could go. I am just about fed up with the seventeenth successive innovative dissertation that is going to rely-on-unstructured-interviews-and-I'll-make-something-of-it-later. Okay. It just is not very innovative after they're going through that, but they think it's innovative because they're not going to be trampled by all the methodological this, that, and the other. So that's my kind of conservative part.

The part of what Dick [Walton] said that I wanted highlighted was when he was taken on by Whitsett and Yorks for being too much of an advocate. Dick's response is ''In fact, I was making two separate but related assertions: (1) that, on the basis of limited empirical evidence and available theory, I was confident that these principles are widely applicable to American work organizations and (2) that, on the basis of my diagnosis of society and my personal values, I favored the wide application of these principles." So there's a data statement and there's a value statement. I think in Dick's work there is the competence base from which he works, and there is a coming to terms with what his values were, which, as I read his paper, then forced him to confront some behavioral requirements that he had to do to try to actualize those values in terms of the kinds of innovations and methods—the kind of variables that had to be addressed that maybe he hadn't looked at before: the opportunism in the work that you referred to. So I am for getting explicit about the values, and I am very much for disciplined activities as a place from which to start.

Walton: Experimental methodology, that "very narrow, non-relevant" methodology, I found, never entered into my repertory, but I tried it. One of the things it taught me was how to go up and down that abstraction ladder, because I eventually had to operationalize something and I realized how much art there was in that, but so that's an example of where I think some disciplinary training teaches you a particular kind of discipline, to master a limited amount of knowledge. I think there's a real advantage to that.

Lundberg: Some people are concerned about role conflict between the consultant/problem solver and the theoretician. In my experience I don't get that role conflict if I understand that what I'm doing is going up and down the ladder of abstraction.

Walton: Where I see the possible role conflict is: Given a set of values, how can you trust me to read the data objectively? Am I not going to find in the data that which confirms my own values? And I think that's a real caution. Now, I don't think that has anything to do with going up and down the abstraction ladder.

The kind of dialogue I have with a practitioner better be pretty close on the abstraction ladder. It is usually more useful if it is either at the lowest level or up one or two levels—whereas in theory, I probably inch up another level or so. I just came from two days of meetings. We were doing the shipping study. The saga is unfolding. We got our data from European shipping industries, and we brought them to the top fifteen CEOs in the shipping industry, nine of the eleven labor leaders, and members of the coast guard and the government there. I am really interested in the theoretical question of how you explain rate of adaptation in one country versus another. If I had worried about that problem in the same terms that I worry about it in my study, if I had talked about it to that group, I would simply have gotten nowhere at all. So I find that I am working at a different level, the lower abstraction level, when I am in a practitioner sort of mode.

Lawler: *Question is addressed to Argyris:* What were you thinking when Richard was singing the praises of discipline training?

Argyris: In one form or another, both Dick and Richard [Hackman] are saying, especially if we are going to be applied, we have a terribly important responsibility to find some way of knowing the validity of statements like "I'm doing something new" or "This is good for you" and so on. I think you can learn this if somebody holds your nose to a grindstone, so to speak, whatever the discipline is. That part I buy. What I don't buy is the rigidity that goes along with it. I think the ethnomethodology approach and the observational approaches have gone hog wild in some schools precisely because students don't have to be rigorous about anything. So I would buy the notion of discipline.

Kilmann: I think if we retrace where we got most of our learning from, at least for me, it has certainly been after the degree. What kinds of experiences have we had? We can go to the internship or the postdoctoral or the kinds of sequences that Dick described in his chapter, but you can't get a lot of that in the doctoral program. So instead of spending our time redesigning doctoral programs, we might say, what is the bare minimum of discipline and background we have to give, and then, in our postdoctoral work and positions of faculty put people into settings where [this other kind of learning opportunity opens up]. I also found that as I got tenure and as I became a full professor, I learned a hell of a lot more. It seems as that freedom opens up, so does the choice for learning. I don't think everyone takes it, but I think that can happen. I don't think it's in that structured experience in graduate school that we learn the kinds of things we are talking about here.

I think the discipline is in the philosophy of science and in research methodology. You can learn the simple-machine models, but I think much beyond that in terms of learning levels of abstraction and learning to work with practitioners and trying to find something that's important and real—I'm not sure that can be done in course work, seminars, and comprehensive exams. I think it has to be done using on-line involvement.

Mitroff: The issues are discipline, structure, competency, rigor. I agree with that. That's not the answer. The question is: What form of discipline? What form of structure and rigor? What form of competency? Look, every one of us in this room can tell one another how we went through and got our competency. That doesn't answer the question. That may be sufficient at best, but it does not answer the necessity question. The question I think really facing us is: If one had to design training for disciplined thinking, structure, competency, and rigor (only somebody who didn't understand knowledge would be against those things), what are the forms that are appropriate for the kind of problems out in the firing line, beyond traditional? That's a different set of questions. I went through the machine and I did my experimental psych, engineering part, human factors, and all that. I'm glad I went through that childbeating to a certain point, but Chris also raised the question, how do you keep from being locked in? I'm afraid most people just get locked in. They just get horribly locked in, and they don't get out of it the rest of their lives. Now, I don't know how to crack that. I don't.

Pettigrew: We are defining this problem of how to produce this chap who is wonderful in theory and wonderful in practice as an individual problem and therefore assuming the answer is the training solution. If we could come up with the best doctoral program, my goodness, it's not suddenly all going to go away. I think that is part of it, of course, but I want to go over some other things. I think the local cultures created by the kind of people that are around this table at the moment are a very important part of that. I think about Richard's comment about these seventeen poor Ph.D. students at Yale all using unstructured methods and Richard standing over them and saying, "Innovate, innovate, innovate." I can imagine looking at the size of Richard, who is quite a big chap, that many of them might feel that the way to answer that problem is to say, "Well, how does Richard Hackman innovate? Well, I'll do it that way." I think climate creation in local academic cultures in particular institutions is a very important factor. A much broader factor, but nevertheless a lever, is the creation of professional climates in the broader sense. It seems to me that most of the people in this room are on the boards of well-known academic journals. In that sense they are in a position to review other people's work. They are also on the boards of, I assume, the National Science Foundation and the Social Science Research Council and whatever bodies there are for handing out money to other people. Therefore they are in a position to influence how money is distributed and what kind of work is defined as worthy. Take, for example, John Van Maanen's issue of the *Administrative Science Quarterly,* December 1979, devoted to qualitative research. That's essentially a political statement: the use of an academic journal in order to say, here is a kind of research, this is what it is, this is how it goes on, this is what people are doing, this can be done, this kind of research.

Another lever can be pulled if we choose to pull it, and I think here we have to be somewhat opportunistic. The extent of the economic change in Europe at the moment is causing universities to rethink considerably their role in society. That kind of basic questioning about what universities are all about also provides an opportunity for those people who want to change standards, norms, issues about reward systems. Changes in economic context and its relationship to the organizations as a unit of analysis offer another opportunity, in fact, to redefine concepts of standards.

All of those things we have to think about as levers to be pulled, not just what is the nature of the doctoral program that we happen to have at our university.

Driver: I agree with what you've been saying. We've been doing a lot of work with companies, and we've been looking at this whole problem of culture and the individual. One of the things that I find are not going to solve a problem like this is an early-on solution. I think it is a sequential one. The thing that strikes me about Dick's career is, the cyclic nature of the generalist's career. There are what we call spiral patterns in their careers, where they expand for a while and get some theoretical ideas, then come in on an application mode for a while, and then expand back out again in a series of cycles, which I think is very nicely described in Dick's chapter. What strikes me as very important in organizations is the support system that either does or does not exist to deal with people during those cycles. I'm not sure we are very conscious of that and how we manage that in almost any organization. Particularly important is the problem of the withdrawal phase, where you're kind of reconceptualizing, you're not producing a lot, you're not grinding out a lot of results. I suggest that until you become a full professor with tenure, it is almost impossible to think that way. And even in some institutions as full professors it's very difficult to do that. So what we tend to reinforce, I think, is increasing specialization, holding on to your technological base and becoming increasingly specialized. It's only some institutions that support the spiral kind of career process.

S. Mohrman: It seems to me that, really, what we are talking about is, are we interdisciplinary or are we not interdisciplinary, and what does that mean? My Ph.D. training, I have since found out, was very strange in that it *was* interdisciplinary. We literally took three courses in every social science department, and we came out with the methodology and the basic theory of every social science, and every one of us has had lots of articles rejected for the same reason, which was "Why are you bringing so many kinds of literature into your literature search?" It comes over and over again. But the things we had to do were learn how to do a good ethnomethodological study and a good quasi experiment and a good social psychological experiment and others. We had to do them all. I expected to come into a department that had people who were good at each. I was absolutely amazed to come into departments of organizational behavior where there were people who were good at only one kind of research, and there was no one to work under if you wanted to do other kinds of research, and not only that, you were not encouraged to go to someone that you could work under. In fact, you were encouraged not to. I remember suggesting to one of our doctoral students here to get a sociologist on his doctoral committee who was good at ethnomethodological studies and sociological theory, and his response was, it would be easier to get my dissertation through if I have OB people because they don't know about that stuff. I think that that is a really telling statement about how we are trained and what we are prepared for.

Lawler: I was struck like Sue [Mohrman]. Why does our OB world end up with a bunch of ethnomethodological studies that are, in effect, bad studies? If we open our arms to new, broader research methodologies and yet we seem to agree that what is going on is simply bad research, not creative, not innovative, just bad research, does it have to be that way? Certainly there can be discipline and rigor and good science in doing ethnomethodology. I also felt a little bit like, well, gee, is it any worse to do a bad ethnomethodological dissertation than it is to do another test validation study?

Finally, I was intrigued, as we were talking about Dick's chapter and Dick's work, that we never raised the issue or challenged the assertion that his work indeed did contribute to both theory and practice. Why is that? Is it because it is incredibly obvious? Do we have clear-cut criteria that led us to say, here's what it is about, could we state why it is that Dick's research seems to contribute to both? Or are we just being polite?

REFERENCES

Glaser, B. G., and Strauss, A. L. *The Discovery of Grounded Theory: Strategies for Qualitative Research.* Chicago: Aldine, 1967.

Walton, R. E. "Advantages and Attributes of the Case Study." *Journal of Applied Behavioral Sciences,* 1972, *8* (1), 73–78.

Whitsett, D. A., and Yorks, L. "Looking Back at Topeka:
General Foods and the Quality of Work-Life Experiment."
California Management Review, Summer 1983, pp. 93–109.

7   Andrew M. Pettigrew

⚜ ⚜ ⚜ ⚜ ⚜ ⚜ ⚜ ⚜ ⚜ ⚜ ⚜ ⚜ ⚜ ⚜ ⚜ ⚜ ⚜

Contextualist Research: A Natural Way to Link Theory and Practice

Contrary to the way the practice of research is often taught and written up, the activity of research is clearly a social process, not merely a rationally contrived act. Further, it is more easily characterized in the language of muddling through, incrementalism, and political process than as rational, foresightful, goal-directed activity. Indeed, it seems naive and two-faced of us to recognize the now familiar notions that problem-solving and decision-making processes in organizations include elements of political process (Pettigrew, 1973a), incrementalism (Quinn, 1980), and garbage can (March and Olsen, 1976) and yet to continue to think of our own research activities in organizations as if they were exercises in technical rationality. As Beveridge (1950), Mitroff (1974), and others have told us, the rationality of scientific activity has its artistic and subjective sides, and cer-

The research reported in this chapter was partly supported by a Personal Research Grant awarded by the British Social Science Research Council.

tainly the starting assumption of this chapter is to regard research as a craft process, not merely as the application of a formal set of techniques and rules.

Although the kinds of research tasks tackled by qualitative researchers are more unstructured than those favored by more quantitative scholars, and although on the face of it the craft metaphor may appear to fit the more interpretative process used by qualitative researchers, all research involves the application of skills, knowledge, and the person to a variety of problems in a variety of contexts. In that sense, it is a craft activity involving skills of individual judgment within a system of collective rules and communication. But of course, as Morgan and Smircich (1980, p. 491) remind us about a system of collective rules and communication, "The choice and adequacy of a method embodies a variety of assumptions regarding the nature of knowledge and the methods through which that knowledge can be obtained, as well as a set of root assumptions about the nature of the phenomena to be investigated." So even while we are members of a community, an invisible and visible college, we are also carriers of different root assumptions nurtured and reinforced in the different societal, academic, and political contexts where we practice our craft. These root assumptions, when crystallized into the various academic subcultures, or paradigms, or rationalities, that quite normally and naturally divide and identify us, provide the systems of meaning that inform the kinds of individual judgments we make in the research process: what we choose to study, how we choose to study it, what literature we do or do not read, how and with whom we develop relationships in research sites, what we are capable of seeing and making sense of, how we make connections between concepts and data, our capacities for intuition, insight, persistence, craftiness, and courage in getting into and out of research situations, and the extent to which our research is useful for theoretical development and practice.

Already in this chapter, I have used the convenient dichotomy between quantitative and qualitative research, although I recognize that, like most dichotomies, it conceals as much as it illuminates. For one thing, much research of a qualitative character involves measurement, and measurement of an opposite nature—that is, created for and sensitively linked to the contextual nuances and systems of meaning in a particular research site or set of sites. Apart from the fact that quantification by qualitative researchers confounds the quantitative/qualitative dichotomy, the more basic objection to the dichotomy is that qualitative research stands for a set of approaches to research informed by the various rationalities or partial world views brought to a problem, rather than just a particular set of techniques. The important thing to recognize is not whether researchers can be divided along the qualitative/quantitative dimension and therefore whether one should give exclusive credence to differences in rationalities, assumptions, and orientations of researchers as they influence theory and method and thus the link among theory, method, and practice. Recent writing by Burrell and Morgan (1979) has been helpful in linking debates about research methods in the social sciences to assumptions about ontology, epistemology, and human nature, but that kind of broad, paradigmatic way of classifying world views of researchers in organizational analysis has to be complemented by expositions of a more practical, down-to-earth kind about the theory or method of research in action if we are to develop our understanding of the craft skills of organizational research.

At the level of mere technique or method, which admittedly is a too limiting way of addressing questions of craft skill in action, one of the differences in the social sciences between quantitative and qualitative approaches is that the techniques and methods of the quantitative work have been effectively turned into procedures that can be described, learned, and practiced. Given that the types of problems and kinds of questions asked by qualitative researchers are, by nature, likely to be more indefinite, it may be unreasonable and is certainly unrealistic to expect the methods of qualitative researchers to be as readily proceduralized as those of quantitative researchers have been. But the fact that describing the craft of any professional activity is difficult—Schön (1983, p. viii) begins his recent book by arguing that competent practitioners usually know more than they can say—does not absolve even those purporting to be tackling indefinite problems through inarticulate methods from trying to describe what they do. This is so because if the qualitative research process includes more than the average amount of intuition, interpretation, and structuring through language, then it is perfectly reasonable for the researcher interested in the analysis of processes to be hoisted with his own petard and asked: ''If this is your outcome, tell me what process you went through to get there?'' It is also because younger scholars interested in doing research the qualitative way may derive some benefit from appreciating the theory of method practiced by a number of more experienced qualitative researchers. Van Maanen's (1983) recent compilation of articles has helped to draw out some of the ideas about theory of method that may be useful, but Argyris (1970, 1982) and Schön (1983) are rare among scholars in consistently and creatively thinking and writing about the craft of intervening in systems for the purpose of research and consultancy.

This brings us to the central question of this chapter— the extent to which research practitioners can say what they know about the craft process of doing research, given that most of their knowing in practice is likely to be tacit rather than expressed. I begin by using some of the argument and language of Schön's (1983) new book, *The Reflective Practitioner: How Professionals Think in Action,* in particular his notion of the constants brought by professionals to their various interventions, to suggest that, at some level, theory of method can be so described. I follow this affirmative answer to the foregoing question by briefly sketching the ontological and epistemological bases of contextualism as a theory of method described in the 1940s by the philosopher Pepper (1942) and recently reinterpreted by Payne (1975, 1982) and then move on to consider weaknesses in the current literature on organizational change and how the theory and practice of organizational change could benefit from research grounded in a contextualist approach. The contextualist approach is then exemplified by my own current understanding of the theory of method of applying contextualism as a mode of analysis. I go on to argue that contextualism offers some of the conditions for a natural identity of interest and opportunity to conduct research that is useful for theoretical development and practice. The chapter ends by briefly discussing criteria appropriate for evaluating contextualist research.

Schön and Professional Reflection in Action

Schön's (1983) splendidly written book looks at five professions—engineering, architecture, management, psychotherapy, and town planning—and asks the question: What is it that these professionals really do when they go about their daily business of solving particular problems? Having identified some constancy and variation in their patterns of working, he then moves on to consider how the skills he identifies can be enhanced and transmitted to others.

Eschewing narrow notions of professional practice as a rational/technical problem-solving process carried on independent of the practitioner's values and views, in which, in consequence, the practitioner has to behave according to norms of objectivity, control, and distance, Schön depicts professionals engaged in uncertainty, complexity, instability, uniqueness, and value conflict. Although Schön begins by assuming that practitioners usually know more than they can say, he does not treat this as a barrier to understanding what professionals do. Artful inquiry, or "artistry," is seen in part as the selective management of large amounts of information, the practitioner's ability to spin out long lines of invention and inference, and the capacity to hold several ways of looking at a situation at once and thus to conduct a pattern of reflection in action in a unique and uncertain situation. This reflection in action, a kind of patterned yet informal improvisation, he calls having a reflective conversation with the situation.

One constancy across the professionals was a mode of artful inquiry composed of a reflective conversation. The practitioner, whatever his or her starting point, gradually turned the encounter into a frame experiment in which a frame was imposed on the situation while the practitioner remained open to the situation's back-talk. While operating in contexts with this pattern of reflective conversation, the practitioners also demonstrated variability in the constants that they brought to their reflection in action. Schön (1983, p. 270) lists these constants as (1) the media, languages, and repertoires that practitioners use to describe reality and to conduct experiments, (2) the appreciative systems they bring to the problem setting, to the evaluation of inquiry, and to reflective conversation, (3) the overarching theories by which they make sense of phenomena, and (4) the role frames within which they set their tasks and through which they bound their institutional settings.

Though labeling these four features of the inquiry process as constants, Schön does not imply that they are set in concrete. He sees them as changing, sometimes in response to reflection on the events of practice, but at a much slower rate than theories of particular phenomena or frames for particular problematic situations. Indeed, without some level of constancy in world view and appreciative system, Schön doubts whether reflection in action is possible. Without that constancy, there would not be the intellectual space or confidence to allow particular theories and frames to engage with and perhaps be dismissed or modified by back-talk from the situation. Inquiry could no longer have the character of a reflective conversation—it would become merely a series of nonadditive, nonassociative, disconnected episodes.

Although the preceding description gives only the briefest account of Schön's (1983) argument, it reveals enough of the skeleton of the conduct of professional inquiry to suggest that there are parallels between it and the particular brand of inquiry called contextualism, featured in this chapter. Like Schön's practitioners, the contextualist does not begin with a unilateral interventionist stance dominated by values of objectivity, control, and distance under the assumption that scientific truth is out there to be discovered by a process of knowing, like some plum to be picked from a tree. Rather, the contextualist begins with a more mutual stance, attempts to steer a middle course between involvement and distance, and recognizes the relative and multifaceted nature of truth among people involved in the research process. Concepts and meanings are thereby shared and traded in the research process. Insofar as acceptable definitions of acts in contexts emerge, they are not so much discovered by a process of detached knowing as they are created by a process of making.

Thus, Schön's notion of having a reflective conversation with a situation parallels the contextualist's desire not to singularly impose his or her concept of meaning on the actors in the research situation. As Spencer and Dale (1979) rightly argue, in the qualitative and contextualist research process, either meanings are decided by the actors and are negotiated among the actors, the researchers, and the practitioners, or it is clearly recognized that there are multiple perspectives in the research setting.

But there are other parallels between Schön and the contextualist approach to research. Chief among them is the situational nature of inquiry. Because in Schön's view practitioners face situations characterized by uncertainty, complexity, instability, uniqueness, and value conflict, practice has at least as much to do with finding the problem as with solving it. Finding the problem obviously requires detailed immersion in the problem setting. As we shall see, one of the core requirements of a contextualist analysis is to understand the emergent, situational, and holistic features of an organism or a process in its context, rather than to divide the world into limited sets of dependent and independent variables isolated from their contexts. These central features of contextualism—the mutual nature of inquiry, the balance between involvement and distance, the notion that knowledge is created through a process of making rather than discovered through a process of knowing, the importance of the situational and multifaceted character of meanings in research settings, and the holistic study of emergent processes in particular and changing contexts—are some of the constants that contextualist research is likely to bring to the process of inquiry which naturally provide opportunities for marrying theory and practice. I will return to develop that point at the end of the chapter, but in the meantime there is more to be said about the ontological and epistemological bases of contextualism and how contextualism resembles and differs from the other world hypotheses propounded by the philosopher Stephen Pepper (1942, 1966) and the useful interpretation of Pepper's ideas by Payne (1975, 1982).

Contextualism and Other World Hypotheses

In *World Hypotheses,* Pepper (1942) distinguishes among the various kinds of evidence about the world that can be used to corroborate claims to knowledge. Two broad types are mentioned: multiplicative corroboration and structural corroboration. Multiplicative corroboration validates claims to additional knowledge about empirical or logical facts through procedures that end up with people arguing and agreeing that such-and-such is the case—for example, that water boils at 100^0 C. Clearly, this process as required by positivists necessitates agreement on a definition of what is being measured empirically, agreement on the form and nature of the measuring instrument, and similar scores made over many different observations.

Notwithstanding the claims of positivists, Pepper (1942) argues that there are other ways to refine cognitions about the world than through multiplicative corroboration. In many fields of knowledge outside certain areas of physics and chemistry, data are often ''rough,'' relying ultimately on common sense. Pepper (1942) argues that a person wishing to propose that data are the only reliable form of knowledge must have a hypothesis about why this position is held. ''The grounds for any such argument could not be based on data, but only on some hypothesis about the structure of the world. Thus we arrive at structural corroboration and world hypotheses'' (Payne, 1982, p. 14).

Within the category of structural corroboration, Pepper describes four world hypotheses and how they may influence attempts to corroborate claims to knowledge. None of these four world hypotheses is deemed superior to the others; all are regarded as relatively adequate because each has some weakness. Pepper explores the origins of each world hypothesis, arguing that each has its own root metaphor and, in turn, its own truth theory. The four world hypotheses are formism, mechanism, contextualism, and organicism. *Formism* is concerned with classifications of similar objects and phenomena into categories or types; the appropriate truth theory is correspondence—that is, descriptions are true as a result of the degree of similarity that they have to their objects of reference, and the root metaphor is therefore similarity. *Mechanism* is concerned with lawlike relationships between classes of phenomena that are divided and linked together according to machinelike principles. Thus, the truth theory of mechanism is cause and effect, and the root metaphor is the machine. Truth derives from observations of whether the machine works and whether one's knowledge allows one to predict the outcomes of any causal adjustments made in the system. *Contextualism* is concerned with the event in its setting; the truth theory has to be qualitative confirmation, since the context will change and knowledge will also need to change, and the root metaphor is the historical event. *Organicism* is also concerned with understanding the historical event, but it differs from contextualism in that time is unimportant. Organicism is preoccupied with enduring patterns of events, irrespective of time and place; the relevant truth theory is coherence of conceptual structures—truth is a product of magnitude of fact, and the root metaphor is harmonious unity.

In two very useful papers, Payne (1975, 1982) chronicles and interprets Pepper's work in greather depth than is possible here. I use the four world hypotheses just listed, plus a fifth hypothesis, selectivism (developed by Pepper, 1966), to categorize examples of research in organizational psychology that have arisen implicitly from pursuing, often imperfectly, the range of world hypotheses listed by Pepper. Payne makes a number of broad points relevant to particular and general themes. He doubts that many researchers were aware of the epistemological underpinnings of their ventures and therefore what they were selecting into or out of in tramping along their implicitly chosen road. Payne argues that the least research activity has occurred in contextualism and the most under the formistic and mechanistic traditions.

Personnel selection and the leadership-style literature, Payne notes, contain two of the largest bodies of empirical data in organizational psychology, and neither has succeeded in maintaining significant empirical or theoretical progress. Both are formistic in that they have tried to compare people and situations and match one to the other to see which forms are congruent. In the Aston studies, for example, Pugh and Hickson (1976) tried to create ways of typing organizations and then relating them to their contexts. Payne uses Starbuck's (1981) criticisms of the Aston studies to say how little new about organizations and their functioning those studies revealed.

Using the examples of behavior modification, much of experimental psychology, ergonomics, and scientific management, Payne argues that the dominating metaphor in organizational psychology has been mechanism. Not surprisingly, Payne (1982, p. 22) notes that the machine metaphor "has been most successful where man is used as if he were a machine, but once one moves to situations where persons interact to achieve something, or where the environment allows the human freedom to select what he will do to satisfy his needs, the machine metaphor has broken down."

With the benefit of Pepper's (1942, 1966) ideas, Payne has clarified the epistemological base of contextualism and exposed some of the strengths and weaknesses of the various world hypotheses that have implicitly or explicitly been put to use in organizational psychology. Payne also nails his own colors to the mast in arguing for a greater use of contextualist approaches in organizational psychology. We will now have to see whether his espoused theory becomes his theory-in-use in conducting his own research in the future. This, after all, is the problem. Valuable as the classificatory theoretical and epistemological maps of Burrell and Morgan (1979) and Payne (1975, 1982) are, the real task is to go beyond espoused classificatory systems and to begin to disentangle, for example, what greater use of the contextualist approach might contribute to theoretical and practical developments in a chosen research area and what "contextualist" actually means in the conduct of professional behavior in a research setting. In the two sections that follow, I address these points, first by arguing for the benefits of contextualism in research on the topic of organizational change and then by specifying further elements of contextualism as a mode of analysis in the practice of research.

Contextualism and the Study of Organizational Change

Discussions about the relative advantages of different research methods cannot be sensibly conducted, as Pepper's (1942) work implies, without reflecting on the epistemological bases and assumptions of the varying approaches. Likewise, debates about method cannot be usefully informed without examining the relation between the chosen method and the chosen research topic and indeed the way different methods open up and constrain opportunities for certain kinds of theoretical, empirical, and practical developments. Nowhere in the study of organizations is the extent to which empirical, theoretical, and practical developments have been bounded by prevailing orthodoxies about method clearer than in the study of organizational change.

A broad review of the literature on organizational change and development (Pettigrew, 1985) makes the following points, essential to the present argument:

1. The organization development (OD) literature (for example, Bennis, 1969; Beckhard, 1969; French and Bell, 1973) has emerged as a rather precious subculture of theory and practice that has not connected itself well with existing work or novel theoretical developments going on in organization theory or behavior or with advances in thinking about change conducted by sociologists and anthropologists (for example, Zald and McCarthy, 1979; Geertz, 1973).

2. Research on OD has been limited by its autobiographical and single-case-study character (for example, Klein, 1976; Warmington and others, 1977).

3. Research on the broader, more inclusive field of organizational change has been weakened by the limited frames of reference and methodologies used to study change. With a few limited but noteworthy exceptions (for example, Kervasdoue and Kimberly, 1979; Berg, 1979), much of the research on organizational change is ahistorical, aprocessual, and acontextual. In this respect, the area of organizational change and development merely reflects the biases inherent in the social sciences generally and in the study of organizations in particular. A consequence is that the field of organizational change and develop-

ment is characterized by limited attempts at theoretical development, few theoretical debates, and very limited empirical findings. Remarkably few studies of change actually allow the change process to reveal itself in any kind of substantially temporal or contextual manner. Studies of innovation are, therefore, often preoccupied with the intricacies of particular changes, rather than the dynamic of changing.

4. The ahistorical and aprocessual form of much research on organizational change results in theoretical limitations that derive from treating the change project as the unit of analysis. Change in this mode of analysis is regarded either as a single event or as a set of discrete episodes somehow separate from the immediate and more distant antecedents that give those events form, meaning, and substance. Not only do such episodic, or project and program, views of change treat innovations as if they had a clear beginning and a clear end, but also, when they limit themselves to "snapshot" time-series data, they fail to provide data on the mechanisms and processes through which changes are created (for example, Bowers, 1973; Franklin, 1976).

The point being made here, of course, is that the research findings on change are method-bound. Time itself sets a frame of reference for what changes are seen and how those changes are explained. The more we look at present-day events, the easier it is to identify change; the longer we stay with an emergent process and the further back we go to disentangle its origins, the more likely we are to identify continuities. Where we sit influences not only where we stand but also what we see. Without longitudinal data, it is impossible to identify the processual dynamics of change, the relation between forces of continuity and change, and therefore the indissoluble link between structure and process.

5. But not only has research on change been limited theoretically and empirically by its ahistorical and aprocessual character, there are also restrictions emanating from the acontextual nature of research on organizational change. If studies of change that do not incorporate antecedent conditions and processual dynamics are limited enough, further problems arise when processes are not analyzed in their present-day and emerging contexts. Although studies of, for example, job design have often

been criticized for ignoring the varying contexts in which such changes have been introduced (Daniel and McIntosh, 1972; Pettigrew, 1976), there is a growing recognition of the role of contextual variables in influencing the content and pace of organizational change (Mohrman and others, 1977; Lewicki, 1977; Elden, 1978).

There are a number of important considerations in delineating and using the contextual variables in any analysis of organizational change. One factor that distinguishes the work of, for example, Mohrman and others (1977), Lewicki (1977), Elden (1978), and Kervasdoue and Kimberly (1979) is how they define context. Of these authors, the first two define context as a combination of intraorganizational variables and some notion of organization environment. Meanwhile, Elden (1978) and Kervasdoue and Kimberly (1979), with varying degrees of specificity, draw on intraorganizational, organization environmental, and socioeconomic contextual variables.

In a forthcoming book, Pettigrew (in press) shows how long-term processes of continuity and change can be profitably analyzed in a contextualist analysis, drawing on features of intraorganizational (inner context) and socioeconomic and political (outer context) levels of analysis.

6. Two other points are worthy of note about existing theorizing on change processes. The first issue relates to the theoretical and practical inadequacies of the highly rational and linear theories of process that drive much of the literature on innovation and planned organizational change. These planned theories, many of them with highly prescriptive and deterministic phases or stages (Lippitt and others, 1958; French and Bell, 1973; Zaltman and others, 1973), are both inadequate ways of theorizing about what actually happens during the change process and overly simple guides for action. The field of organizational change badly needs theoretical development along the lines of the literature on organizational decision making, where there are now a variety of process models of choice ranging from satisficing views of process (March and Simon, 1958) to political views of process (Pettigrew, 1973a) and garbage-can views of process (March and Olsen, 1976).

If the language of process in planned theories of change

is singularly rationalistic, a second problem about the more general study of change is the proliferation of metaphors and images trying to capture, in a phrase, broad processes of development. Each of these phrases is pregnant with its own world view, model of human beings, and explanatory language. How are we to choose among growth and development, continuity and flow, life cycle and phase, contradiction, intrusion, and crisis?

What is analytically clear from this brief look at the biases of method and theory in the literature on organizational change, and indeed from Schön's (1983) advice that, in our reflective understanding of situations, we should leave ourselves open to "back-talk," is: Beware of the singular theory of process and therefore of social and organizational change. Look for continuity and change, patterns and idiosyncrasies, the actions of individuals and groups, processes of structuring. Give history and social processes the chance to reveal their untidiness. To understand organizational change, examine the juxtaposition of the rational and the political, the quest for efficiency and power, the enabling and constraining forces of intraorganizational and socioeconomic and political context, and explore some of the conditions in which mixtures of these occur.

The logic of the foregoing points about theory and method indicates that the study of organizational change is now at the stage where theory and knowledge are required mainly to understand the dynamics of changing alternative contexts, using a framework of analysis that can incorporate different levels of analysis with varying degrees of explanatory immediacy and distance from the change process under examination. In order to do this, the field has to move beyond the useful but mechanical statements of contingency theory that emphasize the interconnections between a state of the environment and certain requirements for structure, behavior, or change. It must begin to examine how and why changes occur in different organizational cultures and political systems, under different socioeconomic conditions, through time.

Such an analysis recognizes that theoretically sound and practically useful research on organizational change should involve the continuous interplay of ideas about the *context* of change, the *process* of change, and the *content* of change, together with skill in regulating the relations among the three. It will require frames of reference and methods of data collection sensitive to alternative antecedent conditions, the organizational culture receiving the change, alternative levels of analysis and explanations, differing change strategies, and alternative change outcomes. Above all, it will require time-series, processual data in order to see how and why these broad analytical factors work themselves through any particular sequence of events and actions.

Contextualism as a Mode of Analysis

So far in this chapter, a number of broad statements have been made both about the epistemological base of contextualism and about the practical process implications of using contextualism as a form of inquiry. Philosophically, contextualism has its roots in the pragmatism of William James and C. S. Peirce, has its focus on the event in its setting, and relies on a truth theory of qualitative confirmation or falsification. In practical process terms, its constants, as seen by this author, imply a mutual form of inquiry, a balancing of involvement and distance, the importance of the situational and multifaceted character of meanings in research settings, and the holistic study of emergent processes in particular and changing contexts.

I wish now to go beyond these broad statements and to sketch out in more detail what contextualism as a mode of analysis is and how the principles so described can be translated into a series of practical components to inform data collection and analysis in any particular study. I offer this glimpse of my own theory of method as a modest attempt to outline a way of thinking about doing contextualist research in the hope that others can be encouraged to do the same. Presented here, it may appear as an intentionally rational strategy conceived before action, but in fact much of what follows has been distilled after the fact from conducting a series of research projects on decision-making processes (Pettigrew, 1973a; Mumford and Pettigrew, 1975) and on long-term processes of strategic decision making and change (Pettigrew, 1983, 1985). What follows should be treated as inarticulate reflections from practice, an idealized view never to be completely realized, and certainly to be tuned according to the vagaries and surprises of different contexts.

In fact, my own understanding of contextualism in use has developed from the experience gained in those research projects. Since the view about to be reported comes from a comparative and longitudinal study of strategic decision making and change in Imperial Chemical Industries (ICI), it may be helpful to describe briefly the core questions of that study before launching into an account of contextualism as a mode of analysis. Elements of the ICI study are reported in Pettigrew (1983, 1985).

ICI is one of Britain's largest manufacturing firms and in 1981 ranked the fifth largest of the world's chemical companies in sales, after DuPont and the German big three—Hoechst, Bayer, and BASF. The research examines ICI's attempts to change its strategy, structure, technology, organizational culture, and quality of union/management relationships over the period 1960–1983. An important and unusual feature of the research strategy has been the collection of comparative and longitudinal data. Interviews and documentary and observational data are available from four divisions and the head office of the company. These data have been assembled on a continuous, real-time basis since 1976 and through retrospective analysis of the period 1960–1975. Some of the research findings have been formally fed back into the company, and I have acted as a consultant to ICI over much of the period since 1976.

The study explores two linked, continuous processes. The initial focus of the research was to examine the birth, evolution, and demise of the groups of internal and external organizational development consultants employed by ICI to help initiate and implement organizational change. This analysis of the contributions and limitations of specialist-led attempts to create change has led to the examination of broader processes of continuity and change in ICI as seen through the eyes and activities of the main board and chief executives of the company, as well as of the board of ICI's four largest divisions—agricultural, bond, petrochemicals, and plastics. The more than twenty-year time frame of the study, plus the author's closeness to people and events in the company, has allowed study of the change processes in relation to changes both in intraorganizational context and in social, economic, and political context.

A contextualist analysis of a process such as strategic decision making and change draws on phenomena at vertical and horizontal levels of analysis and the interconnections between those levels through time. The vertical level refers to the effect of interdependencies between higher or lower levels of analysis on phenomena to be explained at some further level—for example, the impact of a changing socioeconomic context on intraorganizational context and interest-group behavior. The horizontal level refers to the sequential interconnectedness of phenomena in past, present, and future time. An approach that offers both multilevel, or vertical, analysis and processual, or horizontal, analysis is said to be contextualist. Any wholly contextualist analysis would require the following prerequisites:

1. A set of levels of analysis, clearly delineated but theoretically and empirically connectable. Within each level of analysis, depending on the focus of explanation, a set of categories would be specified.

2. A clear description of the process or processes under examination. Basic to the notion of processual analysis is that an organization or any other social system can profitably be explored as a continuing system, with a past, a present, and a future. Sound theory must, therefore, take into account the history and future of a system and relate them to the present. The process itself is seen as a continuous, interdependent sequence of actions and events that is being used to explain the origin, continuance, and outcome of some phenomenon. At the level of the actor, the language of process is most obviously characterized in terms of the verb forms of interacting, acting, reacting, responding, and adapting, while at the system level, the interest is in emerging, elaborating, mobilizing, continuing, changing, dissolving, and transforming. The focus is on the language systems of becoming rather than of being, of actors and system in motion. (Any processual analysis of this form requires a preliminary set of categories as identified in point 1 above. Change processes can be identified and studied only against a background of structure or relative constancy. Figure needs ground.)

3. The processual analysis requires a motor, or theory, or theories, to drive process, part of which will require specifying the model of the human being underlying the research. Within this research on change, strong emphasis is given both to people's capacity and desire to adjust social conditions to meet their ends and to the part played by power relationships in the emergence and ongoing development of the processes being examined.

4. Crucial to this whole approach to contextualist analysis, however, is the way the contextual variables and categories in the vertical analysis are linked to the process under observation in the horizontal analysis. The view taken here is that it is not sufficient to treat context merely as descriptive background or as an elective list of antecedents that somehow shape the process. Nor, of course, given the dangers of simple determinism, should structure or context be seen as only constraining process. Rather, this approach recognizes that process both is contained by structures and shapes structures, either in the direction of preserving them or in that of altering them. In the past, structural analyses emphasizing abstract dimensions and contextual constraints have been regarded as incompatible with processual analyses stressing action and strategic conduct. Here an attempt is being made to combine these two forms of description and analysis—first, by conceptualizing structure and context not just as barriers to action but as essentially involved in its production (Giddens, 1979; Ranson and others, 1980) and, second, by showing how aspects of structure and context are mobilized or activated by actors and groups as they seek to obtain outcomes important to them.

In this analytical approach to understanding the origins, development, and implementation of organizational change, the interest, therefore, is in multilevel theory construction. An attempt is made to formulate models of higher-level factors and processes, lower-level factors and processes, and how they interact. It is recognized that each level often has its own properties, processes, and relationships—its own momentum—and that although phenomena at one level are not reducible to and cannot be inferred from those at another level, a key to the analysis is tracking the interactions between levels through time.

The foregoing are some broad principles informing a contextualist analysis of process. But how might those principles be translated into a series of practical components to inform data collection and analysis in any particular study? Figure 1 lays out in highly simplified, diagrammatic form a possible series of interlinked components in a contextualist analysis. The figure

Figure 1. Components of Analysis: Context and Process.

Context Variability	*Process Variability*	*Outcome Variability*
Outer context		1
		2
Inner context		3

indicates that a contextualist analysis has three basic elements: the context component, the process component, and the outcome component of the process under investigation. In terms of the practical research questions of gathering data and sorting them into broad categories for analysis, the basic steps may be described as follows:

1.   Describe the process or processes under investigation, which, for example, may be processes of conflict, decision making, or changing. (An important pragmatic question here is to be clear about when and why the process under investigation begins and ends. At what time point do you begin and end your investigation?)
2.   Expose in the preceding descriptions any variability or constancy between the processes. This variability is represented in Figure 1 by the different curved lines.
3.   Begin the analysis of the processes by using existing theories of process or developing novel ones.
4.   Begin the task of pinpointing the levels of analysis in the context and some of the categories or variables in those levels of analysis. Are, for example, the levels in the context to be restricted to features of the intraorganizational context

through which the processes immediately flow, or is the analysis to include aspects of the outer context, such as the social and economic conditions surrounding the organization at any point in time?

5. Having established the levels of analysis and categories in the context, begin the task of describing and analyzing any variability across the contexts through which the processes are unfolding. Seek also to describe and analyze trends and developments in the various contexts through time.

6. Begin to consider the alternative criteria that can be used to judge the outcome of the process under study. This is a difficult, practical research problem. Good sources to assist reflection on this problem are contained in the literature seeking to assess the success and failure and other outcomes of social-movement organizations (Goldstone, 1980; Gamson, 1980).

Important as uncovering these components is to the success of a contextualist analysis, the key to the analysis lies in positioning and establishing relationships among context, process, and outcome. In short, what are the relationships, if any, among variability in context, variability in process, and variability in outcome? It is in the craft skills of unraveling and establishing relationships among those three components of the analysis that the major benefits and principal problems of the contextualist mode of analysis lie.

Using Contextualist Research to Link
Theory and Practice

As Spencer and Dale (1979) remind us, one of the frequent objections to case-study research as a form of contextualist inquiry is that even if case studies can provide internally coherent and plausible explanations for individual cases, generalizations cannot be made, and therefore there is only minimal contribution to a body of knowledge. Such an objection, though plausible at one level of interpretation of generalization, may begin to fall apart when the meaning of *to generalize* is reassessed and when outcomes of research other than mere generalization, however defined, are examined.

In comparative statistical studies, generalization is assumed to be possible as a result of the population membership of samples. However, as Fletcher (1974) has documented, such statistical studies often assign population membership without checking more than a few properties of that membership, so that selection of samples may be made according to dubious classification and typologies. As a result of these procedures, generalizations are made that are simply nonsense.

Clearly, case-study approaches cannot offer generalizability in the statistical sense just described, but even single case studies are capable of developing and refining generalizable concepts and frames of reference—for example, Lipset, Trow, and Coleman (1956), Pettigrew (1973a, 1979), Berg (1979). In addition, where multiple case studies are used in the manner suggested by the preceding description of contextualism as a mode of analysis—by seeking to relate variability in context to constant in process or outcome—they move beyond Pepper's (1942) pure treatment of contextualism in terms of analyzing wholes in context and begin to introduce formist and organicist assumptions by dividing the world into analytical categories and deriving generalizable propositions. This is all to the good, for it reminds us that the practical application of principles always muddles up the elegant distinctions of philosophers and epistemologists.

But before I get carried away projecting generalizability as the sole outcome of research, it is important to counterbalance that argument with the contextualist's desire for descriptive understanding. Systematic description of the properties and patterned relationships of any process and of the changes in context through which such processes emerge and, in turn, influence that context is a critical form of knowledge for theoretical development and, as I shall shortly argue, for practice. In conducting such process-in-context research, it is critical for theoretical developments in organizational analysis that context no longer be defined just as intraorganizational context and that organizational environment not be defined just in terms of the activities of other organizations. We have to bring socioeconomic and

political contextual factors into our analyses, not only because
they are in today's world so empirically crucial but also because
incorporating such a broad treatment of context into our analyses
will release organizational analysis from much of the misdirected
and in many cases impotent managerialism that informs the
"theories" guiding management practice.

Irrespective of the pleas of any interest group for useful
knowledge, it is important that historical research, such as Ramsay's (1977) examination of how cycles of management interest
in worker participation correspond to periods when management authority is felt to be facing challenge, be placed alongside
research such as Walton's (1980), which looks at the fate of individual participative projects irrespective of socioeconomic and
political context. The retort that it is pointless to tell managers
about socioeconomic context because it is not a variable they
can control is clearly nonsense given, for example, Miles's (1982)
study of how the six big firms in the tobacco industry sought
to defend their legitimacy against the antismoking lobby in the
United States. More generally, it is clear from my own studies
(Pettigrew, 1983, 1985) that managerial action is fundamentally located in differential perception and understanding of intraorganizational and socioeconomic context and that context is
not merely something that should be understood but must often
be mobilized to create practical effects. An advisory group interested in creating change must itself create a social context
in which it can survive and prosper. A chief executive creating
strategic change has to recognize that a key element of the politics
of organizational change is to know how the context of strategy
can be mobilized to legitimate the content and process of any
strategic adjustment. People who understand the political and
cultural system of their organizations and the impact of changing economic and social trends on the emergence and dissolution of old issues, values, and priorities and the rise of new ones
are at least beyond the starting gate in formulating, packaging,
and influencing the direction of organizational change.

The preceding points illustrate how questions of levels of
analysis, the vertical component of contextualism, can influence
the kinds of theoretical questions posed, empirical generaliza-

tions made, and statements of practice possible. The same logic can be applied to the horizontal component of contextualism, the concept of time incorporated into the analysis. Earlier in this chapter, I argued that the prevailing orthodoxy in the study of organizational change is to treat the change project, episode, or program as the unit of analysis and thereby to detach the analysis of change from the context that provides form, meaning, and substance to that change episode. This episodic view of change can lead to some thoroughly misleading statements about the success of any change project and can misdirect the problem of managing or diffusing particular innovations to the question: How can the change project or proposal be implemented with minimal resistance or maximal support? This kind of honest but theoretically misdirected managerialism has, of course, bred a massive response in the literature on resistance to change, of which some of my own writing may be considered a part. However, a methodological approach that encourages theoretical and empirical developments about long-term processes of continuity and change and, in particular, that addresses questions about the deep-seated, organizational cultural roots of power systems and the strategies emanating from them leads us prescriptively to consider managing change processes in terms of keying into the natural processes of inertia and change occurring in an organization and its context. The practice question is thereby posed less in terms of how the change project or proposal, through whatever form of political agility or "authentic" process, can be implemented and more in terms of how existing processes can be speeded up, how the conditions that determine people's interpretations of situations can be altered, and how contexts can be mobilized to achieve practical effects, in order to move the organization, perhaps additively, in a different direction.

The foregoing discussion of how contextualism as an approach to inquiry can influence the asking and answering of questions of theory and practice should not detract from the essential summary point I wish to make in this chapter—that the analytical approach and process of conducting contextualist research provide a natural opportunity to develop theoretically and practically useful research. I use the word *natural* because of the great similarities between the process of inquiry and action of managers as described by Schön (1983) and what has been described here as contextualist research. Schön (1983, p. 265) argues: "Managers engage in reflective conversations with their situation. The reflection-in-action of managers is distinctive, in that they operate in an organizational context and deal with organizational phenomena. . . . When practicing managers display artistry, they reveal their capacity to construct models of unique and changing situations, to design and execute on-the-spot experiments. They also reveal a capacity to reflect on the meanings of situations and the goals of action."

If that is what managers do, then it should be clear from this chapter that that is what contextualists inquire into and do. The manager and the contextualist both see the world of practice in terms of uncertainty, complexity, instability, uniqueness, and value conflict. Both may be interested in the multiple meanings of events, the placement of acts in contexts, and the recognition that situations of practice can be unique and that practice has to do with finding problems through detailed immersion in contexts, as well as solving problems so found. Both also are wary of standard theories or techniques applied without reference to time or place, look for pattern and idiosyncrasy, wish to balance distance and involvement in inquiry, and, above all, are interested not just in accurate description of what is happening but in the mechanisms that provide opportunities and constraints for making things happen.

Some Criteria for Evaluating Contextualist Research

A fair question to ask any scholar associated with a particular mode of inquiry, whether it be quantitative or qualitative, is: How do you tell a good piece of work from an unsatisfactory piece? In relation to the present attempt to describe the form and potential of contextualist modes of inquiry, the pertinent question, therefore, is: How do you distinguish between good and bad contextualist research?

My views on this question are based on some of the methodological principles outlined in this chapter and the craft-research problems raised by attempting to put that theory into use. I would start with a series of research goals:

1. Precision of measurement
2. Generality over actors
3. Realism of context
4. Theoretical and conceptual development
5. Contribution to particular and general questions of policy and practice

The assumption of this chapter is that scholars conducting contextualist research give primacy to realism of context and theoretical and conceptual development as research goals and, by the very nature of the research process they engage in and the kinds of data they are likely to collect, thereby create some of the circumstances to ask and answer questions of policy and practice. Given that the contextualist explicitly works toward goals 3, 4, and 5, then research of a contextualist character should be evaluated principally around those three criteria. The emphasis given to goals 3, 4, and 5 does not, of course, preclude the use of measurement. Indeed, the generation of opposite measures—measures invented for and sensitively linked to the subtleties and nuances of a particular context or contexts—is an important consideration for the style of research described here. Equally well, the exploration of processes in context does not have to imply single-case-study analyses, although such case studies can be valuable as part of the task of raising new empirical areas for study and articulating novel frames of reference. Where comparisons are being built into the research design, these can involve multiple cases in different settings or multiple incidents in the same physical setting but at different points in time or at different stages in the development of a group or any other system. Where comparisons are being attempted, a prime analytical requirement should be to show how variability in context influences the shape, pace, and direction of the social processes under investigation.

But moving away from these broad goals and considerations, the following more particular criteria can be used to distinguish good from bad contextualist research:

1. Overall, the article (or, more likely in the case of contextualist work, the book) should attain some balance between description and analysis. The role of description is to clarify and establish the context, structure, and process to be explained. In Pepper's (1942) terms, the event should be adequately described in its context—the stream adequately portrayed running through its terrain.

But what is adequate? When does the contextualist researcher stop collecting data? Do you desist peeling layers off the onion only when you or the onion becomes weary or when your eyes begin to weep? Pepper (1942) tells us, of course, that it is a question of qualitative judgment and qualitative confirmation, but that is not very helpful in a practical research setting. Clearly contextualist researchers have to satisfy themselves, their respondents, and their potential critics that the analysis of the process in question has something more than an arbitrary beginning and a perfunctory end. There must be an empirical and a theoretical justification for both the chosen time frame of the study, the horizontal component of contextualism, and the vertical component, the decisions made to restrict the levels of analysis to the group, the organization, or the social, economic, and political context through which the process makes its way.

Another way of approaching the problem of adequacy of description relates to the issue of adequacy of data sources. Was the description of the process based only on interviews with, for example, the OD consultants or with both internal and external OD consultants and with their doubters, supporters, and opponents from various levels of management and, if appropriate, with employee representatives? If multiple data sources were used, have multiple interpretations of events been revealed, and if the researcher has chosen a particular frame of reference to explain the direction and pace of the process, have competing theoretical interpretations been posed or in any sense invalidated by further attempts at data collection and analysis? Similarly, were the interview data cross-checked by archival analysis?

2. These points about interpretation of the descriptive chronology are a reminder that, in many studies, description is not enough. There are, of course, still many areas of life and organizational endeavor where purely ethnographic studies are welcome. Description on its own, unencumbered by theoretical and conceptual elaboration, may of itself be justified when the setting or process under observation is of some significant organizational, social, or practical value or is in some way novel or interesting to professional or practitioner communities. Examples of themes and topic areas in the study of organizations where at this stage in the development of knowledge even purely descriptive work would be valuable include accounts of well-screened and inaccessible phenomena, such as the process of decision making and policy making at the board level and the formulation and implementation of strategic changes.

Even allowing for occasions when right descriptions of normally sheltered organizational processes are worthwhile, a further criterion of evaluation for contextualist work should be the extent to which the descriptive chronology of the process is, in turn, being interpreted by theoretical themes and/or being used to derive theoretical ideas and concepts. These theoretical themes and concepts represent an attempt at generalizability—at placing the work within a wider scheme of things theoretically and conceptually, in a situation where a limited number of cases clearly restrict external validity.

3. Does the contextualist writer also use the descriptive context, the chronology, and the concepts to provide a processual analysis? Are the phenomena under investigation revealed at the "what" level, the "why" level, and the "how" level? Are the social mechanisms operating to guide, develop, and alter the process under analysis clearly specified and empirically established?

4. Finally, as in most areas of social science endeavor, how adequately are the theoretical ideas and concepts in writing connected to the data?

RESPONSE AND COMMENTARY

Larry E. Greiner

The chapter by Andy Pettigrew is one of those tantalizing essays whose title and opening lines I am enthusiastic about but which leave me unfulfilled by what is eventually said. I have the uneasy feeling that Pettigrew has not told us all he really knows about "contextualist" research, or perhaps the subject is such an implicit "craft" that it can only be learned through years of hard knocks in the field.

Pettigrew leads off by challenging academics to look again at how we actually conduct ourselves in the field, ranging from how we gain access to research sites to whether our findings can be made theoretically and practically useful. At this early point —just as Pettigrew was labeling his research a "craft"—I was warming up for an enriching treatise on the realities of field research. We were going to find out how Pettigrew himself had muddled through to produce the excellent studies that he is known for.

But then Pettigrew's abstract "ideology" takes over without delivering on the promise. We are treated to a brief attack on quantitative researchers who cannot see beyond their statistical techniques. Then what follows is a rather vague and general elaboration of something called "contextualist" research that is supposed to show us the way to a more "natural link between theory and practice."

Contextualist research, according to Pettigrew, is designed to capture more of the whole, the history, the process, the environment, and the emergent behavior in organizations. And to do this, he advises researchers to "move into" an organization, do longitudinal research, use multiple methods, and act as consultants by giving feedback to managers.

Now, at this broad level, I agree completely with Andy. He would never get an argument from me that technical rationality overlooks a lot and that we need to encompass better the complex forces acting on important events in organizations. I was weaned on Fritz Roethlisberger, the bank wiring room, and hundreds of case discussions.

So what is it that bothers me, and can I offer anything in place of what I have to complain about? Three issues deserve closer attention: one is the need to establish a better rationale for why contextualist research is essential; second, there are some nagging questions to raise about the adequacy of Pettigrew's conceptual model for developing a holistic perspective; and third is a call for clearer guidelines to link contextualist research with managerial practice.

Establish the Rationale

It is clear that Pettigrew does not like "quantitative" research, since he continuously refers to his own and others' research of a more desirable type as "qualitative." But is numerical myopia an adequate straw man for repelling us toward "contextualist" research?

I do not personally think that the presence or absence of numbers and statistical tests is the troubling issue in our research, nor is it a sufficient basis to persuade me to endorse Andy's model. Let me give some additional reasons that I think Pettigrew would also support. First, we are plagued by a continuing stream of researchers who limit their variable scan so narrowly that they and we already know the unexplained variance will inevitably turn out to be over 85 percent. This same complaint can be made about "case study" types of qualitative research.

A second problem is "snapshot" approaches to gathering data, whether they be quantitative or qualitative. This still-camera approach completely ignores the reality of evolving dynamics in behavior over time. So we end up with superficial correlations that fail to reveal the historical causes or delayed outcomes of behavior.

Still another flaw is the overwhelming use of single-method measurement techniques (usually self-reported questionnaires). I recently thumbed through two of our most respected journals, and I could not find a single article that seriously used multi-methods, either for checking validity or for adding new insights.

Although these three potholes have been pointed out by numerous critics, there are still other subtle and equally troublesome questions. Academic researchers rarely seek or receive open access to organizations; hence, how can they discover what is really going on? Most of us do not even get a five-minute tour through the executive suite. Instead, we dip our rusty fishing hooks in backwater streams and hope to get a nibble.

There is also the issue of whether we are trying to shed light on issues of importance. Serious "real world" problems confront today's managers and organizations, but it is rare to see us speaking directly to them—for example, in examining the organizational and human fallout from leveraged buy-outs. A more preferred research style is to refine our questionnaire for one more try at teasing out a few nuances on an old academic problem.

Establishing validity in our findings is another bothersome frailty in our research. We seem to think that standardized questionnaires, large cross-sectional populations with sufficient controls, and multivariate statistics will do the trick. God forbid we should ever report our data and conclusions back to their virginal sources for confirmation and alternative interpretation! What criteria do managers and workers use to determine whether a research study is creditable?

This last point brings me to our journalese writing style and the obfuscation we use to confuse and bore the reader. Can bad writing be separated from the merits of solid research? I have always contended that bad research can be detected in bad writing that fails to communicate.

A final issue, although my list is hardly exhaustive, is the ignorance many researchers exhibit toward other disciplines and the situational factors bearing on a given business and industry. We still attack problems with a managerial or behavioral bias when a knowledge of economics or technology or political science or marketing might take us a lot further.

Aside from sounding off about my pet peeves, I am concerned that Pettigrew has not articulated the foregoing reasons

252 Doing Research That Is Useful for Theory and Practice

to argue even more forcefully for his brand of research. But perhaps Andy and I mean different things by "good" research, whether it be "contextualist" or some other school of thought. For me the issue is not whether one does qualitative or quantitative research or even takes a contextualist view of the world. In fact, we can do bad contextualist research if we do not have a "nose" for studying important problems or if we cannot communicate our results. The overriding question for me is how we academics can get closer to an important phenomenon in order to describe and explain it in ways that make sense to scholars and practitioners alike so they can act constructively on it. If we took this challenge seriously, then any research that succumbs to the weaknesses I have cited should be called "bad" research and judged unworthy of publication. Unfortunately, this seemingly reasonable standard would put many journals into the bankruptcy courts.

And just to finish off with a further heretical statement, does it make sense to limit our attempts at "knowing" to what we presently call research? Aren't there other justifiable ways of generating knowledge that fall outside the rituals presently legitimated within academe? Surely, much of our society generates knowledge and acts on it without ever going through our traditional hoopla.

My bet is that Andy Pettigrew's approach to knowing embraces many skills besides a disdain for the mathematics of "normal science" research. That is what I expected to hear if he is to call his research a "craft." More about this later, after we examine the conceptual model that Andy proposes for guiding contextualist research.

The Elusive Model

It is a long and arduous task to decipher what Pettigrew means by *contextualist research*. And because the discussion is so abstract, I am not sure that I gleaned more than the general fundamentals, and even then I wavered between confusion and a feeling of "so what else is new?" The concrete meaning of how a contextualist researcher conducts himself or herself in the field is left unanswered.

For much of his chapter, Pettigrew calls on other scholars (Schön, Pepper, and Payne) to tell us about the metaphysical underpinnings of contextualist research. Finally, under "Contextualism as a Mode of Analysis," Pettigrew defines it as "a mutual form of inquiry, a balancing of involvement and distance, the importance of the situational and multifaceted character of meanings in research settings, and the holistic study of emergent processes in particular and changing contexts."

I accept this general definition and am personally sympathetic to it, but the illustrations Pettigrew uses to support it are a bit perplexing. He attacks the large body of organizational change research as "ahistorical, aprocessual, and acontextual," and further asserts that "nowhere in the study of organizations is the extent to which empirical, theoretical, and practical developments have been bounded by prevailing orthodoxies about method clearer than in the study of organizational change." As Pettigrew writes off this vast literature on change, I think of Chandler, Roethlisberger, Gouldner, Whyte, Marrow, Sofer, Lawrence, and Bennis, who have all contributed rich contextual pictures of organizational change. I have no idea what Pettigrew means by the "prevailing orthodoxy" in research method, since there has clearly been much controversy about the diversity of methods used in change research. Why couldn't he have picked on Herzberg's ideological trail of motivation research, or the never-ending satisfaction studies, or the Ohio State leadership saga?

I began to feel more comfortable when Pettigrew turned to his own research at ICI. At last, I thought, there would be a clear description of contextualist research from the author himself. But after only two paragraphs of introduction, the example abruptly concludes with only cursory reference to his contextual model—just at the point where I wanted to ask Andy why a few interviews with top ICI executives could provide sufficient contextual data for tracking the effects of OD change efforts on broader company change processes.

It is only in the last few pages of Pettigrew's chapter that we learn about the key concepts in his contextual model. Basically, the model consists of collecting and examining data from the viewpoint of "vertical analysis" (multiple levels inside and outside the organization) and "horizontal analysis" (processes over time) to determine continuities and discontinuities, as well as something he calls "outcomes."

That is as much as we learn! The reader is left to ask if Pettigrew's way of thinking is any different from the much clearer and far more explicated open systems or natural systems models. I really do not see the difference, but there may be if Pettigrew would draw the distinction.

Perhaps we can discern some unique features if we read between the lines. One is a strong emphasis on history and the belief that the seeds of current events are sown years before. Another is that "context" is everything, not just a murky background surrounding behavior. And beneath all this is the assumption of continuous change in behavior that is captured only in "verb forms." However, Pettigrew neglects to tell us how the stabilizing pull of history can be reconciled with constant change in the present.

We can also infer some theoretical biases. Pettigrew seems more at home as a sociologist with a political scientist's stripe than as an anthropologist or psychologist. Take, for example, his model of the human being, which he mentions only in passing: "Strong emphasis is given both to people's capacity and desire to adjust social conditions to meet their ends and to the part played by power relationships in the emergence and ongoing development of the processes being examined." He justifies the need for such a model by further asserting that "the processual analysis requires a motor, or theory, or theories, to drive the process, part of which will require the specification of the model of the human being underlying the research." Yet, this statement is hard to reconcile with his earlier warning to the contextualist researcher "not to singularly impose his or her concept of meaning on the actors in the research situation."

Another surprising contradiction occurs when Pettigrew, in discussing the problem of generalizability from contextualist research, suggests the need to "introduce formist and organicist assumptions." Although he excuses this step on the grounds of being "practical," we must recall his earlier condemnation of these same paradigms in order to extol the virtues of contextualist thinking. Why can there not be some laws about generalizability that are internally consistent with the contextualist mode?

My quest for clear guidelines about contextualist data-gatherering methods was also met with frustration. Pettigrew argues for "precision of measurement" without acknowledging his prior contention that contextualism is a subjective research process in which multiple meanings are entertained. There is also the recurring mystical statement that "it is in the craft skills of unraveling and establishing relationships . . . that the major benefits and principal problems of the contextualist mode of analysis lie." No description is ever given of these "craft skills."

A final gasp of frustration is reserved for the title of the chapter itself, which promises that contextualist research is a "natural way to link theory and practice." This promise is never fulfilled in any direct discussion, so we are left to inference. Does Pettigrew mean that a more holistic description will lead to better theories, which, in turn, will be transmitted at a later date to managers? What is "natural" about this pedagogical process? Are intellectual insights provided by outside researchers sufficient to move managers into action? How do managers really improve practice when research is going on around them? Shouldn't we at least be treated to a comparison between contextualist research and action research?

The Practice Gap

Despite my carping at the lack of clarity in Andy's paper, I am still in his camp when arguing the value of rich, concrete, and holistic research for bridging the continuing gulf between researchers and managers. This comprehensive approach was once the dominant tradition in the management field with the works of Roethlisberger, Whyte, Blau, and Selznick. But we have seriously deviated from it in our preoccupation with gaining scientific respectability through narrow empiricism.

The values of holistic studies for practice are many: to provide more complete conceptual maps for guiding managers in their diagnosis of organizational problems; to give living illustrations in a language that is understandable to practitioners; and to capture better the realities of an industrial world that moves faster than static truths. Dynamic research is likely to carry far more credibility and utility for managers who see every problem as unique to a moving context.

There is significant value for scholars as well. The perspective gained from holistic research serves to generate hypotheses that can be tested further by our empirical brethren. And the theory developed from this more open-ended research can be just as valid as theory confined to the cross-sectional analysis of a few variables. There is no way that I know of to test the validity of a whole situation through "normal science" techniques.

But the problem of linking theory and practice implies far more than the abstract skills of data analysis and concept formation. Contextual research, in my opinion, requires relatively open access to organizations, and then one has to build a long-term relationship with them. The role distinctions among research, consultant, and employee become blurred and issues of involvement and objectivity are bound to surface. Expectations for feedback are inevitable. But the exchange of data and insight between researcher and manager in ways that benefit both parties is a perplexing task. Such issues lend credence to Pettigrew's notion that "craft" skills underlie contextual research. He defines these skills in terms of "individual judgment within a system of collective rules and communication." But the "rules" are never spelled out, except to invoke Schön's metaphor of holding a "reflective conversation with the situation." What does that look like in practice?

If research is to be a "natural" process, doesn't it have to be an ongoing state of mind and action, whether one is living out in the field or sitting in the bathroom? We should recognize and accept the fact that we obtain data, infer concepts, and test hypotheses in many different ways—by working as an employee in an institution and observing it, as Pfeffer has done, or by teaching cases in the classroom, or by arguing with colleagues down the hall, or by learning from doctoral students, or by going out to consult. If our knowledge-building judgment is honed by all these continuing experiences, shouldn't they be included under the "art" of research? Have we forgotten so easily that Chester Barnard and Peter Drucker never went out to "do research"?

The Managerial Model

I have observed a lot of good managers, and I wonder whether our research styles cannot benefit from their idiosyncrasies. Should we act so differently from managers that neither side feels it can communicate with the other? Are good research skills so different from good managerial practices? Interestingly, the few good scholars I have observed also seem to emulate these managerial traits:

1.   They attack "major problems"—there is no time for trivia or getting lost in the trees. They seem driven to tackle the most difficult and contemporary problems of institutions in our society.
2.   They intervene constantly—without fussing over issues of independence. They learn by going out to the action, not hearing about it from others.
3.   They know an industry in depth after years of long exposure to it. It is a form of knowing that crosses many disciplines and a variety of job experiences.
4.   They act with incomplete data while using their experience and intuition. Events and problems would pass them by if they waited for another study to be done.
5.   They talk in plain everyday language in order to reach common understanding. Hiding behind jargon or abstract terminology only paralyzes action.
6.   They even get confused and call in outside help. There is little arrogance of viewpoint (or paradigm?) as broadened involvement is sought and alternative interpretations are expected.

What if we assume that managers have more to offer us than simply "data"? What might the "mutual stance" that Pettigrew talks about look like in action? I can think of a number of possibilities, beginning with the research site. Why not include a manager as a joint investigator or at least as a sounding board on the research team? Could we not train managers to act as researchers to study their own organizations, just as anthropologists are training native residents to observe their own societies? Managers can also serve as "trackers" who record what is happening when the academic is absent, which is much of the time. The two-way (not one-way!) feedback of data and interpretation seems essential to gain added perspective.

Back in academia, there are likely a number of steps to be entertained. An "executive-in-residence" can be appointed, or even exchanged for an "academic-in-residence." Surely, every doctoral student should be required to go out and write a rich teaching case that has to be read and approved by managers in the situation. Why not make studies of scholars like Andy Pettigrew "in action" rather than asking them to tell us about it? The "classics" of clinical research in our field can be put back on doctoral reading lists and reclassified as "contemporary masterpieces." An applied research center can be established, as we have done with the Center for Effective Organizations here at the University of Southern California, where managers serve on its advisory board and help to make research policy. What about appointing a few managers to the editorial boards of major journals? Should any journal article be accepted without addressing the "practical implications" in more than two cursory paragraphs?

It may seem that I have gone far afield from Pettigrew's concept of the researcher *in situ,* but I am concerned that both he and many of us continue to think of research as a discrete activity that is narrowly proscribed by textbook ritual. Contextual research will not happen simply by saying, "Do more of it" or by writing about it in papers like Andy's and mine. Pettigrew is right in calling it a tacit process, because the judgmental and communication skills it requires are developed and reinforced in many implicit ways that are embedded in our total academic establishment. We will likely have to take a critical and revolutionary look at our own isolated context before real progress is made.

GROUP DISCUSSION

Greiner: Now, when you call it a craft, I don't think it really comes through in your chapter, Andy, what a craft is. In some way I feel like you described a rather traditional researcher going out and gathering data, running it through an analytical model, coming back, and reporting it. Yet for all the rich things you've written, I know there is something else there that makes it a craft.

Pettigrew: All I can do is say in a very imperfect way what some of the elements of craft might be as far as doing research in this manner is concerned. The elements of craft surely have to do with all the aspects of individual judgment that all of us, no matter how we do our research, use. It involves why we choose to study, what we choose to study, what we read and what we don't read, how capable we are of developing relationships with people in research sites, and what we think we see and don't see. I think also the desperately important thing, in this style of research that I'm trying to describe here, is what I would call interpretive skills. The only way I can try to describe this is to again use a metaphor or analogy. Thinking of how a contextualist operates, I think a contextualist has got problems if she or he can only play two chords on the piano, and every time you come into the research site, it's job satisfaction or it's whatever chords one is particularly interested in. I think there is perhaps a stronger requirement for somebody who does research this way to have in his or her head many different frameworks. When the person comes to the piano, as it were, there is actually in principle, if not in practice, the capacity to play the job satisfaction chord, the small-group chord, the organizational structure chord, and so on. One important aspect of how the contextualist plies his or her craft must have something to do with interpretive skill, or you're faced with a mass of material that is very unstructured. The skill of handling that unstructured material could be partly understood as a function of how inclusive the person is in terms of theoretical framework or concepts. It seems that one of the enormous advantages that the more structural or quantitative research approaches have over the contextualist approach as a way of operating is that those approaches have been described and somebody has sat down and said this is how to do a questionnaire. They have been codified in the sense that knowledge has been articulated and clarified, so that in fact it is possible to go and learn how to do research in that particular way. I'm not sure whether it's possible to do that for contextualist research, whether in fact people have tried to codify or produce a sense of discipline for what they are doing. The traditional aspects of this chapter are my imperfect attempt to provide a structure, to describe a sense of discipline that informs what I do.

Argyris: I'm trying to find out how we could specify contextualism a little more. Could I give you an example and you tell me? There are four dimensions, as I understand it, in contextualism. One is process; the others are multilevels of analysis and historical. I forget the fourth right now. Now, if you've had a chance to look at my chapter on the button pushing of the executives and their wives, that is almost no history, to my knowledge, because I saw them for a weekend and we learned something, but it does have process. It ignores a very important dimension that you talk about, which is the more general, social/political dimension, but it has the other one. Now is that contextual? Are those maps contextual, or are they sort of half-contextual, or where would you be with them?

Pettigrew: I'm unhappy with the notion that one has to label things as being contextual. So what is contextual? It seems to me that there are many people analyzing context in different sorts of ways, and that would be very appropriate. It just so happens that in the United Kingdom since 1979, when Mrs. Thatcher arrived, the political context has been very important. Also, the economic context has been crucially important because of major structural changes in economic circumstances. So it seems to me that if any organizational analyst operating in the United Kingdom and studying organizational change ignored certain political and economic contexts in that period particularly, then I would be somewhat skeptical of the analysis.

Mitroff: I think we are missing a fundamental point of this. This chapter comes as close as any thus far to answering the question that Dick Walton raised earlier: How do we know what we know? Andrew lays out a few alternatives, granted that the discussion of contextualism might not be accepted the way it is presented. He says if you take empiricism and rationalism, the traditional, we know that because it matches up with some picture in the outside world, there is good correspondence there. If that doesn't work, we don't have those absolute signposts. What's contextualism? It has all the things Argyris said plus reflectiveness. It has something even more, multiple frameworks, multiple filters if people make clear the particular filter that they are using, which has its own truth test embedded in it. If they spell those things out, then I have a chance to see whether they played their own game. That's the spirit of the way I interpret Andrew's paper. The observer brings with him or her an incredible filter, but now we have some dimensions that he has elucidated that can be used as metacriteria to evaluate a study in this context.

Porter: The only criterion I've heard so far from Andrew is clarity, if I understood him.

Pettigrew: Implicit in my discussion about clarity is clarity of description. If a contextualist can't clearly describe what has happened when a strike is going on, then she or he has got problems. So there is something about being able to go into a situation and clearly describe what happened. I think that Dick Walton was also saying that in terms of how he does what he does. He has to be able to describe clearly what it is he has found when he goes into a research situation. That's one of the starting points for analysis.

Porter: Right. It's clear you see that clarity of description is necessary; is it also sufficient or not?

Pettigrew: No, no, that's not sufficient. In many situations that is enough. In many situations I would be happy for somebody to clearly describe the situation and to regard that as a useful contribution to knowledge. That she or he has actually been able to describe clearly what happens when a group of people have a strike. That in itself is a very important form of knowledge and information.

Goodman: The question is really, then, what does "describe clearly" mean?

Pettigrew: Well, that's got something to do with whom one asks. Again, I would be unhappy with a description of a strike if the people I asked were the personnel manager, the finance director, the managing director of the company, and the production manager of the local factory. I would want to talk to the trade union representatives and to a lot of people on the shop floor. And so the quality of the description will be partly dictated by whom one goes to to ask the question. There is a strong feeling in Europe among many people that perhaps social scientists are often very partial in terms of whom they ask questions of. This is perfectly understandable if one always goes to groups who will give you an easy time rather than groups that give you a hard time. So the quality of the description would be predicated to some extent on whom one goes to to ask the questions.

Hackman: Let's stay with the strike as an example. I want to take seriously your view that knowledge is constructed, a view with which I agree. But it's constructed not only by us, it's also constructed by people in social systems. So if we went to the management group, we would probably find a view of the strike that is their knowledge of that strike. We would find a somewhat overlapping but not totally same view from the trade unionists. If we did the appropriate historical stuff and looked at the processes within those groups, we should presumably be able to document that there are in fact multiple realities associated with that event we label a strike and that those realities are associated systematically with group membership, which is a social science finding. This is the question. Does the contextualist approach then leave us with conclusions like "There are multiple realities associated with multiple groups," or does it leave us with an understanding of the strike? If we were studying the strike, it's the latter we would want to have knowledge about rather than that different groups see things in different ways in constructing reality. How do you go from these multiple realities, the knowledge that has been generated by these different groups, to your understanding, this contextualist understanding of the strike?

Pettigrew: That's where we come into this business of what I was saying earlier about interpretive processes in the head of a particular researcher. It may be an advantage to the researcher, when she or he comes to that point, to have more than one theory of conflict in her or his head. The researcher has this theory and that theory, and at least in principle, she or he can then relate them to this set of events, which may be seen quite differently by different people in the system. At that point, we get to the interpretive process of relating different theoretical ideas and constructs, mode of understanding, abstractions, and language systems to that set of events.

Hackman: Would you say that was a creative act?

Pettigrew: I think that's the most difficult part of the research process, and it's the most creative part of the research.

Hackman: Does the contextualist hold the criterion of disconfirmability in high esteem, and if so, after the creative act is done, how do we deal with that?

Pettigrew: It's hard for the contextualist to get too obsessed with confirmability if the contextualist wants to argue that she or he is a relativist. So the contextualist has got a little bit of a problem there. But I think, in operational terms, the disconfirmability thing is going on all the time, because you're hopefully listening to what the trade union group's interpretation of the strike was. It's a process of making. Knowledge is something that is being made, and so you are leaving yourself open in this reflective conversation that there's somebody to actually convince you that, by God, you really have got ahold of your interpretation of that situation. So in a sense this confirmability issue is part of a process of inquiry that's going on all the time, but at the same time, the contextualist is a relativist. So the contextualist is not, as an end point of the analysis, so uptight about disconfirmability.

Cummings: In this contextualist research, what is the nature of the relationship between the researcher and the people populating the situation, such that those people would see contextualist research as useful?

Pettigrew: Yes, that's a very interesting question. I don't know, really, to be quite honest. Imperial Chemical Industries, which is where I've been working recently, is probably one of the largest and the most visible companies in the United Kingdom. Britain is a very elitist society, and one of the things that Britain does very carefully is to make sure that its elites are not studied. It keeps them very carefully, and the United Kingdom society is nowhere near as open as the United States society. And the elite institutions put blankets over themselves effectively. So the question is, how does one get access to them? And what's the basis for developing access? Because in Britain the game that's played is essentially a networking game. They allow access in a small node or corner of the network, and then you get tested out on that node. And if you're deemed acceptable on whatever criteria, then you pass on to the the next part of the node and then the next part. And this takes a damnable time.

Cummings: So you're earning your right, you're earning your position all the way through.

Pettigrew: It takes a damnable time, but there is some process of evaluation going on obviously while that is happening. One is conscious of that, and one is trying to deal with it in various ways. Maybe this is another part of the craft side of it, of how one improves the quality of the access that one can get in a situation of that sort. I think one of the things that happen in this process, of course, is that people, some of them, will accept that maybe you know quite a lot about their organization. And that part of the inducements and contributions, in a sense, that you're offering them is providing them with an arena where they can have a reflective conversation with you about what you appreciate about their world. So by being around for a long time, you're actually bound to get involved in reflective conversations whether you like it or not. You can't run out.

Driver: Is there any reality in contextualism beyond the perceivers' realities? I am just trying to understand where you are coming from here. If you are familiar with the film *Rashomon*— is there a ghost somewhere that will tell you the real phenomenon? Or is there simply some kind of a summation of all different points of view, which you will try to deal with as your phenomenon?

Pettigrew: That's right, there is no plum there to be picked. You have to construct that plum as a function of the process that I have been describing. That doesn't mean to say that there isn't knowledge about empirical patterns.

Driver: I'm just trying to get at a philosophical view—do you see something beyond the summations of these various people? The second question is: Do you see your technique as leading to prediction or description solely? Is it a technology that you go in each time with to understand that event and only that event, or do you see yourself being able to go beyond and start to build generalizable science in the older sense of that word?

Pettigrew: Yes, I think it would be an attempt to generalize in a number of ways. First of all, by trying to look for empirical patterns, so that when you look at the life history of an organizational development unit or a research unit, you can actually produce process descriptions that showed the OD group in company A was actually rather similar to the one in company B but was really quite different from the one in company C and therefore ask why. And say it was a function of context or a function of process itself or a combination of the two. One would be interested in trying to develop empirical generalizations, similarities, and differences in the conventional sense. One would also be trying to look for concepts that would help one to understand and explain what was going on. There are a variety of process theories, some of which I referred to as political process, incremental process, and so on. The development of those theories is a form of generalization, so there would be two goals. One is to try to look for patterns of empirical similarity and difference, which, of course, therefore means it's rather better if you can do this research using multiple case studies rather than one. The other point is really about the development of concepts or frames of reference—alternative theories of process that can help to inform how well the people analyze particular processes or a variety of processes.

Lundberg: You said at the outset—I mean you sort of told us, but I don't think I heard it and maybe others didn't—that your contextualism is much like being a manager. You said very clearly events, mechanisms, and actions. I hear us, including me and my silence so far, trying to put you into sort of a scientist role. What you've been saying is no, I mean very gently saying, my contextualism is different from the way we've always played the game. If I am even close, I have to report being disappointed at one thing, which is your response to Tom Cummings. He basically said, "Hey, how do you make this relevant, or how is it relevant?" You really didn't say anything. I get two things from that: Either it is a dumb question because contextualism—by definition, I should say—is relevant, or I have to ask you this question: What happens to the people in your research sites when you hand them your contextualist report?

Pettigrew: I think the relevance comes from the closeness that you eventually come to in the worlds of the people that in fact you are involved with. You can actually say: "Well, in agricultural division, don't you recall when they started their OD group, their strategy was not to create an OD department, put a manager at the head of it, and put it on the organization structure? If you set up an OD group and do that, these are some of the dynamics that will happen. In the petrochemical division, do you remember that when they set up their OD group, they chose a different strategy altogether? In fact, they used the network approach for setting up an innovative group. They gave people new roles, and they didn't create an exclusive group of specialists. The consequences of that were these.'' Of course, as you are making these observations, you are starting to posit generalizable statements about the implications of setting up innovative groups that are highly structured and have exclusive styles, and circumstances could prove to have the opposite effect. The relevance comes from the closeness or familiarity with the world and the person one is dealing with but also the capacity to relate that description and closeness to some general principles or ideas that might inform, in the case of this problem, how do we actually create OD groups that survive for more than five minutes? That was the problem. So the relevance thing comes through that sort of dialogue.

Lawler: It seemed to be that we started the discussion of Andy's chapter back at the issue of how do we know when it's done well. I'm not sure we've ever reached a conclusion on that. If I heard the discussion flowing, I think it went along the theme of "You can tell." Those who know how to do it can tell when it has been done well.

Pettigrew: That wasn't the answer I gave.

Lawler: Well, let me finish. At first it troubled me, but as I thought about it more, well, if it is a craft or an art form, no one has ever been able to explain to me what made a good painting or what made a good chair versus a bad chair or what's a good wood carving versus a bad wood carving, but there seems to be some agreement out there. A bunch of people who declare themselves experts write in art magazines or architectural magazines, saying that this is really great. Over time I look at it, yeah, okay, they're probably right, it looks good to me, I'm happy with that. Is that the wrong way to think about contextualist research? I'm not rejecting it; it seems to me this is a reasonable way to look at it.

Pettigrew: I wouldn't apply the metaphor of craft just to qualitative or contextual research. It seems to me that other research modes and styles are also a craft process; maybe the skills might be slightly different, but they all get to the point where intuition or interpretation comes in.

Lawler: Perhaps futilely, but they struggle more with trying to define the dimensions of evaluation when they look at that kind of research. They may not ever make it an objective process, but there is the aspiration at least to make it an objective, replicable, somehow or other, verifiable process.

Pettigrew: Yes. There are problems of subjectivity, of interpretation, and of people making individual judgments in the style of research you just hinted at, as there are in what we are talking about here. That's why I say that all research is a craft process. It's a process of linking the person to a task, to a problem, to a set of circumstances, and the particular chemistry in the relationship between those things will vary as you move from doing this survey to doing that survey, from doing this experiment in the laboratory to doing that experiment in the laboratory. It's all a craft process.

S. Mohrman: The interesting thing to me about this discussion is, nobody seems to be differing that there are those multiple ways of seeing reality. Everybody seems to accept that. But somehow to think you can get around that and to acknowledge it as a wrong way to do research—I'm not sure that any of our methodologies gets us around that.

Argyris: The problem I have is a different one. When I do reflective dialogue, the purpose is to infer a theory-in-use with the intended purpose of helping someone who says he or she has a problem. It is not to get five different points of view. I take a position about what is in the person's head and [decide] I'd better test it, which I think gets to a positivist view of confirmability because I am really taking a position that I can help a person. I can think now of a dialogue that I listen to and go through whatever this is, this craft, and I wind up saying to the woman: Are you saying whenever you're about to deprecate someone, you deprecate yourself first? She says yes, I do that all the time. Next step, how do I know she's not just agreeing with it? So the next step is, we go collect some more data. We wait and see. All this is straight positivist stuff. I think that's what Paul Goodman is saying. "Come on, folks, isn't there an important place for positivism?" I think there is.

Goodman: You're saying yes, but that's not what I am hearing.

Argyris: I know; I like the part of Andrew's chapter where he is talking about the dialogue, but what I think I see him missing is that I take a position that the dialogue is not for the inquiry period. The dialogue is for eventually creating a theory.

Pettigrew: That's precisely what Larry Greiner was reacting to when he was saying, "Isn't this just traditional stuff?" I would guess that there are those basic positivist categories of analysis that can be broadly defined as contextual, and one can look for variability in those factors. There are classes of factors that one can describe in process terms, and one can find differences in process. There are also, if one chooses to use it, classes of things that one can describe as outcomes. Therefore, one can try to posit relationships between variability and context, variability and process, and variability and outcome. That's highly positivistic in terms of its construction and labeling of the world. That's the discipline that I see in this—the understanding of the relationship among those three classes of variables. The outcome of this is not to say that the work can be understood in five different ways. Don't misunderstand that. The outcome of this is not just to say, here are the four interpretations of this situation. One is going to be able to try to draw out interpretations of situations that lead one to certain kinds of conclusions. For example, if you set up your OD group in this way, it will lead to these outcomes. If you set it right up in that way, it's likely to lead to that result. But it might vary as a function of the context. It does have positivistic elements in it in terms of the structure of analysis and the focusing on certain kinds of variables, but doing it in a very open-ended sort of way.

Hackman: I had trouble with the strike. I felt that was more like a historical analysis. I resonated a lot to the OD group, and I would have framed the question: If I am interested in the theory/action thing, how do you create OD groups that survive? If I were going into an organization that maybe had multiple divisions and OD groups, I would do something like the following. I'd first ask at a kind of conceptual level, what do I mean by survival? I would probably come out multidimensionally, and I would ask myself, where do I position myself when trying to get data on those things that I'm taking to be the indicators of survival? Then I would ask, what are some possible forces that might possibly contribute to or detract from the survival as I have now defined it? How can I monitor them? That would be based on some theory, whatever the frames that I come in with, about forces that might enhance or depress the survivability of OD units. Being contextualist, I would pay particular attention to historical things and cross levels of analysis, and I would also ask, what are some of the main groups here? Stakeholders that might generate some forces, including perhaps some forces that I didn't think of based on the theories I brought in here, and how can I get access to and get involved with monitoring what's going on here? Finally, I would ask, what are some main times when there may be a big action about these things that may help me see some things that I otherwise wouldn't see? How can I make sure that I have access to what's going on at critical hot times, budget time or someting like that? Then, I would really try to do all this, probably with a Stanley Seashore Memorial Research Team, because I think it might be hard to get all those things all at once. I would get some data and I would analyze them; and I would create some kind of a picture of what's going on there, but I would also create some conceptual-level hypothesis about what is a relatively parsimonious way of accounting for a lot of the variance and what it is that increases or decreases the viability of the OD groups based on this thing. I would then want to feed back to or talk with the participants to get their views on it and keep that very much in mind as I then continued. Because at this point, I would have some predictions, and I would deal with the disconfirmability by seeing whether the reality that I had constructed had any resonance at all in the system and then use that to keep monitoring in the future, because it should lead me to predict when certain kinds of forces are likely to increase or decrease. I would do that iteratively into the future until I really had a neat theory. Was I just a contextualist or not?

Pettigrew: What you've just described is precisely what I would want.

REFERENCES

Argyris, C. *Intervention Theory and Method*. Reading, Mass.: Addison-Wesley, 1970.

Argyris, C. *Reasoning, Learing, and Action: Individual and Organizational*. San Francisco: Jossey-Bass, 1982.

Beckhard, W. G. *Organization Development: Strategies and Models*. London: Addison-Wesley, 1969.

Bennis, W. G. *Organization Development: Its Nature, Origins and Prospects*. London: Addison-Wesley, 1969.

Berg, P. O. *Emotional Structures in Organizations: A Study of the Process of Change in a Swedish Company*. Lund: Studentlitteratur, 1979.

Beveridge, W. I. B. *The Art of Scientific Investigation*. London: Heinemann, 1950.

Bowers, D. G. "OD Techniques and Their Results in 23 Organizations: The Michigan ICL Study." *Journal of Applied Behavioural Science*, 1973, *9* (1), 21–43.

Burrell, G., and Morgan, G. *Sociological Paradigms and Organizational Analysis*. London: Heinemann, 1979.

Daniel, W. W., and McIntosh, N. *The Right to Manage*. London: McDonald, 1972.

Elden, M. "Three Generations of Work-Democracy Experiments in Norway: Beyond Classical Socio-technical Systems Analysis." In C. L. Cooper and E. Mumford (Eds.), *The Quality of Working Life in Western and Eastern Europe*. London: Associated Business Press, 1978.

Fletcher, C. *Beneath the Surface: An Account of Three Styles of Research*. London: Routledge & Kegan Paul, 1974.

Franklin, J. N. "Characteristics of Successful and Unsuccessful Organizational Development." *Journal of Applied Behavioral Science*, 1976, *12* (4), 471–492.

French, W. L., and Bell, C. H. *Organizational Development*. Englewood Cliffs, N.J.: Prentice-Hall, 1973.

Gamson, W. A. "Understanding the Careers of Challenging Groups: A Commentary on Goldstone." *American Journal of Sociology*, 1980, *85* (5), 1043–1060.

Geertz, C. *The Interpretation of Cultures*. New York: Basic Books, 1973.

Giddens, A. *Central Problems in Social Theory*. London: Macmillan, 1979.

Goldstone, J. A. "The Weakness of Organization: A New Look at Gamson's 'The Strategy of Social Protest.'" *American Journal of Sociology*, 1980, *85* (5), 1017–1041.

Kervasdoue, J., and Kimberly, J. "Are Organization Structures Culture Free? The Case of Hospital Innovation in the U.S. and France." In G. England and others (Eds.), *Organizational Functioning in a Cross-Cultural Perspective*. Kent, Ohio: Kent State University Press, 1979.

Klein, L. *A Social Scientist in Industry*. Epping, England: Gower Press, 1976.

Lewicki, R. "Team Building in the Small Business Community: The Success and Failure of O.D." In P. H. Mirvis and D. N. Berg (Eds.), *Failures in Organizational Development and Change*. New York: Wiley, 1977.

Lippitt, R., and others. *The Dynamics of Planned Change*. New York: Harcourt Brace Jovanovich, 1958.

Lipset, S. M., Trow, M., and Coleman, J. S. *Union Democracy*. New York: Free Press, 1956.

March, J. G., and Olsen, J. P. *Ambiguity and Choice in Organizations*. Bergen: Universitetsforlaget, 1976.

March, J. G., and Simon, H. A. *Organizations*. New York: Wiley, 1958.

Miles, R. H. *Coffin Nails and Corporate Strategies*. Englewood Cliffs, N.J.: Prentice-Hall, 1982.

Mitroff, I. I. *The Subjective Side of Science*. Amsterdam: Elsevier, 1974.

Mohrman, S., and others. "A Survey Feedback and Problem Solving Intervention in a School District." In P. H. Mirvis and D. H. Berg (Eds.), *Failures in Organization Development and Change*. New York: Wiley, 1977.

Morgan, G., and Smircich, L. "The Case for Qualitative Research." *Academy of Management Review*, 1980, *5* (4), 491–500.

Mumford, E., and Pettigrew, A. M. *Implementing Strategic Decisions*. London: Longman, 1975.

Payne, R. L. "Epistemology and the Study of Behaviour in Organizations." Unpublished memo no. 68, MRC, Social and Applied Psychology Unit, University of Sheffield, 1975.

Payne, R. L. "The Nature of Knowledge and Organizational Psychology." Unpublished Memo no. 445, MRC/SSRC, Social and Applied Psychology Unit, University of Sheffield, 1982.

Pepper, S. C. *World Hypotheses.* Berkeley: University of California Press, 1942.

Pepper, S. C. *Concept and Quality.* La Salle, Ill.: Open Court, 1966.

Pettigrew, A. M. *The Politics of Organizational Decision Making.* London: Tavistock, 1973a.

Pettigrew, A. M. "Occupational Specialization as an Emergent Process." *Sociological Review,* 1973b, *21* (2), 255–278.

Pettigrew, A. M. "Strategic Aspects of the Management of Specialist Activity." *Personnel Review,* 1975, *4,* 5–13.

Pettigrew, A. M. "Conference Review: Issues of Change." In O. B. Warr (Ed.), *Personal Goals and Work Design.* London: Wiley, 1976.

Pettigrew, A. M. "On Studying Organizational Cultures." *Administrative Science Quarterly,* 1979, *24* (4), 570–581.

Pettigrew, A. M. "Culture and Politics in Strategic Decision Making and Change." Paper presented at the Symposium on Strategic Decision Making in Complex Organizations, Columbia University, November 9–11, 1983.

Pettigrew, A. M. *The Awakening Giant: Continuity and Change in Imperial Chemical Industries.* Oxford: Basil Blackwell, 1985.

Pugh, D. S., and Hickson, D. (Eds.) *Organizational Structure in Its Context: The Aston Programme.* Farnham, Hants: Saxon House, 1976.

Quinn, J. B. *Strategies for Change: Logical Incrementalism.* Homewood, Ill.: Irwin, 1980.

Ramsay, H. "Cycles of Control: Worker Participation in Sociological and Historical Perspective." *Sociology,* 1977, *11,* 481–506.

Ranson, T., and others. "The Structuring of Organizational Structures." *Administrative Science Quarterly,* 1980, *25* (1), 1–17.

Schön, D. A. *The Reflective Practitioner: How Professionals Think in Action.* London: Temple Smith, 1983.

Spencer, L., and Dale, A. "Integration and Regulation in Organizations: A Contextual Approach." *Sociological Review,* 1979, *27* (4), 679–702.

Starbuck, W. H. "A Trip to View the Elephants and Rattle-snakes in the Garden of Aston." In A. H. Van de Ven and W. H. Joyce (Eds.), *Perspectives on Organization Design and Behavior*. New York: Wiley-Interscience, 1981.

Van Maanen, J. (Ed.). *Qualitative Methodology*. Beverly Hills, Calif.: Sage, 1983.

Walton, R. E. "Establishing and Maintaining High Commitment Work Systems." In J. R. Kimberly, R. H. Miles, and Associates, *The Organizational Life Cycle: Issues in the Creation, Transformation, and Decline of Organizations*. San Francisco: Jossey-Bass, 1980.

Warmington, A., and others. *Organizational Behaviour and Performance*. London: Macmillan, 1977.

Zald, M., and McCarthy, J. (Eds.). *The Dynamics of Social Movements*. Cambridge, Mass.: Winthrop, 1979.

Zaltman, G., and others. *Innovations and Organizations*. New York: Wiley, 1973.

Thomas G. Cummings
Susan A. Mohrman
Allan M. Mohrman, Jr.
Gerald E. Ledford, Jr.

8

✤ ✤ ✤ ✤ ✤ ✤ ✤ ✤ ✤ ✤ ✤ ✤ ✤ ✤ ✤ ✤

Organization Design
for the Future:
A Collaborative Research Approach

I think managers recognize the need to change for a very simple reason: Ten years ago, when they asked a subordinate to do something, it was done. Now, when they ask a subordinate to do the same thing, the subordinate stares at them just a little bit longer and thinks about whether to do it.

I used to manage hardware people. That was easy. I knew just what they did and how to motivate them. Now I manage software people. I don't know what they do. They don't know what they do. Need me? Hell, no, they don't need me. They don't even remember to pick up their paychecks. They're impossible to manage.

We used to be a small, local, paternalistic company. We took good care of our people, related well to the community, and made a lot of money. We're growing and modernizing. We want our people to grow and develop. We want them to think

about their jobs differently. There are a lot of opportunities in this company right now. But all they
want us to do is to continue to take good care of
them. They're indignant that we want them to
change. What's wrong with them?

Opportunity? For what? We haven't had a
promotion in this plant in eighteen months. With
our operational cutbacks, I'm not sure any of us
will ever again move up in this organization. We've
always loved the industry, and living in this area
is great. But I think we're all becoming stagnant.
At least we sure rationalize well about why it isn't
our fault that the status quo isn't working as well
as it used to.

Although the specifics differ, the managers just quoted
share a common concern: They are challenged by changes in
the content of work and the nature of the work force. Organizational and societal conditions are placing new demands on how
organizations are managed and designed. Organization members are spending increasing amounts of time coping with change.
Meanwhile, values are challenged and confirmed, dreams are
built and destroyed, and opportunities are created and thwarted.

This chapter is about doing research with organizations
undergoing change. Our focus is on how organizations design
themselves. We are interested in the range of phenomena associated with organizational design, including cognitive change,
behavioral change, and structural change.

Our interests derive from extensive fieldwork in which
we have actively engaged with organization members in generating and implementing innovative designs. Our roles have been
to join with organization members in the learning process, to
offer advice, to collect data, to guide implementation, and to
study the design process itself. We have been allowed access to
organizations as long as we are considered useful. In order to
contribute to a systematic understanding of organizational design, we have combined the roles of learner and expert. We share
this combined role with organization members.

Introductory Framework

Our attempt to forge a useful research strategy is occurring within a particular framework of understanding, which we will briefly describe as an introduction to this chapter. We believe that organizations are human artifacts created for instrumental purposes (Simon, 1969). Their designs reflect and are constrained by the norms, world views, and knowledge base of the larger society and by the demands of the task environment within which they are embedded. Equally important, organization designs express the values and esthetics of their designers (Ackoff, 1981; see also Chapter Two of this volume).

As societal, environmental, and designer forces change, people try to transform organizations to reflect new purposes, values, and esthetics. The design process is difficult and often incomplete, especially in older, more established organizations. Years later, the characteristics of organizations in a particular industry generally reflect the era in which the industry was formed (Stinchcombe, 1965). It is easier to create new organizations that embody prevailing values, societal conditions, and world views than to redesign existing organizations (Lawler, 1978). Established organizations embody systems and behaviors which are congruent with one another and which reflect the organizing principles that were salient when the organization was created. Reward systems, managerial styles, rules and procedures, and organizational structures often reinforce one another. Attempts to change one aspect of the organization are often countered by stabilizing forces from the other parts (Nadler and Lawler, 1983).

Redesigning existing organizations differs substantially from designing new ones. Redesign cannot be conceived as the work of one person or a small group of persons, such as might occur when an entrepreneur creates a company. Rather, it requires a wide variety of organization members to agree to behave differently. Because organizations are designed to promote certain patterns of behavior, redesigning involves fundamental changes in how people behave and relate to one another.

The problems inherent in organization design are especially troublesome during periods of rapid, uncertain change. In the era of turbulence that most postindustrial societies are undergoing, organizations are being asked to change quickly in an as yet undetermined direction. Traditional and heretofore successful ways of functioning are being challenged. Established organizations with entrenched structures and policies are being asked to be nimble and flexible. Moreover, organization members are being told to embark on a trip with an unknown destination. They are being asked to learn new behaviors with little assurance that the journey will be safe. As one manager engaged in organization design told us, ''We know only that things will be different; we can only hope that they will be better.''

We conceive of research as requiring temporary intersystem linkages between researchers and organizations (Mohrman, Cummings, and Lawler, 1983). Linkages are necessary to achieve cooperation between researchers and organizations. They define the nature of that relationship and determine the purpose and conduct of the research. They have two major aspects: a *content* component, which involves the particular research topic, methodology, and task, and a *relationship* aspect, which is necessary to create and maintain the social connection between researchers and organizations.

Our research content is concerned with how organizations design (or redesign) themselves. This content suggests certain features of the relationship. First, the focus on designing organizations suggests that the relationship between researchers and organizations involves long-term commitments and high levels of psychological intensity. Action-oriented research generally requires long-term commitments because researchers and organization members are jointly engaged in generating new ideas, testing innovative approaches, and trying out different assumptions about organizations. These activities not only take time but invariably produce tension between researchers and organization members. This psychological intensity is inherent in any relationship in which one party is helping the other to change. It is particularly magnified in researching organizational change, where researchers and members are often exploring uncharted waters. The risks of failure and the importance of the stakes are high for both parties.

Second, the joint goals of producing knowledge useful for organizations and useful for the scientific community suggest that multiple stakeholders must be actively involved in the research. Stakeholders comprise those persons or groups having a potential interest in the research, such as research centers, government funding agencies, and organization managers and employees. Traditionally, research has tended to be directed by limited stakeholders, either those from the scientific community, as in basic research, or those from the client organization, as in applied research. What is seen as useful research from one perspective is often seen as useless from the other. Attempts to meet both researchers' and client-organization needs should actively involve multiple stakeholders in generating research issues, designing the research, and carrying it out. This participation increases the likelihood that all relevant stakeholders will see the research as useful.

Now that we have outlined the conceptual framework underlying our research, we can delve deeper into the content and relationship aspects of the research process. We will first discuss the content component, describing certain theoretical and methodological characteristics appropriate for researching organization design. Then we will examine the relationship aspect, providing a richer understanding of research involving multiple stakeholders and high levels of time commitment and psychological intensity among the parties. Finally, we will discuss the larger institutional and transorganizational structures needed to support such research, with special attention to the role of research centers.

The Content Aspect of Research

Research content concerns the substantive part of the researcher and organization linkage. It includes the particular topic of research and the methodology for studying it. A venerable axiom of scientific research is that methodology should be dictated by the nature of the phenomenon under investigation. In our case, research methods derive from assumptions about organizational change or design. (The terms *change* and *design* are used interchangeably throughout the rest of this chapter.) We believe that many traditional research methods are unsuited to studying organizational change, mainly because they are based on assumptions that do not hold in change situations. In the following pages, we first describe a more realistic set of assumptions about organizational change and then suggest requisite research methods, conceptual perspectives, and appropriate uses of research.

Assumptions About Organizational Change

Organizational change is a disorderly, highly dynamic process. Most familiar descriptors for organizational change can be misleading. Our preferred terms, *organization design, organizational development,* and *strategic human resource management,* carry comforting but inaccurate connotations of a rationally controlled process. Yet organizational changes that survive over any length of time typically entail shifting goals, discontinuing patterns of activity, surprising events, and unexpected combinations of interventions. There are many reasons for the chaotic quality of organizational change. Managers must often act without well-ordered plans in order to discover or articulate their goals and strategies (March, 1978; Mintzberg and Waters, 1982). As the change process unfolds, new constituencies may be affected by the change. They may demand modifications in or elimination of the change, reflecting previously unvoiced or even unknown needs and aspirations (Mangham, 1979; Nadler, 1982). Even when organization members have clear initial goals and plans, they may alter them in response to experience (Cyert and March, 1963). Moreover, organizational and environmental changes may render the best-laid plans irrelevant or even dysfunctional (Grinyer and Norburn, 1975).

Processes of organizational change and organizational sense making are interwoven. Organizations channel the ways in which members perceive and act into patterns representing only a small fraction of the possible ways of seeing and acting. These patterns represent socially constructed systems of shared meaning and may be called organizational "paradigms" (for example, Mohrman and Lawler, 1983), "frames of reference" (Watzlawick, Weakland, and Fisch, 1974), "learning models" (for example, Argyris and Schön, 1978), "myths" (for example, Boje, Fedor, and Rowland, 1982), "sagas" (Clark, 1972), "cognitive maps" (for example, Bougon, Weick, and Binkhorst, 1977), or "organizational cultures" (for example, Pettigrew, 1979). Although the perspectives attached to these terms imply somewhat different conceptions of social reality, they share a number of key assumptions. Systems of meaning develop through the repetition of behavior and through socialization processes. They serve as the ground against which figures such as rational beliefs, attitudes, and perceptions are constructed. A system of shared meaning facilitates efficient communication and permits many actions to be carried out automatically or ritualistically. To the extent that a system of meaning is widely understood and shared, it fades from collective awareness and assumes a tacit, taken-for-granted quality. It then becomes relatively inaccessible and difficult to challenge.

Organizational changes and changes in systems of meaning are interrelated. First, changes in observable patterns of behavior are usually associated with changes in systems of meaning. Neither behavior nor meaning necessarily has causal primacy; the causal links between the two are complex and reciprocal (Mohrman and Lawler, 1983). Second, disruptions in shared meaning are extremely uncomfortable for people. Challenges to a group's system of meaning call into question members' views of reality and thus, in a sense, their sanity. Hence, organization members are unlikely to change their systems of meaning unless there are compelling reasons to do so. Moreover, adoption of an alternative or modified system of meaning is often an emotional experience akin to religious conversion. Third, different types of meaning systems vary in the degree to which they are shared within an organization. Different hierarchical, functional, and demographic groups are likely to vary systematically in their constructions of reality (Alderfer, 1977). Some types of meaning systems, however, may be shared almost universally. Argyris (1980), for example, contends that nearly all people share the assumptions of a Model I learning system. Organizational changes may be associated with changes in some elements of an overall system of meaning but not others, and there may be wide variations in the degree to which any new system of meaning is shared in the organization.

Organizational change is a group-level phenomenon. Organizational change is best designed, implemented, and diffused at the group level. It is difficult to change organizations by operating at other levels. Individual change is slow and difficult unless a person's social context also changes, as generations of trainers, educators, and therapists have learned. In addition, individual change as a strategy for changing organizations is too labor-intensive to be practical in large organizations.

Directly changing the organizational and higher levels is difficult. Indeed, major changes in complex organizations cannot be experienced completely by an individual and hence must be comprehended in the abstract. Change agents almost always work with groups, even when their aim is organizational or societal change. Groups exist at a high enough level to influence the organization as a whole, yet they are small enough to be changed without massive infusions of external resources.

Groups are especially important when organizational change involves multiple stakeholders. In our research on organization design, we often create a group representing multiple stakeholders, including researchers, managers, employees, and other relevant persons, such as union leaders. The group manages the design process and attempts to reconcile the different needs of the participants. It serves as a forum in which intergroup dynamics are played out, thus giving researchers a clearer understanding of the forces influencing change and giving organization members greater appreciation of intergroup conflicts and cooperation.

Organization designs cannot be prescribed totally on the basis of prior research. Traditionally, research aims to increase understanding, prediction, and control of behavior. The underlying hope is that if enough research is conducted, social scientists (or those privy to social science findings) will be able to specify appropriate changes for an organization and to predict their consequences accurately. Unfortunately, the relationship between researchers and organizations implied by these goals can result in researchers' sage advice being disregarded. We will address this issue in the next section. It is sufficient to say here that the record does not support the belief that organization designs can be specified appropriately and in detail on the basis of prior theory and research.

Organizational theories can serve as a definitive blueprint for action only if they are elegant enough to have been adequately tested, are supported by the cumulative weight of research evidence, and are powerful enough to account for much of the variance in organizational behavior. These criteria are not met by current organizational theories.

Especially in the area of organizational change, theories are often inelegant, or "ugly" (Mohr, 1982). The temptation to create complex models of organizations is understandable. Many aspects of organizational functioning may be targets of change, and separate theories exist about changes in many of them (job design, reward systems, organization design, and so on). Any attempt to develop an inclusive theory quickly leads to inelegance. Similarly, the systemic nature of organizations means that change in one aspect of organizational functioning affects and is influenced by other aspects. However, any attempt to construct a theory that includes major elements of a system as well as likely feedback loops and interaction effects generates ugliness. The literature is filled with complex, ugly theories (some contributed by us). The problem with inelegance is not merely esthetic. Given the limitations of current analytical techniques, it is simply impossible to test models that include dozens of variables arrayed in nonlinear relationships—particularly when the data used to test these models come from one or a handful of organizations.

A number of reviewers have commented on the lack of cumulative findings in organizational research and in social science research more broadly (for example, Argyris, 1980; Hunter, Schmidt, and Jackson, 1982; Mitroff and Kilmann,

1978; Mohr, 1982). Generally, the more research is conducted in an area, the less consistency there is in the relationships among known variables and the more additional variables are proposed as important explanations of a phenomenon. After hundreds or even thousands of studies have been conducted on a topic, researchers are usually not much closer to cumulative findings than when they began. Instructive examples include the topics of group behavior (Cummings, 1981), innovation (Mohr, 1982), and organizational effectiveness (Cameron and Whetten, 1983), all of which are central to organizational change.

Few traditional theories appear to account for more than a small fraction of the variance in dependent variables (Mohr, 1982). In addition, there is no reason to predict that strong relationships found in one study will be confirmed in later studies, given the inconsistency of research findings in so many areas.

We know of no solutions to these problems. Therefore, our view is that organizational researchers' prescriptions should serve mainly as general guides to organization design rather than as detailed blueprints for action. Organization design is too costly, difficult, and risky to be driven by research findings that may have questionable applicability in a particular situation.

We have presented four assumptions about organizational change: It is a highly dynamic process, it is accompanied by changes in systems of meaning, it is located largely in groups, and it cannot be prescribed on the basis of existing research. These assumptions are not necessarily controversial; indeed, they receive a good deal of support in the literature. We believe, however, that the implications of these assumptions for research and action are inadequately understood.

Implications for Research and Action

Our assumptions about organizational change suggest a new orientation for researching organization design. Specifically, they suggest the following.

Research on organization design should be concerned with change dynamics, sense-making processes, group-level phenomena, and change design as well as with the effects of particular interventions. The research literature on organizational change consists mostly of reports of the attitudinal and performance effects of particular types of interventions (of building autonomous work groups, reward system changes, and so on). It is important to investigate intervention effects, but it is at least as important to investigate other central aspects of organizational change. For example, relatively little is known about the following questions: Why do organizations adopt particular interventions or combinations of interventions and not others? How are new design features actually implemented? What are the patterns by which designs become transformed, diffused, abandoned, or persistent over time? How do different patterns of sense making affect the course of change? When does change precede new interpretations of reality? How do new systems of meaning interact over time? How do we best design groups in order to promote organizational-level change? How do group and intergroup dynamics influence the change process? How do organizations go about designing change when the task is so fraught with uncertainty? When multiple interventions are used, is it better to adopt certain changes first? If so, under what conditions? It would not be difficult to expand this list of questions greatly. Although some research or speculation is relevant to most of these questions, they have not been systematically studied.

We believe that the emphasis on intervention effects, almost to the exclusion of concern for change processes, derives largely from relying on traditional research methodologies. Experimental and quasi-experimental research designs are aimed at making causal inferences about the degree to which a well-defined predictor variable or small set of predictor variables (such as a particular organizational change) affects a well-defined dependent variable. The strongest research designs are those in which researchers can control the field situation in ways that simulate laboratory conditions. Conversely, research designs become weaker and threats to validity become stronger as researchers lose control over such conditions as the nature, scope, introduction, and diffusion of interventions, not to mention the measurement of change.

However, trying to control the disorderly process of change

in order to test for intervention effects may destroy many of the phenomena worthy of investigation. As Kahn (1982, p. 428) recently suggested, ''The suns of organizational change do not revolve around the small domain of the researcher, nor are their large movements defined by the experimenter's small forces. . . . We will learn most about the process of change by studying the full-scale manifestations of that process rather than by reducing it to the size of our experimental powers.'' Generally, researchers cannot control change dynamics. Therefore, change processes are treated as intrusions rather than as phenomena that are important in their own right. Consequently, neither the intervention effects nor the change processes are adequately explored. An example of this pattern is the prevalence of multiple interventions and multiple design alterations. This poses a problem for traditional research methods because it is difficult or impossible to disentangle the effects of different parts of the change process; yet multiple change efforts are closer to the rule than the exception (Cummings, Molloy, and Glen, 1977). Because single interventions are rarely powerful enough to produce significant change in complex, well-bounded systems (Kahn, 1982; Nadler and Lawler, 1983), it is probably fortunate that researchers must suffer through the traumas of having murky change variables.

Knowledge about change processes can only partly come from quasi-experimental studies of each process or subprocess. Even if it were possible to hold all else constant, traditional methods do not capture fully the complex interplay of forces and events that makes organizational change so fascinating and frustrating.

Our strategy for studying change dynamics and intervention effects follows what Lawler (1977) has termed an adaptive research design. It includes several elements. First, there is recognition that the strongest experimental and quasi-experimental designs are difficult to apply in field settings. The best researchers can hope for is some version of what Cook and Campbell (1979) called a nonequivalent control-group design. Second, the researcher tries to cast a ''broad measurement net''—measuring as many variables as possible—in order to capture unintended consequences, unexpected interventions, and other unpredictable turns of events. Third, there is heavy emphasis on qualitative description to supplement moderately rigorous quantitative measurement. Extensive qualitative data are essential in understanding the change process. Fourth, longitudinal research is critical. Finally, semistandardized research instruments are used to investigate multiple cases of a particular type of change. Although comparison is usually difficult because organizational changes, contextual conditions, and change processes tend to be partly idiosyncratic, this approach enhances the opportunities for comparative study.

This research strategy is called "adaptive" because it permits and encourages researchers to improvise and to be responsive to changes in the nature of the interventions. All is not lost if the intervention takes unexpected turns; indeed, unanticipated consequences are expected. This strategy is consistent with the suggestions of other commentators on field studies of organizational change (for example, Cummings, Molloy, and Glen, 1977; Porras and Berg, 1978; Kahn, 1982). However, it is more often suggested than practiced. Generally, field studies fail to provide adequate descriptions of the change process (Cummings and Molloy, 1977) and are limited to relatively brief periods (Porras and Berg, 1978).

We have also begun to explore other approaches for studying organization design. The strategy first proposed by Golembiewski, Billingsley, and Yeager (1973) for identifying "beta" and "gamma" changes (that is, changes in scale calibration and changes in underlying constructs) can facilitate quantitative investigations of change in systems of meaning. Although the idea has received a fair amount of attention in the literature, nearly all studies are concerned with identifying the most appropriate algorithm for calculating beta and gamma shifts. A notable exception is the work of Mohrman and Novelli (1982, 1983) on people's responses to office automation. We are also intrigued by Mohr's (1982) concept of process theory as opposed to variance theory. Briefly, a process theory tells a story explaining a chain of all-or-nothing events rather than variation in dependent variables. Process theories have a different formal structure and are based on a different notion of causality than the ubiquitous variance theories. We are currently developing theories to account for the evolution and persistence of planned change (Ledford, 1984) and are exploring alternative processes for designing organizations (Mohrman and Cummings, 1983).

The usefulness of research for organization design does not depend exclusively on the rigor of the research or the degree to which research findings are cumulative. We have suggested that traditional research is relatively weak in offering prescriptions for organization design. Yet there are other ways of using research findings to facilitate change that do not depend on having well-tested, demonstrably powerful theories. Research can be used to help organization members envision new courses of action, to expose them to new realities, to convey past experiences, and to provide warnings and checklists of issues to consider before taking action.

For example, prior research can help organization members consider new frames of reference. If introduced at the right time and under the right conditions, theoretical frameworks can help organization members expand their views of what is possible. Even simple models and typologies that are too primitive to serve as theories are often sufficient for this purpose. For example, we have found that, in working with people who are struggling to understand the range of possible design options, it is often helpful to contrast the characteristics of traditional organizations with the conditions of high-involvement organizations. This exercise shows that a number of aspects of organizations—job designs, reward systems, management structure and style, personnel practices, and so on—can be changed and that multiple changes can be introduced more or less simultaneously. It also demonstrates that organizations are composed of interrelated systems and that changes in one subsystem can be reinforced or undermined by other subsystems.

Research can also be helpful in conveying prior experience. Case studies go beyond theoretical abstractions to make the possibility and nature of change more real and concrete. Moreover, sharing prior experiences can promote realistic expectations about the change process and about some of its outcomes; it can reassure people experiencing crises that others have overcome similar obstacles.

Existing research and theory can also identify practical issues in designing and implementing change. Models that are too inelegant, or "ugly," to be tested using traditional methods can still be useful in this way. Overdeveloped or redundant models may suggest relevant issues that would otherwise be overlooked.

These practical uses of research are tolerant of findings having certain methodological weaknesses. Such uses are legitimate because the purpose is not narrowly to specify an appropriate course of action but rather to expand the realities available to organization members and, where possible, to help them find comfort, hope, and a healthy skepticism as they learn how to design their organizations.

In this section we discussed the content aspect of our research. We argued that researchers traditionally have made questionable assumptions about organization design, about how design should be studied, and about how research findings should be used in the design process. However, we do not view the content of our research as a radical departure from the best of current practice. We favor, for example, using quantitative methods and research designs that are as strong as possible in capturing the phenomena of organizational change. Our argument is that more modest assumptions about the usefulness of research are needed, that a redirection of theoretical emphasis is called for, and that certain methodological approaches are required to take into account the messiness of the phenomena of interest.

The Relationship Aspect of Research

The relationship aspect of research concerns the nature of the interactions between researchers and subjects. All social research includes a relationship component, although that component typically receives only limited attention. Traditionally, researchers tend to focus on the content aspect of research; they are concerned with generating research questions, designing appropriate methodologies, and collecting and analyzing data. There is considerable evidence, however, that the nature of the relationship between researchers and subjects can have a powerful impact on the research content (Argyris, 1980). For example, subjects may try to second-guess or deceive researchers they do not trust. Relationship effects are pervasive and even operate in such socially impoverished settings as research laboratories (Orne, 1962).

We believe that the relationship component is an integral part of field research, especially in organization design situations where researchers and organization members are jointly involved in the research process. Here, researchers must establish and maintain relationships with multiple stakeholders in the organization. Moreover, relationships must be strong enough to withstand the rigors of a research process requiring long-term commitments and high levels of psychological intensity.

In the following pages, we will discuss the characteristics of the research relationship and then suggest what the researchers' role should be.

Characteristics of the Research Relationship. The relationships between researchers and organization members can be characterized as forming a communications network. The network is composed of different stakeholders, each having preferences, goals, and values. Communication among the participants occurs simultaneously at two levels: the content and relational levels (Watzlawick, Beavin, and Jackson, 1967). The *content* level involves the particular information that is communicated. In our case, this includes information about the content aspect of research—messages about the research focus, methodology, and data collection and analysis. The *relational* level involves the relationship among the participants in the communication network and thus provides information about how particular content is to be interpreted—for example, whether it is a command or request, a compliment or criticism, a hostile or helping act, and the like.

The relational level of communication is relatively tacit and involves subtle contextual cues (often nonverbal) that comment on or qualify the meaning of communication content. Because the relational level communicates a message about how the content is to be viewed, it is of a higher logical level of abstraction than the content. It represents a metacommunication that frames the content and gives it meaning. Hence, different metacommunications, or frames, lead to differences in meaning attributed to the same content. For example, information about organization design research is likely to be interpreted differently by organization members depending on whether it is seen within a frame of trust between researchers and members or within a frame of skepticism between them. The observation of a meeting or conduct of an interview will be experienced differently by individuals who feel the researcher will provide helpful information than by those who feel they are being evaluated. The experience will be different if the researcher is participating in the meeting rather than observing it or is engaging in conversations rather than interviewing.

The relational frame exerts a subtle yet powerful influence on interactions between researchers and organization members. It tends to pattern the relationships, implicitly defining the positions of the participants as well as the nature of their interactions. The challenge for researchers is to gain a position in the network allowing access to information that is critical to the research. In our view, this goal requires establishing effective relations with multiple stakeholders while remaining relatively independent of their different perspectives, goals, and values. This relational strategy is especially difficult in situations in which the multiple stakeholders have well-established frames governing their interactions. Researchers may be viewed as representing a particular viewpoint or stakeholder, and they are likely to be treated in a way that presupposes the response of that stakeholder. For example, unionists may see researchers as representing management's interests and consequently interact with them as if they were managers.

Researchers must explicitly address the relational level if they are to establish an identity in the communications network that is seen as legitimate yet independent of the competing viewpoints already present. They need to understand existing relational frames and may have to change them if necessary, a process called "reframing." Unfortunately, problems at the relational level are difficult to recognize and thus are misdefined as content-level disagreements. For example, researchers often interpret people's concerns and questions about the research as content issues; they respond to those issues by giving more elaborate descriptions of the research content. In reality, questions such as "What are you trying to find out?" and "What are you doing?" often have more to do with "Whom are you working for?" "Whose interests are you serving?" and "How can you hurt or help me?" than with research content. To the extent that people's concerns derive from the relational level, they cannot be resolved by addressing content. Indeed, attempts to resolve relational problems at the content level may escalate the conflict. For instance, the researcher can best establish trust by openly laying out the issues as he or she sees them, not by carefully articulating the research agenda while taking pains to conceal the hypotheses being tested.

Failure to distinguish between the content and relational levels and to solve problems at the requisite level results in disturbed communication (Watzlawick, Beavin, and Jackson, 1967). The quality and usefulness of research conducted when there is disturbed communication between researchers and organization members are questionable. The data are likely to be distorted, and what is useful for one of the participants may be useless to others.

Disturbed communications are typically addressed by unilateral revision of the research content by either the researchers or organization members. Changes are made to render the research either more scientific or more practical. Such changes reduce the value of the research to one party or the other and often result in ill will between researchers and organization members.

Disturbed communications seem particularly prevalent when there is disagreement about whether the relationship betweeen researchers and organization members should be complementary or symmetrical. In complementary relations, one of the participants assumes a dominant posture, the other a submissive one. The two roles complement each other, more dominance leading to more submissiveness, and so on. Symmetrical relations assume equality of the parties.

Traditionally, researchers have tried to act out a complementary relationship with organization members; they tend to treat members as subjects and, by implication, themselves as dominant. They tend to see research as being conducted primarily to serve the interests of the social science community. From a scientific perspective, this relational frame seems rational. Researchers need to control the situation, whether in the laboratory or in the field, so that the findings are "scientifically" valid. Organization members, however, often feel uncomfortable with this complementary relationship. When they do, they may openly rebel, provide misleading data, make arbitrary changes in the research content, or terminate the research relationship altogether. From a practical perspective, these behaviors appear rational, especially when the research is not seen as helping members achieve their goals.

Disturbed communications are an integral part of organization design research and should be addressed at the relational level. Different stakeholders often value different research outcomes and have different frames for the relational part of the research. Unless researchers explicitly address the relationship issue, they may not understand or even be aware of patterns of disturbed communication. Researchers need to create conditions in which the stakeholders, themselves included, can openly discuss their differences (and similarities) and forge a more symmetrical relationship that accounts for the different perspectives. For example, we have successfully used groups composed of multiple stakeholders to design the research content. The group, rather than any individual, makes decisions about research content. Considerable attention is directed at understanding different relational frames and developing a more symmetrical frame for jointly learning about organization design.

Researchers' Role. Researchers play a complex role in our research strategy. They must attend to both the content and relationship aspects of the research, the latter requiring focus on both the content and relational levels of communication between researchers and organization members.

Researchers must maintain long-term linkages with various stakeholders during a design process often infused with politics. Various stakeholders typically try to influence the design in directions favorable to their preferences and values. To remain privy to sensitive information from these diverse stakeholders, researchers must maintain relationships with those who have formal and informal power as well as with those who do not. The organization design that emerges from this political process will embody not only the changed behaviors of those in power but also the new responses of those whose views did not prevail. We have found, for example, that top management often feels that the organization is making a successful transition to a participative culture, while those at middle and lower levels are experiencing neither success nor a serious effort to change. Nevertheless, lower-level participants may maintain a self-protective rhetoric with public statements of success and enthusiasm.

Researchers whose role is defined purely as information gathering have difficulty maintaining effective linkages with stakeholders. Data collection generally requires a commitment of time and energy from organization members, and they are unlikely to continue to cooperate if they see no useful outcome. More fundamentally, organization design involves a great deal of uncertainty and, consequently, insecurity. Rather than seeing themselves as embarking on an exciting and innovative journey, people often feel that they are being pushed into a mode of functioning with which they are uncomfortable, for which they have been inadequately prepared, and in which they may be unable to function effectively. The individuals involved take risks and feel vulnerable. They are likely to feel extremely uncomfortable doing this when a passive observer is recording an "objective" history, particularly when they feel that the researcher is keeping a "report card" on how well they are doing.

Continued access to the design process depends largely on maintaining a "professional" relationship with organization members. Researchers must provide useful services as they acquire privileged access to the organization. "In a sense, therefore, the social scientist begins in practice, however imperfect scientifically, and works back to theory and the more systematic research which may test this, and then back again to improved practice'' (Emery and Trist, 1973, p. 111). A large range of professional services is possible. Researchers might provide systematic feedback of research data; they may play an expert role in providing design information; they might actively intervene in the change process. Each of these roles implies a different relationship to the organization and to the members of the communications network.

Certain roles are more difficult to maintain over time. In the quality-of-worklife studies conducted by the Institute for Social Research of the University of Michigan, for example, some of the researchers who were observers and data collectors found it difficult to maintain this ''hands off'' role (see Lawler, Nadler, and Cammann, 1980; Seashore, Lawler, Mirvis, and Cammann, 1983). Their data gave them potential influence on the design process. Because of their natural inclination to act and because of requests from organization members, they sometimes became active in the change process. They became advocates in the change process, using their interpersonal relationships with the site members and their ''expert'' and ''information'' power to influence the process. This activity caused role conflict among participants in the design process, mainly because other professionals were directly responsible for helping in that process.

There are other problems with the pure observational role in researching organization design. The quality of understanding of the change process depends on how well researchers are integrated into the network of stakeholders enacting the design activity. Understanding a social process requires entering into its flow (Lewin, 1951), or the participation of the knower in the known (Barfield, 1961; Vaill, 1983). Existing measurement tools capture or describe only a part of the richness of organizational change, of the fears and anxieties characterizing a group entering into change, and of the values and esthetic preferences pervading the superficially rational design process. Although it is predictable that these forces will emerge, the particular form they take must be discovered in each situation. We can become aware of them by intense exposure and by being part of the change process.

External observers often fail to grasp the depth of human

reactions to change. Superficial prescriptions for change may result. Take, for example, the common "finding" that participative management was not implemented because supervisors did not change their behaviors, and the resulting recommendation that increased training for supervisors and altered incentives are necessary to enable such changes to occur. Although these findings probably reflect reality and the recommendations are sound, they fail to capture the depth of the change process: the tenuous and delicately balanced position of the supervisor vis-à-vis subordinates, the mixed messages and demands that the supervisor receives from above, the anxiety surrounding behavioral change in what is often perceived as a hostile world, and the inability to envision a new and different role and how it might be played out. Reducing this complexity to a matter of training and incentives misses the dynamics of change; it results in a superficial understanding of what is required to bring about fundamental change in organizations.

Cognitive and structural approaches to understanding design fail to capture the emotional trauma experienced by managers who have operated only with a well-defined set of parameters and who are suddenly asked to invent and create. They miss the political interplay of groups and individuals who are trying to enact a world that confirms their values and preferences. They ignore the desperate search for leadership when a group is embarking into the unknown. Only by being privy to these subtle struggles can researchers capture their profound implications. Researchers who are actively engaged in the change process quickly become aware of the insufficiency of theory as a prescription for change. Those who do not get close enough to the change process to recognize this insufficiency will continue to spin theories of what organizations might be like if they were not populated by people.

Active involvement and a certain humility are needed, then, if we are to grasp the phenomena of change. We must assume our role *alongside* the roles of others with different goals, values, and world views. To do so, we must be open to others' views and explanations of organizational life. We cannot adequately observe a phenomenon so complex as organization design by limiting ourselves to our frameworks. We learn by entering into the world of change, by being open to influence from those whose world is changing, by being willing to learn *from* others rather than defining our task as learning about them.

In short, what researchers bring to organization design is a way of viewing the world, which, when combined with the world views of the others involved, may expand horizons and possibilities. We can share what we see as possible, using our experience with other situations and our theoretical frameworks. We can then learn how organization members treat these possibilities—whether they are assimilated into members' world view, rejected in their entirety, or taken and transformed into a new reality. Organization members' treatment of our theories can serve as a practical source of confirmation or disconfirmation. Likewise, our treatment of their views determines how and whether we contribute to the systematic understanding of organizations. To the extent that we see organizations in a manner that does not accommodate the perceptions of the people who inhabit them, we have spun a set of beliefs that do not fit people's reality. It is questionable whether such beliefs can serve as a guide to organization design and as scientific knowledge.

What, then, is the researchers' role in organization design? Researchers are members of a network of people concerned with change and design. They are enablers of a mutual learning process and contributors to and observers within that process. They differ from other members of the network both in what they bring to the network and in what they take from it.

Researcher Skills. Researchers need to bring multiple skills to the situation:

- Exposure to a wide variety of situations and theoretical frameworks that offer both a rich way of viewing organizations and possible projected futures.
- Ability to present this understanding to others in such a way that they will be able to assimilate it into their own understanding.

- Social skills that facilitate the process by which various stakeholders share their understandings and try to emerge with an agreed-on course of action.
- Ability to view the communications network as a relative newcomer and to make people aware of the patterns and rules that govern and inhibit their interaction.
- Methodologies to observe and record the process systematically so that understandings can be furthered for the designng organization and preserved in the social science literature.

In other words, organization design researchers must be able to bridge the epistemological gap separating the scientist from the practitioner (Bennis, 1983). Looking at the list of tasks composing researchers' role in organization design, it becomes clear that the role probably requires more than one person. Although a researcher might have all the requisite skills, it is difficult for one person to perform all the tasks at one time. Our experience with teams of researchers suggests that trading off the roles of change agent and observer can be done effectively. We sometimes cycle through these role exchanges several times in the same field visit. Likewise, action in the field can be alternated with sense making back in the safe harbor of our research center or university.

The complexity of organization design probably demands multidisciplinary teams, capable of viewing and engaging with a diversity of organizational phenomena. Most organization designing involves both technological and human change. Furthermore, it includes alterations in the cultural, political, and economic aspects of the organization (Tichy and Friedman, 1983). A full grasp of the change process as well as ability to contribute meaningfully to it depends on creating research teams of people who are able to challenge yet complement one another's viewpoints.

Given this complexity and the likely need for research teams rather than individuals, the difficulty of maintaining a research relationship with organizations over time is underscored. The next section of the chapter suggests that effective relationships between researchers and organization members require an appropriate institutional context.

Establishing the Institutional Context for Research

So far, we have argued that researching organization design requires a set of assumptions about organizations differing from the assumptions underlying traditional research methods. Further, we have proposed that research requires a collaborative relationship between researchers and organization members, a relationship in which multiple stakeholders are actively involved in a learning process characterized by long-term commitments and high levels of psychological intensity.

In this final section, we suggest that doing the kind of research proposed here can be facilitated by the existence of an appropriate institutional base. This entity needs to exist at a higher level than the researchers and organization members engaged in a research project so that it can encompass their different interests and help to establish and sustain collaborative linkages among them (Purlmutter, 1965). It needs to provide an infrastructure for integrating the problem-oriented needs of organizations with the knowledge-oriented needs of researchers: a context promoting collaboration and joint learning among the parties.

In the absence of such higher-level support, researchers and organizations are likely to continue to act out their traditional asymmetrical relationship. The key to creating a more collaborative relationship is to break the traditional frame and create a new, more collaborative one. Unfortunately, relational frames are tacit and typically taken for granted. They can be changed only by resorting to some higher logical level (a frame of frames) or by having people external to the relationship (with different frames) help to replace the existing frame with a new one. This is precisely why a higher-level, institutionalized research base facilitates collaborative research. It exists outside the relational frame governing an individual research project and consequently can help researchers and organization members assess that frame and make changes if necessary. Further, it can provide a number of supporting functions that promote collaborative frames.

In order to perform a ''reframing'' function, the institutional base must be sufficiently broad to encompass the interests and values of researchers, organizations, and other stakeholders such as government funding agencies. This requirement argues strongly for what Trist (1967) has called "special institutes," or centers of applied research. They exist intermediately between user organizations and orthodox academic departments and supply the necessary link between them. They may be located at universities, such as the Institute for Social Research at the University of Michigan and the Center for Effective Organizations at the University of Southern California, or they may be independent institutions, such as the Tavistock Institute of Human Relations. In Trist's words, these centers have the following features: "They are problem-centered and interdisciplinary but focus on generic problems rather than specific problems. They accept a professional as well as scientific responsibility for the projects they undertake and contribute both to theoretical development and to the improvement of practice. Their work expresses a *research/application* 'mix'" (1967, p. 11). We do not mean to imply that applied centers are the only feasible arrangement for conducting organization design research. Our main argument is that such centers can help to overcome many of the problems inherent in more traditional researcher/organization relationships. We will draw primarily on our experience at the Center for Effective Organizations (CEO); much of it seems applicable to other applied centers.

The role of CEO can best be understood in terms of a transorganizational framework. People at the center spend considerable time linking with organizations and facilitating interactions between and among them. They try to form a network among different organizations sharing an interest in organization design. This network generally consists of members from relevant organizations, including people from academic departments, university administration, user organizations, funding agencies, and the center itself. The formation of supportive linkages among the different organizations exemplifies the high-level institution building that facilitates the kind of research proposed here. It results in what Cummings (1984) has described as a "transorganizational system" (TS)—a group of organizations that have joined together for a common purpose.

From this perspective, CEO's primary task is building and maintaining a transorganizational system supportive of organization design learning. Cummings has suggested that the development of such systems typically includes three phases: identification, convention, and organization.

Identification. This initial phase is concerned with identifying the organizations potentially composing the TS. Identifying potential organizations involves more than simply having a large number of contacts with researchers, user organizations, and funders. Many possible members are not sympathetic to the view of research proposed here. Moreover, many universities or academic departments and organizations have norms and practices thwarting collaborative relationships with each other. A major task of centers like CEO is to establish relationships with potential members that allow a realistic test of commitment to collaborative learning processes. CEO's forums for exploring commitment have run the gamut from informal lunches and serendipitous contacts to formal conferences. Because the purpose of such meetings is to explore possibilities for collaborative learning, both the content and the relational frame of the interactions tend to reflect this approach. For example, CEO has convened "special-interest groups" to identify areas of common interest among representatives from academic departments, funding agencies, and user organizations. Not all attendees (academic and corporate) leave the conferences wanting to join the TS. They may be uncomfortable with a symmetrical relationship and/or see their organizations' practices as barriers to participating in collaborative learning. In some ways the identification process is a realistic preview of collaborative research. We share our conceptualizations of the research process and solicit their view of it and of what they see as useful behaviors. We try to model symmetrical, collaborative relationships in our interactions. At the same time, they exhibit their ability to respond in kind and their comfort in doing so.

It is important to emphasize that, even among those who eventually join the TS, a considerable number do not become directly involved in a research project. Participation of some groups is important because they are involved in nonresearch relationships with those doing the research. University adminis-tration, for example, not only needs to support the research ap-proach but needs to understand it in a tacit, experiential sense so that support is appropriate.

Convention. Once the potential organizations composing the TS are identified, they need to be brought together, or con-vened, in order to assess whether building the TS is plausible and desirable. In this stage we explore organizations' motiva-tions to join and perceptions of organization design research. We seek to establish sufficient levels of motivation and research consensus to form the TS.

A preliminary issue is who should convene the potential members and manage the event. An applied research center such as CEO is generally seen as a legitimate source of leadership for the TS, especially during its development. Indeed, a primary task of such centers is to provide leadership for building a TS supportive of organization design research.

Organizations' motivations to join the TS typically derive from resource dependencies and mutual commitments to prob-lem solving. Mutual commitment to the organization design problem is inherent in the research relationships proposed here. More problematic is resource dependence. At first glance it seems clear: Organizations need to learn about and do organiza-tion design, and they often need professional expertise to aid them. Researchers need to learn about organization design, and they need ''real life'' opportunities to do so as well as money to support the endeavor. This resource exchange, however, may undermine the symmetry of the interaction, especially if it is the primary motivation to join the TS. How soon does a research center begin to compromise the collaborative relationship in order to sell its services at a rate that ensures it survival?

Traditionally, academic-based organizational research is conducted in a resource-dependency frame. Funding from such sources as the government or foundations is administered by the university, and the particular research project is managed by individual faculty members. Funds from corporations, how-ever, typically go directly to faculty members under an ad hoc consulting agreement, mainly because of the difficulty in creating acceptable standardized approaches to managing the exchange.

Research centers provide a mechanism for managing corporate funds by working out research sponsorship in a way that meets the needs of the researchers, the organization, and the center itself. This is most directly accomplished when funding is administered on a project-by-project basis. Here funding arrangements can be tailored to the needs of the participants directly involved in the project. The center, of course, must have the organizational flexibility to cope with a variety of different project arrangements.

There is a close connection between the nature of the funding arrangement and the nature of the research process. It begins with the way projects and funding become linked. Traditionally, a formal proposal is submitted to a funding source. It specifies the research purpose, the methods and knowledge base, the costs, and the researchers' expertise. The proposal is then evaluated (sometimes by other relevant professionals) according to the purposes and criteria of the profession, the agency, and/or the client organization. The subsequent financial arrangements tend to mirror the standardized procedures of the funding decision. The research is often carried out with similar organization. It is standardized by the specifications in the proposal; the proposal tends to become the blueprint by which the research is carried out. Such programmed arrangements can hinder the kind of research process proposed here.

In practice, however, the traditional approach to funded research is routinely coupled with informal practices that attempt to add symmetry to the relationships in the research process. Most funding agencies, for example, are prepared to collaborate with researchers to find a way of proposing research so that the needs of both the scientist and the funding agency are met. It is usually accepted and expected that research plans will change as the project unfolds. Nevertheless, these tacit acknowledgments of the need for mutuality in research are still within a standardized resource-dependency frame. They are not typically understood as important to the underlying validity of the research but are seen as necessary only because of the pragmatics of the situation. Such informal arrangements are seen as potentially compromising the ideal of rigorous research, not as emerging methodology to be understood and improved.

In convening TS members, resource-dependency motivations to interact need to be kept secondary to shared commitments to organization design research. Hence, the convention phase should emphasize achieving commitment of all parties to collaborative research and developing a framework for institutional relationships to support a long-term, mutual endeavor.

Organization. The final stage of transorganizational development involves establishing the necessary structures and mechanisms to facilitate the ongoing functioning of the system. Here, an applied research center can provide continued leadership for the TS. It can serve a key linking-pin role in integrating the different organizations by serving as a communication channel between them, by linking third parties to one another, and by actively making decisions on behalf of the TS. This leadership role helps to regulate interactions among the members. It is concerned with managing interactions, orienting the members to future trends and issues, mobilizing resources, and establishing linkages with groups outside the TS.

Among the many mechanisms that CEO has developed to maintain organization of the TS are the following. It has an extensive publication series that is routinely sent to all participating organizations. It conducts an annual "sponsors' meeting" where members from academia and private and public corporations share ideas and experiences, assess how well the TS is functioning, and make changes if necessary. Full-time members of the center actively maintain contacts with TS members, including a fair amount of "missionary" work in their respective organizations. CEO has a monthly meeting especially for its academic members and full-time staff where progress on different research projects is reported and emergent problems are discussed. It does continual recruiting of new organizations as well as people to staff the center.

Research centers provide an ideal institutional home for collaborative, problem-focused research. They can pull together multiple constituencies to explore common interests and develop research projects. Management of funding issues by such an institution can help to minimize disruptive effects on the research relationship. Finally, the center community provides a check on the usefulness of the research to the academic and practitioner communities and on the collaborative process itself.

Conclusion

We live in a period of rapid and perplexing change. This chapter has presented a framework for understanding research with organizations that are designing to adapt to this change. We have argued that such research departs from traditional content and methodology because of its appropriate focus on the change process. This means the development of long-term, collaborative research with a high level of intensity. It requires new conceptualizations of the role of researchers in a wider network of key stakeholders in the change process. Although we have made this argument in the context of organizational change, we suspect it has validity for a much broader array of organizational issues. In fact, we believe it applies to all organizational research that seeks to connect knowledge to use.

A key point is that the content of our research is given meaning (usefulness) by the collaborative relationships established to carry out research methodology. Unfortunately, there is little formalized practice in either the corporate or the academic world that legitimizes the collaborative research relationship proposed here. Stakeholders from all sides seem to engage "naturally" in research in an asymmetrical, or exchange, mode. Consequently, we created a higher-level, institutionalized base—a transorganizational system—that legitimizes, socializes stakeholders into, and provides support for collaborative research relationships. It, like other centers of applied research, can be catalytic in the formation of transorganizational systems to frame the collaborative learning process. The ideas presented have profound implications for the conduct of organizational research and the training of organizational researchers. They suggest a fundamental change in how we do research.

RESPONSE AND COMMENTARY

Lyman W. Porter

I would like to begin my comments on the Cummings, Mohr-man, Mohrman, and Ledford chapter by summarizing what I see as the main thrust of this interesting and thought-provoking contribution. Next, I will highlight what I think are several key points. Following that, I will pose some questions that I think are worth pondering in any serious consideration of the type of research methodology urged by the authors. The focus will be on the trade-offs between carrying out research in the manner advocated and more traditional approaches to research methodology in the organizational behavior field.

Thrust of the Chapter

The central theme of this chapter can be captured by quoting several passages. I have selected a series of such excerpts in order to provide the reader with a brief overview of this theme as it appeared to me. It is hoped that this will be a reasonably accurate representation of what the authors themselves would agree is the basic thrust of their chapter. Agreement on what the chapter is all about is the necessary foundation for commenting on some of the key issues.

First, as stressed throughout the chapter, it "is about doing research with organizations undergoing change." The focus is on "how organizations design themselves." The fundamental nature of their approach to carrying out such research involves "actively [engaging] with organization members in generating and implementing innovative designs." More specifically, and quite important in understanding this approach: "Our roles have been to join with organization members in the learning process, to offer advice, to collect data, to guide implementation, and to study the design process itself. . . . We have combined the roles of learner and expert. We share this combined role with organization members.'' Whatever one might think of the merits of this approach, one cannot deny that it represents a substantial departure from the way most organizational research (excluding case studies) has been carried out in the past.

The approach is further elaborated in the early pages of the chapter. For example, the authors note that "we conceive of our research as requiring temporary intersystem linkages between researchers and organizations.'' Further, this approach "suggests that the relationship between researchers and organizations involves long-term commitments and high levels of psychological intensity . . . [that] invariably produce tension between researchers and organization members.''

We now come to the basic thesis of the chapter. "We believe that many traditional research methods are unsuited to studying organizational change, mainly because they are based on assumptions that do not hold in change situations.'' In particular, "researching organization design requires a set of assumptions about organizations differing from the assumptions underlying traditional research methods.'' Such assumptions (that form the basis for the advocated approach) are clearly identified in the chapter (organizational change is a disorderly process, organization designs cannot be prescribed totally on the basis of prior research, and so on). In summary, the authors argue that the approach they propose "requires new conceptualizations of the role of researchers in a wider network of key stakeholders in the change process.'' Furthermore, "we suspect [this approach] has validity for a much broader array of organizational issues. In fact, we believe it applies to all organizational research that seeks to connect knowledge to use.'' The gauntlet could hardly be thrown down with more clarity or more enthusiasm!

Key Points Raised in the Chapter

In my opinion, the authors make a forceful case for the type of research approach they advocate. In so doing, they make several very important points that highlight the nature and potential advantages of undertaking organizational research from this perspective. I would like to select for examination several that I consider especially crucial.

Nature of the Organizational Change. I agree with the authors in their basic description of organizational change processes. That is, I strongly concur with the notion that "organizational change is a disorderly, highly dynamic process." I believe it would be difficult for anyone to make a strong case to the contrary. I also agree with their firmly held view that "organization designs cannot be prescribed totally on the basis of prior research." The problem, of course, is that those faced with the actual task of organization design have to proceed on *some* basis. Therefore, the issue becomes: What kinds of research findings—assuming that those attempting to design or redesign organizations want to take into account what the literature shows—should form a basis for action?

Although we can all (at least most of us) agree that organization designs "cannot be prescribed totally on the basis of prior research," something must form the basis of prescriptions. This leads to the question: Is the type of research approach advocated here likely to lead to an integrated set of findings that will be a better basis for action than the collection of findings from what the authors call more "traditional" research methodologies? (See a later section of this commentary for further discussion of this general question.) The answer is certainly not "in" yet concerning which type of research approach will best provide findings that "account for more than a small fraction of the variance in dependent variables." Regardless of which research approach will be more effective in the long run, I strongly agree with the authors that for the present "organizational researchers' prescriptions should serve mainly as general guides to organization design rather than as detailed blueprints for action." Detailed blueprints are better left to those who provide drawings of physical buildings than to those who would prescribe designs for the human part of organizations.

"Adaptive" Research Strategy. The authors state that "our strategy for studying change dynamics and intervention effects follows what Lawler . . . has termed an adaptive research de-

sign.'' This particular approach, as they point out, has several features, such as casting a '' 'broad measurement net' . . . in order to capture unintended consequences . . . and other unpredictable turns of events,'' a ''heavy emphasis on qualitative description,'' and the use of semistandardized research instruments. They go on to note that such a strategy (combining a number of different elements) ''is more often suggested than practiced.'' It seems to me that true ''field'' research will almost invariably require some form of this ''adaptive strategy.'' The key issues, however, are *to what extent* it must be adaptive and *under what circumstances* an adaptive strategy will be most advantageous. When should a researcher or research team be driven from its planned approach, and what is gained or lost by changing? Will constant or extensive adaptation by the researchers help or hinder the production of useful scientific knowledge (that is, a base on which a systematic set of conclusions can be constructed)? At this stage in the development of our field, we do not have the answers to these questions. The chapter by Cummings and his colleagues, by advocating much more extensive *use* of this research approach, certainly propels us in the direction of learning more about both the advantages and the limitations of ''adaptive research designs.''

''Intensive Involvement'' Research Relationships. One of the major features of the chapter is the strong case it makes for a particular kind of relationship between researchers and the organizations being researched. Specifically, the authors argue for a relationship that involves ''long-term commitments and high levels of psychological intensity.'' Further, they state, with some emphasis, that ''the challenge for researchers is to gain a position in the [communications] network [of organizational stakeholders] allowing access to information that is critical to the research.'' They go on to note, quite correctly in my opinion, that a major part of this challenge is to establish ''effective relations with multiple stakeholders while remaining relatively independent of their different perspectives, goals, and values.'' The key question here, from my perspective, is: Is this realistically possible if *high intensity* relationships are in fact established?

A central feature of the high-intensity relationship urged

by the authors is that the relationship between researchers and organization members becomes symmetrical rather than, as they phrase it, "complementary." What they call the traditional research approach involves complementary relations in which "one of the participants [that is, the researcher] assumes a dominant posture, the other [that is, organization members] a submissive one." In other words, "traditionally, researchers . . . tend to treat members as subjects and, by implication, themselves as dominant." Cummings, Mohrman, Mohrman, and Ledford argue that in such a relationship organization members may "provide misleading data," thereby leading to what they call "disturbed communications." Consequently, they believe that researchers should try to "forge a more symmetrical relationship" that will deal head on with both content and relational aspects of communication. To do this, researchers must adopt a role of much higher involvement than the more traditional field research role of "observer."

In their view, "researchers whose role is defined purely as information gathering will have difficulty maintaining effective linkages with stakeholders." Further, "the quality of understanding of the change process depends on how well researchers are integrated into the network of stakeholders enacting the design activity. . . . External observers often fail to grasp the depth of human reactions to change. Superficial prescriptions for change may result." Finally, this approach to what the researcher's role should be is summed up in such statements as "Only by being privy to these subtle struggles can researchers capture their profound implications. . . . We must assume our role *alongside* the roles of others with different goals, values, and world views." All this adds up to an integrated set of arguments that researchers must assume roles quite different from those that have been typical of most organizational research. As the authors themselves stress, there is considerable challenge in developing such roles. The key issue, however, is: Does this type of researcher role have great advantages that clearly outweigh any possible disadvantages?

Research Teams. If the approach to research advocated here is adopted, it almost by definition requires that projects be carried out by more than a single researcher. This, in fact, is exactly the position of the authors. They note that "the complexity of organization design probably demands multidisciplinary teams." Approaching organizational research by single investigators acting alone in comparison with research teams has, in my opinion, generally not been dealt with sufficiently in discussions of research methodology. I agree with the authors' view that the complexity of the types of organizational problems (in their chapter, organization design problems) that are perhaps of most importance to the field is likely to require much more frequent use of research teams in the future than has occurred in the past. We need to know how to use teams in such a way as to gain maximal effectiveness from the *combination* of researchers beyond the mere addition of more bodies to do more tasks. (The authors also argue for supporting research teams by providing them with an institutional base of applied research centers. The case they make for such centers is both interesting and relevant to the general approach to research on organization design that they advocate throughout the chapter.)

Some Questions

In this section I pose some questions that were raised in my mind when I read the chapter and heard the elaboration of it at the conference. These really are *questions,* because I do not have any firm answers myself. However, they are the kinds of queries that are not only relevant to the chapter by Cummings, Mohrman, Mohrman, and Ledford but also, I believe, important for our field to attempt to answer.

1. *What are the trade-offs between the approach advocated here and "traditional" research approaches?* After reading through the chapter, I found myself asking: Is rigor really mortis? The clear impression that one gets from the chapter is that a great many disadvantages and problems connected with so-called traditional and rigorous research methodologies can be solved or overcome with the approach advocated there. (As an aside, one needs to note that there is a small problem of terminology. The authors rather consistently refer to the former type of research as "tradi-

tional," which, though a venerable and honorable word, typically does have certain pejorative connotations when applied to topics in the field of organizational behavior. Perhaps there is no good substitute shorthand phrase that is less obviously negative-sounding, so in the interest of parsimony—but with some reluctance—I will let the term stand. The other terminological problem is that the authors never really provide a short phrase to describe their own research approach. It seems to me that what they are talking about is "action research" or something so akin to it that I cannot make a distinction. Hence, although the authors might have some objections, I will adopt that phrase as a rough shorthand description of the approach detailed in their chapter.

Back to the question: Are all the advantages really on the side of action research and all the disadvantages on the side of traditional research? I doubt it. In my view, the type of action research advocated here has some clear-cut advantages, such as the ability to generate a high degree of richness of data and the possibility of making creative changes in the research approach as a project moves along. However, those very advantages or unique features of action research also produce their own set of disadvantages (some of which will be indicated in the discussion of several of the following questions). Therefore, for me, the issue is one of relative trade-offs, *not* one of a clear superiority of one type of research approach (action research) over the other type (poor old traditional research). Each researcher (or research team) has to decide which combination of advantages and problems he or she would rather live with and not assume that the pluses are all on one side of the ledger. This chapter, and indeed this book, have, however, clearly helped bring the issue of trade-offs to the forefront and have shown anyone inclined to use the more traditional approaches that he or she should not make that decision perfunctorily but should do it only after careful consideration of viable alternatives, such as an action research approach.

2. *Is it possible to maximize simultaneously the separate goals of researchers and the organization?* The authors do not actually say so, but they strongly imply that it is possible. Again, I doubt

it. It seems to me that efforts designed to jointly satisfy the goals of both parties can often lead to compromises in the research design that in fact impede obtaining valid data about the organization. Of course, as question 1 implies, this certainly would not always be true, and there clearly are instances when research approaches that do not try to take goals of the organization into account end up providing *less* valid data. Nevertheless, I think that there are many instances when researchers have goals that are clearly independent of, or orthogonal to, those of the organization and that the research process is better served by *not* attempting to bring those goals closer together. This is, definitely, a research issue about which we need more research (of both kinds).

3. *How does one generalize from the findings produced by these types of research designs?* In many respects, it seems to me, the approach advocated is a rather elaborate case-study approach. It certainly differs in size and scope from the old single-researcher case study, but it does contain many elements of that kind of approach. If this is an accurate representation, then it raises the questions that are always present in case studies: How can the findings be generalized? How can systematic scientific knowledge be developed? Case studies—and the present approach—have the potential for providing exceptionally rich and detailed knowledge about the organization in question, but how do other researchers replicate the study in order to confirm the findings in a different setting and thereby help to build knowledge that is generalizable? Granted that a large set of case studies can move us in that direction, is this the most efficient and effective method or indeed, as the authors often imply in their chapter, almost always the best method?

4. *What are the criteria for distinguishing between "good" (effective) and "bad" (ineffective) action research studies?* Just as with so-called rigorous research studies, there must be action research studies which are not useful and whose results should not be accorded attention by the field. Most of the journals in our field have for years rejected hundreds of articles using traditional approaches that were in some way, according to the standards of the journals and their editors, flawed. (Cynics would say that

314 **Doing Research That Is Useful for Theory and Practice**

even some of those that end up in print should be similarly evaluated!) The task for those who espouse the approach described and favored by Cummings, Mohrman, Mohrman, and Ledford is to put forth an analogous set of criteria for separating out good studies of this type from those that should be ignored. This perhaps would be beyond the scope of their chapter, but one does get the feeling from reading it that almost any action research study, by definition, is "good." I am sure they would not hold that position, but it would be very helpful to know what they (and others who strongly urge an action research approach) would propose as criteria for determining *which* action studies meet—if one can pardon the expression—the most rigorous standards of quality.

5. *Is organizational change always good? How does one know? How does one separate what should be changed from what should not?* This set of questions nagged me as I read through the chapter. I had the feeling, and this may be totally unfair to the authors, that they were assuming that all change is good and that it is their duty as researchers to help organizations to change. (This is clearly a major departure from a traditional approach, in which researchers would not see it as relevant, let alone as their duty, to help an organization to change.) It seems to me that it is a very open question whether all change is indeed good or whether there may be times when not changing would be in the organization's best interests. At any rate, it is an important research question for our field to study (by whatever method): Under what circumstances is change helpful to organizations and their members, and under what circumstances is it harmful? As Craig Lundberg has said elsewhere, we need to study "stability" as well as change.

Conclusion

The research approach described so ably by the authors is, in my opinion, a very important *addition* to our armamentarium of research strategies. It deserves more attention than it has received to date in our field, and it holds, in my view, great potential. However, I do not see it as a substitute or replacement for more traditional ("classical"?) approaches that emphasize rigor of design and independence of interests between researchers and organizations. There are, as I have pointed out, critical trade-offs between the two basic approaches. What the field needs is more "research on research" so that the two approaches can be directly compared and contrasted to determine when each will be most effective in helping us advance our knowledge of organizational behavior. They each have their roles, and we need to work on developing sharper role definitions. In the meantime, as we proceed to add the action research approach to those that have been around for some time in our field, I am reminded of the statement of a manager quoted by the authors early in their chapter: "We know only that things will be different; we can only hope that they will be better."

GROUP DISCUSSION

The discussion began by focusing on whether the Cummings, Mohrman, Mohrman, and Ledford chapter completely rejected traditional research and therefore was threatening to traditional researchers.

Porter: I believe in pluralism. I don't associate myself with the traditional more than any other type, and I don't feel anything like "My God, the way I've been doing research is going out of style!" I believe there are many ways to get research findings, and clearly here we are talking about a category of approaches that have been underemphasized before and not used a lot in organizational research, and I think that's good. But I also think that we should explore and look at those things and not just say, well, they're new and therefore they're 100 percent accepted, just as we don't accept 100 percent traditional approaches because they've been around.

S. Mohrman: I'd like to respond to some of the questions. First of all, I do own this chapter. We struggle with it, but we believe it. I think we are very pluralistic. We have people analyzing data, and we have people doing correlational studies, and we have people doing traditional interview studies. In our team we have all those things. It didn't come across properly in our chapter, and I think that's a very important stylistic comment. The *only*s are intended. There are some phenomena we find in change situations that we find we can get at only in certain ways. And I think those *only*s are important.

A discussion between Argyris and Porter followed. This discussion revolved around Argyris's criticism of traditional approaches and Porter's defense of them and led to focusing on one example.

Porter: It is interesting, Chris, you and I had this discussion back at Yale in 1966. You kept telling me I was too far from my research data and I should get more involved with the research subjects and offer a service. I am not sure you have to provide a service. It creates other problems.

Lawler: But you can't understand the phenomena and get the access to the data unless you provide the service.

Porter: I'm not sure that is true, that you have to provide a service. Or, to put it another way, I think in exchange for providing service, other problems may be created that make it difficult to do research.

Walton: Was Graham Allison providing service when he did his research on the Bay of Pigs?

Argyris: I spent four hours with Graham Allison on this issue. Graham says to me, in no uncertain terms, he had no interest in serving anybody. He has no interest in change. He wanted to write a case study that gave understanding. One of the problems the Kennedy School is having now in its senior executive program is that they're getting those kinds of cases. The executives at the Kennedy School get angry and hostile because they're saying an understanding that does not give you some degree of bridge is a hostile act for you to communicate to us in this classroom. We're only going to do whatever research methods we can use that combine understanding with action, so that when we face our client, we don't create the hostility and so on that

Graham Allison unintentionally creates. I don't think you'd condemn that contention.

Porter: I just want to know what the trade-offs are. What do you gain by doing that, and what do you lose?

Argyris: Well, you just heard one. You reduce the long-range hostility of the stakeholders.

Hackman: I want to say one word on the other side. The psychological intensity that is involved when you are working collaboratively on the consulting thing is very hot. Sometimes that gets in the way of my learning what I need to have. What provides us the opportunity to get out of the psychological intensity and reflect back?

Cummings: Richard, a good example: Jerry and I came back from the field two weeks ago, badly bruised. I have never been hurt that much. We spent hours talking through conception, what the hell happened that froze us out there at a very deep psychological level?

Lawler: I think clearly on the down side that it is an extremely time-consuming process. The more your emotions get involved, obviously the more you are open to distortion of the situation. You may get more data, but you may distort those data in ways that are much more associated with where you are and how you've been attacked by the system.

S. Mohrman: I was struck by some of the observations of the people in your Michigan studies [*referring to Lawler and Seashore*] who were in an observer capacity, who talked about interviewing people from many levels in an organization, and they talked about the clamoring of the organization members to find out what they were finding out. They were cornering them in the hall and saying, what are you finding out in your interviews? How are we perceived? How do you experience us? Or even just to vent. The service of listening to them venting was an exchange; it was not a planned-for one, I'm sure. But it happened.

Several questions were asked about how the Center for Effective Organizations actually operates. This led to a response from a member of the center.

S. Mohrman: We create a series of extremely rich longitudinal studies. They tend to involve subgroups, so that two of us may be involved with one company. We really spend a lot of time in what Hackman calls looking for the problems and seeing what the common sort of phenomena are that come out of them. We are consciously dealing with different kinds of technological settings and different industrial settings so that we can figure whether the same kinds of common problems arise in all of them. Right now, for instance, we're dealing with several service organizations in the banking industry, we're dealing with several high-tech organizations, and we have some very low-tech, basic production sytems. We are altering and modifying the approaches being used to help people generate alternative ways of designing. Right now we're using a dialectical process, for instance, in the high-tech setting to try to generate a new way of designing systems because they say nothing they've done so far will work. But we have to constantly come back together and share and help interpret the phenomena. We figure out what is general, and it's a very time-consuming process.

Lundberg: I'm finding this an incredible discussion in a sense, because there is an enormous literature about it. Anthropologists for umpteen dozens of years have come down, it seems to me, and documented elaborately that there are exchanges between participant observer, observer, or whatever the researcher role is and those people that you're dealing with in the field. The classic, of course, at this point, is the appendix from *Street Corner Society*. Whyte is shot through with the exchanges that he does, partly for general access, but mostly to access the sensitive stuff, being able to eavesdrop, to look at anything. The nature of the exchange is hard to nail down, you're right. In my own work it has ranged as far as letting the vice-president of a division take me to a cocktail party and introduce me as from an Ivy League university. It's good for his ego. The little things. Lots of exchanges.

Lawler: You get very different kinds of post hoc reactions from people when you provide a service like being associated with a Yale research project versus providing them with something "that makes their life more effective or their organization more effective." I think that being associated with the Yale research project kind of wanes in their eyes and they feel rather had. At least now when I enter organizations, I find an awful lot of organizations who feel in the past that they've been had by researchers who came in and sold the glory of science and the association with the university, and then they left, leaving nothing else behind. The organization felt that was a rather hollow thing.

REFERENCES

Ackoff, R. L. *Creating the Corporate Future.* New York: Wiley, 1981.

Alderfer, C. P. "Group and Intergroup Relations." In J. R. Hackman and J. L. Suttle, *Improving Life at Work: Behavioral Science Approaches to Organizational Change.* Santa Monica, Calif.: Goodycar, 1977.

Argyris, C. *Inner Contradictions of Rigorous Research.* New York: Academic Press, 1980.

Argyris, C., and Schön, D. A. *Organizational Learning: A Theory of Action Perspective.* Reading, Mass.: Addison-Wesley, 1978.

Barfield, O. "The Rediscovery of Meaning." In R. Thruelsen and J. Kobler (Eds.), *Adventures of the Mind.* (2d series.) New York: Vintage Books, 1961.

Bennis, W. "Utilization of Organizational Behavior Knowledge: The Improbable Task." In J. Lorsch, *Handbook of Organizational Behavior.* Englewood Cliffs, N.J.: Prentice-Hall, 1983.

Boje, D. M., Fedor, D. B., and Rowland, K. M. "Myth-Making: A Qualitative Step in OD Interventions." *Journal of Applied Behavioral Science,* 1982, *18.*

Bougon, M., Weick, K. E., and Binkhorst, D. "Cognitions in

Organizations: An Analysis of the Utrecht Jazz Orchestra.''
Administrative Science Quarterly, 1977, *22*, 606–639.

Cameron, K. S., and Whetten, D. A. *Organizational Effectiveness: A Comparison of Multiple Models.* New York: Academic Press, 1983.

Clark, B. R. "The Organizational Saga in Higher Education." *Administrative Science Quarterly*, 1972, *17*, 178–184.

Cook, T. D., and Campbell, D. T. *Quasi-Experimentation: Design and Analysis Issues for Field Settings.* Chicago: Rand McNally, 1979.

Cummings, T. G. "Designing Effective Work Groups." In P. C. Nystrom and W. H. Starbuck (Eds.), *Handbook of Organizational Design.* Vol. 2. New York: Oxford University Press, 1981.

Cummings, T. G. "Transorganizational Development." In L. L. Cummings and B. Staw (Eds.), *Research in Organizational Behavior.* Vol. 6. New York: JAI Press, 1984.

Cummings, T. G., and Molloy, E. S. *Improving Productivity and the Quality of Work Life.* New York: Praeger, 1977.

Cummings, T. G., Molloy, E. S., and Glen, R. "A Methodological Critique of Fifty-eight Selected Work Experiments." *Human Relations*, 1977, *30*, 675–708.

Cyert, R. M., and March, J. G. *A Behavioral Theory of the Firm.* Englewood Cliffs, N.J.: Prentice-Hall, 1963.

Emery, R. E., and Trist, E. L. *Towards a Social Ecology: An Appreciation of the Future in the Present.* London and New York: Plenum, 1973.

Golembiewski, R. T., Billingsley, K., and Yeager, S. "Measuring Change and Persistence in Human Affairs: Types of Change Generated by OD Designs." *Journal of Applied Behavioral Science*, 1973, *12*, 133–157.

Grinyer, P. H., and Norburn, D. "Planning for Existing Markets: Perceptions of Executives and Financial Performance." *Journal of the Royal Statistical Society*, Series A, 1975, *138*, 70–97.

Hunter, J. E., Schmidt, F. L., and Jackson, G. B. *Meta-analysis: Cumulating Research Findings Across Studies.* Beverly Hills, Calif.: Sage, 1982.

Kahn, R. L. "Conclusion: Critical Themes in the Study of Change." In P. S. Goodman and Associates, *Change in Orga-*

nizations: New Perspectives on Theory, Research, and Practice. San-San Francisco: Jossey-Bass, 1982.

Lawler, E. E., III. "Adaptive Experiments: An Approach to Organizational Behavior Research." *Academy of Management Review,* 1977, *2,* 576–585.

Lawler, E. E., III. "The New Plant Revolution." *Organizational Dynamics,* Winter 1978, pp. 2–12.

Lawler, E. E., III, Nadler, D. A., and Cammann, C. *Organizational Assessment.* New York: Wiley, 1980.

Ledford, G. E., Jr. "The Persistence of Planned Organization Change: A Process Theory Perspective." Unpublished doctoral dissertation, University of Michigan, 1984.

Lewin, K. *Field Theory in Social Science.* New York: Harper & Row, 1951.

Mangham, I. *The Politics of Organizational Change.* Westport, Conn.: Greenwood Press, 1979.

March, J. G. "Bonded Rationality, Ambiguity, and the Engineering of Choice." *Bell Journal of Economics,* 1978, *9,* 587–608.

Mintzberg, H., and Waters, J. A. "Tracking Strategy in an Entrepreneurial Firm." *Academy of Management Journal,* 1982, *25,* 465–499.

Mitroff, I. I., and Kilmann, R. H. *Methodological Approaches to Social Science: Integrating Divergent Concepts and Theories.* San Francisco: Jossey-Bass, 1978.

Mohr, L. B. *Explaining Organizational Behavior: The Limits and Possibilities of Theory and Research.* San Francisco: Jossey-Bass, 1982

Mohrman, A. M., Jr., and Lawler, E. E., III. "The Diffusion of QWL as a Paradigm Shift." G81-13(18). Center for Effective Organizations, University of Southern California, 1983.

Mohrman, A. M., Jr., and Novelli, L., Jr. "Adaptively Learning About the Impacts of Information Processing Technologies in the Office." G82-8(27). Center for Effective Organizations, University of Southern California, 1982.

Mohrman, A. M., Jr., and Novelli, L., Jr. "Three Types of Change in the Automated Office." G83-10(41). Center for Effective Organizations, University of Southern California, 1983.

Mohrman, S. A., and Cummings, T. G. "Self-Design Processes in Organizations." Working paper, Center for Effective Organizations, University of Southern California, 1983.

Mohrman, S. A., Cummings, T. G., and Lawler, E. E., III. "Creating Useful Research With Organizations: Relationship and Process Issues." In R. H. Kilmann and others, *Producing Useful Knowledge for Organizations*. New York: Praeger, 1983.

Nadler, D. A. "Managing Transitions to Uncertain Future States." *Organizational Dynamics,* Summer 1982, pp. 37-45.

Nadler, D. A., and Lawler, E. E., III. "Quality of Work Life: Perspectives and Directions." *Organizational Dynamics,* Winter 1983, pp. 20-30.

Orne, M. T. "On the Social Psychology of the Psychological Experiment with Particular Reference to Demand Characteristics and Their Implications." *American Psychologist,* 1962, *17,* 776-783.

Pettigrew, A. M. "On Studying Organizational Cultures." *Administrative Science Quarterly,* 1979, *24,* 570-581.

Porras, J. I., and Berg, P. O. "Evaluation Methodology in Organization Development: An Analysis and Critique." *Journal of Applied Behavioral Science,* 1978, *14,* 151-173.

Purlmutter, H. "L'Entrepure internationalerise: trois conceptions." *Revue économique et sociale,* 1965, *2,* 1-14.

Seashore, S. E., Lawler, E. E., III., Mirvis, P. H., and Cammann, C. *Assessing Organizational Change.* New York: Wiley, 1983.

Simon, H. A. *The Sciences of the Artificial.* Cambridge, Mass.: MIT Press, 1969.

Stinchcombe, A. L. "Social Structure and Organizations." In J. G. March (Ed.), *Handbook of Organizations*. Chicago: Rand McNally, 1965.

Tichy, N. M., and Friedman, S. D. "Institutional Dynamics of Action Research." Paper presented at a Conference on Producing Useful Knowledge for Organizations, Pittsburgh, Oct. 28-30, 1983.

Trist, E. "Engaging with Large-Scale Systems: Some Concepts and Methods Based on Experience Gained in Field Projects at the Tavistock Institute." Paper contributed to the Mc-Gregor Conference on Organization Development, Endicott House, Endicott, New York, 1967.

Vaill, P. B. "Process Wisdom for a New Age." In J. Adams, *Transforming Work*. Alexandria, Va.: Miles River Press, 1983.

Watzlawick, P., Beavin, J. H., and Jackson, D. D. *Pragmatics of Human Communication: A Study of Interactional Patterns, Pathologies and Paradoxes. New York: Norton, 1967.*

Watzlawick, P., Weakland, J. H., and Fisch, R. Change: Principles of Problem Formation and Problem Resolution. New York: Norton, 1974.

9

Paul S. Goodman

❧ ❧ ❧ ❧ ❧ ❧ ❧ ❧ ❧ ❧ ❧ ❧ ❧ ❧ ❧ ❧ ❧

Critical Issues in Doing Research That Contributes to Theory and Practice

This book is about our work—doing research in organizations. It is an analysis of the nature of our work, the assumptions underlying our work, and the broader implications of this work for knowledge and practice. I feel privileged to be part of this exploration.

My role is to contribute an integrative chapter. The strategy is to identify a critical set of themes that permeated the chapters, the discussants' presentations, and the proceedings of the conference. The themes represent some of the critical issues that must be resolved in designing research that is useful for theory and practice.

I have tried not to describe in detail what people said about these issues but rather to highlight some of the critical questions and unresolved problems inherent in each of these issues. The topic of this book precludes stating what we know or pro-

viding needed resolutions to issues. Rather, this book is about
values, how we should conduct our professional lives, our assumptions about the world, and general questions of epistemology. The reader will note many personal research odysseys in
the preceding chapters. These accounts are informative and
make concrete many of the abstractions that flow through this
book. My personal statement is that I value research that contributes to theory and practice. My strategies have been pluralistic in methods, collaborative relationships, and the application of positivistic criteria to how we know and generate scientific knowledge. My impression is that my own strategies differ
from the modal orientation that characterizes the research activities described in the previous chapters. This will become apparent in the discussion of the following issues.

A Problem in Meaning

It may be presumptuous, after the reader has worked
through the chapters, to ask what this book is about. The answer
seems obvious. The book is about doing research that is useful
for theory and practice. Indeed, a cursory review of the chapters,
particularly their opening sections, would generate topic sen-
tences that concern the characteristics of research that is useful
for both theory and practice (Walton), research that contributes
simultaneously to theory and practice (Hackman), research that
might better serve theory building and effectiveness in practice
(Seashore), and so on. So it would seem that there is no ambiguity among the contributors about the thrust of this book.

But to talk about research that contributes to theory and
practice evokes multiple meanings and interpretations. Consider
the following cases: In case one we are interested in research
that simultaneously contributes to theory and practice. This
statement means that the products of research facilitate or enhance theory development *and* practice. In case two—action
research—the boundaries between research, theory, and practice are blurred (see Susman and Evered, 1978). Action research
is a cyclical process of diagnosing, planning action, taking action, evaluating a particular learning, and then beginning the

diagnostic process again. In this context, the processes of doing research, theory building, and practice are ordered among the three concepts. In case three we are interested in doing research that contributes to theory and practice. The word *simultaneously* has been omitted. In this case, research typically contributes first to theory, and subsequent translations of this research affect practice.

The reason for distinguishing among these three cases is to sharpen our meaning of research that affects theory and practice. In all three cases research may affect theory and practice, but how that research is conducted and the nature of its impact may differ. For example, if one adopts the action research perspective, the relationship between the researcher and client will be much more closely linked than in case three. Or the criteria for evaluating the goodness of research will differ if one adopts the action research perspective rather than case three. The action researcher will look more toward whether planned organizational changes occurred, whereas the researcher in case three is more likely to adopt positivistic criteria such as disconfirmability through prediction and control as measures of good research.

The purpose of this discussion is to argue for a more careful delineation of the meaning of the relationship among research, theory, and practice. If we want to do research that simultaneouly affects theory and practice, that takes us down one road. If we see the three concepts as blurred or as really one activity, that leads in another direction. We may see the three concepts as analytically independent but only loosely connected (case three). The modal orientation of the chapters is to adopt case one or two. The idea in case three, where research affects theory and theory affects practice, was not well received. My own tastes are to adopt case three. It permits many avenues for research to affect practice, including case one.

Another source of ambiguity concerns the meanings of *research, theory building,* and *practice.* I raise this issue not simply as a linguistic exercise; rather, it is essential for understanding how to conduct research that is useful to both theory and practice. The goal is not for everyone to endorse a common meaning. However, it is probably useful to acknowledge the multidimensional structure of these concepts and follow through the implications of this structure when tracing the impact of research on theory and practice.

Research. Research is ascribed different meanings in the different chapters. Pettigrew talks about research as a craft process, not merely as the application of a formal set of techniques. Argyris talks about research as a process that includes describing reality, specifying causal relations, producing generalizations, and public testing. Some think about traditional research in terms of understanding prediction and control; others think about it in terms of products or forms of knowledge.

What we see in the chapters is not simply different definitions of research but different aspects or dimensions of the meaning of research. Research can be thought of as process. Argyris's notion of research as describing reality, specifying causal relations, fits into this category. Research can also be conceived as production of a type of knowledge. Walton separates written products into those with no generalization specified, ad hoc insights and hypotheses, and systematic theory. The latter two categories would be labeled as forms of research products. Seashore provides a list of types of knowledge that includes skills and arts for dealing with others, descriptions of events, theoretical formulations of knowledge, and so on. Research can also be thought of as a set of formal and informal institutional arrangements. That is, the array of universities, funding agencies, professional meetings, conferences, and so on constitutes another dimension of research.

The point of focusing on the meaning of research is that it is crucial to making sense of the broader questions of the relevance of research for theory and practice. It is the intersection among research as a process, forms of knowledge, and institutional arrangements that is the key. Seashore talks about this when he says, ''Different methods of inquiry [process] have their respective advantages in generating the different classes of knowledge. Practitioners . . . find that a particular instance of application calls on some of these categories of knowledge, perhaps not on others. The issue is one of fit among (1) type of knowledge . . ., (2) method of inquiry employed, and (3) context for practical application.'' The meaning of this to me is that application, or practice, requires certain kinds of knowledge, which, in turn, require certain kinds of inquiry. Stated in another way: If one wants to make research more relevant, one needs to identify (1) the form of knowledge required, (2) the process of inquiry that fits the form of knowledge, and (3) the appropriate institutional structure.

Practice. There is also ambiguity in the meaning of practice. What do we mean by practice? When the action researcher brings about organizational change, is this an example of research or practice? Again, the reason for this exploration of meanings is that we cannot design research that is useful for theory and practice unless we are clear what *research, theory,* and *practice* mean. In my analysis of the chapters, I found surprisingly little attention given to the meaning or conceptualization of practice. Argyris is an exception. He views practice as ''the implementation of a set of ideas in order to achieve intended consequences in a world of practical affairs. The act of implementation may be at the level of formulating a policy or executing it.'' This definition has a clear operational implication. If we wanted to assess the effect of research on practice, we would look for a new policy.

At issue is whether there are other viable definitions of practice and how to determine the impact of these definitions on the relevance of research. For example, let us broaden the interpretation of *implementation* used in Argyris's definition. Implementation may mean not only generating new policies but also generating new ways to organize information or to analyze problems. That is, research may not only change our policies or roles with respect to others but also change how we organize and analyze information. In this case research influences our cognitive processes, not simply our overt behavior. This broader definition has implications for tracing the effect of research on practice. Now we are willing to consider changes in how people think about their world as well as in what they do. We will also be open to forms of research that are more likely to affect how we think about the world of practical affairs than what we do in that world. Consider briefly the impact or relevance of books like *Theory Z* or *In Search of Excellence.* These writings are based on some forms of research. They have been read by hundreds of thousands of managers. Whether or not you endorse these books, it is clear that they have influenced how people organize or perhaps analyze their worlds. Using the broader definition of practice, most people would say that these and other, related books have been influential and relevant. I raise this issue simply because the two books cited represent a particular type of research that has probably had a particular type of influence on practice, and this type of research and influence is not a modal strategy in this book.

There are other points of ambiguity that might be explored (for example, the relation between research and theory building), but it is probably better to end this discussion with the following observation: Doing research that contributes to theory and practice would be valued by most readers of this volume. At one level of meaning, that assertion seems perfectly clear and acceptable. At another level, there are many meanings that could be attributed to the concepts and their interrelationships. It is at this level that the problem statement becomes interesting and complex. It is at this level that the meaning assigned is likely to lead to different strategies in research and different kinds of effects of research on theory and practice.

Traditional Models of Science

Most of the chapters criticize traditional models of research and their lack of relevance for informing practice. The basic argument is that traditional research methods from the physical sciences are based on a view of the world that is incompatible with the world of organizations and therefore that research inspired by these methods is unlikely to have relevance for practice. Mitroff opens the book with this argument when he offers pictures of the machine model of the world and the world as a complex hologram. The machine model is a world of reductionism, economic rationality, and simple cause and effect. The world of the hologram is complex, made up of a diverse set of stakeholders engaged simultaneously in economic and psychodynamic transactions.

Traditional research methods are seen as inappropriate.

330 Doing Research That Is Useful for Theory and Practice

Pettigrew's discussion of contextual analysis takes a similar position: "One of the core requirements of a contextualist analysis is to understand the emergent, situational, and holistic features of an organism . . . rather than to divide the world into limited sets of dependent and independent variables isolated from their contexts." Hackman takes a different approach but draws similar conclusions. He does a nice job in pointing to the limitation of traditional approaches such as laboratory experiments in developing practical theory about performance effectiveness. In general, the picture of the traditional model of research is one dominated by positivistic science, experimental methods, observations of the present, methods that are supposedly value-neutral, detached relationships with clients, and so on.

The issue for the reader is how seriously he or she should consider the criticism of the traditional research paradigm. The following questions may help. *Is the field of organizational research dominated by methods from the physical sciences?* I think not. A cursory review of the major journals will show a diversity of methods used in different research problems. Varying levels of rigor are demonstrated in theory development and empirical analysis. *Do organizational researchers subscribe to the machine model of the world?* I think not. The systems model dominates much of the thinking. In the field, concepts such as equifinality, reciprocal causation, and garbage-can models permeate our thinking. *Why, then, is there a common attack by the contributors of this volume on the traditional model?* I think there are two reasons. First, traditional research methods are often used to test trivial topics. That is, certain aspects of using traditional methods lead one to seek more and more refinement, which often leads, in turn, to researching unimportant issues. We probably do not need the 500th test of a job-design model. So one criticism of traditional methods is that the values of precision lead to trivial research. My own view is that this criticism is misplaced. The problem with the 500th test of a job-design model is not inherent in traditional research methods but rather in taste. If one tests whether age moderated the effect of job design on satisfaction in a nursing population, that is not caused by traditional methods. Precision does not necessarily cause trivial problem selection—taste does.

Second, the criticism of traditional research methods represents a dialectic position forcing us to think about how we want to conduct research. That is, by attacking traditional methods, one is forced to think about alternative ways of doing research. That, in my opinion, is the primary rationale for criticizing traditional methods. The problem with this dialectic approach is that it forces us into "either/or" thinking, which may not be appropriate. Traditional models of research are viewed as the opposite of research designed to influence theory and practice. What we do not want to do is to adopt an "either/or" stance. That is, if the criterion of confirmation for traditional research is "x," then if I want to adopt research relevant for practice, I should select "not x." This seems to me to be dysfunctional reasoning. As I will show, characteristics of traditional research can be incorporated into research that contributes to theory and practice.

An Alternative Research Strategy

Much of the criticism of the traditional model was initiated to provide a rationale for alternative models of designing research useful for theory and practice. As the reader moves through this book, a variety of approaches for designing research with dual relevance are presented. At the same time there are commonalities that cut across the chapters. Let's start with the differences.

Walton presents a practical approach to designing research that will affect theory and practice. His suggestions include mixing research and consulting activities, selecting appropriate questions and variables, and emphasizing hypothesis generation over hypothesis testing and relevance over rigor.

Argyris's proposals for dual relevance are intimately linked to his theory of Model I and Model II behavior. His basic argument is "If human beings use maps for action to inform their actions, then one way for social scientists to help ensure that the knowledge they produce will be usable is to organize, or package, it in the form of maps for action." The beauty of Argyris's chapter lies not so much in the substantive merits of his theory but in that his substantive theory dictates a research methodology that increases the probability of dual relevance.

As a third example, the chapter by Cummings, Mohrman, Mohrman, and Ledford endorses research defined by a symmetrical collaborative relationship between researchers and organizational stakeholders. One of the ways that chapter differs from others is in explicating an institutional structure (namely, a transorganizational system) for supporting this type of research on organizational change.

Although these and other perspectives in the book differ in their strategies for designing research with dual relevance, there are also some apparent commonalities. One common theme, and probably one of the most important, is the collaborative nature of research in the alternative mode. Researchers and organization members work together and assume joint responsibility for the research process. Values in the alternative model are more likely to be explicated. The purpose of the epistemological activities is to improve the well-being of the individual and the organization.

Relevance is preferred to rigor. Problem selection is more often focused on creating change than on questions of solely theoretical interest. There is a strong interest in the contextual perspective, and the time perspective is on the present and the future. This enumeration of factors is presented to illustrate the common structure among the alternative research strategies presented in this book.

Some Limitations

This is an important book because it articulates an alternative strategy for conducting research. The espoused strategies probably have more commonalities than differences. The emphases on collaborative relationships between researcher and client, alternative criteria for confirmation, exploration of the values underlying the research process, and so on all speak to a different approach to creating dual relevance for theory and practice.

With this advocacy for new strategies should also come some acknowledgment of limitations. Only Walton's chapter seems to address some of these limitations. Walton mentions two points. First, action assignments shape the nature of the theoretical questions and methodology used. The implication is that these assignments may affect practice more than theory development. Second, the dual role increases the potential for self-serving or defensive explanations.

There are, of course, other limitations, which I will briefly enumerate. My interest is to evoke a more balanced dialogue about the merits of the proposed strategies for dual relevance. First, does a collaborative, symmetrical relationship between researcher and client generate better-quality information? I think the answer is that different forms of collaboration generate different types of information—not necessarily better-quality information. For three years I was associated with a sophisticated action research team that subscribed to the collaborative relationship position. I was an evaluator of this team's change project, operating in the more traditional detached role. Both the action and the evaluation team had access to the data on change. Let me give you an example. There were several walkouts during this organizational change project, and these are important events in the history of this organization. The evaluation team knew when these walkouts were going to occur and who was involved. Information on some of the walkouts was not available to the action team. Now, anyone who is familiar with the union in question or the secrecy surrounding such action will appreciate that access to prewalkout information is difficult to come by. I cite this example not to criticize the action team but rather to point out that although the evaluation team was detached in a research sense, we had a different role relationship with the participants that generated different and relevant data.

Second, a common theme throughout the chapters was identifying the relevant stakeholders and integrating them into the research process. This position appears somewhat naive. Stakeholders or constituencies by definition represent different interest groups. Why should we believe that these individuals will operate in a cooperative manner if the institutions they represent are in conflict? For example, we are currently working with a national labor/management committee in an industry where safety is a major problem. We are the researchers for this committee. Although the individuals may be personally interested in participating in the research process, what they do will be shaped by political considerations. For example, when national negotiations began, this committee was "on hold" until a new contract was signed.

Third, to develop the kind of collaborative relationships advocated in this book requires an organization of employees who have the ability and the interest to work in this form of collaborative research relationship. Although I would hope that these abilities and interests would develop over time, I doubt that the modal organization willing to participate in organizational research is sophisticated enough (in terms of interests or abilities) to operate in the collaborative model suggested in the book.

A related limitation is that the researcher must have an extraordinary amount of personal, intellectual, and research skill to pull off this alternative approach. I am sure the reader will acknowledge that the contributors of the preceding chapters are leaders in the field. They have extraordinary skills and have made extraordinary contributions. They may be leaders of a new methodology, but they surely do not represent the modal researcher in the organizational field.

A fifth limitation is that the current institutional structure may not support the alternative strategies for dual relevance advocated in this book. Let's take a simple case. Much organizational research is conducted in university settings. Universities expect faculty members to be productive in both research and teaching. By anyone's account the proposed alternative form of research is tremendously time-consuming. Years, not weeks, are invested in this activity. So my arguments are not about the scientific merits of the new research; the fact that it is time-consuming will make it less attractive under current institutional reward systems.

Let me conclude this section with a quotation from Seashore's chapter. The point being made is that we have different kinds of knowledge that require different kinds of research strategies: "The varieties of knowledge we work with and need exceed the capacities of research methods that are constrained by the unique case, by direct involvement in the phenomena under study, and by 'experience' accessible to participants in such approaches to knowledge generation.''

Institutional Change

In previous sections I have enumerated some of the advantages as well as limitations of research strategies designed to produce dual relevance for theory and practice. Many of the limitations are tied to the institutional research structure in our society. That is, the network of universities, funding institutions, and journals controls the type of research that gets produced. It is doubtful that a particular form of research will survive unless it is supported by this institutional structure. It should be clear from the various discussions in this book that the current institutional structure supports the traditional model, rather than the alternative models for conducting research with dual relevance. So an important question is, what are the ways to modify this institutional structure to provide a more supportive environment for research designed to promote dual relevance?

Changing this institutional structure is important for two reasons. First, research designed to forward dual relevance will survive only in a supportive culture. Second, most of the people advocating the dual-relevance position have experienced feelings of defensiveness and feel threatened by people who believe they have abandoned the traditional model. A careful reading of the chapters and the discussions of those chapters reveals how strong these feelings of defensiveness are. Attempts to bring about an institutional structure supporting this type of research will have important psychological benefits for the participants. So the basic question is, how does one legitimate this type of research?

The chapter by Cummings, Mohrman, Mohrman, and Ledford presents the boldest attempt to answer this question. Their discussion of the transorganizational system provides a clear picture of one type of organizational structure that will support research designed for dual use. The chapter is particularly useful because the delineation of the transorganizational system is grounded in a real organization—the Center for Effective Organizations.

Other forms of institutional change appear throughout the chapters. The role of funding organizations is obviously critical. Major grants for research on dual relevance would provide an important source of legitimation. Universities will also play a major role. Much of our initial taste for doing research is shaped during our doctoral training, so the form of that training and its consequences for the alternative model of doing dual-relevance research are critical. A different educational change might come in the form of special internships or new types of postdoctoral training. Another central feature of universities is the operative reward system for financial and promotional benefits. As previously mentioned, if the reward system does not support the type of output produced by dual-relevance research, that work will not get done. Another institutional area for change is the journals. Creating journals is one way to disseminate and to legitimate forms of research. *Organizational Behavior and Human Performance* is a good example of a journal legitimating one type of research.

I have included this issue in my discussion because I think it is central to whether research designed to promote both theory development and practice will be viable and influential. My own view is that significant institutional changes will be difficult to bring about. True, organizations such as the Center for Effective Organizations are up and running. But will this organization be viable five years from now? What would happen if the principal researchers of the Center for Effective Organizations or the other constituents of the University of Southern California wanted to change its mission? Setting up a new journal is trivial compared with changing the institutional research structure in universities.

The dilemma is that institutional change is necessary. Some change has occurred, but it is fragile and there are strongly opposing forces.

How Do We Know

The questions of how we know what good research is, how we know whether research affects practice, and how we know whether research will affect theory permeate all the chapters. Indeed, the book is about epistemological issues in organizational research. I identify this as a central theme because if one wants to advocate a new form of research, it is desirable to specify how one would evaluate that research or distinguish good forms of that research from poorer forms.

It seems to me that, by the end of the book, there is less consensus on this topic than on any of the others I have outlined. Some of the authors approach these questions by arguing that our assumptions about the structure of the world determine our "theory of truth." This position can be seen clearly in Mitroff's and Pettigrew's works. Walton discusses some of the trade-offs between rigor and relevance, two possible criteria for judging the value of research. Explicit or implicit in most of the expositions is that the rules for "knowing" from the traditional model of science might not fit the alternative model of research designed for dual relevance. So other criteria should be proposed. Argyris provides one of the clearest discussions of the "how do you know" question. On the one hand, he adopts some of the approaches of the traditional model by advocating describing reality, specifying causal relations, producing generalizations, and public testing or refutation. On the other hand, objectivity achieved by distancing the researcher from those being studied, or precision through quantitative analysis, is incompatible with his view of creating research with dual relevance.

"How do you know when research aimed at practice and theory is good?" is a very difficult question to answer. The chapters highlight the importance of this question but do not provide many coherent arguments for its resolution. I can sketch out some parameters for how one might attack the questions. First, many of our evaluations of goodness come from our own values or tastes. Do we think the research is an important problem? The definition of *important* may be inherent in the research problem or in how I think the research might bear on theory and/or practice. This evaluation is clearly in the realm of personal taste and probably explains a lot of the judgment of "goodness." A second parameter in evaluating the goodness of research designed for dual relevance is selection of criteria. Which criteria are selected depends in part on which scientific community serves as one's reference group. The general concept of confirmability or disconfirmability would be one powerful criterion to use in evaluating the goodness of any research. The difference would appear in the bases of confirmability. Logical consistency, prediction, and control are means of assessing confirmability. The traditional model would probably use all three bases of confirmability, whereas research for dual relevance might select only control (where *control* means the ability to create a more desirable state). The important point is that specification of the bases of confirmability is necessary for assessing goodness. It is important for the reader to note a point stated earlier: One can embrace research designed to enhance theory and practice and also embrace criteria of confirmability drawn from the traditional model. Argyris's discussion of the criteria of confirmability drawn from the traditional model illustrates that point.

A third parameter in evaluation is judging the appropriateness of methods. That is, we will evaluate goodness by whether the methods fit the problem and by our position on confirmability. A theme throughout this book is the inappropriateness of traditional methods of experimental design, instrumentation, and quantification in analysis for research designed for dual relevance. This position is probably derived from the nature of the problem under study—understanding organizational change. Creating changes leads to a complex set of phenomena not easily captured by these traditional procedures. An unfortunate implication of this type of reasoning is that we should discard these traditional procedures and focus solely on more qualitative case studies. However, it is not clear to me that new qualitative approaches are the only appropriate method for the problem. It is true that most research on organizational change concerns a unique event, not easily generalized, and characterized by complex systems of causation. That does not mean, however, that methods from traditional science cannot be effectively utilized. For example, there are no true control groups in organizational change projects. But does that mean one should not use some adaptation of the concept of a control group in one's research on organizational change? (See Goodman, 1979.)

The fourth parameter in evaluating the goodness of research designed for dual relevance concerns assessing the impact of the research on theory and practice. That is, how do we know that research has caused a change in theory or practice? This question brings us back to the first theme of this chapter, which concerned the meaning of *research, theory,* and *practice.* Unless the meaning of those terms is clear, it will be difficult to evaluate the effects of research on theory and practice and hence to evaluate the goodness of the research.

Some Concluding Remarks

This book is critical because it challenges some of the basic assumptions about how we do our research on understanding organizations. I have tried to highlight some of the important themes or issues in this discussion. There are no simple resolutions to any of these issues. Rather, I have tried to present some of the similarities and differences in order to sharpen our understanding of the basic problems.

The central issue in furthering our understanding of the general question of how to design research relevant to theory and practice is the delineation of the meanings of *research, theory,* and *practice* and their interrelationships. This question touches on values and topics in the philosophy of science. We will not make any progress with loose and metaphorical narratives. If changing practice means changing behavior, that is one valid definition of *practice.* So when we look at the link between research and practice, we look for specific changes in behavior. If we say we want to design research that simultaneously affects research and practice, this is a very different meaning from a problem statement that permits us to look at research that affects theory, which, in turn, affects practice. It is difficult to examine whether theory follows practice or practice follows theory without clarifying the meaning of the central concepts. We generate verbal links such as *lag, inform,* and *relevance for* without specifying the linking process.

The dialectic between the traditional form of research and the alternative strategies for dual relevance permeates every chapter in this book. This form of discussion, with its "either/or" quality, is useful because it clarifies our understanding of the alternative research model by identifying the underlying assumptions or contract dimensions. For example, the client in the alternative strategies for dual relevance is a collaborator in the research process, not an object of study. Research that informs practice is considered more valuable than research directed solely at theory.

Although the dialectic serves as a useful heuristic, I have tried to sketch out some limitations particular to the alternative model. I did this because most of the discussion was about limitations of the traditional model compared with the alternative model. For example, in the alternative, close collaboration between researcher and client is assumed to create better data. That is, of course, an assumption, not an empirical fact. In addition, I argued that different forms of collaboration lead to *different, not necessarily better* forms of information. Another potential problem with this dialectic dialogue was the inference that if one accepts adopted strategies for dual relevance, one cannot simultaneously adopt positions congruent with traditional research. I used Argyris's chapter as an exception. Argyris clearly embraces research designed for dual relevance, with many of its implications (for example, high collaboration between researcher and client). At the same time, he adopts some conventions of confirmability from the traditional model.

I discussed the issue of changing the institutional research structure because I think it is basic to whether research aimed at dual relevance will survive. The issue of "how do we know" is a dilemma facing anyone interested in the relationship of research, theory, and practice. Much of the discussion of that issue also had the "either/or" orientation. Do we want high rather than low uncertainty, certainty rather than usefulness, and so on? I believe that type of questioning is not very useful or likely to lead to any useful responses. I tried to approach this question by identifying four parameters, or classes of decisions, that should be examined when asking the "how do we know" question. That is, we need to think about ways of structuring the question before trying to resolve it.

Will research designed to create dual relevance for theory and practice be viable over the next decade? The answer at one level is obviously yes. This type of research is not at the proposal stage; it has been an important contributor to our knowledge about organizations over the past decade and earlier. The real question is whether research designed for dual relevance will become a more dominant influence in the literature on organizational behavior. There are forces pushing for more influence. Government sources offer less funding for doing basic research on organizational functioning. Organizations becoming more sophisticated in their understanding of human resource issues are less likely to fund or participate in research that has little application to improving the well-being of the firm. Opinion leaders such as the contributors to this volume are advocating research with dual relevance. Organizations such as the Center for Effective Organizations provide real models for designing this type of research. This particular organization and others like it serve to legitimate the need for this kind of research, as well as stimulate dialogue about it and other forms of research.

However, there are counterforces that will work against the diffusion of research designed for dual relevance. The most important force is the current institutional research structure, composed of funding institutions, universities, journals, and so on. This structure is more likely to legitimate research with a more traditional orientation than that focusing on dual relevance. Unless that institutional structure changes, I doubt that research with dual relevance will increase markedly. In addition, there are trends that will strengthen the legitimacy of more traditionally oriented research. Major development has occurred in other disciplines in such areas as statistical modeling. Those techniques

342 Doing Research That Is Useful for Theory and Practice

are slowly moving into empirical research on organizations. The assumption underlying the application of these techniques is that finer quantitative precision is desirable. So while the strategies articulated in this volume call for new methods and ways of knowing, there are also new technological developments in our field that move toward legitimating the traditional model.

This book is an important part of continuing dialogue on the relationship among research, theory, and practice. There are still many unanswered questions and unexplored areas. Some of our discussion is too parochial. To a great extent our focus is within the field of organizational behavior. Many other disciplines—for example, social psychology, engineering—have wrestled with this issue. Similarly, we probably should broaden our experience in the philosophy of science. Many of the problems we are examining have a long tradition in philosophical analysis. We should also pay more attention to the research on research utilization and diffusion of knowledge and practice.

Our inquiry into this central question of the relationship among research, theory, and practice should be broader rather than narrower. There are many routes to linking research with theory and practice. We should look at how to design research that simultaneously affects theory and practice. We should also examine the nature of research that affects practice but not theory and the kind of research/theory connection that does not affect practice. How does our consulting lead to new insights about theory? How does evaluation of organizational practices affect the diffusion of those practices into other settings? Many of the contributors to this book teach in professional schools where the goal is to help managers in practice. Which aspects of our teaching affect practice and which do not?

There are different types of knowledge, some pertinent to theory building, some pertinent to practice, some pertinent to both. For each of these types of knowledge, there are different methods of intellectual inquiry and different ways of "knowing" that either the knowledge generated or the application of the methods of inquiry is appropriate. The task is to examine the fit among the type of knowledge, the methods of inquiry, and the ways of knowing.

GROUP DISCUSSION

Lawler: You raised the issue of legitimation in several ways. Are these styles of research legitimate, respected, and valued in the field? That is a strong concern. There is a tension around me that fails to reflect the record of visibility of the people sitting around the room. Literally hundreds of books and thousands of articles have been written by the people at the table, and they have received probably every award the field has to offer. Why are we tense about being change agents, worried about being legitimate? I don't have a ready answer for you.

The other issue of legitimation concerns the work of people who don't have all the credentials. I wonder what would make it easier for other people to do this kind of research at an earlier stage or a different stage without feeling that they were doing something inferior or incredibly risky.

Kilmann: One piece of data is from a study I did last year with Ken Thomas. We sampled 1,000 people from the Academy of Management on issues of rigor, relevance, and the ideal purpose of the organizational sciences versus the actual. When we asked what they personally valued, rigor and relevance came out absolutely equal. When we asked what they thought others in the field value, they came out strongly as high on rigor and low on relevance. That was referred to as pluralistic ignorance. Somehow, this circle first has to be exposed, then corrected.

Whetten: My concern is that, coming out of this conference, we might legitimate something that is accessible only to the elites within the field—those people who have made it, who are in highly visible institutions, who are in action research centers such as CEO that are well funded, who have the skills and knowledge. How is this going to play in Peoria? What can we say to the people in Lawrence, Kansas, and Champaign–Urbana who have these aspirations? They want to make a contribution, but they don't have the kind of institutional support that makes this sort of conference possible.

Lawler: When I hear Dave's comment, I find myself very ambivalent. On the one hand, I'm all for egalitarianism, with everybody pitching in from every nook and cranny of the world, because we need all the knowledge we can gather. On the other hand, I think one of the problems of the field is that we've been a field of little tiny studies done by people with inadequate resources, small samples, and inappropriate conceptualizations. Perhaps we're in trouble because of mass egalitarianism. Maybe we need more big research efforts, whether in teams, institutions, or large-scale studies.

Whetten: I think we have to be careful in our attributions about why those little studies are coming out all over the country. My sense is there is considerable desire on the part of researchers in our field to become more relevant, but they don't know how to do it. There aren't many institutional devices for legitimating this kind of research, providing training, and providing access to organizations by teams of researchers. Mechanisms like CEO are lacking, and that, as much as lack of interest in or desire for relevance, explains the kinds of studies we're seeing.

Argyris: What's terribly important is that CEO is something that can happen in Lawrence, Kansas, for example. You need some faculty members who will risk their careers on creating an organization that will connect with practice. Like CEO, they can get their funding largely from organizations that they're studying. There's no reason that can't be done in Peoria, unless those in Peoria don't have the competence. And if so, thank God people in Peoria aren't doing this kind of work.

Whetten: My response is, let's get the people in Peoria trained. Right now they don't know where to start. They don't have the access they need.

S. Mohrman: Access is a big issue but not a simple one. One way to get access is to be a Lawler or to piggyback on him. But there are other ways. I wonder about the role of the faculty member and the junior faculty member in this kind of research. Getting access is giving a whole lot of free speeches to groups that might be able to get you into their organizations. It is spending a lot of time in lunches that go nowhere. It is doing what

Richard [Hackman] described, working with an organization for a year and a half before you find out that they don't want to do anything or, worse, before you find out they're going to quit in the middle of the project. It is a very, very time-consuming process that has as much to do with whether you are willing to pay the dues to get access as it has to do with competence. I'm not sure that faculty members, especially junior faculty members, are willing to spend the time necessary to do that kind of work.

Walton: Universities have got to be willing to support faculty members in the following ways. They've got to be willing to give credit for being a member of a team. They've got to be willing to take dry periods where you're out there kicking the bushes and give credit for that. They've got to restructure the reward system. And restructuring the reward system won't be easy.

REFERENCES

Goodman, P. *Assessing Organizational Change: The Rushton Quality of Work Experiment.* New York: Wiley, 1979.

Susman, G. I., and Evered, R. D. "An Assessment of the Scientific Merits of Action Research." *Administrative Science Quarterly,* 1978, *23* (4), 582–603.

Susan A. Mohrman
Allan M. Mohrman, Jr.
Gerald E. Ledford, Jr.
Thomas G. Cummings
Edward E. Lawler III

Epilogue

❧ ❧ ❧ ❧ ❧ ❧ ❧ ❧ ❧ ❧ ❧ ❧ ❧ ❧ ❧ ❧ ❧

Walking the Tightrope
Between Theory and Practice

During the past year, we have spent considerable time reflecting on the significance of this book and the conference. Their subject is the very lifeblood of our work at the Center for Effective Organizations (CEO). We can continue to prosper only as long as our research meets collegial standards of theoretical excellence and the equally demanding practitioner standards of practical utility. We continually try to assess the viability of this goal, the appropriateness of our research approaches, and the quality of our relationships with both the academic and the practitioner communities.

We believe the conference was a success. Many of the finest researchers in the field joined us in a discussion of a topic central to CEO's mission. Our own perspectives have been considerably enriched, and our assumptions challenged. The conference highlighted the tightrope we must walk between theory and practice. It reminded us that our fellow academics sometimes are a force for imbalance in our highwire act.

Prior to the conference, several colleagues accused us of assembling a group of participants who "think alike" about matters of rigor and relevance. Some suggested that we ought to stage more of a debate among divergent viewpoints. Others felt that practitioners should be included. Our inclination was to address differences at a later time. This conference was aimed at coalescing what we felt to be an already rich diversity of approaches used by leaders in the field who share a concern for both theory and practical relevance.

We feel that our inclinations proved correct. The participants were indeed diverse, both in terms of what they do and how they think. Some adhered strongly to the tenets of positivist science; others found the traditional research model too limited; still others were not concerned about epistemology at all. Several participants had a clear and consistent model for gathering and analyzing data; some stressed the need to employ different approaches in investigating different problems; others advocated the simultaneous use of multiple methodologies to investigate the same phenomenon. The research history of some participants has focused on the development and testing of a particular theoretical framework; others have migrated from one theoretical framework to another; some have employed multiple frameworks and levels of analysis. The participants varied in the way they approached ambiguity in field research. Some carefully structured their activities to remove and overcome it; others embraced it and designed their studies to capture it.

There were other differences. Some worked in teams; their writing was characterized by periods of intense collaboration with certain colleagues. Others were essentially loners who had made significant solo contributions to our field. Some operated as members of an academic faculty; others were housed in research centers. They ranged from being highly concerned to being relatively uninterested in building research institutions.

The commonalities among the participants were equally interesting. The chapter writers were organizational "campers," not office researchers. They had submerged themselves in organizational life in order to understand it better. Despite epistemological differences, they shared a practical orientation. Their concerns and activities were field-determined, driven by specific experiences with organizations and the issues facing them.

Equally noteworthy was the general concern with rigor and discipline. There was unanimous agreement that excellence demands well-thought-out and carefully executed studies. "Doing a couple of interviews to see what's out there" would not meet the professional standards of any of the participants.

Without exception, the participants viewed themselves as social scientists. They have continued to research and publish at a prolific rate throughout their careers. They are *not* tenured academics who have stopped doing research and concentrate solely on consulting. Rather, they have amply demonstrated that, given the values of relevance and science, field and academic skills, and perhaps a little luck, it is possible to build a career that addresses compelling needs for organizational practice and contributes to organization theory.

The participants' difficulty in feeling comfortable with the topic of this book seems ironic and even paradoxical. As is evident in the transcripts of the discussions, the conference addressed issues that were not easily or openly tackled.

The participants' values, preferences, and world views were deeply rooted and were sometimes defended with great emotion. Openly confronting these differences seemed to risk splitting organizational researchers into factions and perhaps forcing conference participants into one faction or another. Most participants have built their careers on transcending such academic divisions. Thus, discussing individual careers seemed potentially threatening to some participants. We anticipated some of this awkwardness. Indeed, the decision to emphasize commonalities rather than foster debate was based on the belief that initial treatment of the topic should be thoughtful and supportive rather than confrontational.

Conference discussion was made difficult by another factor that we had not anticipated. Not only are the values and world views that underlie the work of many of the participants fundamental and personal, they have also not always been fully articulated. Several participants expressed surprise at the initial list of questions to which they were asked to respond and indicated that this was the first time they had addressed such issues as how they had developed their research styles, what drove their investigations, and so on. The activities of this group did not seem to have gained impetus from introspection.

Yet most of the participants had clearly pursued a career of relevant research because of personal inclinations and interests. Even those who had been educated in applied research centers did not necessarily feel encouraged to proceed in that direction. This fact, together with the lack of relevant research being conducted, raises the critical issue of how this kind of research can be sustained.

There are certainly a number of prominent research centers whose mission is to conduct practical research. Historically, they have found it difficult to walk the tightrope; they have tended to move toward pure academic research or toward pure consulting. A sobering thought, from our perspective, is that applied research centers may be inherently unstable because of their competing missions and constituencies. Despite this, there is a recent growth in their numbers and the number of academic scholars who are attempting to build such research institutions.

We have also learned much about the institutional viability of CEO from the reactions to the conference by our colleagues at the University of Southern California. Those who attended the conference and a follow-up seminar have had a variety of responses. There has been little reaction from the senior faculty, most of whom have defined their orientation to the field through research records that speak for themselves. Many of the senior faculty were involved in the conference in some capacity and are committed to bridging the gap between theory and practice.

The reactions from some of our junior colleagues and doctoral students were more intense. Several new faculty members found the issues to be pragmatically troublesome for their own careers, which are heavily influenced by the ''publish or perish'' mandate and a short-term orientation toward what is quickly studied and easily published. For some, ironically, the conference crystallized a short-term strategy of avoiding deep involvement in the long-term, team-based studies that are described in Chapter Eight by Cummings, Mohrman, Mohrman, and Ledford. One young faculty member expressed a certain sadness that his short-term career dilemmas had become quite clear: for the present he must orient himself to an institutional reward structure that precludes dealing with the pressing organizational concerns that led him to the field in the first place. Yet another junior faculty member said that for the first time he could appreciate that CEO was in fact doing research, although it certainly was not the kind of research that he had been trained to do or value. Another expressed confusion that conference participants, as prominent researchers, were describing ways of doing research that appeared quite discrepant from his training and the requirements of the journals he must satisfy.

Doctoral students also were quite mixed in their responses to the conference. For some, it offered hope that the seemingly endless seminars, theories, and papers might lead toward research careers linked to practical organizational concerns. For others, the content of the conference was irrelevant to the knowledge in which they were becoming "expert." Some graduate students have even been counseled by faculty advisers to avoid deep involvement in CEO projects. Perhaps the most intriguing reaction was from students who expressed surprise that practical, programmatic research demanded disciplined mastery of the basic quantitative as well as qualitative methodologies of the social sciences. They had hoped for a haven from "needlessly structured activities."

In summary, our colleagues reacted to the conference with a full spectrum of emotions, ranging from approval and concurrence through skepticism and confusion to disapproval and rejection. This diversity of values and orientations makes possible a dialogue that is fundamental to continued academic strength. It also risks exposing the divisiveness that has always characterized an extremely diverse field of study, a field that often seems ready for cacophonous disintegration. We admit to mixed feelings. The balance remains tenuous—perhaps more than we had imagined at the onset. We hope that this book will stimulate similar activities elsewhere, not because they will remove the need for the tightrope or even make walking it easier, but because they will force us all to keep on trying not to fall.

Afterword

Warren Bennis

❖ ❖ ❖ ❖ ❖ ❖ ❖ ❖ ❖ ❖ ❖ ❖ ❖ ❖ ❖ ❖ ❖

Observations on What We Have Learned About Useful Research

Ralph Waldo Emerson used to greet old friends he had not seen in some time with the question, "What's become clear to you since we last met?" What has become clear to me since the conference was held at the University of Southern California where the chapters included in this book came to life is my response to the leading question Ed Lawler posed to all participants: "How can we do research that is useful for both theory and practice?" Three key concepts have emerged in my thinking about this question: role ambivalence, the need to transcend the duality of theory and practice, and the importance of coming to terms with the fact that there are no easy answers.

Role Ambivalence

My ideas on ambivalence stem from a remarkably sensitive observation Alexis de Tocqueville made about those who pursue knowledge and truth and those who engage in action.

> I have come across men of letters, who have
> written history without taking part in public affairs,
> and politicians, who have only concerned them-
> selves with producing events without thinking of
> describing them. I have observed that the first are
> always inclined to find general causes where the
> others, living in the midst of disconnected daily
> facts, are prone to imagine that everything is attrib-
> utable to particular incidents, and that the wires
> they pull are the same that move the world. It is
> to be presumed that they are both equally deceived.

The concept that Tocqueville's remarks elucidate is not psychological ambivalence—the state of experiencing two opposite emotions, such as love and hate, at once. Instead, it is sociological
ambivalence—incompatible normative expectations within a
single role in a single social rank. The two are frequently linked,
to be sure, and as conference participants pointed out, sociological ambivalence is one major source of psychological ambivalence. Indeed, all who engage in the interstitial world of knowledge—we happy few!—are afflicted by sociological ambivalence
insofar as we occupy at least two domains: that of seeker of
truth and that of applier.

When we reckon with the role of doing research that is
useful, we are compelled to confront the ambivalence inherent
in that effort for at least two reasons. First, unlike engineers,
pharmacists, or even surgeons, who can dispense their knowledge without much, if any, human contact, those of us interested in application must be deeply involved with our clients.
Affective neutrality is impossible when profound human changes
are at stake. The fact is that the realm of classical science is at
odds with the messy, unwieldy, deeply human findings of the
social sciences. Furthermore, in classical science one can carry
out experiments on one's subjects; but the situation is very different in applied behavioral science. The "subjects," as the
chapter by Cummings, Mohrman, Mohrman, and Ledford implies, must become coinvestigators if the research is to have any
meaning and ultimately lead to change.

The second, more arguable, reason for confronting the

ambivalence is embodied in the strong idealism the conference participants bring to their tasks. Although they frequently, and almost always unsuccessfully, try to mask their strong desire to help create more democratic, more humane, more liveable human systems, the people assembled for the Center for Effective Organizations conference are perhaps unusually idealistic. For George Orwell, there was no higher ideal than the humanistic one, and the inner tension between his idealism and his humanistic values led to his unique political philosophy. When I reflected on the words and actions of the participants at the conference, I was struck by this same tension being expressed through debates that always seemed confrontations between our scientific superego and our impulse to "do good." I suspect that those of us engaged in the pursuit of practical theory are failed saints; our practice and our ideals are all too frequently out of sync.

The ambivalence of which I speak is further deepened because there are essentially two strategies for truth gathering. In the exoteric mode, knowledge is produced for the public interest and springs out of the direct experience of an immediate, intimate relationship to the sources of data. In the esoteric mode, knowledge is produced for one's learned colleagues and is consciously more detached, socially disengaged, and remote. Most of us, certainly all of us who participated in preparing this volume, were trained esoterically and practice exoterically. (Even Lyman Porter and Chris Argyris, despite their stated differences, have this in common.) This is the major determinant of the inevitable ambivalence we must reckon with.

Transcending the Duality

The phrase *useful for both theory and practice* does more than imply a duality; it implies a challenge as well. And, as the reader will note from the discussions that occurred among the participants, all too often the duality—an essentially false dichotomy —blocked our view.

Cummings, Mohrman, Mohrman, and Ledford state in their chapter that "useful information cannot be produced *for* organizations, but must be generated *with* them.'' They argue that if ''organizational research is to be useful, researchers and organizational members must become partners in the research effort.'' That about sums up the duality and the challenge to transcend it. What fascinated me was the chorus of voices around the conference table supporting the principle of *with* not *for*, despite occasional lapses into false dichotomies.

I believe that this emphasis on collaboration that most of us extolled has less to do with ethical considerations than with pragmatic ones. The only way any client will successfully adopt new knowledge is by receiving it with a cooperative attitude in a climate of positive support that will balance opposing forces and eventually bring them to a new and desirable level. Kurt Lewin told us this at least forty years ago. He also argued that a ''new and desirable level'' can be reached only by facilitating communication within the client's organization as well as between the client and the researcher qua change agent. Without that communication, how can the researcher discover the data needed to diagnose the situation? The information has to come from the client organization itself; thus it will become available only if the client will make it so. Field researchers studying different societies have long acknowledged their reliance on trust to counter their clients' strong resistance to yielding important information. Without the trust that is generated through collaboration, the applied researcher and the client's organization will be forced to struggle with limited and often distorted data.

One last point should be made about collaboration. The process of developing a collaborative relationship between an applied researcher and the client's organization may contribute to an understanding of problems in the client's environment. Somewhat similar to transference in psychoanalysis, the conditions of the relationship can create analogies between the past and the present, between the clients' outside world and the client/practitioner relationship. To this extent, the collaborative relationship provides not only an affective prop (while change is occurring) but may pave the way for cognitive revelations. Many applied researchers use problems in the evolving relationships they have with their clients as exemplars of the other relationship problems the client must deal with. In short, insofar as the collaborative relationship constitutes a microcosm of other relationships, it can augment the researcher's knowledge of the client's organization.

In reality, it is difficult to find a purely collaborative relationship; the best to be hoped for is a commitment to work toward collaboration on the part of both the knowledge provider and the knowledge seeker. Ambiguities and irregularities almost always accompany such a commitment. All the same, I view collaboration as a necessary condition for successful research, necessary not only because it generates trust and facilitates the collection *and* interpretation of data but also because the positive aspects of the relationship help overcome the client's inevitable strong fears and resistance to change.

The duality posed by Lawler's question about how to make research enrich practice as well as theory dissolves upon close analysis. Theory, no matter how rigorous and vigorous, will not count unless there is a collaborative relationship between researcher and client; nor will our theories be sufficiently robust without the client's contribution. Thus practice and theory are indivisible. Neither can fully exist and flourish without the other. As Kurt Lewin once said in response to a question from a colleague, "Close cooperation between the theorist and the practitioner can be accomplished if the theorist does not look toward applied problems with a highbrow aversion or with a fear of social problems."

No Easy Solution

We tend to think of action researchers or applied behavioral scientists as experts, analysts, advisers, consultants, theoreticians (at times), designers, and sometimes merely "temporary help." But most of these terms have little to do with the contribution that applied social science exists to provide. At its most influential and professional level, applied social science is profoundly important to what is occurring in the world today and is essential to our realizing the full potential that organizations represent for human lives. That assertion derives from the following two propositions:

1. Organizations are self-referencing systems and therefore

tend to have an inaccurate perspective on themselves. One role of applied social science is to provide the tools an organization needs in order to know itself, to be visionary about itself.

2. Some of the most challenging problems facing the world today have to do with the management of institutions. Applied social science, at its most powerful, can be a significant force in addressing those problems because it exists not as a "thing to do" or as a set of tools or techniques, but as a relationship between an organization and a body of knowledge. As we develop more advanced theoretical and methodological skills, perhaps those of us who serve both theory and application will be better able to foster the growth of this relationship.

H. L. Mencken, that arch and cynical critic, was probably right: "There's an easy solution to every human problem—neat, plausible and . . . wrong." There is certainly a lot we do not know about the mysteries of change. But despite the problems and obstacles, the disclaimers and precautions expressed throughout this volume, the truth is that social science research has made a difference in how we conduct human affairs. Changes have occurred at the workplace. Organizations have enhanced the quality of their employees' working lives. It is not always clear how and why, nor do we fully understand the conditions under which improvements take place, but certainly progress has been made in applying research findings to organizations.

It may be fitting to end my observations with a quote from a practicing psychoanalyst speaking about the divine mysteries of a patient's positive changes (Malcolm, J. *Psychoanalysis: The Impossible Profession.* New York: First Vintage Books, 1980, p. 98):

> At the end of *A Midsummer Night's Dream,* the human characters wake up and rub their eyes and aren't sure what has happened to them. They have the feeling that a great deal has occurred—that things have somehow changed for the better, but they don't know what caused the change. Analysis is like that for many patients.

Perhaps we are all the Pucks and Oberons who make things happen, sometimes without even knowing why. But this should in no way deter us from trying to understand, far better than we do now, how and why those remarkable things that occur to humans in the organizations with which we work actually happen.

Appendix

✢ ✢ ✢ ✢ ✢ ✢ ✢ ✢ ✢ ✢ ✢ ✢ ✢ ✢ ✢ ✢ ✢ ✢

Questions for Chapter Authors

I. How is research that is useful for theory and practice different from traditional research?

    1. Does theory- and practice-relevant research require a different relationship with the subject? Is there such a thing as the research subject? Is there such a thing as a researcher?

    2. Does research that is targeted for both theory and practice require a different kind of relationship with the client than does traditional scientific research?

    3. Is there a necessary trade-off between rigor (as defined by the traditional research literature on methodology) and relevance? To what extent can you use traditional research methods and do research that is relevant to practice?

    4. Do different criteria need to be used to assess whether a research project aimed at influencing practice meets scientific tests of validity?

    5. How do you know when research that is aimed at practice and theory is good?

6. Can you do research that is relevant for practice without studying change?
7. What is the role of normative models in doing research that is relevant to theory and practice?
8. Can we learn about improved practice without creating normative-based new organizational conditions or practices?
9. What is the role of evaluation research in producing knowledge? Can it be structured to produce both practically and theoretically relevant research? Is it destined, by its very nature, to provide more information for one than the other?
10. What is the relationship between consulting and useful research? Can they be one and the same? Must they be one and the same?

II. How can a social system be created that promotes research that is useful for theory and practice?
1. What are the best ways and places to publish research that is relevant to both theory and practice?
2. How do you respond to the point that only a few superheroes can do research that is both practically and theoretically relevant?
3. George Stigler, the Nobel Prize winner in economics, has said that "new knowledge on the working of economies is almost certainly specialized and technical in nature, so it will be known first primarily to one's professional colleagues. Hence, the influence of the economist's work and even the popular esteem in which he is held are most likely to be negatively correlated." Do you think this is true for the field of organizational research? If not, why?
4. Is there a way out of the dilemma that organizational behavior research is seen as irrelevant by practitioners and as nonscientific by our more physical-science-oriented colleagues? Should we even be concerned about this? How far along are we toward developing a paradigm in which we establish our own research, turf, methods, and credibility?

    5. What kind of training is needed in order for someone to do research that is relevant to both theory and practice?

III. What is the pattern of your personal evolution as a researcher interested in practice-relevant research?

    1. In the early development of your professional interests, were you more interested in research or practice?

    2. Who were your early mentors or role models?

    3. What training or experiences were particularly crucial in your development as a researcher doing practice-oriented research?

    4. To what extent have your needs changed over time around such issues as meaningful interpersonal relationships, approval from scientific colleagues, and desire to be respected and accepted by the business community? How are any changes related to the developmental pattern of your research interests and methods?

    5. When did you first become interested in doing research that would influence practice? Did you see yourself torn between maintaining scientific standards and doing ''relevant'' research? If so, how did you resolve this conflict?

    6. Did your training emphasize theory- or practice-relevant research? Did it equip you to do research that was relevant to practice?

    7. What research studies of your own would you identify as being particularly good examples of research that is relevant to both theory and practice?

    8. Does doing research that is targeted to both theory and practice cause you to expand your thinking? To look at problems differently? To do better research from a theory point of view?

    9. At what point in your career would you say you began to try to do research that would influence both practice and theory? Were there any critical events that caused you to be concerned with this duality?

10. What would you say the biggest problems are that you faced in having your practice-relevant research accepted as being scientifically valid and useful?

11. To what extent would you say your research has pushed forward the development of a creditable research methodology around doing research that is jointly useful for theory and practice?

12. Does your research that is relevant to both theory and practice constitute a trail of research or simply stand-alone studies? Does doing research relevant to both practice and theory require longer time perspectives and more of a trail of research?

13. How do you know when your research is relevant to both theory and practice?

14. In your own research, what do you think about in deciding whether it is a good study or not?

15. To what extent do the methods you use reflect your own needs around such issues as meaningful interpersonal relationships, approval from your scientific colleagues, and desire to be respected and accepted by the business community at large?

16. To what extent do your research methods reflect your own comfort or lack thereof with statistics and the more esoteric methodologies that are part of traditional research methods?

17. How do you differentiate between consulting and research, or do you?

18. Do you find yourself in ethical binds because of an overlap or confusion about relevant research and consulting? How do you resolve the two so the binds do not occur?

Index

A

Academy of Management, 343
Ackoff, R. L., 24, 25, 26, 27, 28, 43, 277, 319
Action maps: accuracy of concepts in, 110–112; advantages of, 109–110; analysis of, 79–125; and complexity, 107–108, 114; concept of, 80–81; conclusions on, 103–107; and consequences of responses, 89–90; and context, 120–121; creating, 94–96; and data collection, 96–97, 121–123; and easing-in actions, 100–101; examples of, 81–91; features of, 91–94; and generalizability, 93–94, 108–109, 112–113, 120; and governing conditions, 88–89, 92; group discussion on, 115–123; and interdependence, 91; and jargon, 109–110; and Model II learning, 88, 90, 94, 95, 102, 108, 113, 114, 118, 119, 120; and motivational factors, 113; nested features of, 99–103; and objectivity and distancing, 103–104; and observers, 110–112, 115–117; and paradoxes, 90–91; and passive proactive responses, 89; and pretraining, 114–115; and psychological assessment, 111; response and commentary on, 107–115; and sloppy causality, 91–92; and social systems, 92; and supraindividual systems, 93; testability of, 97–99; and theories-in-use, 93, 102–103, 119; and theory of defense, 95; and unfreezing, 98, 104
Adams, J. S., 8, 17
Adaptive research, for organization change, 286–287, 308–309
Advocacy: issue of, 70–72; as usefulness dimension, 64–65
Agency for International Development, 178
Alderfer, C. P., 133–134, 135n, 173, 281, 319
Allison, G., 43, 316–317
Ansoff, H. I., 80, 123
Argyris, C., x, 46, 60, 69–70, 72, 73, 74, 76, 79–125, 146, 158, 159–160, 163–164, 165, 166, 168, 172, 173, 180, 213–214, 216, 217, 225, 260, 261, 268–269, 271, 281, 282, 283, 290, 316–317, 319, 327, 328, 331, 337, 340, 344, 353
Argyris, D., 79n
Aston studies, 231, 273
Athey, T., 114, 124

B

Bache, W., 121–122
Barfield, O., 295, 319
Barlow, D., 66, 77

Barnard, C., 54, 76, 257
BASF, 237
Bayer, 237
Beavin, J. H., 290, 292, 323
Beckhard, W.G., 232, 271
Beer, M., 135*n*, 173
Bell, C. H., 232, 234, 271
Bell System, 183
Bennis, W. G., xi, 60, 72, 73, 76, 171, 172, 232, 253, 271, 298,319, 351–357
Benson, J. K., 62, 76
Berg, P. O., 232, 242, 271, 287, 322
Berger, P., 64, 76
Berkowitz, L., 132, 173
Beveridge, W. I. B., 222, 271
Billingsley, K., 287, 320
Binkhorst, D., 281, 319–320
Blake's aid, 60
Blau, P., 255
Blumberg, M., 135*n*, 173
Boje, D. M., 281, 319
Bok, D. C., 163–164
Bougon, M., 281, 319–320
Bowers, D. G., 233, 271
Bradford's aid, 60
Brett, J. M., 138, 173
Brittain, J. W., 105–106, 124
Brown, L. D., 135*n*, 173
Bryson, J., 114, 124
Burns, T., 181
Burrell, G., 224, 231, 271

C

Cambridge, Massachusetts, science issue in, 163–164, 165
Cameron, K. S., 284, 320
Cammann, C., 295, 321, 322
Cammann, E., 66, 76
Campbell, D. T., 172, 207, 286, 320
Case studies: generalizability from, 241–242; and performance effectiveness, 138–139, 154; usefulness of, 52, 56, 57, 65–66
Center for Effective Organizations (CEO): and convergence, 74; in institutional context, 300–305; 318–319, 336; and research conference,

xi, 346–350, 353; role of, ix, x, xii, 258, 341, 343, 344, 350
Central Intelligence Agency, 178
Certainty, usefulness versus, 12
Chandler, A. D., 253
Change: conditions for, 99–101; metaphor for, 19–20; study of, and research, 12–14. *See also* Organizational change and design
Churchman, C. W., 20, 28, 34, 43
Clark, B. R., 281, 320
Coleman, J. S., 242, 272
Communications Workers of America, 183, 194
Complexity: of action maps, 107–108, 114; issue of, 40–41, 42–43; of models and of use, 170–171. *See also* World, pictures of
Conflict avoidance, and action maps, 81–84
Conflict management, dual-relevance research on, 178–179, 187, 200, 203
Consulting: and research, 14; and values, 164–165
Contextualist research: and action maps, 120–121; analysis of, 222–274; background on, 222–226; components of, 240; concept of, 228, 230, 236, 252–255, 260–261; as craft process, 223–225, 249, 256, 259–260, 267–268; criteria for evaluating, 245–248; and data access, 264–265; and descriptive understanding, 242–243, 247–248, 261–262; and disconfirmability, 263–264; and generalizability, 241–242, 254–255, 265–266; goals of, 246; group discussion on, 259–270; and managerial model, 257–259; as mode of analysis, 236–241; and organizational change studies, 232–236; and performance effectiveness, 131–132, 154–155, 165–168; and practice gap, 255–257; prerequisites for, 238–239; and qualitative/quantitative dichotomy, 223–224, 250; rationale needed for, 250–252; and reflection in action, 226–229, 245, 268; relevance of, 266–267; response and commentary on, 249–259; steps in, 240–241;

theoretical biases of, 254; for theory and practice link, 241–245; and variabilities, 269; and world hypotheses, 229–231

Cook, T. D., 286, 320

Cummings, T. G., ix–xii, 119, 121, 122, 264, 266, 275–323, 332, 335, 346–350, 352, 353–354

Cyert, R. M., 280, 320

Cyprus, and conflict management, 179

D

Daft's research, 207

Dale, A., 228, 241, 273–274

Daniel, W. W., 234, 271

Data collection: and action maps, 96–97, 121–123; and confidence, 15–16; for contextualist research, 264–265; for dual-relevance research, 188–189; in research, 3–4

Deci, E. L., 8, 17

Denison, D., 51–52, 76

Denmark, shipping industry of, 184

Denny, A. T., 137, 174

Dickson, W. J., 11, 17

Directive control, and action maps, 81–84

Distancing, by researchers, 70, 72–73, 103–104

Donnerstein, E., 132, 173

Driver, M. J., 74, 107–115, 117–118, 120, 124, 170–171, 211–212, 218–219, 265

Drucker, P., 257

Dual-relevance research: analysis of, 176–221; case example of, 176–185; conclusions on, 201–204; on conflict management, 178–179, 187, 200, 203; contributions to, 205–208; and data access, 188–189; general strategies for, 198–201; group discussion on, 211–220; on high-commitment work systems, 180–181, 187, 200; implications of, 206–207, 208–211; on information technology, 181–183; on interinstitutional innovations, 183–185; issues in contributing to, 185–198; learning strategies for, 185–201, 205; limitations of, 332–335; motivation for, 200–201; objectives for, 191–192; orientations of, 186–187, 202–203; question formulation in, 192–195; research strategy for, 199; response and commentary on, 204–211; and rigor, 198; and role conflicts, 206, 215–216; of shipping industry, 183–185, 189, 192–193, 215–216; and subjectivity, 190–191; theory and methods for, 195–198; transcending, 353–355; and values, 199–200; variables appropriate to, 195–197, 207; on work innovations, 179–183, 194–195, 200, 203

DuPont, 237

Dutton, J., 178

E

Einstein, A., 106

Elden, M., 234, 271

Emerson, R. W., 351

Emery, R. E., 60, 294–295, 320

Equifinality, principle of, 137, 141–142

Erikson, E., 36

Esthetics, of science, 21–23, 33, 34, 41

Ethiopia, and conflict management, 179

Evaluation criteria: for contextualist research, 245–248; for organization change, 313–314; for research, 337–339

Evered, R. D., 66, 77, 325, 345

F

Facts: or frames, 10–11; models, theories, and paradigms related to, 62

Fedor, D. B., 281, 319

Feedback, error-enhancing, 84, 93

Feren, D. B., 137, 174

Feyerabend, P., 35, 43, 156

Fisch, R., 281, 323

Fitness for future action, construct of, 38–39

Fletcher, C., 242, 271

Franklin, J. N., 233, 271

Freeman, J. H., 105–106 124, 125
French, W. L., 232, 234, 271
Freud, S., 31, 111
Friedman, M., 23
Friedman, S. D., 298, 322

G

Gamson, W. A., 241, 271
Garner, W. R., 147, 173
Gebhart, R., 66, 76
Geertz, C., 232, 271
General Foods, 179–180
Generalizability: and action maps, 93–
    94, 108–109, 112–113, 120; from case
    studies, 241–242; and contextualist
    research, 241–242, 254–255, 265–
    266; and organization change, 313;
    and performance effectiveness, 134
Giddens, A., 239, 272
Glaser, B. G., 199, 220
Glen, R., 286, 287, 320
Goldstone, J. A., 241, 272
Golembiewski, R. T., 287, 320
Goodman, P. S., x–xi, 160, 161, 262,
    268–269, 324–345
Gouldner's research, 253
Greiner, L. E., 119, 158, 169, 249–
    259, 269
Grinyer, P. H., 280, 320

H

Hackman, J. R., x, 41, 50, 68, 70–71,
    76, 126–175, 213, 214–215, 216,
    218, 262–263, 269–270, 317, 325,
    330, 345
Hakel, M. D., 135n, 173
Hannan, M. T., 105, 125
Hardy, G. H., 149, 173
Harvard Business School, 55, 57; and
    convergence, 74
Hersen, M., 66, 77
Herzberg's research, 253
Hickson, D., 231, 273
Hitachi, and trade secrets, 31
Hoechst, 237
Holistic studies, benefits of, 256
Holland, shipping industry of, 184

Hulin, C. L., 207
Hunter, J. E., 140, 173, 283, 320
Hypotheses, generating versus testing,
    197–198

I

IBM, and trade secrets, 31
Imperial Chemical Industries (ICI), and
    contextual research, 237, 253, 264
Institute for Social Research (ISR), x;
    and organization change, 295, 300;
    and personal issues, 58–59, 68–69
Intellectual synergy, in dual-relevance
    research, 188, 202

J

Jackson, D. D., 290, 292, 323
Jackson, G. B., 140, 173, 283, 320
James, L. R., 138, 173
James, W., 236
Job design research: and applications,
    50–51; and context, 132n
Johnson, M., 20, 43
Johnson & Johnson, 40
Jung, C. G., 31, 111, 113, 125

K

Kahn, R. L., 137, 174, 286, 287, 320–321
Kaplan, R. E., 135n, 173
Kast, G., xii
Katz, D., 137, 174
Kearney & Company, A. T., 58
Kenya, and conflict mangement, 179
Kerr, S., xii, 36–40, 41, 159
Kervasdoue, J., 232, 234, 272
Kilmann, R. H., 41, 70, 75, 116, 120–
    121, 123, 149–155, 156, 158–159,
    169, 171, 174, 216–217, 283, 321,
    343
Kimberly, J., 232, 234, 272
Klein, L., 232, 272
Knowledge: abstraction of, 64–65; and
    action maps, 79–125; and advocacy,
    64–65; construction of, 262–264;
    and inquiry gap, 150–151; kinds of,
    35–36; multiplicative and structural

corroboration of, 229–230; needed,
48–49; practice related to, 53–54
Ku Klux Klan, 164–165
Kuhn, T. S., 22, 23, 43

L

Labeling, issue of, 171–173
Lakoff, G., 20, 43
Lawler, E. E., III, ix–xii, 1–17, 34, 66,
70, 71, 76, 121, 122, 123, 145, 158,
159, 160, 162, 164, 165, 166, 168,
174, 191, 212, 213–214, 216, 220,
267–268, 277, 278, 281, 286, 295,
308, 316, 317, 319, 321, 322,
343–344, 346–350, 351, 355
Lawrence, P. R., 253
Ledford, G. E., Jr., ix–xii, 66, 71, 76,
275–323, 332, 335, 346–350, 352,
353–354
Lewicki, R., 234, 272
Lewin, K., 2, 17, 69, 70, 71, 295, 321,
354, 355
Likert, R., 69, 70, 71, 180
Lippitt, R., 234, 272
Lipset, S. M., 242, 272
Locke, E. A., 137, 174
Louis, M. R., 64, 77
Luckmann, T., 64, 76
Lundberg, C. C., xii, 60–66, 67–68,
77, 160, 169–170, 215, 266, 314,
318

M

McCaleb, V. M., 137, 174
McCarthy, J., 232, 274
McGrath, J. E., 130, 174
McGregor, D., 180
McGuire, W. J., 143, 174
McIntosh, N., 234, 271
McKersie, R., 178
Malcolm, J., 356
Mangham, I., 92, 125, 280, 321
Mann, F., 60, 69
March, J. G., 222, 234, 272, 280, 320,
321
Marcus, M. L., 131, 174
Marrow, A., 67, 253

Maslow, A., 157
Mason, R. O., 26, 28, 29, 42, 43
Massachusetts Institute of Technology,
73
Matrix management, and action maps,
84–91
Mencken, H. L., 356
Michigan, University of. *See*. Institute
for Social Research
Miles, R. H., 243, 272
Mill, J. S., 24, 44
Mintzberg, H., 280, 321
Mirvis, P. H., 295, 322
Mitroff, I. I., ix, xii, 16, 18–44, 62, 64,
71, 75–76, 77, 119, 123, 152, 156,
157–158, 159, 174, 213, 217, 222,
261, 272, 283, 321, 329, 337
Models, facts, theories, and paradigms
related to, 62
Modus operandi method, 139
Mohr, L. B., 65, 77, 283, 284, 287, 321
Mohrman, A. M., Jr., ix–xii, 71, 275–
323, 332, 335, 346–350, 352, 353–
354
Mohrman, S., ix–xii, 219–220, 234,
268, 272, 275–323, 332, 335, 344–
345, 346–350, 352, 353–354
Molloy, E. S., 286, 287, 320
Mook, D. G., 130, 174
Morgan, G., 223, 224, 231, 271, 272
Moses, J. L., 135*n*, 173
Mulaik, S. A., 138, 173
Multiple possiblity theory, and per-
formance effectiveness, 141–142
Mumford, E., 236, 272

N

Nadler, D. A., 277, 280, 286, 295, 321,
322
National Academy of Sciences, 183, 189
National Training Laboratory, 60
Newton, I., 106
Norburn, D., 280, 320
Northern Ireland, and conflict manage-
ment, 179
Norway: shipping industry of, 184;
technology agreements in, 183
Novelli, L., Jr., 287, 321

O

Occam, W., 118
Office of Economic Opportunity, 178
Office of Naval Research, Organizational Effectiveness Research Program of, 126n
Ohio State University, leadership studies at, 253
Oldham, G., 50, 76, 162
Olsen, J. P., 222, 234, 272
Olson, M. L., 66,77
Organization: concept of, 277; models of characteristics of, and applications, 51-52; research needed on, 59-60
Organization change or design: and adaptive research, 286-287, 308-309; analysis of research on, 275-323; assumptions about, 280-284; and communications network, 290-293; conceptual framework for, 277-279, 306-307, 308; conclusion on, 305, 314-315; content component of research on, 278, 279-289; and contextualist research, 232-236; criteria for evaluating, 313-314; as disorderly, 280; and disturbed communication, 292-293; and generalizability, 313; and goal maximization, 312-313; group discussion on, 315-319; as group phenomenon, 282; implications for, 284-289; issues in, 311-314; and multiple stakeholders, 279, 282, 290-291, 293-294, 305, 309-310, 317; nature of research on, 307-311; relationship component of research on, 278, 289-298, 309-310; research centers for, 299-305; research directions for, 284-288; research teams for, 310-311; researchers' role in, 293-297; researchers' skills for, 297-298; response and commentary on, 306-315; and sense making, 280-282; and theories, 282-284, 288-289; and traditional research, 311-312, 315-317
Orne, M. T., 290, 322
Orwell, G., 353

P

Paradigms, facts, models, and theories related to, 62
Payne, R. L., 225, 229-231, 253, 272-273
Peace Corps, 178
Peer groups, suggested, 56
Peirce, C. S., 236
Pepper, S. C., 225, 228-231, 232, 242, 247, 253, 273
Performance effectiveness: analysis of research on, 126-175; and case study, 138-139, 154; concept of, 128-130; conclusion on, 146-149; and contextualist research, 131-132, 154-155, 165-168; and contingency models, 139-143; and evaluation research on productivity improvement programs, 143-146; and field experiments, 133-136, 169-170; and group discussion, 156-173; and laboratory research methods, 130-133; and nontraditional forms, 145-146; principles for, 151-153; proposal for, 154-155; and research partnership, 135-136, 155; response and commentary on, 149-155; and stakeholders, 152-154; and unitary causes, 136-139
Person variables, neglect of, 170
Peters, T., 3, 17, 123, 328
Pettigrew, A. M., x, 42, 157-158, 160, 161, 165, 166-167, 168, 169, 170, 171, 172-173, 181, 217-218, 222-274, 281, 322, 327, 330, 337
Pfeffer, J., 131, 174, 256
Pondy, L. R., 62, 66, 77
Porras, J. I., 287, 322
Porter, L. W., 42, 121, 157, 160, 261, 306-315, 316, 317, 353
Poza, E. J., 131, 174
Practice: concepts of, 79-80, 328-329; and contextualist research, 241-245, 255-257; facts or frames needed for, 10-11; research related to, 53-54; theory related to, 4-5
Pringle, C. D., 135n, 173
Prouty, C., xii
Pugh, D. S., 231, 273

Purlmutter, H., 299, 322
Putnam, R., 79n

Q

Questions: evolution of, 193–195; formulating appropriate, 192–193
Quinn, J. B., 222, 273

R

Ramsay, H., 243, 273
Ranson, T., 239, 273
Reality: as construct, 20; distortions of, 39–40
Reich, R., 123
Research: alternative approaches to, 45–323, 331–332; applications of, 49–52; assumption about, 2; and breadth issue, 11; and change studies, 12–14, 275–323; comparing approaches to, 324–362; concepts of, 327–328; and consulting, 14; contextualist, 222–274; and counterintuitive findings, 7–8; data gathering in, 3–4; with dual relevance, 176–221; epilogue on, 346–350; evaluating, 337–339; and expertise issue, 6; future of, 341–342; group discussion on, 67–76, 343–345; importance of, 355–357; and important learning, 104; institutional and organizational issues in, 45–78; and institutional change, 335–336; institutional context for, 299–305; interest in, 1–2; issues of, 1–44, 324–345; knowledge needed in, 48–49; and legitimation issue, 343–345; meaning issues in, 325–329; observations on, 351–357; on organization change, 275–323; overview of issues in, 339–342; parties at interest in, 54–56; partnerships for, 135–136, 155; on performance effectiveness, 126–175; personal issues in, 57–60, 67–76, 176–185; and pictures of world, 18–44; practice related to, 53–54; and project size, 8–9; propositions on, 47–48; and questions issue, 9–10; questions on useful, 359–362;

reorientation of, 147–149; response and commentary on, 60–66; and subjects issue, 6–7; suggestions on, 56–57; traditional assumptions about, 1–17; traditional models of, 329–331; usefulness of, 2–4
Researchers: distancing by, 70, 72–73, 103–104; generalist or specialist, 209–211, 212; as interdisciplinary, 219–220; personal experiences of, 57–60, 67–76, 176–185; role ambivalence of, 206, 215–216, 293–297, 351–353; security of, 75; skills of, 297–298; teams of, 68, 310–311; training of, 212–218; ultimate values of, 105–106
Roethlisberger, F. J., 11, 17, 250, 253, 255
Rowland, K. M., 281, 319
Runkel, P. J., 130, 174

S

Salancik, G. R., 131, 174
Schein, E., 73
Schlesinger, L, 180
Schmidt, F. L., 140, 173, 283, 320
Schneider, L., 183
Schön, D. A., 46, 76, 124, 168, 224, 225, 226–229, 235, 245, 253, 273, 281, 319
Science, values of, 156–165
Scriven, M., 139, 174
Seashore, S. E., x, 42, 45–78, 160, 164, 212, 270, 295, 317, 322, 325, 327, 334–335
Security, of researchers, 75
Selznick, P., 255
Shaw, K. N., 137, 174
Shepard, R. N., 60
Sherif's work, 39
Shrank, R., 191
Simon, H. A., 118, 234, 272, 277, 322
Slovic, P., 141, 174–175
Smircich, L., 223, 272
Smith, D., 79n, 81, 82n, 85, 86n
Smith, K. K., 135n, 173
Social Science Research Council (United Kingdom), 222n

Sofer, C., 253
Somalia, and conflict management, 179
Sorcher, M., 135n, 173
Southern California, University of, 38;
  School of Business Administration
  of, xi. *See also* Center for Effective
  Organizations
Spencer, L., 228, 241, 273-274
Stakeholders: issue of, 333-334; and
  organization change, 279, 282, 290-
  291, 293-294, 305, 309-310, 317;
  and performance effectiveness, 152-
  154; and world view, 23-24, 26-27,
  28, 29-31, 37-38, 41
Stalker, G. M., 181
Stanley, J. C., 172
Starbuck, W. H., 231, 274
Steele, J., xii
Stigler, G. J., 16-17, 360
Stinchcombe, A. L., 277, 322
Strauss, A. L., 199, 220
Susman, G. I., 66, 77, 325, 345
Sutherland, C., xii
Sweden, shipping industry of, 184

T

Tavistock Institute of Human Rela-
  tions, 60, 300
Technology Change Committees, 183
Thatcher, M., 260
Thematic Apperception Test, 113
Theory: concepts of, 61; and contex-
  tualist research, 241-245; facts,
  models, and paradigms related to,
  62; levels of, 61-62; and organiza-
  tion change, 282-284, 288-289;
  practice related to, 4-5; zones and
  tradeoffs for, 62-64
Thomas, K., 64, 77, 343
Thorngate, W., 62, 77
Tichy, N. M., 298, 322
Tocqueville, A. de, 351-352
Toffler, A., 24, 44
Tolman, E. C., 126-127, 175
Topeka, Kansas, and work innovations
  study, 179-180, 182, 187, 190, 191
Transorganizational systems (TS): and
  applied research centers, 300-305;

convention phase of, 302-304; fund-
  ing for, 302-303; identification phase
  of, 301-302; organization phase of,
  304-305
Treufert, S., 112, 124
Trist, E. L., xii, 46, 60, 78, 294-295,
  300, 320, 322-323
Trow, M., 242, 272
Tylenol case, 29, 38, 40
Tyler, L. E., 141, 175
Tymon, W. G., Jr., 64, 77

U

Unions, and dual-relevance research,
  183, 194, 200
United Auto Workers, 194
United Kingdom: chemical industry in,
  237; context in, 260-261; elites in,
  264; shipping industry of, 184
United Nations Institute for Training
  and Research, 179
U.S. Departments of Commerce; Defense; Health, Education, and Welfare; Housing and Urban Development; Labor; and State, 178
U.S. Steel, 58
Usefulness: background on, 45-48; certainty versus, 12; concept of, 64-65; of
  contextualist research, 266-267; of
  counterintuitive findings, 7-8; issue
  of, 2-4. *See also* Dual-relevance research

V

Vaill, P. B., 65, 78, 295, 323
Values: and consulting, 164-165; and
  dual-relevance research, 199-200; of
  researchers, 105-106; of science,
  156-165
Van Maanen, J., 218, 225, 274
Vidmar, N., 127
von Neumann, J., 150, 175
Vroom, V. H., 140, 175

W

Walton, R. E., x, 73, 74-75, 115-116,
  156, 160-161, 163, 164, 165, 166,

172, 176-221, 243, 261, 274, 316, 325, 327, 331, 332-333, 337, 345
Warmington, A., 232, 274
Waterman, R., 3, 17, 123, 328
Waters, J. A., 280, 321
Watzlawick, P., 281, 290, 292, 323
Weakland, J. H, 281, 323
Weick, K. E., 62, 65, 78, 130, 171, 175, 281, 319-320
West Germany: chemical industry of, 237; shipping industry of, 184
Western Electric studies, 11
Whetten, D. A., xii, 204-211, 212, 284, 320, 343, 344
Whitsett, D. A., 190, 214, 221
Whyte, W. H., 11, 17, 253, 255, 318
Wickes, T., 43
Wilber, K., 32, 44
World, pictures of: analysis of, 18-44; background on, 18-23; as complex hologram, 29-32, 37 38, 40, 152; as complex system, 25-29; and complexity issue, 40-41, 42-43; conclusions on, 33-36; and experimenta-
tion, 24, 28, 33; group discussion on, 40-43; hypotheses about, 229-231; implications of, 32-33; left brain view of, 22-23; orders of, 106-107; as organism, 27; and psychodynamic transactions, 31-32, 33; response and commentary on, 36-40; as simple machine, 23-25, 152; and stakeholders, 23-24, 26-27, 28, 29 31, 37-38, 41

Y

Yakushi, A., xii
Yale University, program at, 213-214, 319
Yeager, S. 287, 320
Yetton, P., 140, 175
Yorks, L., 190, 214, 221

Z

Zald, M., 232, 274
Zaltman, G., 234, 274